Valentine Ackland

Also published by Handheld Press

Valentine Ackland

A Transgressive Life

Frances Bingham

Handheld Research 4

This edition published in 2021 by Handheld Press
72 Warminster Road, Bath BA2 6RU, United Kingdom.
www.handheldpress.co.uk

ISBN 978-1-912766-40-6

1 2 3 4 5 6 7 8 9 0

Series design by Nadja Guggi and typeset in Open Sans.

Printed and bound in Great Britain by Short Run Press, Exeter.

FSC
www.fsc.org
MIX
Paper from
responsible sources
FSC® C014540

Dedicated to my dear mother

Caroline Bingham
1938–1998
Historian and Biographer

Illustrations

Contents

Frances Bingham writes across the literary spectrum, focusing on gender-transgressive lives like her own. As well as editing *Journey from Winter: Selected Poems of Valentine Ackland*, she has also published fiction, plays, and poetry, including *MOTHERTONGUE, The Principle of Camouflage, The Blue Hour of Natalie Barney* (Arcola Theatre, London), *Comrade Ackland & I* (BBC Radio 4), and most recently *London Panopticon* (with images by Liz Mathews).

Introduction:
It Is Urgent You Understand

Valentine Ackland, poet and inveterate self-mythologising autobiographer, is best-known for cross-dressing, and being the lover of Sylvia Townsend Warner; she was proud of both attributes, but saw herself firstly as a poet. Her life encompassed Communism and Catholicism, war-work and pacifism, a life-partnership and many affairs, and – above all – the contradiction of being a fine poet and remaining little-known. Even if she hadn't written, Valentine's life would have been a remarkable one, representative of that extraordinary generation in Britain whose intellectual maturity coincided with the mid-twentieth century, and who rose to the challenges of that time with such verve and courage. But she did write: poetry of witness, commenting on the political state of the world and the plight of the powerless individual; poetry celebrating the natural world while lamenting its loss to the encroachments of war and progress; love poetry of passionate complexity, and metaphysical poetry which meditates on the human place in the universe. This writing, by a poet deeply connected to her time and committed to interpreting its events and their impact on her own life, gives that life another dimension. Valentine's work expands the history of one fascinating individual into that of a wider community.

Her own life Valentine saw as a story; she retold it to herself and others, in its various versions, almost obsessively, as though without narrative to sustain her she might vanish, become merely a blank page. Some autobiographers can swing like a spider on their linear plumb line, the straight story of their life so far; others circle earlier events at an ever-greater distance, rounding outwards like an ammonite growing. Valentine was the hermit-crab variety, carrying her past everywhere, embellishing it and inhabiting it, using it both as camouflage and display, yet ready at need to jettison it for a similar, larger version of heavy identity. Her willingness to shape her life story to different artistic ends, and the parallel text of her poetry (not explicitly autobiographical, but a translation of experience) makes writing her biography an unusual task.

The outwardly significant events of her life, their places and dates, are well-documented through multiple evidence, and duly appear in this book. The detailed record of an inner life, a writer's creative narrative, is also here, often in Valentine's own words. Autobiography offers insights (both intentional and unintentional) to the writer's mind, the colour of her thoughts, the weather of her relationships, which is why I've quoted so extensively from Valentine's writing on herself. She was well aware that her diaries were revealing, of her weaknesses as well as her humour and passion. Once, after quoting something self-complimentary she added 'Of course I ought not to copy this, but no one will know until after I'm dead, if then, so what odds?'[1] This throwaway remark could be taken to apply to her entire life-writing oeuvre, so much of which is about her work, as well as the – sometimes dramatic – events of her life.

As Virginia Woolf ironically observes, in a frequently-quoted passage from *Orlando*: 'life ... is the only fit subject for novelist or biographer; life ... has nothing whatever to do with sitting still in a chair and thinking ... this mere wool-gathering; this thinking; this sitting in a chair day in, day out, with a cigarette and a sheet of paper and a pen and an ink pot. If only subjects, we might complain (for our patience is wearing thin) had more consideration for their biographers!' And she completes the faux-diatribe by declaring that, as we all know, 'thought and imagination – are of no importance whatsoever'.[2] And yet, in Orlando's life, as much as in Valentine's, the invisible inner life of thinking and writing is as eventful as the outer life of action.

Apart from her books and (many but scattered) magazine publications, Valentine's writing has been preserved in the Sylvia Townsend Warner – Valentine Ackland Archive. When I was first researching both authors, these papers were still in Dorchester Museum, housed in an attic lined with oak cupboards – a haphazard treasury; part library, part paper-heap. There are dozens of notebooks, ranging from large ledgers and leather-bound account books through diaries of every size and format to tiny memorandum books for the pocket. All of these are crammed with poems, both finished and unfinished (some in many versions), notes, quotes, diary entries, travel journals, accounts, lists, reminders, prayers, jokes, menus, fragments of ideas. There are also shopping-lists, used envelopes, telephone message-pads, old photographs and post cards, with poems scribbled on the back. The history of a writer's mind is here. There are many boxes and files of typed paper: short stories, articles, a play, a novel or two, a children's book, the poems and – of course – memoir and autobiography in many versions and revisions. Some of Valentine's writing is not represented in the archive at all, some pieces are duplicated many times.

Also in the archive is the mirror-image of all this; Sylvia's papers, just as varied and unchronological, often telling the same life story from the opposite viewpoint. There are also innumerable mementoes of a shared life: love-letters, Christmas cards, notes, postcards, telegrams, their hotel room reservation card for 'Mr and Mrs Ackland'. There is an intense immediacy about these relics. The notebooks are covered in tear-stains, cigarette-burns, cat's paw-prints, wine or coffee splashes; full of pressed flowers, dried leaves, cuttings and scraps, the feathers which Valentine picked up and kept, as they symbolised to her descending poems. The books smell of the river which ran past their damp house, the ghost of Gauloises cigarette smoke, the vanishing trace of scent from the writer's wrist. On opening one of the rarely-disturbed oak cupboards, one was assailed by this fragrance of the past, slowly fading in the attic of a museum.

Valentine was strongly aware of this future; the imagined reader of her diaries is sometimes addressed with apparent directness: 'It is growing dusk already and I must go.'[3] No doubt this is why she cross-referenced her diaries, dated her poems (sometimes to the hour), and carefully noted revisions; some of her typed poems carry explanations of origin, such as 'written at about the time Sylvia was writing *The Sea Change*'.[4] This is all most constructive, and her self-cataloguing certainly made the task easier when I was editing her poetry. But explanatory notes, asides, later added comments addressed to the future researchers Valentine evidently expected, can seem disturbingly personal. (Although one grows used to it, even I was startled, admittedly, when I received a letter in the post, the envelope unmistakeably addressed to me by Valentine's instantly-recognisable typewriter. Fleetingly imagining that it might contain some imperious instructions, I opened it to find an affectionate letter from the inheritor of the machine.)

With such careful provisions made for the future, it can seem that the dead use us, indifferent as they must be to who we are; so long as we're resurrection-men, we will do. By the same token, it's often presumed that the writer of life stories is just a kind of grave-robber, ransacking the catacombs for choice relics. But our mutual aim – a considered life – should be a kind of time-travelling co-operation between the quick and the dead; an exploration of one character by another, completed by the reader's participation. It's easier than usual to imagine this ideal when writing about Valentine, an avid reader of even the most obscure biographies, who actually typed up volumes of her own diaries with numbered pages; so helpful. (When quoting Valentine's own words, her characteristic long dashes and ampersands are in the original texts, but ellipses indicate a word or phrase left out, unless marked as original in the notes.)

~

I was first commissioned to write a biography of Valentine twenty years ago, in 2001, but a few years later the publisher folded and the book didn't come out. In a way this was lucky, from a research angle. Then, I met people who are no longer here to be interviewed and was given generous access to the archive in its original form. Now, I have access to documents such as de-classified MI5 files and the Elizabeth Wade White Papers which weren't available until more recently. So this new biography contains both up to date research and memories which are older, and closer to its subject.

Within the ever-expanding definition of biography I personally prefer those books about people's lives – or aspects of them – which leave one with the sensation of having met, known, liked or loathed someone, in all their complexity and contradiction. So I aim to give the impression of getting to know Valentine as one does get to know people, through a mosaic of their own anecdotes (and those others tell of them), meetings with their friends and relatives, discoveries about their pasts, revelations about their thoughts. However, there is no fictional writing here. If there's a conversation, it's a conversation somebody noted down; if a fast car drives along a lane between summer hedgerows, it did.

Of course, we now know far more about Valentine's life than one would ever know about a living person, and also far less; no amount of research and scholarship can replace the briefest meeting. My interpretation is, however, based on a premise she would understand; that many stories make up a life, not in its entirety, nor in any final version, but as it is lived – changeable, vivid, real.

'Reading my own works', the poem which gives this introduction its title, is addressed directly to the reader, that imagined other in the future who will hear Valentine's voice and see her words. It's an extraordinarily direct statement of the poet's need to communicate and belief in the power of poetry, and a perfect introduction to her authentic voice, which rings with integrity and self-awareness, as it sounds out powerfully, compelling attention. This poem encapsulates the often conflicting emotions of writing; the joyful experience of reading her own work, the fearful possibility that creativity may be merely a mirage. As a commentary on Valentine's entire poetic life, the poem is completed by its specific inclusion of the reader; we may pour her poem away only half-emptied, but our very existence offers some sort of hope that we may, just possibly, understand.

> I hear my own voice, over the desert of days,
> Across the sandy stretch of the war I see my own words;
> And I had almost forgotten that once I could speak.
>
> You who read words when you want them,
> Who turn on the tap of a book, who pour a poem
> Half-emptied down drain – It is urgent you understand
> How bounteous the words looked, how coolly the mirage
> Flowed over sand.[5]

1. Valentine in her trousers, Chaldon, 1930s.

Chapter One:
Becoming Valentine

One November evening in 1925, two young women from London arrived at the village of Chaldon, in Dorset. They brought with them two suitcases, a gramophone, and a wooden boxful of records; the bare necessities. Both wore trousers ('unheard-of then except among perverts'),[1] and had Eton-cropped hair, but this was the androgynous fashion of the moment; they were not a couple. The taller of the two, Mrs Turpin, had come to the country to recover from a recent operation to remove her hymen. Her friend Mrs Braden thought this was tremendously funny.

It was already evening when they reached Wool station, so on the dark journey to the village they would have sensed, not seen, that in turning off the main coast road they were entering an extraordinary hilly landscape. The winding, narrow lane was unmetalled in 1925, a mere cart track to an isolated place, and the cottage they had rented was all that two escaping Londoners could wish. Mrs Wallis's was pleasingly primitive; tiny, lit by oil lamps and candles, with an earth closet at the bottom of the garden, and a sampler in Molly Turpin's bedroom picking out the text 'God is Love'. The two women had tea as soon as they arrived, followed by Bovril with cheese and biscuits for supper shortly after. Molly lay awake for a long time, in her delight at being alone in bed.

In the morning, she saw that they had approached the village along a valley. All around it, great shoulders of the downs heave up, and the little settlement is cupped in a hollow of hills. It seems cut off from the inland world. The drove lane labours up over an immense fold of the downs, skirts the Five Maries – a row of prehistoric barrows – close to the sky, with a view way across country, and drops sharply down to the coast road. Yet in the opposite direction, no road goes on towards the sea two miles beyond, for there are high chalk cliffs, and although the sound of the waves reaches the village sometimes, and storms can blow seaweed up to the sheep-fields, there is no way down to the beach here. The village itself, a few picturesque thatched cottages of pale local stone grouped round a triangular green, was obviously poor, but it had, most importantly, a pub, *The Sailor's Return*.

The villagers observed these out-of-season visitors with interest. Rachel Braden, who had been there before, was shorter and curvier than her companion, and obviously 'fast', with a touch of theatrical glamour, if not quite a stage person herself. She was chatty, friendly, and argumentative. Her friend Molly Turpin, nineteen years old, almost six feet tall and extremely thin, could easily be mistaken for a youth (there was some discussion about her gender) and seemed more reserved, though very polite. She did not look well, being so thin and pale, but the two of them set off walking first thing in the morning, in the direction of the sea, taking some biscuits.

The inhabitants of Chaldon were quite used to artistic visitors renting their cottages. The place had been discovered by a sculptor, Stephen Tomlin, on a walking holiday in 1921. Tommy, as his friends called him, was a charismatic alcoholic (briefly married to Lytton's cousin Julia

2. Looking inland over Chaldon towards the Five Maries ...

Strachey), who caused emotional havoc with every gender wherever he went, and died suddenly in 1937, after having a tooth extracted. He admired the work of T F Powys, a hitherto unknown writer whose wife, Violet, was a local woman and who lived in the village. Visiting Theodore Powys had become a reason to see Chaldon; David Garnett (Duncan Grant's lover in a uncomfortable triangle with Vanessa Bell), Sylvia Townsend Warner (unhappily in love with Tommy), Ralph and Frances Partridge, Leonard and Virginia Woolf, and most of the rest of Bloomsbury passed through.

Once the villagers had seen Lady Ottoline Morrell (the Bloomsbury patron and eccentric host of Garsington) in one of her outrageous hats, two women in trousers would not scandalise them. Chaldon was now fashionable; an artistic colony migrated there every summer, and in the 1920s the place was cheap, unspoilt, and beautiful. But beyond that, it had a special atmosphere, a sense of secrecy, of being entirely separate from the rest of the country, not on the way to anywhere.

3. ... and the view seawards towards Chydyok, over the downs.

(The feeling persists; Dorchester taxi-drivers joke 'Back to civilisation!' with obvious relief as they turn out onto the main coast road from the narrow village lane.) 'It was an extraordinary place,' Valentine wrote later, 'extraordinary things happened there and extraordinary people were to be found there: and [like Communism] to everyone according to his capacity it gave according to his need.'[2]

On that first day in Chaldon, Rachel set off along an imperfectly-remembered route, to introduce Molly to some of the residents. First they walked across the downs towards the sea, to a remote farm-house called Chydyok where Theodore's two sisters, Gertrude and Katie, were living. Gertrude, an artist, wanted to paint Rachel; Katie, a poet, was to fall painfully in love with Molly. Even in summer, Chydyok can seem eerie and windswept; in November it must have been grim. (I stayed there in January once, when the wind howled round the house and the ghosts of Powyses past seemed to grin from the sheep's skulls on the mantelpiece. It was indescribably dour. Apart from the discouraging atmosphere, the lavatory was frozen, there was rat poison in the bedrooms and my hopes of a romantic weekend were dashed when my girlfriend discovered a dead mouse folded inside the sofa-bed. Our car, an aged Citroën 2CV, had managed the semi-vertical gradient on the farm track perfectly well, and only shown a tendency to slide backwards on the final icy mud-slope up to the house, but when we wanted to leave – early in the morning after a sleepless night in front of the sitting-room fire – there was some-thing very wrong with it. I thought our despair at the idea of being stranded there was perhaps a Londoner's response but, when we had escaped, there was general consternation that we had gone 'to that terrible place' in the dead of winter. 'The walls drip with despair,' a Dorset friend commented. At least neither of us had just had an unpleasant operation.)

Rachel's walk continued, miles further on, to the coastguard cottages along the cliff path where Llewelyn Powys (another of Theodore's writer siblings) lived with his wife, the American critic and author Alyse Gregory. She would later become a great friend, and 'Lulu' (as they called him) a boon companion, but on that day Molly could hardly speak to them for exhaustion. The journey continued round to Beth Car, Theodore and Violet's house just outside the village, which

Valentine later reckoned to be a ten-mile round trip. Theodore, whose writing was much admired by this period (and parodied so accurately in Stella Gibbons' *Cold Comfort Farm*), was a rural patriarch Molly came to revere greatly, but then she could only sit by his fire in silence. To meet so many of the Powys clan at once would have been an ordeal at the best of times, perhaps.

The next day, still feeling the ill-effects, Molly stayed at home. Rachel kept her company, dancing to the gramophone and high-kicking at the cottage beams; later, they tried to smoke the pipes they had acquired. Molly was starting to worry about imminently returning to her husband, Richard, at whose instigation she had undergone this medicalised rape. In hospital, when she was afraid before the operation, Molly had realised that she had no one to rely on. Neither her mother, her sister, her lover nor any friend had been able to help her escape from the terrible situation she was in; she had not even been able to extricate herself. Then, she had vowed to learn self-reliance, and quickly. For three days after the operation (which she found painful and humiliating) she refused to see her husband; to her surprise, the hospital thought this quite natural. When he did visit, he made her cry and a kindly nurse turned on him 'like a tiger',[3] and forbade him to visit again. Molly had to stay in the clinic for two weeks, rather than the expected one; before she went in she was unable to eat or sleep, drinking heavily, and physically run down. The nurses had protected her there, but now she had to look after herself. She wrote Richard a letter saying that she would never go back to him, and posted it at the village post office.

When Rachel heard what she had done, she was amused and excited, but she pointed out that Richard would arrive shortly. What could Molly do then? Molly said she would refuse 'steadfastly' to go back with him.

'He is very dull,' Rachel agreed. 'He's quite the wrong person for you, darling; I don't know *what* sort of man you would like? Perhaps you'd rather have a woman?'

Molly already knew that she would, much rather, but she was amazed at Rachel's perspicacity.

'Do you love women, then?' she asked.

'Anything that comes!' Rachel assured her.[4]

Molly's lover Bo Foster was a mutual friend; a charming, well-educated woman, ten years older, who lived with her parents and was very discreet. Molly had promised never to tell anyone about their relationship, but she could not resist talking about Bo, thus innocently confirming all Rachel's suspicions.

Richard arrived on Saturday, wearing town clothes. They booked him a room at the pub in the next village. He was a fair, good-looking young man, slightly more cultured than most of the 'nice, normal people'[5] Molly's family knew, and he was bitterly angry. (He did not know about Bo, any more than his wife knew about his male lover – but they were both well aware of the other's preferences.) It was annoying for him to find Rachel in Chaldon, since he disapproved of her, but Molly had begged her not to leave them alone together. Richard was taken on the Powys trail, and kept at it till dark. Eventually he had to ask Rachel 'Will you please let me talk to my wife alone?'[6] It did no good. Molly remained, as she had said, steadfast, and Mr Turpin returned to London without his wife.

~

When Richard Turpin first met Molly Ackland six months before, in May 1925, he was deeply disturbed by his homosexuality, which he hoped to eradicate by marrying. Molly had been converted to Catholicism by Bo, and passed it on to Richard, who probably thought that religion would help, too. As for Molly, she was in a desperate situation; her affair with Bo, which she had romantically imagined would lead to a life together, was still secret. She was so unhappy at home that she had recently become engaged, by letter, to Rodric Heming, a tea-planter in Java she'd last seen eight years before, when they were both eleven. As the date for sailing to Java grew uncomfortably close, Bo still made no move which might defer it. On 9 July Molly wrote only two words in her diary: 'Married Dick'.[7]

They had known each other barely six weeks, Richard having proposed on their fourth meeting. When in answer Molly showed him the pearl engagement ring Rodric had sent her, Richard took it off her finger.

'It comes off quite easily,' he remarked. 'I shall keep it and you can put on our wedding ring instead.'[8]

This at last was the tempestuous passion, carrying all before it, for which Molly had hoped. Otherwise, Richard's behaviour did not come up to her expectations for a whirlwind romance; when Molly asked if he loved her, he answered 'I suppose I do.' However, this 'disjointed and lukewarm' courtship suited the 'almost total unreality' of Molly's state of mind. She did not even consider whether or not she 'felt desire' towards Richard, perhaps because (as Valentine theorised later) her 'body was wholly given over to Bo, whose love excited and satisfied' her. Valentine described Molly's confused feelings: 'the situation was amusing; it was modern and emancipated ... I was shy of him, anxious to impress him ... anxious – above all – to appear sophisticated and competent to deal with this or any other situation.'[9] Perhaps more importantly, if she sailed to Java it would mean a permanent goodbye to Bo, and Bo did not seem able to offer any alternative solution.

Richard was not the ideal saviour of the situation, but Molly accepted his offer. He kissed her, roughly, which she found utterly distasteful; her mother entered the room in time to witness the unwelcome embrace. Ruth Ackland – beautiful, widowed and rather silly – was not the woman to pass up such an opportunity for a scene:

Ruth: (screams) What is all this? What?
Richard: (with aplomb) Your daughter is going to marry me. I hope you don't mind?
Ruth: But you are engaged! How dare you do this?
Molly: I am sorry. I could not help it. I have fallen in love with Richard!
Richard: I'm very sorry. It is all very awkward. But we can't do anything about it. I am sorry for the man in Java. But she is going to marry me.

(After much debate, and mention of the tickets for Java, the trousseau and wedding presents, it is agreed that Richard will only communicate with Ruth, until Molly has written to Rodric. Richard makes to exit.)

Molly: Have you got a card? I don't even know your right name. I don't know where you live.
Richard: (gives her a visiting card, and hands the engagement ring to Ruth) That is done with now, thank you. (Exit)
Ruth: Well, my God! I think you are quite mad.[10]

Having played her appointed role in the drama, Ruth was in high good humour, and ordered oysters and champagne for supper in honour of the occasion. Richard wooed her with flowers, presents and letters beginning 'O Shenandoah [I love your daughter]',[11] and she became a staunch ally. Rodric was cabled, the passage to Java cancelled. (Molly sometimes wondered about that unimaginable life as Mrs Heming; Rodric was murdered, only two years later, by a Chinese workman.)

Richard probably thought that when he said to Molly 'I haven't kissed a young woman before', she took his meaning, especially when he hinted at unmentionable vices.[12] He underestimated Molly's inexperience; she had been disablingly shy, but learnt to conceal this beneath a poised, apparently urbane, social manner. His social carapace was, less successfully, 'a mixture of cringe and swagger'[13] which by turns alarmed and impressed Molly. Presumably their very lack of sexual chemistry was an attraction; if they had been content with an unconsummated *mariage blanc*, it could have been a convenient partnership. Molly would have escaped from her family, and gained the freedom accorded to a married woman, Richard would have been protected from the dangers of his illegal preferences by a public appearance of heterosexuality. But Richard was not interested in a mutually beneficial arrangement; he wanted real conformity, normality, paternity. He was also apparently motivated by an exaggerated competitive instinct, and a public school determination to overcome all obstacles; any opposition made him frantically determined.

After the experience of kissing him, Molly was seriously put off the idea of marrying Richard, but the less enthusiastic she became, the more obstinately he insisted. At this juncture, her dangerous sister Joan – herself eight years older and recently married – gave Molly vehement advice:

> She told me I *must* marry; never mind who – Richard as well as anyone else. I could not otherwise escape from my mother ... Even if I did not think I loved Richard – or any one else – I must at least *marry* ... Even if I did not love my husband (and probably I would) then at least I should be free from home. Look at her, she said, she was free.[14]

Molly was desperate to escape from her past and have the opportunity to become her own person. She did not pause to consider that Joan was untrustworthy, even malicious, and that their characters were very different. Joan might be perfectly contented with such a situation, but Molly had a great need of love, and capacity for it. Neither did it occur to her that she might merely exchange one kind of bondage for another.

Molly telephoned Richard, and arranged to meet him at a restaurant. 'I will marry you if you will marry me tomorrow,' she told him. 'I won't if you put it off for a day.'[15]

Richard obtained a special licence, and caught the train to Devonshire, so that he could tell his mother the news. Molly was to drive to Ilfracombe, collect him there at midnight, then drive straight back to London, and be married on their return. Ruth accompanied her, bringing a hamper from Fortnum's. Molly loved driving and they went fast, singing. (Just before they left, Molly telephoned Bo with the news, and was hurt that she made no attempt to stop her.)

They arrived in the small hours to find Richard standing in the dark street. He had changed his mind. His parents had never met Molly, there could be no Catholic wedding yet since they hadn't completed their conversion. It was all impossible. Molly was enraged; it was now or never, she said. As far as the Catholic thing went, once the civil marriage had taken place, the church would hastily receive them whether they had finished their instruction or not, and marry them before they sinned by consummating their merely legal wedding. Forcing the issue by blackmailing the church particularly appealed to Richard, and he got into the car. (Ruth, whose recurrent cry to her daughter was 'Why CAN'T you be *simple*?',[16] must have been relieved.)

Molly and Richard were married at Westminster Registry Office that afternoon; the only untoward event was that Joan publicly refused to be a witness.

'My husband has forbidden me to countenance this marriage,' she announced, doubtless with great enjoyment.[17]

One of Molly's schoolfriends obliged instead, and the ceremony proceeded. That evening, when she was alone, Molly gazed with satisfaction at the ring on her finger. 'There,' she thought to herself. 'I've done it.'[18]

She did it again, a week later, in Westminster Cathedral. (As she had predicted, their spiritual directors had swiftly enacted the rituals of reception into the church, and the marriage was performed by the Cardinal.) Before the wedding, Bo collapsed. She did not, therefore, attend, but insisted that Molly should wear one of her large and noticeable jewels. Molly was embarrassed by the whole event, which she refused to take seriously; on the way up the aisle she murmured to a friend in the congregation, 'I'm fainting for a sausage.'[19] This flippancy, most unsuitable to the formality of the occasion and the grandeur of the surroundings, was Molly's childish form of denial as well as aspiration to behave like a Bright Young Thing. Immediately after the ceremony, to celebrate the end of familial authority, she had her hair cut in a short Eton crop. Her wedding dress, 'the ordinary kind of thing, pretty and white',[20] had a medieval coif beneath the veil, so her haircut was concealed during the wedding reception.

When Molly appeared in her going-away clothes, Eton crop revealed, the sensation created was all she could have hoped. (It was still considered daring for a woman to have such short hair; on a bride it was outrageous.) One of the guests told her it was disgusting, which gratified her. Richard, however, was thrilled; 'possibly,' the worldly Valentine suggested, 'because it made me look extremely boyish.'[21] There was a postponement of the second wedding night, as there had been of the first, this time for a medical, rather than religious, reason. Richard needed a minor operation and, bizarrely, it had been arranged for the following morning. Molly hardly understood why this was going to be kept quiet, but she obligingly set off with Richard as though they were leaving for a continental honeymoon. They drove once round the park instead. This charade symbolised the marriage perfectly.

For a week all was well; Molly visited Richard in his nursing home and enjoyed the novelty of being addressed as 'Mrs'. She saw Bo every day, and although they had agreed that they should no longer be lovers, this was a technicality. They had a heartbreaking parting when Richard left hospital, and Molly arranged for flowers to be sent to Bo every day during the honeymoon, with a daily love letter. These arrangements made, the newlyish-weds set off for Winterton in Norfolk, where the Acklands had a country house.

(Winterton was not a good choice. It was in Winterton, as a child, that Molly had first experienced the ecstasy of freedom, left alone to play on the beach, climb trees, and read. The Ackland holiday home, Hill House, was a large Victorian brick villa with extensive gardens, somewhat incongruously sited beside the beach, separated from the sea only by the dunes, and with no other houses in sight. The endless open skies, wild landscape, and exposure to the elements had appealed to Molly enormously as a child, and brought out her own toughness. Here, she wrote, the London child became 'a privately-adventurous, ageless and sexless being',[22] and it was here that she learnt to swim, ride a bicycle, row a boat, fish, and then later drive, shoot, and, more unusually, box. The Winterton people respected her, and nicknamed her 'the young master' because of her resemblance to her father, Robert; she felt popular and accepted. It was her childhood retreat, but also the place where she was most independent, most like the Valentine she became.)

On the train, Molly compared her husband with her lover, to his detriment; she already thought he seemed meagre, now she noticed that his hands looked insensitive. 'My mind misgave me now',[23] Valentine recalled, with some understatement. At Winterton, where she had learnt the skills she prized, where she was known and recognised, she was put in the spare room like a stranger, and the embarrassed servants (usually her friends) would hardly speak to her. Trina, the maid who had been her sympathetic confidante in the past, was especially shy; she knew about Molly's sexuality.

To get herself into the marital bedroom at all, Molly drank a large brandy, standing alone in the dining room in her dressing-gown. (Like a scene in Julia Strachey's *Cheerful Weather for the Wedding*.) This spare room had two beds, which was perhaps not conducive; the bridegroom was nervous and the bride unco-operative. 'We did not accomplish anything that night',[24] Valentine wrote drily, many years later. The inability to consummate their marriage was the result of a deeper problem than the mutual embarrassment or inexperience which marred so many honeymoons of the time; both were committed to other lovers and other lovemaking, neither could force themselves to it, but Richard's heterosexual credentials were at stake. 'I did not

4. The husband (briefly) – Richard Turpin ... and the lover – Bo Foster.

understand,' Valentine recalled, 'more than vaguely, why Richard would commence making love, as it were quite gaily, and then collapse into bitter tears and next day walk in gloom and silence.'[25] (The word 'gaily' is probably intentionally ambiguous here.)

When Richard tried to reach a satisfactory conclusion with speed and force, he only succeeded in hurting Molly, whose passive non-co-operation turned into active resistance. This Richard found more exciting; he tried to assert his marital rights by violence, Molly fought him off. She was physically repelled by him, and frightened;

he was mortified, and terrified of what he perceived as failure. They were awkward together in the daytime, remembering their nightly ordeal, and scared of each other in bed. Thus was their miserable honeymoon passed.

After a fortnight, Ruth joined them on her usual August holiday by the sea, and noticed nothing amiss; after a month Bo joined them. Not being on their own together all day eased the social mortification of the honeymooners, and Molly was overjoyed to be with Bo again. They returned to loverlike intimacy, and it was inevitable that soon their resolution faltered and they made love 'under a haystack in the bright sunshine.'[26] With Bo, Molly had no difficulty or pain during lovemaking. (Many years later, writing of the 'commonplace cause of trauma' which was her honeymoon, Valentine recounted that she had dreamt about it – a nightmare – but that anyway 'I invariably dream frustration, when I dream about men', even though there had later been slightly more successful episodes with other men which hadn't been 'very satisfactory' but had 'gone off alright'. She added: 'It was much easier for me to be lover than beloved.'[27] This insight not only relates to Molly's easy sexual relationship with Bo, but is also a glimpse of the emerging Valentine Ackland.)

Their ghastly honeymoon over, Mr and Mrs Turpin moved to their new flat at 32 Colville Terrace in Bayswater, conveniently close to Bo. On Richard's insistence, they consulted doctors who, predictably enough, decided the problem was Molly's; her hymen was unusually *tough*. Richard was in danger of getting inhibited, and must succeed in deflowering his wife or risk a 'nervous injury'.[28] (Neither of them would, of course, have mentioned their preferred sexual practices to these doctors.) A weekend completely alone in the Golden Cross Hotel, Oxford, was prescribed, without success. By now, Molly had discovered a fact about the married state which was even worse than the sexual aspect; she had exchanged the confines of home for a more complete tyranny. Richard was not a monster, but he wanted to have a completely conventional marriage. Molly was determined not to surrender:

> I fought against Richard's excessive possessiveness ... his insistence on his 'rights' as master of everything – of me. I wanted

to read, to do nothing else but read and write: I didn't want to cook, to listen, to companion him, to be his wife. I wanted to be my own. This I fought for all day and all night ... I was in extremity...[29]

Molly avoided Richard's attentions by claiming to be ill (Ruth's favoured avoidance technique), and indeed she was not eating or sleeping, but was drinking heavily, so her health was getting worse.

Richard went out to work at his father's office, and in his absence Molly and Bo made love. This made Molly physically happy; although she felt guilty about committing adultery, she was incapable of refusing Bo's love. Bo stoutly maintained that what they did was not adultery; if Molly really thought it wrong she should stop it immediately. (Perhaps Bo felt that the invisibility of lesbianism could work in her favour for once.) Molly recognised this as a spurious argument, but she would not repudiate Bo, who still represented an ideal of romantic love, even if that ideal had proved unattainable. She had, however, given in to social pressure to marry, and now there was an enormous pressure to make the marriage work. By marrying, she had achieved the goal for which her entire upbringing had prepared her, satisfying her mother's ambitions and her class expectations; there was too much invested in it to allow an easy escape.

Molly consulted a woman doctor about being 'sickened by Richard's lovemaking',[30] and she recommended an operation to remove the hymen, making it easier for Richard to enjoy his conjugal rights. There is no record of any suggestion being made to improve Molly's side of the situation. The doctor also suggested that it would be dangerous for Molly to have a baby. Molly's priest vehemently commanded her to have the operation, allow her husband to impregnate her, and obey him. When Molly made the mistake of talking about it to Richard, he enthusiastically agreed that it was his Catholic duty to beget a child, and insisted that she should have the operation. The beleaguered Molly confessed to another, unknown priest, who sympathised so much that he wept for her, but still abjured her to have the operation, give her husband 'every chance to enjoy his rights', submit to him in everything, and leave it to God whether or not she died in childbirth.[31]

Once the church and the medical profession had pathologised marital incompatibility as physical inadequacy (hers, not his), and prescribed the cure, Molly was trapped. 'Physically revolted'[32] by Richard, she was under intense pressure to conquer her aversion. Although she was terrified by the prospect of childbirth, let alone death, and frightened by the idea of the proposed procedure, she seemed to have very little choice. Guilty, confused, anxious to do the right thing, Molly agreed to have this unusual operation.

~

No wonder the cottage bedroom seemed like heaven. Chaldon, cold and windswept and isolated, was safe; an enchanted place. It was here that Molly began to 'moult away' her 'draggled adolescence'.[33] She stayed on, eating Bovril and biscuits, trying to smoke her pipe, writing poetry, and exploring the countryside. Gradually, she recovered, her health slowly improved, she slept better, her appetite returned, her strength grew from walking, swimming, sunbathing and gardening. She made friends with the people who lived there; the pub landlady Florrie Legg, who was tactful about selling her brandy, Mr Goult who let her drive the village bus unusually fast, Shepherd Dove who greeted her from the height of the downs, Grannie Moxon, known as the local witch, who took a great liking to Molly. Ruth continued her allowance of £300 a year, on the understanding that Molly might yet return to Richard, but Molly felt relatively poor (for her class). Still, she was determined to divorce her husband, and here she found an unexpected ally in the Catholic church; non-consummation was one of the few reasons for which annulment could be granted.

Bo visited Chaldon often, and they 'embarked together on a new phase of love-making'.[34] It was with Bo that Molly decided to take a new name, to mark the emergence of her new identity. She would return to her maiden name as a matter of course, but she decided to choose a new first name as well, as an act of individuation and taking possession of her self. 'We made a list of about six, I think,' she recalled, 'and I chose Valentine in the end.'[35]

Valentine Ackland. This piece of profound self-invention was euphonious, and sounded like the name of a poet. Equally importantly, it was ungendered, if not positively masculine, expressing the contemporary fascination with androgyny, and emphasising Valentine's new image. Whether envisaged as coming out or growing

5. Young Valentine, her transition from Molly almost complete.

up, this naming was the means by which Valentine publicly proclaimed her new identity. It was not a pseudonym; Valentine was known to all by that name all her life, it was her official signature, it is on her gravestone. Although there were other ways in which she claimed her preferred identity, this was the most fundamental. It was the cause of frequent gender confusion, which she did not bother to correct, even in correspondence. However, the final *e* feminises the name in France; Valentine was already expert at being acceptably unacceptable.

The decision made with Bo also fell on that choice in clear reference to Valentine's self-proclaimed status as a lover, whose patron saint and namesake is the high priest of love. The pagan rituals of St Valentine's Day were important to Valentine, who treated it as her name day, and always wrote rhymes like this for the occasion:

> Let who will proclaim
> There's nothing in a name
> One name's powerful – mine –
> Chosen your Valentine. [36]

Perhaps Shakespeare's Valentine in *The Two Gentlemen of Verona* was also an influence; as the handsome leader of a band of outlaws, his unfaltering love wins him his beloved who is, of course, the auspiciously-named Silvia.

Most importantly, this name change was a repudiation of the childhood self, the Miss Molly who had been miserable, abused and powerless. That sad child was no more. It also expunged the hetero-sexual wedded self – Mrs Turpin – that Molly was unable to become. Later she wrote of this act, only half-jokingly, as necessary to her very survival. 'Why don't more people change their Christian names? I did. It would not have been possible to live so long if I had been called Molly – now, *would* it?'[37] By repudiating the names – and the roles – given her by other people, Valentine was free to assume adulthood, to become the poetic self she chose to be, and to express her potency – both sexual and poetic. The process of becoming Valentine completely would take several years, but living independently in Chaldon was the first step towards it.

Bo, who had contributed so crucially to this transformation, must have been dubious when she saw what kind of butterfly was emerging from the chrysalis. Even now that the situation was so changed, she could not offer any acknowledged relationship, just as she had not spoken to prevent either of Molly's intended marriages, because she had no alternative to offer. Valentine would no longer remain exclusively Bo's lover without Bo's commitment; Bo wanted exclusivity, but would not make this commitment openly. Disagreement was inevitable.

~

When they first met, back in 1924, Bo was twenty-eight, Molly not quite eighteen. Bo was an official speaker for the Conservative Party; Molly had been volunteered by Ruth to work in the Young Conservative Union, while she prepared for the voyage to Java. Bo gave Molly worldly advice about drinking burgundy and gin for her period pain, or not smoking too many cigarettes, and her warmth and charm quickly made her a real friend to Molly. Joan, extremely jealous of such a friendship, invited Bo to lunch and warned her that Molly had an unsavoury past, including a lesbian relationship at finishing school which had broken their father's heart. Bo, doubtless encouraged by this, began her careful courtship.

Molly was 'deeply flattered' by the suggestion that they should stay the night together at a house Bo knew of in Camberwell, near their work. In Glengall Road, Madame Daloge cooked French food, her companion Miss Woollard was an accomplished violinist, and it was possible to have an adventure. Bo was so discreet that everyone was convinced she was a good influence on Molly (even Joan never suspected her), and Molly was allowed to go. Their first visit was on 5 January 1925, when Molly was too shy to enjoy herself. She wrote in her diary: 'Bo is a fascinating person ... She spoke about Java that it would be unwise to go – I know in my heart she is right, but she stopped just when she might have helped ... She held my hand and kissed me goodnight. An odd affair'.[38]

A fortnight later they went again, and had champagne at dinner. With commendable foresight, Molly had extracted from her trousseau the clothes intended for her wedding-night: a dressing gown of white figured velvet with a swansdown trimming, an apricot crêpe-de-chine nightdress with heavy Irish lace, and white leather slippers with heels. Thus attired, she met Miss Woollard in the corridor and overheard her reporting back to Bo: 'She looks like an angel – like a duchess – Miss Foster – you never saw anything so beautiful in all your life.'[39] They talked for a long time in front of the fire about going to Spain together; Molly had a legacy of £50 from her grandmother for the journey. After their conversation turned towards love, Bo kissed Molly 'slowly and so intently that [she] almost fainted.'[40] Then the cautious Bo sent Molly to her own bed. In the morning, when Bo came to her, Molly tried to adopt a sophisticated manner and said,

'Well, I suppose it is all over?'

'Over?' Bo answered. 'This is only the beginning of the beginning.'[41]

They set off for Spain via Gibraltar on 6 February, on the SS *Caledonia*, accompanied by Bo's brother Boyo, whose protective presence was necessary to secure Ruth's permission. (She was now fond of Bo, but had never met Boyo, who was a rather loutish Army officer.) As soon as they were alone in their cabin, Molly and Bo made love. Valentine knew, in retrospect, that Bo had been 'considerate and gentle',[42] but at the time their lovemaking seemed violent, sweet, exciting and terrifying. 'Bo made love very well indeed,'[43] Valentine recorded, giving credit where it was due. Molly had 'dedicated',[44] as she put it, all the loveliest things in her trousseau to Bo, and considered this as their honeymoon. When she woke, with Bo looking down at her, she felt afraid of her own passion ('I am lost') and then gave herself up to its dangerous power ('I WILL not hide from this').[45] It was a decision she abided by always.

Ever afterwards, Spain meant sex to Valentine. It seemed intensely romantic, travelling third-class on the train from Grenada to Seville to Algeciras. Once they passed a green young poplar tree standing alone in a brown field. Bo wrote a note – Boyo was asleep – 'My beautiful – you are like that tree', and gave it to Molly, who wrote in answer 'Let a gale blow on the tree.'[46] Afterwards, Molly wrote in her diary 'Spain was the most marvellous thing that ever happened';[47] her only regret was that it had to end. As she lay in her cabin on the return voyage, the dance band played Irving Berlin's 'What'll I do when you are far away', and the cheap music seemed unbearably potent. Molly imagined confessing this affair to Rodric, the ensuing parting … but this triangular romantic drama was not on Bo's agenda.

On their return, Molly realised that although Bo did love her, and enjoyed being with her, there was no question of living together; talk of their cottage was pure fantasy. Bo made Molly promise to be extremely careful and keep their relationship absolutely secret. Perhaps one day, after her parents had died, she might be in a position to change her life. Molly's passion had made *her* wild and bold; she wanted the violence of a commitment which overwhelmed all other considerations, to be everything to Bo now, not in the future. This intensely romantic approach seemed dangerously impractical to Bo, but in refusing it, she ultimately lost her lover. Once Molly had shunned the hypocrisy of her marriage, and become Valentine, she was not prepared to sacrifice her life to a perpetually un-acknowledged love.

~

In 1926, after escaping her marriage, Valentine embarked on a period of sexual experimentation, typical enough for her age and era, if not popular with Bo. Despite the obviousness – to sophisticates like Rachel – of Valentine's sexual orientation, she did not exclude men from her repertoire, as yet. Perhaps, separated from her husband, she was testing her own heterosexual responses, which she could hardly judge from her marital experiences. Unlike Richard, however, she made no attempt to deny her homosexual impulses. Rachel belatedly became a lover, as did Rachel's lover, Sydney Sheppard. Elizabeth Muntz, a sculptor who lived in the village, was an admirer who took to sketching Valentine when she sunbathed naked on the beach. Katie Powys, who had a difficult history of falling in love with unobtainable people, inevitably fell for Valentine and was hurt to discover that Valentine's attentions to her were by no means exclusive. Realising too late that Katie was a vulnerable person with whom it was difficult to keep a relationship casual, Valentine attempted to be kind without giving too much encouragement; a near-impossible task. Several other women who lived in the village engaged in less emotionally-involved but happier experiences with Valentine; this was the 'light love' which she expected.[48] Considering her sexual practices at that time, Valentine wrote:

I was naturally more inclined to love women than men; I found deep pleasure, true pleasure and complete satisfaction from making love with women, and less complete pleasure, but still good pleasure, from being made love to by men. I did not ever really and completely make love with men: but with women I was released and happy, and I gave happiness and pleasure; and I did not need any kind of help from drink, to make me feel competent and secure in making love.[49]

The vocabulary she uses is significant – she is made love *to* by men, whereas she makes love *with* women. One activity is passive, the other collaborative. Valentine tells us that Bo, on their first night together, made love *to* Molly, thereafter she describes it as a mutual activity. Her comment that she never 'really and completely' made love with men could be a definition of sexual practice, or a revelation of Valentine's own sensations of an incomplete act. All the positive aspects of sex which she affirms with women seem, by implication, to have been lacking with men. (There is also the implication that she needed alcohol to function in sexual situations with men, as on her wedding night.)

Although she still lived in Chaldon, Valentine also took a studio in London, at 22 Doughty Street. It was here that she 'walked in Mecklenburgh Square in trousers',[50] an act which caused great amazement, even in Bloomsbury, and became in her recollections one of the seminal images of herself in youth. It was here, she believed, that she became pregnant, despite her avoidance of 'complete' sex with men. Valentine was not interested in the paternity of the child she intended to have; she intended to be a single parent. Her daughter would be called Tamar, and brought up in the country, by women; Valentine would love her unconditionally, and protect her. Bo, after her first rage at this further proof of infidelity, promised to help her when the time came to have the baby, and adopt it if Valentine died. Ruth pretended to believe that the child was Richard's, and that there might yet be a reconciliation, so she was able to be pleased. Valentine was radiantly happy; all her life's problems and emptinesses would soon be over. She began to collect her favourite poems into a *Miscellany for Tamar*.

Richard was still legally her husband, and after Christmas 1926, Valentine told him her good news. The discovery that his wife had conquered her aversion to sex sufficiently to become pregnant by another man must have been a severe blow to Richard's pride – and made a nonsense of his insistence that their problems had been all her fault. However, he perceived at once that the situation was one he could turn to advantage – or perhaps he was being gallant? He answered Valentine immediately: 'All right. If you come back to me I'll accept it as my child.' This suggestion, whether generous or self-serving, totally misjudged the new Valentine. Rather than being penitent and grateful, she was outraged. Not tactfully, she swore that she would never *dream* of letting her precious child enter his house, far less believe that she had a father like Richard. He thought it inevitable that she would change her mind, faced with disgrace and social disaster. 'Never, never, never!' Valentine replied.[51] She was determined not to put herself, or her child, in his power again.

Divorce proceedings now began in earnest. The Catholic marriage was to be annulled too, on the same grounds of non-consummation. Such annulments were not easy to obtain, and were humiliating public examinations of private failures of desire. Valentine was no longer a Catholic; understandably enough, she was somewhat disillusioned with the church. The incident which finally convinced her that it was incompatible with her life was when a priest ordered her to destroy her copy of James Joyce's *Ulysses*, and Valentine, as she later recounted the story, 'told him where to put it'.[52] However, she wanted the annulment; the operation for removal of her hymen was taken as sufficient proof that she had emerged from her marriage with it intact, and nobody noticed that she was currently pregnant. She said what was necessary in the various courts, several times over, and did not consider that she was committing perjury, since she told the truth about her marriage to Richard – which was the matter in question – even if she was no longer, by most definitions, a virgin.

Early in 1927, before her pregnancy had reached the end of the fifth month, Valentine had a miscarriage, caused by a fall. Walking on the downs near Chaldon, she slipped down a bank; there was no apparent damage done, but an hour later she started to haemorrhage. Valentine was truly distressed; the object of all her loving concentration had suddenly gone. She mourned Tamar deeply, and it was years before she became reconciled to the loss. Yet, there was another side to the story; sometimes there had been mixed feelings for Valentine about her state; 'the strange ambiguity going on inside one … at one moment violently protesting against this pressured-on, overhastened adjustment and then, terrifyingly, accepting it as a matter of course.'[53]

The loss of Tamar bereft Valentine of a vividly-imagined future, and the chance to re-invent her own childhood as a happy one. (After Valentine's death, Sylvia was touched to find a Kate Greenaway *Mother Goose* inscribed to Tamar. She dreamt of Valentine 'stately and happy, cradling a child in her arms – lost Tamar. And I rejoiced to see that loss restored to her.')[54] Part of Tamar's significance was that she remained unsullied, an imagined child never compromised by reality; the 'dearest child' of Valentine's later poems about the innocent soul.

At the time, Tamar was a repository of what might have been, and her loss became a turning point. During the spring of 1927 Valentine continued to have brief affairs with men; Garrow Tomlin, Stephen's brother (a pilot who died in a spectacular aeroplane crash a few years later), Francis Powys, one of Theodore's feckless sons, and Thomas Horder, an older doctor who gave critical encouragement to her work. But she avoided another pregnancy – indeed, she soon stopped having sex which included men at all. On the morning of her twenty-first birthday (20 May 1927), she made a resolution about her future preferences, and asked the young man who had spent the night there to leave. There was a brisk early breakfast, he departed, and Ruth arrived almost immediately. 'Breakfast?' she exclaimed, 'How nice! May I have – oh!',[55] her glance having fallen on the second, used, cup, with its inescapable implications. This complete acceptance of her own sexual nature was another move towards becoming Valentine.

Chapter Two:
An Essential Part Of Me

In London, as in Chaldon, Valentine was writing poetry, using a typewriter which Bo had given her. Some of her poems were accepted by poetry magazines, and it became known that she was a writer, although she showed her work to few people. Theodore and Violet Powys knew of her writing, and one afternoon in 1927 invited her to 'Come to tea and meet a poet.'[1] (Valentine often helped with Powys teas; on one occasion a visitor indicated her and asked 'Is this your eldest son, Mr Powys?' Theodore could only reply helplessly 'No.')[2]

The poet was Sylvia Townsend Warner, whose poetry Valentine knew well and appreciated; recently Miss Warner had become a best-selling novelist as well, with the enormous success of *Lolly Willowes*. This thoroughly modern fable intrigued Valentine with its mix of proto-feminism, witchcraft, and Englishness; the elusive, dapper figure of Satan perhaps contributed something to her urbane-rural persona. Valentine was an ideal reader – when Sylvia looked at her copy of *The True Heart* (a later novel), she saw that Valentine had underlined 'almost all the strokes I had supposed no one would notice but myself'[3] – and hoped to talk to Sylvia about poetry. Sylvia was a celebrity; her sharp, intelligent face was familiar from photographs and she had recently been portrayed by Cecil Beaton, 'that amiable, suggestible and complying young man.'[4] Her fashionably-cut short dark hair, long earrings and uncompromising spectacles immediately identified Sylvia as a sophisticated woman, absolutely modern in outlook.

The Powyses would certainly have gossiped to Valentine about Sylvia's first visit to Chaldon with Stephen Tomlin, possibly they intimated that she was also involved with a married man in a long-term, low-key relationship. Her background was no secret; she had been brought up at Harrow School, where her father was a much-loved teacher. She was an only child of great gifts, who trained as a composer but had worked for over a decade as a musicologist, co-editing a massive research project on Tudor church music. She was twelve years older than Valentine, lived self-sufficiently in London, and had many friends. These things Valentine must have known. What no one had conveyed in advance was the sheer force of Sylvia's personality, the speed of her conversation, the sharp wit with which she dominated every conversation. Valentine felt she had met a worldly tornado, rather than a poet, and she was silenced. Sylvia, in her turn, had heard about the trousers, if not the poetry, but was unprepared for this new Chaldon resident to be scented, aloof, and disturbingly good looking.

The meeting was not a success, although it was so important to them both. (Indeed, when they eventually found themselves in bed together, Valentine reminded Sylvia that she had been 'rude'.)[5] As she did all her life, Valentine had confused the creative artist with the social person, and been disappointed. Perhaps she had hoped to show Sylvia some of her poetry about Chaldon which, when she eventually read it, Sylvia would admire.

Indeed, the poems Valentine wrote in Chaldon capture the spirit of the place, and the young poet's centrality in the landscape, with boldness and originality in lines like these from 'Space is invisible waves':

> And I on a hill-top in summer, when grass is brown,
> Lying beneath the sky, and likely to drown
> In the vast ocean of space passing to and fro ...[6]

Valentine was different now. Both her trousers and her poetry writing had made her a celebrity in Chaldon, and in London, too, she began to be recognised. Her height, androgynous looks and cross-dressing made her an object of interest, and her distant manner gave her an other-worldly air; she made people think of a faun or a unicorn. She was physically flamboyant, however, with a confidence which then seemed typically boyish, especially combined with the forelock of hair which continually fell forward onto her brow. This impression was confirmed by her 'viola' voice, which was low, slow and musical,[7] and by a dandyish interest in (male) clothes and meticulous neatness. The contrast between her boyish look and female physique was very of the moment artistically, and Valentine found herself in demand as a model by artists 'eager' that she should 'sit to' them; she was drawn, painted, sculpted, photographed.[8] Fellow-Catholic Eric Gill exploited this fashionable look in a series of nude drawings. Valentine was suddenly a citizen of the bohemian world she had always longed to inhabit.

Rachel introduced her to the hard-drinking, high-living circle centred on the 'monstrously expensive'[9] Eiffel Tower restaurant in Soho, which Valentine enjoyed, although she couldn't really afford it. Here, Augustus John, Nina Hamnett, and most of the other inhabitants of Fitzrovia (at its intersection with the societies of Bloomsbury and Mayfair) drank, danced and occasionally ate. Valentine met all of 'em, and recorded some of her encounters in a drunken 'Limerick Diary':

> An erudite artist called Gill
> In print has announced: 'Well, I still
> > Believe in the Fall
> > And in Adam and all,
> And in Art and in Love and in Gill.'

> Today saw the carver called Muntz:
> She is not now a lady, but wuntz
> > She lived in a shack,
> > Far off, and Way Back –
> But now lives on babies and kuntz.[10]

One was about Nancy Cunard, the glamorous rebel who rejected her wealthy family to embrace Black culture and scandalous living. Valentine's occasional relationship with her probably began around this time:

> Nancy Cunard came to meet
> Me, and came as well to eat –
> > How angry she
> > That I should be
> So bloody gentle – so discreet.[11]

Another, more illuminating:

> To-night I spent at thirty-nine
> Half-dressed and quite prepared to shine –
> > And did, but Hinks
> > (Roger) still thinks
> I'm hers – and she is not quite mine –

Then we three went to Boulestin,
A place both to eat and to rest in,
    And she managed the two
    As a veteran should do –
And he paid – Mais, ça c'est le destin.[12]

The unnamed woman in this jingle is Dorothy Warren. She was the niece of Lady Ottoline Morrell, and owned the Warren Galleries in Maddox Street, where she curated the kind of scandalous, successful exhibitions which were raided by the police. Dorothy was tempestuously lovely, and had a reputation which did her shows nothing but good; she was said to be promiscuous, and a sadist. She was certainly bisexual, later being simultaneously involved with Vita Sackville-West and Vita's unusually (for her) male lover Geoffrey Scott, and then consoling the poet Roy Campbell when Vita began an affair with his wife, Mary. Geoffrey Scott was the victim of another of Valentine's limericks:

'Really, my darling, you've got
One evening to meet Geoffrey Scott –
    I promise – the sight
    Of a good poet tight
Is certain to help you a lot.'[13]

Valentine fell for Dorothy, hard, but by the summer of 1928 she was in desperation, for Dorothy was elusive. Sometimes Valentine was treated like an intimate almost-lover; invited to Dorothy's flat at the Galleries to watch her have her bath and drink and smoke inordinate amounts, they'd then take the car for an 'adventure' to Whitechapel (where it was inevitably stolen) or the docks, dine out on nothing but caviar and champagne, and talk into the small hours. At other times Dorothy would be cool, difficult, make blatant excuses on the telephone, and disappear. Once, she became confiding, only to break off in mid-sentence exclaiming 'God! Have we copulated without knowing it?'[14]

In certain moods Valentine believed that Dorothy 'has all this loveliness herself and gives it freely. People desire and she gives'.[15] But when Dorothy seemed inimical, Valentine quoted bitterly 'For I

6. 'Don't be afraid ...' – Newspaper cutting of Dorothy Warren.

have sworn thee fair and thought thee bright / Who art as black as hell, as dark as night.'[16] Dorothy's ability to inspire obsession, to make her lovers experience terror and agony, was, it seems from Valentine's diaries, because of her strength in communicating her own horrors. Laudanum is the only drug Valentine mentions taking with her, but Dorothy's emanations of despair read like drug-induced states. The physical aspect of their affair was not the conclusive lovemaking which Valentine had hoped for. Instead, Dorothy initiated her into techniques of inflicting pain, with the words 'Don't be afraid, darling one – you will love what I teach you ... You are so lovely – you are so young, too, and there is time to get used to pleasure, as well as pain.'[17] Dorothy did not, apparently, discuss her rituals beforehand; she explained afterwards, on seeing the copious blood flow, that Valentine should have stopped her.

On hearing of Dorothy's death in 1954, Valentine wrote of

> the hallucinated, almost *resigned* way she took my hands and drew me to her on that first night ... the wild despair on her face as she woke in the morning, before she had come to consciousness – that *damned* look ... I lay beside her, aching and trembling still, and scarcely able to breathe because of the strangeness and glory and – in some sense – horror of the night with her ... and looked down at her as she lay with her head on my arm and her wonderful, matchless hair flooding over my skin. No one else has ever given me such decisive rapture as she did – nor such bewildering pain of loss and evasiveness and collapse. But whatever pain – and it very nearly spun me into madness, too – she gave me knowledge ... [18]

This knowledge Valentine used. Power and its abuse had already been a central concern in her life, but she had not previously made an explicit connection with sexual practice, nor seen the possibility of playing with responses to power. Though she was ambivalent about lovemaking that made her bleed literally rather than figuratively, Valentine found it intriguing. Her sexual persona had never been mild, but the liaison with Dorothy added an element of ruthlessness and authority to her repertoire which more conventional lovers found deeply exciting. This also influenced her poetic persona, and the use of power dynamics in her later work. At the time, Valentine felt herself to be completely dominated by Dorothy in her imagination, unable to forget her strange scent, her copper-beech leaf coloured hair, and her indefinable sadness. Valentine's youthful observations of Dorothy were remarkably shrewd: 'it is always that way with artists who do not follow their art. She is only wholly at ease with herself when she is dressing, and making up. That is because it is a miniature art.' [19]

Valentine wrote some of her experiences into poetry. The neatly turned Housmanesque lyrics which were her apprentice pieces she could write with great effect:

> I never played a stranger game,
> You were so sweet, so new, so dear,
> But now the dream is gone, the night
> Closed on corruption, shame, delight,
> And I am left alone with fear. [20]

Although she had become so adept at rendering this kind of measured (if unsettling) verse, she was also experimenting with more contemporary styles, more suited to the urgency of her emotions. 'See you tomorrow night', which was published in her first poetry collection, opens:

> Night ends, day comes. Sitting alone,
> Silence loses flesh, skeleton bone
> Rattles and is still again ...

and concludes:

> ... Endurance is this –
> Sweetness seen like distant trees, still-remembered kiss
> Still half-believed. Day stretches on –
> Tomorrow's day more dreary still – Longed night gone.[21]

Dorothy was the inspiration for some of this poetry, and the fount of much knowledge. Not all of it was comfortable for someone of Valentine's age; she was determined not to be shocked by the pornographic postcards she was shown at the Galleries, or the curious company she found herself keeping. Bo, predictably jealous, judged Dorothy 'Nothing better than a street-woman!' Valentine, with both more experience and involvement, considered her 'better – but as coldly-burning ... as careless. I shall go to her again. I have not learnt enough.'[22] Valentine kept returning to Dorothy, whenever Dorothy was welcoming, but neither of them expected an exclusive relationship, and Valentine continued living promiscuously, much to Bo's displeasure. These experiences would form the basis of her 'bedtime stories', told for the amusement of later lovers, and also for her own autobiographical statement of herself as a lover of many women.

By the end of 1928 Valentine could write in her diary 'Of course I am a Lesbian', adding irreverently 'Bo hates the idea of Lesbians!!'[23] This was certainly not, at that time, a label which a cheerful and pleasant woman like Bo would find relevant or wish to assume, with its connotations of monstrous behaviour linked to sexual deviance. Valentine wrested a more positive image in a poem boldly titled 'Lesbian', in which the conventional view of lesbians as 'lovers ashamed of love' is subverted by the suggestion that lesbians are 'darkly driven to sin where no sin is' by a society in which '"must not love" shadows "cannot".'[24] Radclyffe Hall's impassioned plea for social acceptance of 'inverts', *The Well of Loneliness*, was published in July 1928, and perhaps influenced this poem, and Valentine's perception of herself as a lesbian, written in December. She already had good reason to know that the prevailing view of lesbianism was violently antagonistic.

~

When she was fifteen, in 1922, Molly had been sent to a finishing school in Paris after leaving school early because of ill-health. She was rather young for this rite of passage but an older schoolfriend, Emily Black, was going, and it seemed a good opportunity to send Molly too. The school at 9 rue Ybry was a typical Ackland choice; not exactly what it seemed, but adequate to give the impression to their wealthy neighbours that Molly had all the luxuries that their class expected. It was not in Paris proper, but the suburb of Neuilly-sur-Seine, which in comparison seemed like a provincial town.

The house was in the same street as Coty's scent factory, which spread its heady perfume over the surrounding area, and indicated the social level of the place. Anne-Marie, Yvonne and Germaine de Rigny, three not-very-kind sisters, received English girls into their house to impart sophistication. But, far from being well-bred, they had no particular education, and one of them worked secretly in an embroidery shop. The girls were shocked when they discovered this, and their parents would not have been amused by the irony that women sullied by trade were preparing their daughters for society. However, perhaps aided by their own sharp consciousness of class distinction, the sisters could deliver the training. Their charges were chaperoned to art galleries and concerts (a commute into Paris), and taught to speak and read French, keep 'company manners', dance, dress and make up like adults. They also learnt more nebulous skills: how to oblige a young man to ask you to dance, how to refuse. Best of all, they acquired 'polish', a patina of elegant good manners, 'for which,' Valentine commented, 'I have been passionately thankful through all my life; it is the best protective skin I know.'[25]

The process of developing it was initially painful. Everyone was homesick, the food was awful and none of them could speak French.

There were four English girls in the house, and Molly shared a room with Emmy. To entertain her, Molly wrote a serial Gothic novel called *The Ravens*. Whenever there was a love-scene, she resorted to a long row of dots; when Emmy grew restive and complained, Molly explained loftily that this was propriety – in fact she was vague on the missing details. After a while, the novel was abandoned ('the first of my prose-works to run their inevitable life-cycle')[26] and Molly took to writing poetry far into the night. She wrote by candlelight, with a purple quill pen and purple ink, smoking gold-tipped Turkish cigarettes, in front of a plaster skull resting on a book. The other girls began to succumb to French decadence, too, drinking liqueur miniatures in their rooms, playing bridge for money, and making shopping trips into Paris. Mlle de Bergerain, who accompanied them, was a cultured woman who sought to educate her charges about French literature and contemporary art, and Molly responded to this new world enthusiastically. Her education hitherto had been singularly mundane, and intellectual endeavour was regarded with suspicion; the trip to Paris was intended to impart a fashionable veneer, nothing more. But this was still the Paris of Gertrude Stein, Romaine Brooks, Natalie Barney, Djuna Barnes, and the icons of Modernism; by inhaling the atmosphere of this foreign city, Molly was beginning to be aware of the important issues of her adult life.

In April, a new girl arrived. Lana was eighteen, very attractive, already spoke fluent French and, most importantly, was sophisticated. She was 'extremely well-dressed, her hair ... was beautifully-waved, she was made up, but properly, with much more powder and lipstick, and much more tactfully applied'[27] than the other girls had yet managed. Molly's compatriots decided that Lana was common, and promptly closed ranks to exclude her. An enormous row broke out over the fact that her father smoked his pipe in the street, which was allegedly 'not done'.[28] Molly couldn't remember if her father did or not, when appealed to, and the implications of the row apparently passed her by. Although she could sympathise with the Rignys' difficult struggle to maintain their position in post-war Paris, she was vague about the signifiers which differentiated Robert Ackland FRCS, CBE from other fathers who were not quite gentlemen. Perhaps her reading of Edward Carpenter's *Towards Democracy* (in which she underlined almost all of the section *Love – Sex – Friendship*) had inspired her with its vision of a socialist, homosexual utopia. It's also probable that about social hierarchy, as most other matters, she was still very naive.

One afternoon in the spring, Molly was ill in bed. The house was empty, the others were all out, except for Lana, who had stayed to keep her company. She sat on the bed, and they talked, until Lana interrupted Molly's vivid description of a leper colony by kissing her on the mouth. 'Don't you know how much I love you?'[29] she asked. Molly, inexperienced as she was, 'recognised the face of love at once.'[30] Her response was immediate: in a

> wild confusion of ecstasy and shyness, I clasped her in my arms and she kissed me again and again … my blood burned me, my heartbeat stifled me, I felt as though something had exploded inside me and I had been blown to atoms.[31]

Valentine always remembered and idealised this moment when young Molly discovered the romantic universe; the lilac was in flower outside the window, Lana was gorgeous in silk and perfumed with *Quelques Fleurs*, the spring nights were warm.

Lana exchanged her privileged single room with Emmy, so as to share with Molly. There was a stay of consummation when Ruth came to Paris to celebrate Molly's sixteenth birthday, and booked them both in to the Hotel Roosevelt. Here Molly scored a minor triumph; she arrived first, fully made up and in evening dress, and her mother walked past without recognising her. When Molly spoke to her, Ruth cried out in her histrionic way 'Darling – they have made you grow up!'[32] and kept staring at this unfamiliar adult. Molly's height was now an attribute, she walked elegantly, with a smooth gait, her thinness was fashionable, and her hair was a chic shoulder-length bob. Her paralysing self-consciousness was disguised by a cool reserve which Lana, for one, found fascinating and enigmatic. Ruth's awkward child had blossomed suddenly into a striking young woman.

In the hotel, Molly received her first love-letter, from Lana. After reading it, she examined herself in the mirror for visible signs of change, and was amazed by the 'intense, burning, amorous excitement' she saw looking back at her out of her own eyes. On her return, Lana had filled the room with flowers – white irises and lilac – 'like you', she said.

7. Molly as a debutante.

They had to endure a long evening of formal dinner, company manners, conversation practice and dancing – although they danced together. When Molly at last hurried upstairs she found a note: 'Do not be afraid, my darling.'[33] She undressed behind a screen and scrambled into bed; after a discreet interval Lana joined her. The memory of that night made the experienced Valentine a little sentimental; she recalled their innocence and delight. 'We lay awake all the time, finding absolute joy in kissing and caressing and beholding – amazed to find each other so beautiful.'[34] Valentine recounted this episode with nostalgic tenderness not because it represented sexual enlightenment (for she gave Bo the credit for her real initiation into sexual love) but because it embodied a more complete epiphany.

Molly now experienced a profound revelation, which dispelled all her previous shyness and anxiety. She had been dimly aware 'that there was a considerable expanse of Me as yet untouched and unknown', and by acknowledging this identity, begun the search for it. 'But when I lay down in love,' she wrote, 'I was instantly released into my whole own self … I knew that I possessed myself as well as, because of, possessing her.'[35] In that moment, Molly discovered the key to herself, and recognised the unknown 'Me'. She recorded the significance of the affair with Lana: 'That less-than-month in the Spring of 1922 controlled the whole course of my life.'[36] It was the first step on the way to becoming Valentine.

The idyll was intense, but brief. Molly believed that this had never happened before to anyone, that 'it was a miracle, a special grace.'[37] Lana was, perhaps, a little more experienced, for she urged discretion on Molly, explaining that other people would not understand, and might therefore want to put an end to it. When the time came to return to England, 'to separate lives, and to a society both powerful and ignorant',[38] Molly began to have misgivings, too. Despite the pledges of faith, the gifts exchanged and love-letters written, Lana's villa at Green Lane in Eltham seemed very far from St James's Court, the Acklands' enormous London apartment, reassuringly near Buckingham Palace. Ruth's well-meant remark that Lana was 'a pretty little thing'[39] enraged Molly by its understatement. Her family obviously found it 'horribly important'[40] that Lana's mother worked, as a buyer for a wholesale dressmaking company, that they lived in the suburbs, and were not (as Molly's friends had immediately known) in the same class. Molly still loved Lana devotedly, but among her own family she began to see how difficult this love was. Joan, known for her gift of 'venom-speaking',[41] saw the possibilities in the situation immediately.

~

Ever since this sibling-interloper Molly had appeared on the scene, Joan had tried to do her harm. The situation of displacement and jealousy wasn't unusual; it was Joan's pertinacity which was extraordinary. She never forgave her parents for their betrayal, and she hated the young pretender with an intense and murderous fury which never abated; all her life she suffered from nightmares in which her parents did not recognise her. Molly realised that Joan was a 'tormented spirit', and 'in an odd way ... was always passionately sorry for her',[42] but she was also terrified of her. 'Joan was a hard, hard scourge on the back of a child', Valentine wrote, 'and I bear the marks still and I always shall.'[43] (This was not mere metaphor – Joan's bullying violence was physical, as well as psychological. 'I was terrified', Valentine recalled, 'of the violent flush of anger and the way her eyes blackened just before she abused or struck me.')[44]

While Molly was a child, Joan told her quite seriously that they were Cain and Abel: 'I am fated to kill you',[45] she said, and as an adult she wrote articles under the pseudonym Kane. Towards Molly, she adopted a policy – prior to the intended murder – of watching her continually, criticising her every move, allowing her to have no privacy and ridiculing her very ordinary childishness. Under this regime, Molly developed an intense self-consciousness, and the habit of observing herself and commenting – before Joan did – became so strong that the adult Valentine bemoaned her lost spontaneity, doubting that she ever acted without 'the shadow of that double-vision "This is me doing this –".'[46]

Joan was an expert at long-running persecutions, such as the pretence that Molly was really 'an Idiot'[47] (with a mental disability which explained her stupidity), which she maintained for years. She told Molly that her parents wanted it kept secret so they would deny it if she asked them, and of course she never dared to. Joan seized every opportunity to distress Molly; when they saw a woman with an enormous bosom on the bus, Joan assured Molly that hers would be like that when she grew up. (How did she know that this would horrify Molly?) And, as a matter of course, Joan spied on her sister, read private poems, letters, or diaries which she attempted to hide, and mocked them mercilessly.

When thirteen-year-old Molly fell in love for the first time she was with her parents in Alassio for Christmas 1920, having been ill with the Spanish flu epidemic. She was smitten by Italy, and by a fellow-guest at the hotel. Myra was eighteen, liked to be admired, and was happy to hold Molly's hands and tell her she was like a knight in shining armour. Molly knew she was in love, and the obvious plan seemed to be to run away, disguise herself as a man, and return to marry Myra. (She had a slight anxiety that Myra would mind that Molly was actually 'a long, badly-dressed schoolgirl' when she noticed, but Molly decided that 'she would be so much in love with me that a small thing like that would not trouble her.')[48] This adolescent love might have passed relatively painlessly, since Myra was evidently not one to discourage adoration – although she might have declined marriage – if Joan had not joined them. When their parents returned home, Joan swiftly relegated Molly to a child's place, and secured Myra's affections for herself. 'During those two months,' Valentine recalled, 'I experienced every pain and humiliation I have since felt.'[49] Her jealousy was adeptly tended by Joan, who sent Myra notes, enjoyed private jokes, danced with her, brushed her hair, and read Kipling to her – to Molly's acute agony.

Even when Joan was a married adult and Molly still a vulnerable adolescent Joan never relented, though sometimes she pretended to. 'My sister loathed me,' Valentine stated baldly, 'and occasionally staged dreadful scenes of reconciliation or confession: in which she told me how much she hated me and how tormented she was.'[50] This was Joan's ultimate weapon, to offer Molly love, apparent kindness, a redeemed relationship. And Molly never learnt to say no and avoid another humiliating rejection.

As adults, Joan intervened in her sister's private life by warning off potential friends, lovers, husbands or employers with poison pen letters or confidential chats, explaining that her sister was an 'unstable' character. She was still doing this when Valentine was in her fifties, and wrote of the 'great, continuing injury'[51] Joan had done her – but Valentine judged that she would never know the full extent of the damage. Possibly Joan could not leave this troubled relationship behind her because she could not abandon her own pain. As Valentine sagely observed, she was always 'one to embrace anguish, and to run back for another hug, too.'[52] This was Joan's tragedy; it drove her to sabotage her sister's happiness and divide her family, confirming Sylvia Townsend Warner's judgement that even if Joan did not intend harm, 'She *is* harm.'[53]

~

Joan was soon aware of the situation between the Paris-returned Molly of 1922 and her new love Lana. She read Lana's love-letters and understood their implications, and spied on the pair at Winterton. When she showed Ruth the letters, her mother did not question the propriety of Joan intercepting them, but managed to deceive herself as to the exact meaning of their content. She had a little talk with Molly, suggesting with much embarrassment that perhaps her friendship with Lana was 'just a little too strong'. Molly asked aggressively what she meant? Ruth, rather flustered, mentioned the possibility of schoolgirls getting 'too devoted' and then going mad as a direct result of 'being horrid'.[54] She also, confusingly, mentioned a hat shop in Maddox Street which the police had raided because of the girls there being very horrid. (Valentine later remarked on the curious coincidence whereby it was in Maddox Street that she learnt 'the very things my poor mother was now trying to tell me.')[55] But at the time she had, unsurprisingly, very little idea what Ruth was talking about. It was just like *The Ravens*: 'there was always a row of dots just where the explanation should have come.'[56]

Ruth was reassured when Molly told her that it was 'all right' (whatever it was), and promised that the friendship would not become 'too exaggerated'.[57] Joan was thus temporarily foiled, mainly by her mother's determination to avoid unpleasantness if at all possible. Molly was extremely confused – especially about the mysterious hat shop – but she did realise that the love between herself and Lana was not a unique miracle devised especially for them, but something which happened to other lovers too – and 'apparently some people thought it wrong'.[58]

Although they wrote and telephoned every day, Molly missed Lana, and was delighted to be invited on a motoring tour of the Continent with her family, in September 1922. They set off in an enormous Studebaker car, Lana and Molly in the back seat, ecstatically happy, holding hands under the fur rugs. But the drive across the battlefields of Flanders appalled Molly; the trenches were still stinking and choked with debris, reminding her of the mud-caked and battered helmet her mother had brought back from a tour of Flanders as a grisly 'souvenir'.[59] She never forgot the sight of the devastated land, nor what her imagination could picture there.

It was not an entirely easy trip for other reasons, too; to begin with, Molly was appalled by the opulence and bad taste of Lana's home, startled by her mother Peggy's dyed hair, and shocked to discover that their male escort was not Lana's father but Peggy's lover, as was obvious even to innocent Molly. Then, she had all the wrong clothes for the journey, and her parents had neglected to give her nearly enough money; kind Peggy offered to buy whatever she needed, but Molly had been taught to refuse such acts of generosity. After a blissful week alone with Lana in Grindelwald, in sight of the Italian Lakes, they turned homeward. In Paris they stayed at the Hotel Continental (according to Molly's parents 'too vulgar for anyone to stay in')[60] and in its excessive splendour she felt humiliated by her shabby clothes. Despite this ridiculous mortification, there was Lana. 'She was sensitive,' Valentine recalled, 'full of delicacy, full of amorousness and subtlety. She made love with exquisite fervour and abandon.'[61] This must have been some compensation for the other difficulties of the holiday.

On her return, Molly felt that her life had changed; she was growing up. Valentine summed up her experiences:

> I had been abroad three times; I had lived in Paris; I had discovered poetry; I had fallen in love. And these are bare statements, like the outline maps we used to be given in the Geography class; filled in with their rivers, railways, county-boundaries and cities, they covered quite a considerable part of the country I was learning to live in.[62]

This glimpse of an adult country she could inhabit, of possible happiness, was brief. While Molly was away, Joan (who was recently engaged) had taken the opportunity to show Lana's letters to their father and make sure their implications were fully understood. The results were all she might have hoped.

Robert Ackland was the Senior Dental Surgeon at Bart's Hospital; he had received his CBE for pioneering reconstructive surgery on facially-disfigured soldiers during the First World War. Despite Robert's apparently humanitarian vocation, he was not a compassionate or gentle man. His colleagues respected but did not like him, his family feared him. He was eloquent in his anger, physically daunting, and prone to ungovernable rages and bleak depressions, with the result that his daughters did not know him and were 'completely unable to be at all frank with him.'[63]

Nevertheless Molly adored him, admired his height, his pride, his magnificence, and longed for his approval. She occupied the unnerving position of being considered his favourite; their close resemblance evidently pleased him, and he indulged her in unexpected ways. His high expectations, and the allowances he made for Molly, suggest that she sometimes enabled him to forget that there were no Ackland sons. Certainly he allowed Molly to learn skills unsuitable for her gender (although her education was typically female in its insufficiency). Molly naturally emulated him, but she knew she could not rely on his affection. On her return from this holiday with Lana, she realised something was badly wrong when he told her to pack and be ready to leave immediately.

Lana, on the telephone, was able to explain – through her weeping – 'I can't speak to you. We mustn't ever meet again.'[64] Robert, presented with evidence of the affair, had confronted Lana's father and extracted a promise from him that she would be prevented from seeing Molly again. The interview at Eltham must have been extraordinary; Robert was a formidable man with a nasty temper, and this revelation about his daughter seems to have deprived him of rational judgement. He did not wait to hear Molly's side of the story, but arranged for her to go directly to a domestic training college in Eastbourne; an inexplicable destination for this Paris-returned young lady. When Molly understood why this was happening (typically, not through any communication from her family), she tried to talk to Robert about it.

He turned on her with a ferocity which no empathy with his view-point or sense of contemporary values can entirely account for. In a series of interviews which she never forgot, they quarrelled, violently and irreparably. Under the extremity of Robert's anger and disgust, Molly answered her father back, for the first time. Although she was badly frightened, her sense of injustice was roused and she denied that she had done 'the most horrible thing in the world.' When Robert told her that her behaviour was 'totally unnatural' she answered, logically enough, 'How can it be unnatural? I didn't know anything about it and I did it – it must be natural.'[65] Told that she had done 'the worst, filthiest, most unforgiveable thing that anyone could do',[66]

Molly stubbornly maintained that she and Lana had fallen in love, and there could be no sin in that.

Taking up this essentialist position on natural homosexuality probably convinced Robert of his daughter's depravity; he doubtless imagined that they had been lovers 'in the News of the World sense',[67] as Valentine scornfully put it. (Since Robert's idea of lesbian sexual practice would have been most likely to come from the lavish pornography of the period, his suppositions might well have been lurid. There's an oft-told story – repeated by Sylvia Townsend Warner to her cousin and her literary executor – that after taking Molly with him on his hospital rounds Robert would make his regular visit to the brothel he frequented, while his daughter waited in the parlour downstairs.) He was clearly not the kind of man to understand Molly's ideal of love, gained from poetry, in which sex could not be anything other than an expression of love. Even if Robert had understood this, or been given a careful explanation of the sexual practice which Valentine later described as 'innocent', he would not, of course, have been mollified. Any eroticism between women was taboo; to use the vocabulary of romantic love and claim similar validity for their relationship could only make it worse. Robert was so horrified that he could not endure the presence of his once-favourite daughter.

Robert's extreme response was not merely the obverse of his previous indulgence towards Molly. He took Molly's adolescent first love affair as proof of absolute, permanent lesbianism, apparently recognising it immediately – as she had – as an expression of her true self. There seems to have been no possibility of treating it (as Ruth had attempted to do) as a misapprehension of strong feelings into which young girls sometimes slipped almost by accident. Robert knew, and perhaps felt guilty, complicit. He had been flattered by his daughter's resemblance to him, amused by the Winterton people nicknaming her 'the young master', proud of the gentlemanly skills he had allowed her to acquire. Although Robert hadn't exactly treated Molly as a surrogate son, he had certainly indulged her taste for pursuits which were – in contemporary terms – masculine. In an era which equated 'female inversion' with 'mannishness', it suddenly seemed that he had colluded with his daughter's learning of lesbianism. Her imitation of him, which had seemed harmless and doubtless pleased his vanity, had gone too far, and become an enactment of his sexuality, as well as his gender. (Robert probably had his own guilty and problematic areas here, to be included in his anger against Molly; no doubt his Victorian medical training had also left him with strange ideas about women's sexual capacities.) Never having bothered to take Molly seriously before, he was now confronted with the difficult truth that she possessed a sexual nature which was an intrinsic part of her self, and she was prepared to fight for the independence to express it. Robert's only response was to turn against her savagely.

'My father never forgave me,'[68] Valentine wrote sadly. His bitter anger extended to Ruth, who had tried to protect Molly from the worst excesses of his rage. Ruth had tried to avert the crisis, however ineptly, and was now appalled by the scale of the catastrophe, the ruin of their lives upon which Robert seemed determined. She was aware that Molly was 'almost unhinged' by grief and anxiety, but Ruth was powerless; all she did was weep. Joan was in the ascendant; Robert tried to console himself for his 'great horror' of Molly by 'cleaving' to her.[69] Molly was escorted, with threats and angry scenes, to her exile; Joan, left in sole possession at last, was Daddy's girl again.

The choice of the domestic college was clearly intended to punish Molly, as well as get her out of the way, and to remind her of her female role and her ensuing complete dependence on her parents, who had the power to banish her, de-class her and strip her of that carefully-acquired Parisian polish. After the few selected other girls in Paris, there were fifty women at Eastbourne; after having been too delicate for boarding-school, there was a regime of cold and discomfort. (Fortunately childhood in Mayfair had hardened Molly to this.) The students were well below Lana on the social scale, and the main subject taught was cooking, which to the Acklands was a subject for Cook. The education was not limited to the topics on the syllabus; Valentine noted with grim humour that the place was what Robert 'would have understood by the phrase "a hot-bed of vice".'[70] She thought Joan would have got on well there; it had the same 'treacle of manliness'[71] as her surnames-only, Kipling-reading boarding school, Crauford House.

The collar-and-tie Principal, Miss Randall, had favourites who vied for 'Ranny's' private talks on religion, and she hinted to Molly in an avuncular way that she knew all about Lana, and understood. Molly was appalled to encounter this institutionalised lesbianism, but it did not impinge on her own perception of love between women. She was disgusted, not so much by the 'gross attentions' of the girls to each other, as by the 'gross sentimentality and gross materialism ... Splendid Vice, Fine Sentiments, religion, patriotism'[72] which the college encouraged. Her own ideal was untainted.

> I was innocent as well as ignorant: just being made less ignorant did not in any way touch the innocence. I realised quite clearly what was going on in the house on Silverdale Road, but I never connected that with myself or Lana; nor was there any connection.[73]

After one enforced trip to the common room ('Girls – here's Ackland at last'), and one downstairs for the ritual hot-water-bottle filling ('Ranny KISSED me goodnight!'), Molly retired to her room.[74] One further indignity was that she had to play games, an ordeal hitherto avoided.

> Since she did not know how to play hockey she was put to keep goal ... There she stood, detached as a heron, all scorn and misery, till she saw twenty-two beefy young women rushing towards her, brandishing hockey-sticks. She cast down her stick and RAN for her life.[75]

As a final torture, Robert attempted to enforce heterosexuality by arranging that the Principal's brother, Major Randall, should take Molly dancing; his attentions were inappropriate and extremely unwelcome. She remained adamant, she would not forswear her true self, or betray her love by calling it unnatural. If Robert had been less extreme, he might have realised that trying to insist on this would only make his adolescent daughter feel more wronged, romantic and determined, but he continued to threaten her with medically-inevitable blindness and death, and the imminent loss of her reason. Under such pressure, missing Lana and home, cold, hungry and unable to sleep, Molly might well have begun to doubt her sanity, and believe her father. 'But he did not know', Valentine wrote, 'that I had the poets to protect me.'[76]

Robert's anger did not decrease; he was implacable. Ruth, however, was worried by the reports of her nephew Alec, who visited Molly at

Eastbourne, and also by the opinion of her maid, Trina, who thought that, judging by Molly's letters, she was 'almost beyond help'.[77] Ruth arranged for Lana to meet Molly, with Trina as chaperone; stoutly loyal, she promptly left the disgraced lovers together. It was an unhappy meeting; Lana had decided to marry as soon as possible, since their love was hopeless, and Molly had to accept that the affair was over. She'd waited for blindness to descend; in the same way Lana had been convinced that no one would marry her, and she was anxious to make sure someone did, quickly. Molly was powerless to offer any alternative, so she and Lana wept and kissed goodbye. Just before Christmas, Molly was removed from the college; a move she attributed to Ranny's decision that she 'didn't quite fit in',[78] rather than any mercy from her parents. She was not allowed to come home, but sent instead to her aunt Bessie, Ruth's sister, who had a farm at Apsley in Sussex.

This was not much of an improvement. Although Molly enjoyed the job of looking after horses which was supposed to earn her keep, her cousins teased her unmercifully about poetry, intellectual activity of any kind, and 'Unnatural Tendencies'. Possibly they thought they were doing her good; it is curious that none of them noticed her state, 'very much astray, very bewildered and far too near being mad.'[79] Her inability to eat sounds like anorexia; she was also insomniac, and developing a compulsion to tell obvious lies and commit blatant thefts. Early in 1923 she stole money from her aunt's purse, and ran away. There was nowhere to go but home, and she threatened to commit suicide unless they allowed her to stay. Robert was now ill, although this was not spoken of, and he did not have the strength to persecute Molly. She kept out of his way, hiding in Trina's room much of the time. The attention of the household was on Joan, engaged to be married in April to Phillip Woollcombe. Molly also heard that Lana was engaged to her cousin John.

In May, when Joan was safely wed, Ruth gave Molly a coming-out dance (presumably sanctioned by Robert as a necessary preamble to respectable marriage), and she was presented at Court. ('It's quite alright,' she was told in advance, 'if you don't catch anyone's eye.')[80] Once she was Out, with Ruth determinedly treating her as an eligible girl, and Robert strangely indifferent, Molly's life improved. She even survived having dinner with Lana and John, with whom she quarrelled violently and publicly. After Robert, John's attempts to frighten her seemed pathetic, but Molly was disillusioned by the way Lana 'flattened herself beneath'[81] his blustering. But his insults, and his threats to expose her and cause a scandal, remained with Molly, as did the distressing experience of attending Lana's wedding to this boorish man who intimidated her. Valentine would later take her own kinds of revenge on marriage and its male perpetrators.

In that summer of 1923, Robert went into a nursing home for X-rays, but returned home, still not speaking to Molly. She went to Winterton for the summer holidays as usual, and on 6 August Joan and her husband arrived there unexpectedly. They gave no reason for this unpleasant surprise, and it was left to Molly to guess – there was something wrong? Was it Daddy? Was he dead? Joan merely smiled at these foolish questions, but it later transpired that Robert had, indeed, died suddenly. Only Ruth had been present, but Joan nevertheless supplied Molly with a vivid eye-witness account of their father choking to death, and added her version of the process of cremation described 'with appalling realism and detail'.[82] Molly had nightmares for months afterwards. She was not allowed to attend Robert's funeral, or acknowledge her sorrow. Ruth insisted that their holiday should continue as usual; her refusal to accept that her husband's death would change anything seemed to Molly 'barely sane'.[83] At least she had managed to restore Molly to some place within the family before Robert died, and now, far from continuing his policy of trying to alter her sexuality, Ruth 'accepted the whole position with a kind of generous shrewdness – adapting herself to the inevitable so as not to lose me.'[84]

Robert had lost his daughter, before she lost him irrevocably to death. Valentine remembered the 'frantic grief' she felt, knowing that her father had died 'not loving me but hating me and that ... what he had hated was an essential part of me.'[85] She made no attempt to evade this truth. Molly would not have changed, Robert would not have relented. Ruth realised that her choice lay between accepting this aspect of her daughter or losing her; Robert would not accept it, but he was strangely certain that it was an essential part of her. He recognised her, so like himself, and hated what he saw.

Chapter Three:
Valentine's Trousers

For many years afterwards, Valentine lighted a bonfire on the anniversary of Robert's death, and marked the day with commemorative poems. The suddenness of his departure, and the way in which he had failed to make peace with his family, left her with a frightening sense of life's fragility, and a determination to be ready for death whenever it came. His bitter and unforgiving end pained her, but she recovered with extraordinary rapidity from his persecution; less than five years later she identified herself as a lesbian, and she wanted this identity to be visible. Valentine wished that 'lesbians could wear a distinctive dress, as men do',[1] and considered that her trousers were the nearest she could get to a lesbian uniform; this was the significance of wearing them when she arrived in Chaldon. Trousers proclaimed her Robert's true heir, while simultaneously declaring herself in the sexual role which made him want to disown her.

Trousers also signified the sexual potency her husband had lacked, as well as the gentlemanliness Richard Turpin had failed to show towards her. As a sartorial choice, trousers indicated that she had usurped certain masculine privileges, particularly from these two men, husband and father, who had shown themselves incapable and undeserving. In a more obvious way, trousers were pleasurably shocking; an announcement that she was not a conventional woman, and did not intend to be bound by social expectations. There was a limited range of clothes available with which to intimate lesbianism, and male dress – not only trousers but also the tie Valentine usually wore with them – was a shorthand for being 'like men' in possessing the power to be a lover of women. (Although this power was not exclusive to men in any inevitable sense, it was still perceived as naturally belonging to men, so to advertise it was both an act of bravado and a satirical gesture.) Performing some aspects of masculinity was one of the few ways available to Valentine to expose her true self, that hitherto hidden non-heterosexual, not-conventional woman, and if she felt that the binary system of gender-coded clothing was inadequate for her needs, she did her best with it.

Valentine certainly enjoyed being subversive, and confounding gender expectations. On the occasions she passed as a man – like the Powys tea-party – she was always amused by the confusion, and rarely corrected it. But she did not actively try to be mistaken for a man; rather she borrowed certain aspects of masculinity for her own uses, and improved upon them, enjoying certain attributes usually forbidden to women but without the disadvantages of actual maleness. This would enable her to be towards women as men had so utterly failed to be towards her. However, in an era of continuing strict binary gender division (despite a fashionable interest in androgyny and lesbian chic), since Valentine apparently had no wish to be a man, but felt that she was not really a woman either, she must find some other description.

The term 'invert' was never adopted by Valentine. Contemporary sexologists used the word to describe 'a man trapped in a woman's body',[2] so it might well have seemed pseudo-medical and pathologising, or slightly outdated for her, associated with an older Radclyffe Hall generation. It could also have felt inappropriate as Valentine didn't suffer painful gender dysphoria, which came with the territory. The other contemporary label, 'third sex' or 'intermediate sex', implying a distinct role in between the two binary opposites, is closer to Valentine's understanding of herself as a Lesbian with a capital L; a trouser-wearing being, not a woman but not exactly a man either. This suggests that despite her masculine appearance she'd have been unlikely to identify as a transgender man, had that nomenclature then existed.

However, when writing poetry Valentine referred to the poet and narrative voice as 'he', not only within the conventional usage of the period but also specifically as an 'Englishman' or describing the writer's 'boyhood', which reveals that she had an internal non-female identity, although she didn't use masculine pronouns in daily life. (Sylvia, who reminded her that 'the sex of your body, without prejudice to the rest of you, is female', always referred to Valentine as 'she' – so I've followed her example).[3] Sylvia's apparent sense of biological sex and chosen gender as separate entities prefigures our twenty-first century right to self-define as anything from non-binary, non-gender-conformist,

8. The quintessential image of Valentine enacting her masculinity.

to trans, gender-free, or any of the constantly-emerging and evolving identities on the gender spectrum.

As such identities are only valid if self-chosen, it's subjective and speculative to imagine which, if any, Valentine might have adopted as well as, or instead of, her contemporary recognition of herself as Lesbian. She might even have felt able to identify as a woman if she could have added 'butch' or 'boyish' to the title. To me Valentine looks like a butch in her dapper male clothes, with her challenging direct look and swaggering yet ironical performance of masculinity – although my personal view does not, of course, preclude or inhibit other interpretations. (Butch could be defined, among other things, as an exemplar of female masculinity, especially when coupled with the complementary Femme woman, who performs femininity with a similar swagger.)

At the time, lacking labels, Valentine invented her own continuum. Her sense of a complex uniqueness of gender was expressed in her response many years later on hearing that an old acquaintance had described her, to Ruth, as a 'charming woman':

> This made me feel extraordinarily odd ... it is such a strange kind of shock to be reminded ... that one is seen and can appear as a "charming (or any other kind of) woman" ... Nothing could be more remote from what I feel myself to be. And what do I feel myself to be? Simply myself.[4]

That self indulged in many pursuits which, at the period, could be read as masculine signifiers – aside from trouser-wearing. There was her love of cars and driving, which formed an important aspect of her character always; in a still-recognisable trope she liked to drive fast, in a sports car, and was proud of her skill. Later in life, in a larger 'dear, dear car',[5] this was transformed into other kinds of power; the driver's knowledge of the route (such as short-cuts through London) and offers to convey passengers wherever they wanted to go. Other skills – such as repairing gadgets or restoring antiques, filling Sylvia's lighter and lighting her cigarettes, plying a corkscrew and filling wine-glasses, maintaining their bicycles, lighting the fires – would usually have been perceived as within the male domain.

Far more categorically male were Valentine's country skills of digging and wood-chopping, catching fish, shooting rabbits, skinning and gutting them. Guns, especially rifles, and knives were favourite possessions; apart from their obvious Freudian symbolism (of which Valentine was well aware) weapons, even for field-sports, allowed the demonstration of male prowess. Many other quasi-masculine accoutrements were important to her – sword-stick, compass, field-glasses, telescope, equipment for picnics and camping paraphernalia – and all her possessions, whether town or country, were of the best quality and chosen to complement this 'gentlemanly' style.

Researching this book, I spoke to many people who remembered Valentine, and without exception, when I asked what she looked like, they all said a version of 'She always dressed as a man, you know, all in men's clothes; she wore trousers always.' In fact, Valentine occasionally had to wear a skirt on formal occasions, from backless evening gowns in her early life to tailored tweed suits later, and never lost her finishing school ability to walk well in high heels.[6] But this was a 'disguise' or 'imprisonment';[7] even during the war she managed to wear 'slacks' as part of her uniform. Although it is probable that she wore trousers more consistently as she got older – and Sylvia does not mention anything else among the clothes Valentine left at her death – it seems more to the point to say that she is only *remembered* in trousers.

The archetypal Valentine, summoned up for the person who never met her, appears trousered, not merely trousered but actually cross-dressed, as she perceived herself, and this is how she remains. (Valentine was not, of course, unique in her time as a persistent cross-dresser; contemporaries noted for doing the same include the artists Gluck and Marlow Moss, the writer Bryher, the motorboat racer Joe Carstairs and many others who passed occasionally, most notoriously Vita Sackville-West.)

In Chaldon, and in London, the implications of Valentine's revelatory trousers were apparently well understood, but this could bring its own problems. Now she sometimes worried that she was invited out merely to be exhibited in the famous trousers, and she objected to being the local 'eccentric or show-Lesbian'.[8] Bo would certainly have disliked this idea, as she disapproved of Valentine's sporadic continuing

9. Valentine explores new freedoms.

involvement with Dorothy Warren, and was enraged by her casual holiday romances when they went abroad.

Holidays with Bo were opportunities Valentine never resisted. When they went skiing in Andermatt she immediately began a romance with a young German woman called Marianne, with much dancing together and skiing to remote mountain huts to make love. When Valentine found herself locked out of Marianne's bedroom, she climbed down onto the snowy balcony from above, and appeared through the French windows, with satisfactory results. At Portofino she immediately embarked on another fling, this time with a beautiful Greek woman staying at their hotel. 'How lovely!' Valentine exclaimed at the sight of her; Bo, 'already pensive and bitter', reluctantly agreed.[9] Aspasia was married, but this did not deter Valentine from her seduction, as usual, whether on Bo's theory of lesbian sex not constituting adultery, or as part of a post-Lana revenge on husbands in general.

Valentine's attitude at this time encompassed an upper-class Edwardian acceptance of discreet adultery – the English idea of French morals – and the Bloomsbury-Bohemian ethos of free love, open relationships and sex as a healthy necessity. Ironically, Valentine's thoroughly modern version of the traditional male prerogative to pursue and seduce made her, during this period, into a fair imitation of the old-fashioned predatory lesbian – usually a mythic figure. If she *had* been a man, of course, her behaviour wouldn't have seemed particularly unusual. This raises the interesting possibility that her performance of gender inevitably imitated the most notorious male traits and exaggerated them, enacting a travesty of toxic masculinity?

In the summer of 1928, Valentine had an affair with a 'strange romantic creature'[10] who worked a fairground, with whom she later recalled having been much in love. Valentine always had a deeply romantic approach to gypsies and travelling people, although she did not underestimate the hardship of life on the peripheries. Bo was so distressed by this particular liaison that Valentine reluctantly broke it off; it seems likely that the disreputability of the woman was what made it so unacceptable. The only other occasion on which Bo's annoyance was so great that it made Valentine modify her behaviour was when she was taken to a brothel in Hanover Square (which she found disturbingly like a grand hairdresser's) by a woman she had 'picked up (rather stupidly) at Boulestin.'[11] Bo claimed that she knew about the place because Boyo went there; Valentine was startled to find it so expensive that she went overdrawn at the bank.

Possibly imitating her father's habits, and with the curiosity of youth, Valentine also visited brothels in Paris during the late 1920s. Initially a male friend persuaded her to try Jeanne, who was best for first-timers. 'I was wax in her hands, of course,' Valentine remembered:

> She took everything with great speed and encouragement and said 'Alors' and shot out of her clothes in a moment ... She did instruct me in quite a number of what a London tart I met later called 'those artificial things foreigners use' and yet managed to be very flattering so that I felt full of self-confidence when I emerged.

Valentine returned whenever she was in Paris, and also sampled some of Jeanne's colleagues, including an older woman who was frequently disappointed in her clients' abilities. She confided to the intrigued Valentine that 'the best time she'd ever had was from the elderly wife of a shopkeeper.'[12]

~

Juggling lovers, Valentine was keeping several irons in the fire in Chaldon, too. Katie Powys was still in love with her; once Valentine turned from her typewriter to find Katie at her back brandishing a dagger. Alyse Gregory believed that Valentine's attempted kindness, after she realised the damage her casual attitude to love had done, was misinterpreted by Katie as encouragement. Llewellyn, characteristically, encouraged Valentine in her exploits, exchanging laddish letters with her about women (and, one can't help suspecting, getting vicarious thrills in the process). Closely connected with this circle, yet outside Valentine's romantic entanglements, was Sylvia Townsend Warner, with whom Valentine was now cultivating a friendship.

After their unsuccessful introduction, they had made no effort to meet – quite the reverse – but in the small community of Chaldon some contact was inevitable. First impressions were somewhat revised. Sylvia was one of those unfairly gifted people who can do anything with great success. Aside from her musical, literary and conversational talents, she was a fabled cook (whose recipes are still appreciatively remembered), a remarkable gardener, a skilful and inventive maker, especially with the needle; her idiosyncratic turn of mind made everything she created recognisably hers. (No wonder she unnerved some people.) But although she could be alarming, and did not suffer fools gladly, Sylvia had great sympathy and compassion. One of her best qualities was to recognise talent in others and summon it briskly forth. She now began to realise Valentine's true value. And Sylvia liked Valentine more the more she became Valentine.

A shared experience, which perhaps made a bond, was the death of fathers. George Townsend Warner had been a profound influence on Sylvia, and she was 'mutilated' by his early death when she was twenty-two.[13] 'My handsome father, who died young'[14] was a huge figure in Sylvia's personal mythology; he had been a charismatic, inspirational teacher whose death was hastened by the shocking loss of many pupils in the First World War. But her close relationship with him was not without its difficulties. George gave formal teaching only to boys; like Valentine, Sylvia was almost entirely self-taught. Her formidable breadth of knowledge, fluent French and cultured mind were either acquired piecemeal from him when off-duty, or gleaned from her unfettered reading. Languages were instilled by her equally brilliant mother, Nora, or by her grandmother. Sylvia was always anguished by her exclusion from George's intellectual working world, and her love for him contained this element of pain.

There was also a problem with her mother, who was difficult, charming, and a natural story-teller, too like her strong-willed daughter for an easy relationship, perhaps, but also deeply competitive for George's attention. The two never forgave each other for his death, or his love, although Nora exacted duty from her daughter. Only when Nora re-married (to Ronald Eiloart, one of her husband's ex-pupils, an architect who had built their house, Little Zeal) was Sylvia able to escape to an independent life in London. As they got to know one another better, Valentine found out more about Sylvia's past, and offered her own history in exchange. She did not yet know the other curious fact about Sylvia's relationship with her father, which was that Sylvia's long affair with a married man, twenty-two years older, had begun when she was nineteen and he was in his forties – and her father's friend and colleague.

Percy Buck had taught Sylvia music since she was sixteen; she called him Teague. (Valentine later admitted that she always winced slightly at the mention of him, 'deplored' his age and 'resented' his grown-up daughters.[15] She ascribed this to retrospective jealousy, being far too careful of her reputation for broad-mindedness to voice the unavoidable truth that Teague had abused his position; however precocious and brilliant Sylvia was at nineteen, however forceful a personality, she was still his pupil, and the daughter of his friend. Their relative situations would normally have put her out of bounds to him; failure to accept this would later lead both Sylvia and Valentine into some questionable decisions themselves.) Aside from Teague's position of power, and her youth, by the standards of the Edwardian era he had ruined her reputation – without any prospect of making reparation, as he was already married – thus destroying any hope that she could now make a 'good' match, if any. In contemporary terms this was a shocking betrayal of her father's trust in him, ungentlemanly, grossly improper – but not illegal.

Sylvia remained fond of Teague, and was always impatient with societal norms of this kind. It's possible that her father was aware of the situation, at some level, or even gave it his approval. Or was this a complicated revenge on the father who adhered to public school traditions even when they excluded his beloved daughter? Or did Sylvia fall in love with a figure who was the closest she could come to possessing her father herself? Whatever the complexities of the situation, Teague remained a link with Harrow, Sylvia's past, and her lost father.

As solitary girl-children, more used to the company of adults than their contemporaries, sketchily educated yet voracious readers, Valentine and Sylvia had certain parallel experiences during their childhoods. But Sylvia was treasured and encouraged, however unconventionally, and her exceptional gifts recognised, while Valentine was at best ignored, and often tormented. Her knowledge was harder-won, her isolation far more complete. If Sylvia had felt excluded and alien at Harrow School, how much more alone had the child Molly been, hiding in the attic from her sister's persecution, or sitting on the dark stairs outside the lighted kitchen to escape the cold of the night nursery. Nora had not loved Sylvia as she felt she should be loved, had competed with her for George's attention, but was an intelligent and principled woman. Ruth had smothered her daughter but neglected her real needs, and manipulated her with tears, threats of illness, moral blackmail and pious silliness.

Both Valentine and Sylvia had developed independence, self-reliance and an individual viewpoint from reading; literature had influenced their development far more than anything else, and remained paramount. Sylvia was interested in Valentine's commitment to writing; she admired hard work and determination, and saw that Valentine was serious. Valentine, in her turn, began to think of Sylvia as, potentially, something more than the ideal reader of her poetry.

In 1929 Valentine moved her London rooms from Bloomsbury to 2 Queensborough Studios which was – surely not by coincidence – within sight of Sylvia's house in the parallel road, Inverness Terrace, opposite Kensington Gardens. Once, driving by, she saw Sylvia in the street 'haunted and despairing',[16] the private, unhappy woman rather than the busy, successful writer. Valentine wrote to her, offering the use of her Chaldon cottage; Sylvia declined gracefully. Then Valentine read one of Sylvia's poems in a magazine, which told Valentine what she needed to know about this sorrow; the poem comments on the writer's oddly contented behaviour when her lover is absent. Valentine was intrigued; from her writing, let alone her social personality, Sylvia seemed too passionate a person for such a lukewarm love-affair. (If Valentine had heard gossip about Percy Buck, she'd have guessed that the sixteen-year-old relationship was stagnating; Sylvia might be independent and confident, but something that mattered profoundly was missing from her life.) Valentine noted Sylvia's emotional famine, and added her to a mental list of possibilities.

Currently, Valentine herself was enjoying an uncomplicated affair with the American-Chinese film star Anna May Wong, who delighted Valentine by telling her 'If I could make love like you, I guess I'd father half the world!'[17] (Valentine was certainly doing her best; Sylvia's cousin told me that Valentine's affairs numbered 'dozens and dozens and dozens!')[18] These early experiences, though apparently trivial encounters, formed the basis of the scandalous rumours about her past, the dangerous reputation which she did nothing to discourage.

Even so, Valentine found time to write poems. In July she inscribed

'Ah, did you once see Shelley plain ...' (the title is from Browning) 'To S T W', and the poem acknowledges Sylvia's powers as a poet, marvelling that she'd ever seemed just one 'among the rest'. 'No sound / Came to me there / From this deep distant music that you tell ...'[19] Used as she was to critical praise, Sylvia must have felt complimented at the implied comparison with Shelley's genius. Her friendship with Valentine deepened.

~

Early in 1930 Valentine's involvement with Dorothy Warren intensified again, perhaps because her marriage – which she had described to Valentine as a union of people with similar tastes – had turned out to be 'soft, too-gentle ... unhappy.'[20] They were mixing business with pleasure; Dorothy planned to have an exhibition of paintings by John Craske, an artist Valentine had recommended to her. Craske was an untrained ex-fisherman invalided out of the war who painted naive seascapes and harbour scenes, and also worked carefully-observed maritime subjects in wool, all with extraordinary vigour and originality. Valentine had seen his work by chance when she was at Winterton, and instantly recognised his natural talent. For Valentine, Craske was representative of all that she loved most about Norfolk; the independence of its people, the sea's perpetual presence. Although comparisons with Alfred Wallis of St Ives annoyed her, Craske is inevitably considered a Norfolk Wallis; stylistically similar and equally an outsider artist.

Valentine wanted to help Craske financially, and had the connections to be able to promote his work; she decided pragmatically that he should benefit from the current interest in Primitive or Folk Art. Sure enough, Dorothy, having seen one picture in Valentine's flat, handed over her cheque-book with instructions to buy enough of his work for an exhibition. Although it was difficult to put a monetary value on his work, which at first he could hardly believe anybody would actually pay for, Valentine reached a compromise whereby Craske felt well-paid and Dorothy pleasantly surprised. The show was critically well-received, and the danger that Craske might be briefly fashionable and then ignored was averted. Valentine did not forget him; her recommendations brought him new collectors and patrons for the rest of his life, creating a large body of work, much now in public collections.

Valentine's social conscience was increasingly active. The time she spent in Chaldon, close to rural workers who were living in real poverty, made her aware of the economic problems of the Depression in human terms. Her seriousness about poetry as a vocation meant that this growing sense of social responsibility was inevitably reflected in her work. As well as the pastoral poetry she was writing in Chaldon, still heavily influenced by John Clare, which dealt with the realities of shepherding in the snow or working the fields, she also began to consider other lives, further away from her own. Without any political agenda, she wrote poems which were starting to show political awareness of social injustices of various kinds. A poem of this period about 'The Lonely Woman', whose independence leaves her solitary, is related to a poem about a youth 'who ... will be executed tomorrow'.[21] In both works the poet empathises with another person whose situation is different, but part of the communal whole. Ever after, Valentine wrote poems to commemorate judicial executions taking place near her; they are protest poems of the most subtle sort, asserting a common humanity by bearing witness to unacceptable acts and speaking on behalf of those who are, for one reason or another, silenced.

Sylvia was now profoundly connected, in Valentine's mind, with the business of poetry, and she was no longer elusive. In London, they met regularly; many years later Sylvia recalled Valentine's exact costume when she came to tea at 113 Inverness Terrace, down to her 'pigskin shoes (faun's feet)'.[22] Although Valentine was usually cautious about allowing anyone to see her poems, Sylvia was persuasive. Soon she was reading Valentine's work regularly. On 13 April 1930 Sylvia wrote:

> I am very grateful to you for showing me these. I think I should have guessed them yours anywhere. It was a true pleasure to read them, though sometimes rather a shy pleasure: for it is rare to find poetry that is genuinely out of its author ... I like your way of writing, the lines that are sleek and cold like the pebbles the sea has but just now left. And I like, too, your sparseness.[23]

She signed 'Yours ever'. Some hope which had been extinguished, some belief in the possibility of joy, was being revived in her by

Valentine. In her diary, Valentine noted some of Sylvia's advice about poetry; she was worried that poems by Henry More, which she admired and wanted to emulate, Sylvia thought only 'pleasing minor verse'.[24] Valentine thought that perhaps this meant that she was on the wrong track, but Sylvia reassured her. 'As for poetry,' she wrote, 'I continue to think yours the genuine article – and you can no more renounce that than you can renounce a leak in the roof.'[25]

In the spring of 1930, Sylvia had a new project: to buy a cottage in Chaldon. Valentine could look after it during Sylvia's absences in London; they would co-habit when they were both in the country. This was a reversal of the situation with Bo: the dreamed-of shared cottage, but without the love-affair. The available freehold cottage was ordinary enough but solid, with a good garden, and it was situated conveniently opposite the pub, where the drove road started to climb up from the edge of the village towards the Five Maries on the downs' crest to landwards. The previous inhabitant had recently died, at a great age, so the cottage was known in the lawyer's letters as The Late Miss Green's Cottage. The scheme became so important to Valentine that when one of the Powyses helpfully informed her that Sylvia had failed to buy the cottage she 'decided to die within two days'.[26] Fortunately, a letter from Sylvia 'made it all right', and Valentine confided to her diary: 'I have good hopes.'[27]

What, exactly, Valentine hoped became gradually clearer over the next few months. Sylvia bought the cottage successfully, repairs and alterations were started, and Valentine began work in the garden. (She was delighted when a neighbour remarked, of the wild poppies coming up all over the lawn, 'They fled there and grew theirselves.')[28] The organisation of all this required much communication, naturally, and Valentine took to noting Sylvia's letters in her diary. 'Letter from Sylvia – very charming indeed. She is most of anyone composed of things I like. A most judicious admixture of metals ... Letter from Sylvia. *Very* much as I like ... I had a letter from her today. That makes four this week.'[29] (Sylvia wrote gleefully many years later: 'Even then I was wooing her with every word.')[30]

Valentine's hopes were almost too delicate to name in writing; she could openly admit to herself 'I long for Sylvia to come down while I am here', but then she worried:

foreseen and expected happiness is a threat, as much of disappointment as anything else. The promise of happiness is
intoxicating and a little unnerving. I hope to be happy here, but
my position is still not defined.

When Valentine considered what it would be like living with Sylvia, she
was unsure what might develop:

> Her sensibility will react possibly towards ... complete withdrawal
> – and that is death – or else towards an offering of intimacy – and
> that is life. So that is all very uncertain and insecure. But it is
> started.[31]

Meanwhile, Valentine did not neglect her existing relationships. In
January, she'd enjoyed an emotional night with Dorothy, with whom
the power-balance had shifted; Valentine was less obsessed, Dorothy
more. Then in June they went away together, and Valentine 'made love
to her' on Valentine's, rather than Dorothy's, preferred terms. Dorothy
was pleased and impressed by this new authority, and started to
discuss Valentine's sexual persona.

'I have always wanted this', she declared (somewhat to Valentine's
surprise). 'Two people as sensitive and aware of each other as we are
must meet like this as well – must have our naked bodies close together
sometimes ... You are very stern with me, darling! Why mayn't I touch
you? Oh, of course, I know that – But why not just stroke and love you?'

'That is for me tonight!' Valentine answered.

'Do you really feel like that about it?' Dorothy asked, impressed.

Valentine laughed as she said no, leaving Dorothy none the wiser as
to how set her preference was for 'being the lover'.[32]

The satisfactory culmination of a difficult and sometimes very
unhappy affair gave Valentine enormous confidence. She wrote:

> the intensity of passion I knew that night was not only mine, but
> shared fully with her ... I had her and I took her, and I deeply and
> passionately adored her. She cried in my arms and her tears were
> my joy and were her happiness and ecstasy as well ... She gave me
> so generously that triumph and power.[33]

This 'blessed night' appears to have been much more satisfactory for

Valentine than her laudanum and razor-blade experiences, and also pleased Dorothy who 'was not left unsatisfied.'[34] She was interested in spending more time with this newly exciting lover, but Valentine vanished back to her duties in Chaldon.

Here she found that the reaction to her new but undefined position was anything but positive. Everyone told her – separately – that it looked as though her motives for cultivating Sylvia were financial (that age-old manoeuvre to separate the conveniently-single who are about to form a couple). The Powyses solemnly advised her against 'toadying', and simultaneously warned her against Sylvia. According to them 'she might be the sister of the devil', Valentine recorded wryly; 'God knows what they would do if there was no one to hate.'[35] Since Sylvia was still under the impression that Theodore and Violet thought of her as a daughter, it didn't take too much imagination to guess that they were not entirely charitable when they talked about Valentine in *her* absence. Feeling embattled about The Late Miss Green only made Valentine more determined, though she was sorry that it was evidently going to make things socially difficult in Chaldon.

Sylvia, unaware of these disturbances, was now sending her own poems to Valentine regularly. Valentine searched them for clues to Sylvia's feelings more obvious than those offered by her calm behaviour, but had to admit: 'Her poems, to date, do not guide me much more clearly.'[36] After her experiences with Lana, Bo and others, Valentine knew that she could afford to wait; she did not intend to jeopardise the intimacy she had achieved so far by hurrying Sylvia.

In August, Sylvia came to Chaldon, to inspect the progress of the cottage. She flattered Valentine by exclaiming 'What a perfect steward! who can cut wood and make good tea!'[37] and they enjoyed flirtatious conversations which raised Valentine's hopes. She noted: 'Sylvia's clothes are always most attractive', and was encouraged by Sylvia's determination to feed her.[38]

But at tea with the Powyses, Sylvia annoyed Valentine by trying to coerce her into politeness when their hosts were antagonistic towards Miss Green; she was presumably trying to save a social situation, without realising its antecedents. Valentine angrily vowed 'I shall not any longer look to Sylvia ... for house-room and companionship ... I go my way.'[39] But the following day she was more reasonable:

> I wish I did not want to live with Sylvia. I do. However, I could not repay her ... While I can easily bear and most often enjoy her love of power and the consequent dominion over my liberty – I cannot and will not endure a demand for forced tact and diplomacy and above all that social submission which anyway I cannot give. So today I am a sadder and a wiser woman – not so much of a woman, either, in grey flannel and a white shirt open at the neck.[40]

That night, Valentine dreamed that she said 'I love you very much' to Sylvia, who replied 'And I love you, my dear, and I love you.'[41]

If things had not progressed quite thus far by day, Sylvia was certainly sending unmistakeable signals. 'I love it when you look like a fourth form schoolboy', she told Valentine, 'Won't it be heavenly to have a house of our own?' and 'This has been a delightful foretaste.'[42] After a week of this, Valentine was writing frankly 'I should have liked to get into that bed beside her.'[43] Sylvia – who was reputed to be a witch, and startled Virginia Woolf by explaining she knew so much about witches 'Because I am one'[44] – told Valentine the spell to compel a lover to come to you, by burning a red flannel heart soaked in your own blood, and intensely wishing for the one you desire. Encouragingly, Sylvia spoke of the object of this magic summoning as 'she'. By now, Valentine was wandering about the lanes after she had walked Sylvia home at night, and returning to wait beneath her window. When Sylvia went back to London, Valentine went too, and here Sylvia was equally charming. After a long afternoon discussing poetry, Sylvia gave her a snuff-box full of cigarettes, and a parting kiss. 'Look after yourself,' she said, 'and write a lot of poetry, and write a lot of letters to me'.[45] Valentine was exultant.

Sylvia sent her a long ironic poem, 'Father, most fatherly', about Joseph Staines Cope, the Victorian vicar of Chaldon, which Valentine loved and probably understood better than anyone. She described the experience of reading Sylvia's work, and the closeness which it made her feel, in a poem for Sylvia, 'The Cottage at Night', which opens:

> I sat reading your poems as the night went on,
> Bread was beside me and there was a glass to hand,
> While the fire burned clearly and outside all was still ...

and concludes with an image of this shared ritual amounting to a religious experience, in which the absent poet is transubstantiated into a real presence:

> ... my heart was a quickened lover –
> Familiar words became blest. I could understand
> The plait of your craft, the divine half-awareness of will,
> And I broke bread, took wine, and over
> Far spaces offered for you my sacrament.[46]

The prestigious (and paid) publication of several of her poems in *Time and Tide* passed virtually unnoticed by Valentine; so did Bo's visit in September. Miss Green was almost ready, and its future occupants were amassing furniture and household paraphernalia – even their storage jars pleased Valentine, who interpreted them as 'tangible proof'.[47] As they drove with a last load from Inverness Terrace, Sylvia gave herself up to a future with Valentine: 'Watching her hand on the wheel, abandoning myself to a suavity of driving which was like the bowing of a master-violinist, I felt that everything was bound to go right.'[48]

Initially, it went wrong when Sylvia was bitten by the dog from the vicarage, a notoriously nasty Great Dane. (Sylvia was bitten quite often, arbitrarily, but on this occasion she was rescuing her affable Chow, William.) She continued on to tea with the Powyses and said nothing to Valentine until they got back to her room late in the evening, when she remarked 'Now I can take my coat off. I didn't want Violet to see the blood.'[49] Valentine had to take over the preparations for moving in, and the all-important lighting of Sylvia's cigarettes. This was no hardship for either of them. Valentine was confiding in her diary 'She looked most tensely beautiful ... her hands are quite exquisite ...' and so on, while Sylvia was simultaneously admitting to watching Valentine's legs, admiring her hands, envisaging 'joy and trousers', and more along the same lines.[50] She told Valentine they would be like the Ladies of Llangollen, and Valentine recorded these conversations which came close to declarations:

S: What do you think I got the cottage for?
V: I have never been quite sure.

S: Surely it was obvious enough? That one reason (and that was, apparently my poetry).

S: You have got a real gooseflesh quality – when one stops in the middle of reading a poem and says – 'Oh, my dear' – that surely is a criterion?[51]

They moved in to Miss Green on 4 October 1930. Sylvia was there first, and when Valentine arrived kissed her in greeting, and then felt that perhaps she had been too forward. Valentine recalled:

> a duck cooking and one large dubious-looking horse-mushroom which she had picked on the Five Maries that afternoon. We ate that good dinner and drank some beaujolais and then some brandy ... In the morning I came downstairs in my fine silk man's dressing gown and morocco slippers, and lighted the first fire. It burned very brightly and kindled without trouble.[52]

So the omens were good. Valentine and Sylvia settled in to their cottage, with its coral-pink woodwork, milk-white walls, gold-scrolled oval mirror lit by candle-sconces above the fire. They were rather grand, conversing with company manners in finished Paris style, listening to music seriously and cooking elaborate meals. Within this formality, their intimacy increased; Sylvia recorded that Valentine had told her more about her childhood 'embellished with a mad nurse.'[53] The stories Sylvia now heard of her friend's background accorded oddly with the person she knew with 'the composed low voice and the sardonic turn of mind and velvet good manners'.[54] She listened.

~

Valentine could claim 'I was born and bred a Londoner' and 'Scotland is two-thirds my native country' with equal conviction.[55] London-born she certainly was, in Mayfair, at 54 Brook Street – a tall red-brick Victorian extravaganza opposite Claridge's Hotel. (It was a Sunday, 20 May 1906, and poor Ruth 'so horribly feared and suffered' during childbirth that Valentine thought 'she shrank from' physical contact with her children ever after.)[56] The Scottish connection was ancestral; Molly was christened Mary Kathleen Macrory Ackland, to commemorate her mother's Scots maiden name. Robert's middle name, Craig, was also a Scots surname from his mother. 'My father's father was pure Devonshire,' Valentine admitted, but 'I am entirely Northern: Northumberland and Scotland.'[57] This Northern blood seemed romantic to Valentine, but other parental inheritances she considered more problematic.

> I have a really sinister heritage ... extravagance, half-wittedness or at any rate flounciness, sombre melancholy, splenetic rage, violent and self-righteous determination, ambition, dramatic intensity, and a total disregard for accuracy ... plus Robert's almost lunatic scrupulousness.[58]

Robert's scrupulousness could take strange forms. His expectations of his children were unrealistic; ordinary childish nervousness about playing the piano at the school concert was transformed by him into proof of cowardliness, weak character and disgrace. He had a lucrative private dental surgery in the house, but his children's teeth were so neglected that Valentine had none left by the time she was forty. During the First World War, he expected little Molly to accompany him on his ward rounds to visit his plastic surgery patients, all horribly disfigured and many blinded, young men who despite his best efforts would never be anything but dreadfully damaged. (It can only have added to their ordeal to have to play cards or haltingly converse with a shy ten-year-old child.) This experience left her with a terror of blindness, and a horror of what she saw as her own cowardice. In later life, Valentine believed that her father's unbending strictness and formidable manner probably masked intense shyness like her own, and she certainly identified her own adult melancholies or furies with those of his she'd witnessed as a child. (The one person who remembered Valentine talking about her relationship with her father could only say to me 'These are very deep waters, deep and dark.')[59]

Ruth did not hide from her daughter that she was afraid of Robert, and she often wept over his brusqueness. It was comforting to pray together for Daddy's conversion – he was not a church-goer. Ruth, by contrast, was highly if idiosyncratically religious; she confided in Molly that she was a Saint and a Mystic, and inculcated in her daughter a tormenting sense of guilt. Molly knew that Ruth worried about Joan, who frightened her, and considered herself 'very delicate in health', overworked by the running of the house and supervision of the servants, and also 'that she set for herself a standard of "unselfishness" which ... she considered she almost always attained.'[60] Ruth's vague pious remarks had a disproportionate impact on such an imaginative child as Molly, who agonised about her sins, dreaded God's anger, and practiced what she later described as 'spiritual masturbation ... hardly pleasurable at all – and more tiring than anything I've felt since'.[61]

With this parental background, and the ever-present Joan, it was inevitable that Valentine should tell Sylvia of her isolation: 'I do not remember ever being comforted or supported through any ordeal by anyone, through the whole of my childhood', she wrote. 'I never had any sense of there being anyone I could turn to for protection or shelter ... There was never anyone to rely on.'[62] But, with the robust toughness which her father could not see, Molly created for herself a moral framework, a safe place, a private world; like so many lonely children, she read. Books had an enormous influence on Molly's character, and the development of her individuality. She read anything she came across, but found that poetry gave the most direct access to the realm of the imagination. (Valentine remained a passionate and committed reader all her life, with the result that she was extremely erudite.) Once Molly understood the power of poetry, she decided to become a poet herself; her childhood ambition was to write, as well as to read, to engage in the conversation from both directions. Even playing in the attic, dressed up as a bard to sing *Land of my Fathers*, she was acting out the idea of being a poet. When she was a child, she believed the poets were her 'friends and protectors',[63] since she had no others.

'I see', Valentine wrote in 1951, 'that my "upbringing" was really disgraceful. We were totally impoverished'. She was referring to cultural deprivation:

> I do not think that, in my own class, I have ever known any family as benighted as ours was. A *complete* blank in every place: No pictures, no music, no books, no plays, no philosophy, no theology, no science, no languages, no history, no architecture. Absolute chaos on the walls – all horrible.[64]

The 'mad nurse' whose existence struck Sylvia so forcibly was a typical part of this household. Despite being extremely well-off, the Acklands spent very little money on their children. Nanny was given an allowance out of which to buy whatever little Molly needed. As a result, unsurprisingly, Molly was often ill-clothed and underfed – although there were unexpected interventions, when she would suddenly be kitted out in immaculate bespoke riding clothes and boots. Nanny was so short-tempered and violent that Valentine later thought her actually insane; at the time she was more concerned about her missing pocket-money. When she was sent to school at eight years old – belatedly, since she'd had no home tuition – Molly found herself short of basics like socks and lacking crucial bits of school uniform. (Ever after, she was fanatical about good clothes, fine leather shoes and lavish accoutrements.) Her parents were oblivious, so long as she was booted and suited for riding, and she was unable to communicate with them. As Valentine later understood, their neglect was a form of self-deception; so long as nothing was said 'my parents could easily

10. Ackland family motoring – L to R: Robert, Molly (at the wheel, aged 5), Joan, Ruth, and (as Valentine inscribed on the back of the photo) 'my awful nurse'.

believe that I was satisfactorily provided for; and no doubt they did believe that.'[65]

No doubt. The school they selected was not an unreasonable choice, once Ruth had convinced herself that Molly was too delicate to be sent away to boarding school. (Joan's school had been selected because one of the proprietors was the sister of the vicar at Winterton; it had apparently nothing else to recommend it.) Queen's College was chosen because of its proximity in nearby Harley Street, where it is still an expensive private school. Although it was originally founded with great intentions for the education of women, the school magazines for the period of Molly's attendance indicate that the pupils emerged to marry, rather than pursue further education; many of the previous year's sixth formers are congratulated as married women. (When I visited the school, ninety years later, the helpful archivist introduced me to one of the departmental heads, who raised her eyebrows with a weary smile when the word 'feminism' was used.)

Molly was accompanied there and collected by Nanny; she was terrified of being late, but Nanny did not share this anxiety, so poor Molly always arrived in a panic. Although she was very 'backward' in arithmetic when she first attended, her reading was 'fluent and intelligent' and her teachers noted that she had a 'desire to get on.' This was perhaps partly because of her lack of any intellectual stimulation at home; one of her more alert teachers commented on her 'particular interest in the English subjects.' Beyond this, it was only observed that Molly was 'steady'; she maintained a position of near-invisibility, she never had a bad mark, and her conduct report always stated 'very good indeed.'[66] For the five years she attended the school, Queen's College never witnessed the slightest trace of her individuality.

Molly's friend Emmy Black was, by contrast, an outgoing, cheerful girl who was always in trouble for being too talkative in class. Valentine afterwards claimed that when she realised it was normal to have friends she 'attached one or two casually', but never felt intimate; indeed, it would have been virtually impossible to have a truthful personal conversation without revealing her parents' neglect, her sister's abuse, and her own insecurity. Her oddness was evident enough for Emmy to say frequently 'Molly's a very quair girl really', and she was right.[67] Molly's queerness was quite obvious:

she was different, but no one quite knew why, yet. Still, with these schoolfriends and their families she was able to experience ordinary childhood amusements and naughtinesses in London, or during the summer holidays when they came to stay at Winterton, and played bicycle-polo on the lawn.

At Winterton, Ernest the chauffeur taught Molly to drive, as soon as she could reach the pedals, and Ham the shabby butler, who claimed he'd won a Lonsdale belt, taught her to box. He coached her on the lawn, shouting 'Sock him one! There you go! Bring out your left – your *left*!' and occasionally forgetting himself and swearing or hitting her properly. (If Robert saw this, he would interfere – 'Steady on' – which annoyed them both.) Other delights included the singing dog Leo, who belonged to Mr Powles the gardener, who did not allow Molly to set Leo howling as often as she would have liked, out of consideration for his emotional state.[68]

The Acklands collected particularly eccentric servants, as Valentine recalled, 'there were so many – so dear or so queer.'[69] Her favourite was Nobby the ostler, but there was also factory-girl Rosa who called Molly a little bitch, Gladys the kleptomaniac, Edith who was roughly kind but talked to soldiers in the park, Gertrude who helped herself to champagne from the cellar and was once too drunk to serve dinner. But it was Nanny who nursed Molly through severe illnesses – Spanish flu, pleurisy, colitis – who looked after her when she had her tonsils and adenoids out, and her appendix removed on the kitchen table. Nanny was irrational, expert at pinches, slaps and hair-tugs, but perhaps worst of all she was good at frightening children with stories of the terrors outside the nursery.

Valentine remembered 'fear and rapture'[70] as the most common emotions of her childhood; she remained able to experience both extremes to an extraordinary degree. Her fear of other people manifested itself in disabling shyness (of which she'd trained herself to give not the slightest sign), and a desire for powerful influence over others. Her search for rapture took her to some strange places. But most of all, her childhood had left her with an insatiable longing for the love and admiring attention she'd been denied. And as Sylvia would discover, even when that need was met, it had to be proved, tested, and proved again.

Chapter Four:
Sylvia's Lover

Her experiences of being powerless and unprotected had given Valentine a strong sense of identification with the underdog, and her determination to be in a position of strength henceforward was partly so that she could protect those who needed her help. It was famously said of Sylvia by William Maxwell: 'her heart was with the hunted, always',[1] and this shared characteristic was, fittingly, what would bring Valentine and Sylvia together. Sylvia was due to return to London for the winter, after only a week in the shared cottage – the building work hadn't been completed in time for her to spend the summer there. As the week drew towards its end, she knew more of Valentine's background, but no definitive move had been made to alter their relationship to that of lovers, rather than close friends. On 11 October they went for a walk, and an unusual light on the familiar landscape created a curious atmosphere, which Sylvia interpreted as threatening. Valentine assured her that the imminent feeling presaged something good. Their discussion was interrupted by the arrival of some village news.

The dangerous dogs from the vicarage were kept by a mother and daughter named Katherine and Joan Stevenson. They also kept five young women from the county asylum, and received one pound per week per inmate from the council for training them as servants. Mrs Stevenson was extremely unpopular in the village, as she was believed to ill-treat her charges, whom she called 'mentals'. Several people had remonstrated with her about the conditions in which she kept the trainee servants, only to be told that the young women were dangerous sex-maniacs who needed a strict regime, and only wailed all night long because they were mad. One of them, Lily Roberts, had run away several times because she was so unhappy, and been brought back by police who were sympathetic to her story. She had just made another attempt to escape, begging to be allowed to go home to her mother.

As soon as they heard the news, Valentine and Sylvia hurried to the vicarage. According to Miss Stevenson's account, they suggested that the furious villagers wanted to burn the vicarage down, and warned her about the ancient custom of 'rough music',[2] when crowds of women noisily crashed pots and pans together in a percussive show of disapproval. (This was traditionally used to protect women from wife-battering, but as a way of expressing communal disapproval of domestic violence, it could reasonably have been applied to the Stevensons.) It was obviously Valentine and Sylvia's intention to frighten them into common decency, since politely indicating that their behaviour wasn't acceptable had not worked. Sylvia – who was notoriously terrifying when angry – was thrilled by Valentine's rage: 'Valentine shook her stick in the air like a squire. Righteous indignation is a beautiful thing, and lying exhausted on the rug I watched it flame in her with severe geometric flames.'[3] This opportunity to observe each other passionately committed to a just cause was stirring; their first united exercise of power. It broke down social barriers which previously had been insurmountable.

Usually, when they went to their separate beds in the adjoining bedrooms, they did not chat from room to room, but that night they broke this rule of silence and continued talking excitedly through the wall about the vicarage, the owl hooting outside, the merits of eiderdowns, different kinds of liking. About this, Valentine remarked in her low melancholy voice 'Sometimes I think I am utterly loveless' (or unloved, or without love).[4] Whatever she meant by this, it was the cue Sylvia needed. She came through the dividing door, knelt on the floor by the bed, and took Valentine in her arms, to tell her how much she *was* loved. Valentine drew Sylvia into the narrow bed, held her, kissed her, and at last they were lovers. Ever after, the sound of the inn-sign creaking and the wind rattling the thorn-trees along the drove would remind them both of that first night together.

In the morning, Valentine asked her usual morning-after question, a stern 'Well?' (Or, as Sylvia sometimes recalled it, 'Do you know what you've done?' and 'Do you regret it?') Sylvia noticed with amusement that she had changed into clean pyjamas, and was more struck by this than by the question. For she had 'found love'; already she 'was at home in an unsurmised love, an irrefutable happiness'.[5] They laughed together that morning, with relief and thankfulness and delight; it seemed that they might so easily have missed each other.

Valentine recaptured their joy when she wrote, years later:

> Our lives for the next few weeks scarcely knew night or day or any change in the weather: we knew nothing except our joy and pleasure and the thousand-and-one, infinitely fine adjustments we were making, to fit always closer and closer to each other.[6]

Telling this story, as they both did so many times over, the nature of their love was presented as immediately apparent, as it no doubt seemed in retrospect. But at the time, nothing was quite so certain or so obvious; although they both knew that this was not an ordinary love, they were uncertain as to its future. Their first day together as lovers was Sylvia's last in Chaldon, 'a bridal of earth and sky'. Sylvia wrote of lying on the Five Maries scandalously with Valentine: 'It is so natural to be hunted and intuitive. Feeling safe and respectable is so much more of a strain.'[7] She was delighted by Valentine's insistence on cutting short the social round of farewells and hurrying through dinner so that they could return to bed. The next morning, Sylvia went to London, as planned, for dinner with Teague. She felt hardly present in London, her thoughts were so strongly still at Miss Green, and this experience made her decide there and then that she must take the risk of accepting the different future which now seemed possible. In her diary that night she wrote:

> life rising up in me again cajoles with unscrupulous power, and I will yield to it gladly, if it leads me away from this death I have sat so snugly in for so long, sheltering myself against joy, respectable in my mourning, harrowed and dulled and insincere to myself in a pretext of troth.[8]

(Describing her relationship to Teague as a death suggests it was moribund indeed, but was Sylvia also, at some level, acknowledging its darker aspects? Her choice of the word 'harrowed' – *Harrow*ed – is also interesting.)

The morning post brought her a parcel from Valentine, Chaldon snail shells in a box, 'one orange, one lemon-yellow, smelling of Valentine'[9] (she'd marinaded them in her scent, *Fougère Royale*); Sylvia was as disturbed as was intended. Valentine also sent a ring that she usually wore herself, and sealed the letter with black wax imprinted with her signet; the heraldic device of a falcon on a fist with the Ackland motto *Inébranlable* (Unshakeable).

Sylvia was due to be absent in London for a month – she was very social, and had engagements booked into November; Valentine adjured her not to forget. Valentine couldn't yet realise how impossible Sylvia would have found it to forget; Sylvia's return to London as previously intended, asking Valentine not to tell anyone about their affair, suggested that she wasn't entirely lost to love. Alone in Chaldon, Valentine perhaps wondered whether Sylvia felt as strongly as she did, or had other doubts (or even another sexual encounter); she destroyed her diary entries for a few crucial days. But an exchange of letters swiftly clarified how deeply Sylvia felt; she wrote, after smelling the scented shells, 'Oh, strip off these hours one by one, till I feel your flesh against mine again'.[10]

Valentine wrote to her

> ... the sure rightness of your words, your wit and understanding, wisdom and courage and steadfastness. All this is an endless delight to me, and ... the beauty of your body, which I worship, and the achievement and mastery for which I adore you.[11]

When Valentine's diary resumes (meditating on her lover in the manner of the seriously smitten), she has no anxieties about whether the love is reciprocal:

> Her wit and her understanding, her wisdom and courage and directness and finesse – All these qualities I adore. All of them compel me to love her ... Sylvia – what a most lovely name that is![12]

Four days after Sylvia had left for London Valentine followed her, and their reunion was all that she could have hoped. Days spent separately culminated in romantic picnics at Valentine's studio, champagne in bed, much love-making and little sleep. Valentine wrote:

> Everything smiled upon us and I did not know that such joy could be found – or ever beguiled to stay. She was so sweet: so tender and compassionate and full of understanding. Delicate and kind.

Besides the exciting glory of her desires. Conversation still keeps to an explorative mood. [13]

This exploration of each other as lovers, rather than friends, was sensitive. Sylvia had divined the complexity of Valentine's nature, and its difficulties. 'How to house, and yet not to tame, this wild solitary heart,' she mused, 'so fierce even in its diffidence.' [14]

Sylvia understood that Valentine's inscrutable façade, haughty and remote, sometimes hid real melancholy; she romanticised this difficult side of her young lover, seeing her as a 'lonely, mysterious creature grieving alone'. [15] The other extreme aspect of Valentine, swaggering and extrovert, was a wild character – daring, autocratic and passionate – who reminded Sylvia of 'a very young, fastidious and urbane pirate'. [16] Sylvia celebrated all the elements of her lover, hailing her as 'my more than music, my true sky, my light and my gravity', calling her a unicorn, a mermaid, a leopard, a true poet. She delighted in describing Valentine's long legs, her lovelock, her dark eyes, her suave bearing, her ability to dig like a man and drive like an angel (or on occasion, 'like God'), her power to rescue Sylvia from 'resignation' and 'smite this away from me with a kiss'. [17] The fairytale prince awakening her from enchanted sleep was how Sylvia envisaged her sudden transformation, after some years of feeling old, dull, and emotionally dusty, into seeing herself as a glamorous woman whose maturity and sophistication required an attentive and demanding lover. Valentine's strength and passion were a revelation to Sylvia, who always maintained that Valentine was the best lover she ever had, and explained her own life-long fidelity as entirely natural.

Their relationship did not remain clandestine for long; Sylvia's initial wish that no one should know was swiftly replaced by the desire that everyone should know. Her early instinct for secrecy indicates that Sylvia understood the implications of taking such a visible lesbian as her lover, but ever after she was openly proud of the relationship, and – bravely – expected her friends to be unshockable. Her epiphany on the Five Maries, when she recognised that being 'respectable' and heterosexual was far more difficult for her than the 'natural' state of being outcast with Valentine, was the culmination of Sylvia's lifelong experience of otherness; it explained everything.

Valentine thought acceptance would be easier if they could marry, and wrote about this (then) social impossibility: 'I see the vital importance of Lesbians being recognised as a third sex ... which will come naturally one day, but too late to profit me.'[18] Her belief that she'd been born different, and her reading around the subject, led to much pleasurable discussion about their sexuality and what it all *meant* – although they sometimes mocked the earnest conclusions of the sexologists. Thus Valentine wrote to Sylvia in 1931: 'Perhaps you had better read all about extroverts, which is me, and introverts, which is you, before you develop any more desires.'[19]

Sylvia now took a great interest in stories about lesbian couples (as she always did ever after, as well as taking particular pleasure in the friendship of other lesbians). Among the many stories they relayed to each other, Sylvia ended a long account to Valentine about Little Zeal's local lesbians 'how romantic and delightful it all is ... I hope one day someone will be writing a letter about us'.[20] She also hoped that 'in the future the little girls [of Chaldon] should play at being Miss A and Miss W.'[21] But this sentiment co-existed with satire at the expense of institutionalism; she and Valentine had a running joke about being advised to join the Order of Woodcraft Chivalry because of being bi-sexual (by which they meant of dual gender, rather than attracted to two sexes).

Of her conversion, Sylvia later wrote to Valentine:

> Do you remember the ceremony of the Brides of France – that on the frontier they were undressed and crossed it only in a shift? And on the French side, the shift was whisked off, and the bride clothed in the husband's country – I crossed my frontier in my shift, my darling, and left everything but myself on the other side of that flimsy wooden door painted pink.[22]

This vividly describes Sylvia's crossing the border from heterosexuality into another country, a new found land of sexual transgression in which Sylvia found herself entirely at home.

Not all the inhabitants would welcome her. The problem of Bo had occurred to Valentine very quickly; her new love was not like the previous ones which could exist concurrently with a continuing relationship. An unfortunate episode was recorded by Sylvia: the moment 'when Bo broke in on us at 2: I tousled on the floor, no doubt about it, and serene. And [Valentine] sprang up and stood defensively between us.'[23] Bo had endured what she regarded as frivolous infidelities before; now Valentine needed to convince her that this was a different thing. 'I cannot bear to hurt her,' she wrote, thinking of their long relationship. 'It has to be done – it is cruel to keep her love, but I hate losing it.'[24] A week later, having been to Winterton with Sylvia, she wrote about Bo in her diary again: 'I feel such a swine, and yet what can I now do? ... this is so swiftly the whole centre of my life.'[25]

After a distressing visit from Bo, when she played 'My Old Dutch' on the gramophone 'a little ironically',[26] Valentine realised that Bo intended to persist in treating Sylvia as just a phase. It wasn't until several months later that Valentine could bring herself to write a letter reminding Bo that there had been a time when it was Valentine who wanted more from their affair than Bo would offer. Valentine explained that Sylvia had given 'everything, without any possible reservation'. She continued: 'I do not want to hurt you. Our love was far too dear to me. But the last yielding was not there. You had a separate life. Our love did not ever compel us to live together.'[27] At this, Bo had to accept Valentine's departure as permanent.

After visiting Winterton (and less than three weeks with Valentine), Sylvia also decided to end her long involvement with Teague, and tell him why. Previously, like Valentine with Bo, Sylvia had considered herself free to have simultaneous affairs (like the one with Stephen Tomlin), but had never felt the need to break off the background liaison. She had known, however, that their relationship was all but defunct, and Teague could hardly have expected Sylvia to remain living alone, apparently single, forever (however convenient this might have been for him). He was approaching sixty, she was thirty-six, there was no question that he could leave his wife and family, or even acknowledge that he and Sylvia had any relationship; it must presumably have crossed his mind that she might like to marry and have children of her own. If he had half-expected some such revelation, Sylvia's news was still a surprise. 'It was not an easy thing to say',[28] she wrote in her diary with some understatement – but she managed. He was civilised and made no scene, accepting that their affair was over, whatever his private thoughts about Sylvia's unconventional choice.

~

Winterton was Valentine's test, not so much of her lovers, but of her response to them in that special place (which was where Richard had so absolutely failed). They drove there at night, on 28 October, at a speed which left Sylvia feeling that the journey had been an epic flight; although they arrived at 1.15am, she was shown all over the house, and the dark greenhouses. In the morning, there was a tour of the garden and outbuildings. Sylvia was particularly interested in the room above the stables which Ruth had allowed Valentine to use as a separate flat; it was full of interesting clues to her character such as jeweller's scales, microscope slides, and poems written on the wall or scratched on the window. The house she saw as 'like being in a liner',[29] which was tactful; the large garden (with its bluebell wood, lilac grove by the pond, Aldeburgh Garden of daffodils, and donkey drawing water from the well) was perhaps easier to admire. Since Robert's death, the grounds and house were no longer so carefully kept, and this neglect seemed poignant to Valentine. In Sylvia's company, her childhood love of the place seemed closer: 'Nothing is changed and I am come back,'[30] Valentine wrote.

The rather ugly house was made romantic, Sylvia thought, by the presence of the sea; they ran across the dunes and paddled, wrote each other's names in the sand, and walked barefoot back to the house. Sylvia was not in the least embarrassed to be an object of interest in the pub as 'Miss Maaalie's latest'; she was fascinated to observe Valentine's swagger on her home ground, and hear her referred to as 'his Lordship' behind her back.[31] Her resemblance to Robert, thus commented on, perhaps seemed stronger at Winterton; the dilapidation of The Hill House was a constant reminder of past glories – and less happy memories. Sylvia was introduced to Trina, who delighted her by showing photographs of Molly, her face transfigured with pride and love as she did so. All the inhabitants of Winterton, even the village youths Valentine had once boxed with, seemed allies to Sylvia because of their regard for Valentine; the visit was a demonstration of her popularity. Later, Sylvia said that it was with Valentine that she first experienced the spell of the sea, and she suspected her of having mermaid blood.

It was significant that Sylvia enjoyed her visit to this so-significant place, and that her presence there made it all the more important to

Valentine. Sylvia was aware of how central she had become to Valentine, so quickly, when she wrote in Chaldon in early November that she had 'vowed and prayed that I might never hurt this wild sensitive love.'[32] They argued often, usually over questions of precedence (accepting presents, respecting dignity), but also resolved such issues easily; as Sylvia wrote: 'We are both of us tethered to savage senses of honour, no arrangement to which we have consented would have cast on either a slight.'[33]

Valentine was fascinated to discover that Sylvia really *was* a witch, or at least took the practice of witchcraft seriously, as Valentine's poem beginning '"Call up the Devil!" cried Sylvia' suggests.[34] Some of the pages removed from Valentine's diary apparently refer to this; one of the remaining scraps reads tantalisingly '... [not] "bubble bubble" but worship and grave evil and feasts ... But [Sylvia] did not take easily my joke about a coven to be held last night'.[35] Sylvia's flamboyant love-spells or blasphemous cat-christenings (and her familiarity with the historic literature of witchcraft) found a counterpart in Valentine's home-made rituals, and the personal superstitions which had always been one of her strategies for countering internal fears.

Sylvia now realised that Valentine's unpredictable emotional weather was the result of the abuses she had suffered, but their exploration of each other as lovers rather than friends revealed strengths, as well as sensitivities. Sylvia was delighted by Valentine's Noël Coward impersonations, and her habit of interspersing hymns with Coward songs 'without a waver of tone.'[36] And she was overwhelmed by the eroticism celebrated in poems like 'The eyes of body', with its explicit sensual exploration:

> The eyes of body, being blindfold by night,
>   Refer to the eyes of mind – at brain's command
>   Study imagination's map, then order out a hand
> To journey forth as deputy for sight.
>
> Thus and by these ordered ways
>   I come at you – Hand deft and delicate
>   To trace the suavely laid and intricate
>   Route of your body's maze.

My hand, being deft and delicate, displays
Unerring judgment; cleaves between your thighs
Clean, as a ray-directed airplane flies.

Thus I, within these strictly ordered ways,
Although blindfolded, seize with more than sight
Your moonlit meadows and your shadowed night.[37]

~

Valentine and Sylvia saw in the New Year of 1931 together in London, and on 12 January they went to a concert of Mozart and Beethoven piano concertos at Queen's Hall. Afterwards, they dined at the Monte Carlo restaurant (where a typical menu was sweetbreads followed by ptarmigan). In the taxi on the way home, Sylvia told Valentine 'I looked at all those people during the interval, and knew that I wanted none of them, I only wanted you.'[38] Valentine took this as it was intended, as a declaration of permanent and absolute commitment. When they got home, she recorded, 'God spoke to me and I performed his word – we knew our greatest happiness together.'[39] In the morning, Valentine went out and bought two wedding rings; for the rest of their lives, they celebrated this day as the anniversary of their marriage. It had taken them not quite three months to decide that this love affair was the great love they had both imagined, and longed for; a relationship which they hoped would last lifelong.

Now that Sylvia no longer wanted to keep their liaison secret, indeed wanted to flaunt it, she was amused by Valentine's discomfiture when she realised that two women had seen them making love outside, in Chaldon. 'I have been teased all evening,' Valentine noted. 'Sylvia was not abashed at all.'[40] (Sylvia cheered her up by suggesting that it would re-open the village debate about her gender – one faction 'had known for certain she was a man'.)[41] There were other hazards in making their love public. Bo cut Sylvia when they met, the Powys faction in the village was deeply disapproving (with the exception of Llewellyn, who wanted Valentine to supply detail). Ruth merely commented 'Well, at any rate she's a gentlewoman',[42] and lost no time in taking Sylvia aside to confide that she didn't expect to live long. There was no question, for Ruth, that any other relationship might ever lighten Valentine's responsibility towards her; she could accept her daughter's eccentric choice of lovers, on the understanding that she remained Valentine's first obligation. Dorothy Warren was initially civil toward Sylvia, but only while under the impression that she was one of many; she was affronted to discover that this new love was to replace the old ones.

One evening (when Sylvia was out dining with her extinguished old flame, Teague) Dorothy came to Valentine's flat, to look at Craskes. Presumably, she'd expected dinner to lead on to bed, and Valentine declined; certainly, when Dorothy understood the new situation she became very angry. Valentine, leaning elegantly against the mantelpiece and refusing to fight, was suddenly attacked; Dorothy knocked her down, banged her head against the floor, strangled her with her tie, and threatened to throw her out of the window. When gentlemanly Valentine wouldn't retaliate, Dorothy tried to destroy her poems in the fire, which had the desired result; enraged, Valentine flung her to the ground. After this ugly struggle, Dorothy's abuse and threats turned to howls of reproach and talk of suicide, but she eventually departed. Valentine summoned Sylvia to see the wrecked flat with its overturned furniture, scratched floor and ink-spattered carpets; she was shocked at this evidence of physical combat, and unimpressed by Dorothy's later explanation: 'You see, when I am angry I am always violent.'[43] Negotiating Valentine's past wasn't always so dramatic, but it was to be a major preoccupation for Sylvia.

For Valentine this new life inspired an outpouring of poetry. Her transformed situation meant that she had the perfect subject for her work in Sylvia, who was also an enabler of creativity; both muse and mentor. Sylvia placed great importance on working; as a professional, she presumed that their life together would be structured to allow time and space for writing, and this was propitious for Valentine's poetry. The emotions which Valentine was experiencing with such intensity every day were the personal yet universal themes best expressed in poetry, and a new maturity appeared in her work, which flourished. Love provided her with inspiration, something essential to write about.

The poems to Sylvia both create and celebrate her identity as Sylvia's lover, and explore an imaginative landscape which Valentine never ceased to map. Some of these love poems are tender, others intensely absorbed in the lover's dread of loss: 'What must we do if we cannot do this – / Lose ourselves in our dark autumn kiss ...'[44] She could also write with fierce humour, as in 'The clock plods on', which describes waiting for her lover in a storm: 'If she came and love's storm should arise – / What then – / With the gale outside, and within / A fiercer wind blowing? / If she came with the storm in her eyes / There's no knowing.'[45]

> The moment I woke up in the morning I looked at her. She lay, still asleep, her black hair on my arm close to my face & her face turned towards me, burrowed into my breast.
>
> I stayed still, lying easily on my back, remembering the night very clearly.
>
> Then, after a while, she stirred gently and opened her eyes – looking straight at me. She remembered instantly & smiled at me so sweetly & confidingly that I felt like weeping. I held her closely in my arms, & she said 'My darling!'[46]

Valentine often wrote like this about Sylvia's love. Certainty of that love was important; it was not popular or easily accepted.

In March 1931 Sylvia's step-father died suddenly of heart failure. Sylvia was upset, as she'd liked and respected Ronald, but she was also appalled on her own account. Nora was alone, living in their isolated house in Devon; she considered it her daughter's duty to return home and look after her permanently. But Sylvia had no intention of extending her emergency visit indefinitely; Valentine's trust in her was not misplaced. Sylvia wrote to Valentine from Little Zeal 'if I am not to be yours on easy terms I am the more yours; and the better wife in my own eyes for being thought a bad daughter.'[47]

Even in her state of shock and anguish, Nora was avid to control Sylvia, and needle her. She remarked about Sylvia's ring 'with intent to startle and shame ... It looks just like a wedding-ring,' to which Sylvia answered 'Yes, doesn't it?' ('and who was then shamed?')[48] Sylvia didn't immediately enlighten Nora about her new marital situation, but she hardly needed to; Nora had obviously guessed.

Valentine found enforced separation unendurable, and could imagine how the bereaved Nora would be treating Sylvia. On the pretext of a condolence visit, she arrived with Ruth, who was immediately questioned by Nora about their daughters' 'sudden

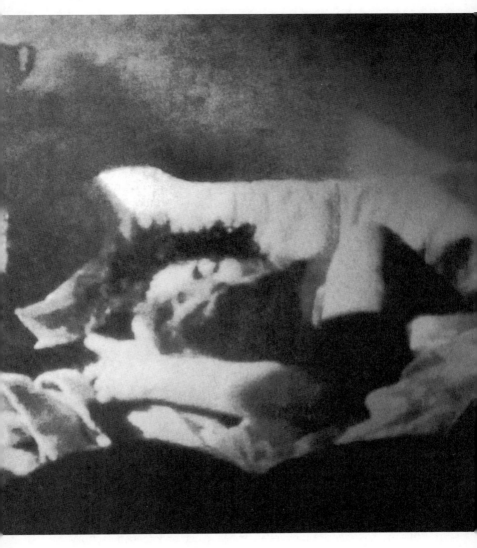

11. Valentine's lover – Sylvia asleep.

and intense friendship', over which she and Sylvia had by now 'had words'. Ruth assumed her well-practised naive air and observed that it was 'so nice' for them – but afterwards she warned Valentine that Nora really hated her.[49] This antipathy would probably have extended towards anyone who established an acknowledged relationship with Sylvia, but was particularly virulent because Valentine was a woman – Nora only liked men. She made it clear that she considered Sylvia undutiful for her decision to live with Valentine.

Ruth had managed the situation far more skilfully. By accepting Sylvia and absorbing her into the Ackland sphere, she maintained her hold on Valentine, who wouldn't have tolerated any antagonism towards Sylvia. Nora, by contrast, lost Sylvia's respect through her rudeness about Valentine and, by behaving as though Sylvia was a bad daughter, made it difficult for her to be a good one. Sadly, for memories of a loving mother Sylvia had to go back to her early childhood, when Nora told wonderful stories of *her* childhood in India. After that, Nora was always barbed. In 1932, with the words 'I found this and thought that you and Miss Ackland might like it', she gave Sylvia a Victorian china pomade pot, decorated with the Ladies of Llangollen walking out in their top hats. Sylvia optimistically interpreted this as 'a spirited and affable little dig in our ribs';[50] Miss Ackland may have doubted the gesture's goodwill.

Charles Prentice, an erstwhile lover of Sylvia's, was another whose reaction was difficult to gauge. He appeared at Chaldon in July 1931; Sylvia had a scheme for his firm, Chatto & Windus, to publish Valentine's poems. Charles was a gentle, cultured man but his history with Sylvia did not endear him to Valentine (who was already hyper-sensitive about her poems being read as a favour to Sylvia). Valentine concluded that he did not admire the poems though he did admire 'the brandy, the Craskes and, I fear, Sylvia.'[51] When Charles read Sylvia's poems, some of which responded to hers, Valentine found it extraordinary that he still ignored their relationship. Whether intended tactfully or dismissively (or whether it was genuinely invisible to him), this led Valentine to speculate on the disadvantages of their unofficial status:

> If Charles asked Sylvia to marry him, I wonder if it would make her look askance on me, and strangely? Which is truth? He or I?

Socially that is a madman's question; actually only love can answer it.[52]

Although Valentine was always insecure and prone to test love beyond any reasonable endurance, she did not really doubt 'Sylvia's heart'. But she found it galling that her own status was unrecognised, socially as well as legally, while a 'real' offer of marriage would have absolute validity. This slippage between the absolute reality of their relationship, to them, and its official invisibility would always be painful to Valentine; it was an area in which she was powerless.

A happier summer visit was that of Sylvia's aunt Purefoy with her husband, the writer Arthur Machen, and their fourteen-year-old daughter Janet, who was a great favourite with Sylvia. Valentine taught her to drive and they had water-fights in the garden with soda-water siphons; Janet, for one, was delighted with Sylvia's new companion. Later in August, Valentine and Sylvia had to part for holidays with their respective mothers; Ruth in Paris, Nora at Little Zeal.

This separation confirmed how much they loathed being apart; it also clarified other areas of their relationship. Hitherto, Sylvia had declined to expect fidelity from Valentine, while freely offering it herself. Indeed, as she later said, 'with refusing of vows and rejecting of contracts ... I paid out such yards of free reins and long ropes that it is a marvel to me now we didn't get strangled in them.'[53] Valentine wrote to her from Paris: 'I have seen some pretty and even two beautiful girls here – but to my horror and wry joy, I look dispassionately and then my gaze travels to you'.[54] When a French friend offered to set her up with a woman, Valentine extricated herself and assured Sylvia that she had no interest in anyone else – 'But what violent storms of desire I suffer for you.'[55]

In reply, Sylvia departed from her previous policy, and even ridiculed herself for it:

> I was just going to put my head on one side and say O what a pity that not one of the slenders or the slys or the willings caught your fancy. And only just in the nick of time did I find myself out – my deep female pride and content that they didn't.

Doubts about the wisdom of this admission constrained her to add:

> And as soon as I'd written *that* I found myself cautiously going on
> to say that if by any chance one of them had done so since your
> letter, I was, of course, delighted.[56]

Sylvia knew that Valentine had terminated her existing love-affairs,
but now that she'd voluntarily refrained from embarking on new ones,
Sylvia was emboldened to admit her preference for mutual exclusivity.
Whatever happened later, this could not be unsaid.

~

Although based in Chaldon, Valentine and Sylvia moved about
frequently, travelling between London and Winterton, and also staying
regularly at Lavenham (where they borrowed a house), on a houseboat
at Thurne in the Norfolk Broads, and at a favourite pub, The Lamb at
Tinhead. These miniature holidays romantically alone together were
always part of the pattern of their life. To make it easier, Sylvia bought
a red and cream Sports Triumph car which Valentine adored driving.
Sylvia's confidence as a learner driver was permanently dented by her
devoted cleaner Mrs Keates' lugubrious advice: 'O Miss, I hope you
won't be too venturesome.'[57]

Their pleasures were again threatened by an outbreak of familial
obligation. Ruth decided to let the London flat and spend the entire
winter economically in Norfolk, because of largely illusory financial
anxieties. Valentine perceived it as her duty to share this self-imposed
penance, and even pay rent for the flat above the garage at Winterton.
Sylvia determined to make the best of this 'new sort of winter', but when
she witnessed the Ackland family in action – Ruth's continual demands
and encroachments on Valentine's privacy, Joan's competitiveness
and needling – she utterly deprecated their treatment of Valentine,
especially the 'recurring cry of justify yourself by being a typist'.[58]
Unsurprisingly, Valentine sank into a suicidal melancholy (fortunately
alleviated by love-making), drank heavily, and suffered from hangovers,
migraines and gastric ulcers.

Joan's campaign against Valentine continued unabated, though her
usual tactics did not work with Sylvia, needless to say, and Sylvia's
love afforded Valentine some protection. Yet the pattern continued

in which the two sisters were twinned in parodic mimicry. Joan was now gaining some journalistic success, which she emphasised by employing Valentine to type, and passing on certain commissions to finish. These articles, on calculated subjects such as female pilots or the transvestite 'Colonel' Barker, Valentine knew to be 'hideous nauseating hypocrisy',[59] but she still felt inferior because poetry wasn't so lucrative. By the Ackland family's materialist standards, Joan was the successful one, though she knew her writing was of no intrinsic worth. Valentine's was the ethical victory, Joan's the worldly one, and Joan's life was a travesty of Valentine's. Throughout their later lives, this uneasy distorted mirroring would continue: in Joan's increasingly masculine appearance, her relationships with women after her husband's death, her war work, her conversion to Catholicism and so on. This imitative tendency of Joan's suggests a competitive obsession with taking over Valentine's private spaces, as had happened throughout her childhood. Yet it only emphasised the absolute contrast between the two sisters.

Over the winter of 1931-32 Valentine was writing well, despite family pressures, publishing poems in periodicals such as *The New York Review of Books* and even getting (modestly) paid for them. She was anxious if she didn't write poems in enormous numbers – five a day was quite average – and she dreaded being 'a bloody little minor poet'.[60] In this she was influenced by her family's conventional idea of success, however inapplicable to a poet. Bouts of depression about her work and her finances continued even after they returned to Chaldon in the spring of 1932, but alternated with ecstatic delight. Most importantly, Valentine wrote,

> I have – my deep and true and dark and passionate love for Sylvia – our life together of warmth and passion and continued desire – our mutual rekindling, constant planting of fireseeds, constant budding and leaving and shedding and dark rooting and fresh spring again – this is exactly the stuff of poetry.[61]

In a letter to Bo, Valentine wrote a detailed description of daily life in Chaldon in 1932 which – although it has an understandable note of self-justification – gives a fair idea of how she intended most days to be spent. It demonstrates the importance of creative work in her life, and the relationship between life and work in which she believed.

> Most days I write in the morning, after doing the rougher part of the housework – coals and oil and wood-cutting and lighting the copper. Then lunch, and I go out to work in the garden or drive or talk to the people at the pub or I walk – then tea, and I read while dinner is getting and read afterwards too – or we play chess or the gramophone and Sylvia sews and mends sometimes, or writes. Then we go to bed. We sleep together always and I am very happy. It is a particularly full life, very productive and intensely happy. And passionate, which fills a need I have always had, and makes my poems come alive ... I see no difference between our state and the state of normal true marriage between a man and a woman. As long as pleasure and physical enjoyment lighten the deep passion and *as long as the deep passion, which is equally animal and spiritual goes on burning redly to the core* – then this love in which we live is true and produces truth.[62]

(Not exactly what Bo wanted to hear, perhaps.)

Many more glimpses of this happy and productive life come from Valentine's diary: her delight to be back in trousers after a brief 'imprisonment' in a skirt; her forthright comment on an article about perversion ('Balls!'); her experiments on Sylvia with kisses: 'Which did she prefer?'; a scrap of reported speech: '"Hurry up, now" I said – "Whaffor?" she answered – lingering – "Bed" I answered – and she was gone in a flash.'[63] Sylvia's writing also flourished under this Chaldon regime. Valentine recorded that she was busy 'writing the beginning of her Lesbian novel',[64] an illuminating reference to *Summer Will Show*. On their second October anniversary Valentine wrote of her gift of a mourning-ring 'Let it be a pretty mourning for the sad days and nights she spent out of my arms – for I was ready for her so long before she came.'[65]

Later in October Valentine and Sylvia heard that Charles Prentice had accepted their joint book of poems for publication. Cautious Charles would run few risks by publishing the unknown young poet together with one of his firm's established writers, but it was a compromise for

12. 'This kind paradise where we were so happy' – Valentine and Sylvia
    in the looking-glass at Frankfort.

them both. Valentine was, she calculated, '⅔ in favour and ⅓ not,' for her conscience was troubled by Sylvia's involvement. But, reminding herself '*Honi soit* –' (although she must have known that Joan would always think evil) she overcame these scruples and agreed to the 'new scheme'.[66] The book would be out in about a year.

In 1933 Valentine and Sylvia left Miss Green. The honeymoon cottage seemed too small, their village friends Granny Moxon and Shepherd Dove had died, other neighbours (notably the Powyses) were difficult, Valentine was drinking too much. Frankfort Manor at Sloley in Norfolk was a good place to re-establish their enchanted realm;

the beautiful dilapidated seventeenth century brick house was romantically too large for them, and sparsely furnished. The lawn in front of it had never been mown except with a scythe, a tradition the new tenants had to promise to uphold. There were abandoned outbuildings and ruined greenhouses, like Winterton, and an ancient orchard, remarkable old trees. Their stay at Frankfort was not long (they lived there for just over a year, across two summers) but its imaginative impact was great.

Valentine called Frankfort

> the perfect house ... the loveliest small manor house that I have ever seen ... We lived in a kind of solemn, fairy tale splendour ... every day, every evening, every night and every dawn there was some new, strange beauty or curiosity or discovery. And we were very very happy.[67]

Among the pleasures of the place was the wild garden which produced bumper crops of asparagus, whitecurrants, chestnuts and rare varieties of pears. They both loved the seclusion, left alone with few visitors – although one evening they met a hedgehog walking up the mossy drive. 'Another day, in full sun,' Valentine recalled,

> I was picking green peas into a colander, and saw the earth near my feet heaving, and a mole emerged, and I caught it instantly, in the colander, and carried it to Sylvia, who was writing in her room, and set it down beside the typewriter on her table.[68]

Valentine was in her element. She shot record numbers of rats in the stables, observed birds' nests in the wood, studied the stars through the telescope Sylvia had given her. (Knowing the Ackland penchant for 'expensive and devouring passions' Sylvia imagined Valentine announcing 'Sylvia, we must sell the car and the silver and all that we have and buy an astronomer's telescope ... I shall be perfectly happy, I shall wish for nothing else. We must get it instantly.' But she was content to study the moon and 'the expressions of the hens in the field across the lane'.)[69]

In love, too, she was intensely happy, writing of her physical relationship with Sylvia 'No one has ever answered to love as she does – Love itself is matched by her.'[70] Only occasionally her old fear of death intruded, when she remembered the great sorrow that such a great love would inevitably bring. 'Last night,' she wrote in her 1933 diary, 'after such an intense happiness, I lay awake for all the night, swung between despair and despair'.[71]

Valentine's poetry could absorb such thoughts; at Frankfort she wrote well and prolifically. In just one of her extant notebooks there are ninety-two poems, written between March and September 1934, as well as short stories and notes. Yet it was hard work living at Frankfort, with the time-consuming demands of the house and garden. Money was tight; as well as paying the £50 a year rent, they needed a servant to help with the labour-intensive housework. (She was a young local woman, Irene Peake, who sensibly ate the cats' meat when there was nothing else for breakfast.) They were as self-sufficient as possible, stored and bottled produce for the winter, sold jams and pickles, and delivered their potatoes to the local chip shop in Valentine's beloved motor car (now a racing green MG Midget). It was hard work, and to survive there at all required total commitment to the place. Yet, despite these prosaic hardships, there was something unreal about it all.

The fairy tale atmosphere of Frankfort gave the time they spent there a magical significance in Valentine's memory. Writing of 'this kind paradise where we were so happy, so hard-working, so good', Sylvia sadly asserted 'we were never again so unimpededly good as we were at Frankfort Manor.'[72] But the good, as in all fairy tales, were tested; the strange house had its dark side. Although in sunlight it was propitious and enfolding, during thunderstorms the atmosphere was sinister; the trees seemed to crowd around, while Valentine and Sylvia sat on the sofa calming cats and expecting to be struck by lightning. Shortly after they arrived, Chow William had to be put down. Valentine dug his grave, and remembering the dog's 'simple-hearted love' she determined to 'take on some of William's simplicity of goodness towards her – for even my great love can do with that.'[73]

~

Early in 1934 their book *Whether a Dove or Seagull* was published by Chatto (having come out in America at the end of 1933). It was named – approximately – after the first line of one of Valentine's poems 'Whether a dove or a seagull lighted there / I cannot tell.' The book had an introductory note explaining that fifty-four of the poems were by one author and fifty-five by the other, that they had not been worked on collaboratively (an important point for Valentine) and that they were not individually attributed, to ensure that each would be read without bias, not pre-judged by the individual poet's reputation.

Valentine had always had reservations about publishing with Sylvia, but she had been persuaded by Sylvia's enthusiasm – and doubtless tempted by the irresistible idea of seeing her work in book form, and vindicating herself to her family. It may now seem obvious that publishing jointly with a famous author, who happened to be her lover, was an error of judgement. But at this stage of her career it wasn't so obvious to Valentine; she had an optimistic belief that the quality of her work would silence any criticism, that it only had to be available to be appreciated. She was twenty-seven, ambitious for success, with impossibly high expectations. Perhaps she secretly hoped to wake up and find herself famous, certainly she imagined that those who had previously been unconvinced by her writing would now recognise it, and acknowledge her talent. Writing twenty years later, Valentine recalled 'I was simply, placidly *sure* that I was a poet – a writer – and that it would be made clear to everyone, just like that.'[74]

With hindsight, Sylvia noted: 'Probably, it would have been better to wait until she had sufficient poems to her liking for a book of her own',[75] which carefully understates the gravity of the mistake. However, Sylvia makes the reasonable assumption that – with her existing record of magazine publication – Valentine could have built up a collection which would have found a publisher, even in the Depression. As it was, she appeared to be merely Sylvia's protégée (or, to the less charitable, her dilettante lesbian toyboy).

When the reviews began to arrive at Frankfort, Valentine realised her mistake. They were universally positive. But it was not enough for her to be hailed as 'a remarkable new poet', one of 'two good poets', 'a good technician ... with fine sensibility', and so on.[76] She was enraged when one (admittedly idiotic) critic commented that her verse 'moves sweetly' and sardonic about remarks such as 'Valentine Ackland brings a more obviously passionate note into his work' or 'Miss Warner is ... less deliberately an artist than Mr Ackland.'[77] These comparisons were possible because everyone had been so distracted by the authorship puzzle that a key was added to the English edition, which at least prevented Valentine's best poems being presumed Sylvia's and Sylvia's weaker ones assigned to Valentine. But confusion remained; it's still often thought to be a book of jointly-authored poems, and both poets have been credited with the other's work at various times.[78]

The nepotism of the project was perhaps too obvious to need mentioning; it could be assumed that Chatto had been obliged to take the book since Sylvia was, after all, one of their best-selling authors. A more curious silence was maintained over the authors' very obvious relationship. It's unclear whether Valentine and Sylvia envisaged their readership as an extension of their own bohemian, sexually liberated circle, expected a *succès de scandale*, or optimistically believed that their work would be treated as entirely separate from their life. Certainly to avow their love so passionately and publicly was an act of daring. In that era it took courage for any woman writer to proclaim her sexuality as an urgent driving force; to acknowledge this powerful force as directed towards another woman was outrageous. The recent *Well of Loneliness* obscenity trial demonstrated that openly lesbian writing could be interpreted as a danger to society, and censored.

Lacking overt political statements about lesbianism, *Whether a Dove or Seagull* was unlikely to attract the legal attention Radclyffe Hall's work had received. But there are other kinds of trouble, and the book takes real risks. The love-poems in it are not disguised with a fictional framework, or distanced by classicism and encoded references to Sappho. Only an extremely blinkered reader could miss the way the poems echo and answer each other, and it would be difficult to interpret them as heterosexual, despite Valentine's androgynous name, when both poets write explicitly about women's sexual experience. Despite this there was no public comment, many reviewers named Valentine as Mr Ackland, all moved sweetly. Presumably Charles Prentice had relied on this heterocentric public response, if he'd thought about it at all.

Privately, some people were less pleased. Robert Frost, the poet to whom the book was dedicated by an admiring Valentine, was disgusted. He wrote to Louis Untermayer, the mutual friend who had sent him the book, 'if *you* could have got along without two or three of the more physical poems in the book, you can imagine how much more philosophically I could … Don't you find the contemplation of their kind of collusion emasculating? I am chilled to the marrow, as in the actual presence of some foul form of death, where none of me can function.'[79] His castration anxieties, triggered by two women he didn't even know, may be unintentionally comic, but his inability to see past the poets' sexual orientation enough to consider their poetry makes distasteful reading. Evidently his prejudice was shared by Untermayer, and the two men sympathised with one another over their dreadful experience.

The scale of the disaster was not immediately obvious. The reviews *were* excellent, and Valentine had expected comparisons with Sylvia; early the previous year she had noted 'I still wish, though I no longer hope, to get read on my own merits.'[80] She sent the book with great pride to all her relations – mostly highly unsuitable recipients – and friends, as well as everyone she'd ever slept with. The realisation that most people did not instantly recognise her as a poet (that, indeed, they hardly noticed the book) came gradually. Joan, inevitably, delivered the final blow, scornfully pointing out that in the index of Chatto's list, Valentine's entry read 'Ackland, Valentine, see Warner, S.T.'. Valentine's fury and humiliation knew no bounds; she vowed a violent revenge on Charles, damned his firm to boil in hell, embarrassed Sylvia by 'behaving most *dread*fully badly – in really bad taste', and altogether almost 'spoiled everything'.[81] The damage lasted longer than the rage.

Valentine was disillusioned in the faith which had sustained her through every crisis hitherto, the great certainty of her life. 'I bitterly resent having been so childishly simple,' she wrote, 'so innocent and eager to clutch my posy and wear it as an official bouquet.'[82] It was painful that her lover had been involved in this tragedy; their private relationship had been exposed, without the art they had made from it being acknowledged. Sylvia, although she was careful not to admit it, had seen another side of Valentine; envious and resentful of her name being the more famous. They never collaborated on a writing project again, which remained a great sorrow to Valentine – especially as it was her own behaviour which made such collaboration impossible. She did not lose the sense of herself as a poet, or her belief in the power of poetry, but she came perilously close to it. In a manuscript book she noted: 'N.B. *About my poems* – where I had true hope before, I have none now. It isn't that I have lost my faith in the truth of my poetry, or of my poems – *but where I had hope before, I have none now.*[83] She also quoted, as she often did in times of trouble, John Clare's sad line 'Poesy is on the wane.'[84]

Sylvia, an established poet, did not publish another book of poetry for almost twenty-five years, although she continued to write it. This was surely self-censorship to spare Valentine's feelings – although there were other reasons too (of which more later). It's impossible to assess the exact damage done in an incalculable situation, but it appears to have been great. Valentine was relegated to a netherworld of 'difficult' minor poets, the literary equivalent of box-office poison. She never had another book accepted by a major poetry publisher in her lifetime, although her poems were regularly published in magazines and broadcast on the radio. This wasn't what she'd imagined, in her childhood dreams of becoming a great poet. When she began to realise that her work would always be overshadowed by Sylvia's brilliant talent, she wrote 'Sylvia makes the best cakes', a dialogue comparing Sylvia's effortless baking with her own more painstaking cookery: 'Oh, yes, I care. That's how my cakes are made.'[85]

But, the book has an interesting afterlife. Despite being too long to contain only the strongest of the authors' work, and lacking a unifying theme (as the love-poems are included among many other subjects), it is a considerable achievement. Some of Sylvia's love-poems are among her best work: 'What weather with you now, / You, my true sky?' or 'I would give you Alexander's Bucephalus', with its searing conclusion 'I would give you Alexander's Bucephalus / Though you should mount and ride away – / Though you should ride away.' Valentine's, too, are some of her most successful, from the erotic power of 'Overnight' to the tender love of 'Beneath this roof-tree' and many moods of love in between.[86] Read together, with their echoes and answers, these poems stand as an extraordinary work of art created by two young poets who were inspired to turn their passion into words. *Whether a Dove or Seagull* is obviously important within the lesbian literary canon; women's voices in overt poetic dialogue about love between women were rare at the time, or at any time. But these subtle poems speak fluently about diverse experiences of love with a universality beyond the writers' gender and sexuality.

For many years *Whether a Dove or Seagull* was out of print, very expensive to buy secondhand, but available in libraries such as the National Poetry Library in London's Southbank Centre. When Valentine's collection of poetry books was left to this library (then the Arts Council Library), on the typewritten list of these bequeathed books Sylvia added the title by hand, in her distinctive elegantly spiky writing. She wrote as authors 'V. Ackland – S.T. Warner' which was alphabetical, but also a careful recompense for the long ago distress caused by 'for Ackland see Warner'.[87] The text was reprinted in the 2008 edition of Valentine's Selected Poems, *Journey from Winter,* in its entirety, with the poems individually attributed.

Chapter Five:
Comrade, Darling

In March 1934, Frankfort showed its frightening side again. A plague spread unstoppably among Valentine and Sylvia's animals; all the cats there died, and it was feared the murrain would spread to the farm animals (as they were told it had seventy years before). The house seemed dark and unfamiliar, the suffering of the cats distressed them, and the sudden destruction in a hitherto benign place struck them both deeply. This disaster at Frankfort would become a repeated theme in Sylvia's writing, in her elfin stories and others such as the Introduction of *The Cat's Cradle Book*, where 'the house smelt of sickness, death and disinfectant'.[1]

During this dark time, they heard from Llewelyn Powys that another of the Chaldon vicarage inmates had attempted to escape. He was organising a petition to the Council, to demand an enquiry and insist that the young women 'should be treated with sympathy and understanding'.[2] They both signed, of course.

One cat, Meep, survived by being quarantined at Winterton and she produced kittens, so Frankfort was not without cats when the disease subsided. Summer returned, Valentine celebrated her twenty-eighth birthday, she had poems printed in *New Republic*, her state of mind improved. Even the news that their old enemies at the vicarage were now suing them for libel did not impinge on Frankfort's other-worldly atmosphere. Yet they were contemplating leaving. There were obvious reasons: the exhausting physical work needed to run the place, its burdensome expenses, the proximity to Winterton which made Ruth's visits too frequent. Also they were homesick for Chaldon in some ways, and the impending court case there needed to be faced. Unsettled by this, Valentine began drinking too much again, worrying about her work, fretting over money. She had, Sylvia sadly concluded, 'outgrown Eden'[3] and it was time to leave their paradisal garden and set out into the cold world.

They departed in September, grieving for the loss of the house, the end of a dream. It would remain central to Valentine's imagination, and she would ever after look at beautiful, empty houses as potential Frankforts which she and Sylvia could rescue, restore, and live in happily ever after.

Valentine and Sylvia returned to Chaldon, but not to Miss Green. The cottage would have seemed tiny after the grand scale of Frankfort, and they were loth to move their friendly tenants, May and Jim Pitman. Indicating their changed state, they rented an isolated cottage on the downs of High Chaldon. Its remoteness from the village and uncompromising character appealed to Valentine; 24 West Chaldon had no running water or electricity and no road to it. Merely living in the house was still extremely hard work, and the damp of the building soon had a bad effect on their books and other possessions, as well as their health. But this hard and simple life suited the new Communist ideal Valentine was exploring.

Valentine's personal response to social injustice had always been strong, but her political sense had developed since the unquestioning days when she had joined the Conservative Youth League. Her instinctive reactions were independent of party politics; she always maintained the position of a writer whose vocation gave her a special responsibility to speak about political issues in personal terms, and lend her voice to the silenced and dispossessed. Her experiences as a sexual outsider and gender rebel, in exile from her own class and home, had given her insights which were unusual for someone of her background. She had observed the desperate conditions in which rural working people often lived during the Depression, the insecure position of servants, the situation of vulnerable people like the 'mentals' at the vicarage. Poverty was not something she read about in newspapers, but a condition of life she witnessed daily, and she understood that it inexorably led to the erosion of freedom.

Sylvia always gave Valentine the credit for their conversion, but they were in the vanguard of a swing to the Left among many of the British intelligentsia, who saw Communism as the only active alternative to the rise of Fascism. As Sylvia observed, 'at that date for anybody of intelligence, that was the only way for them to go.'[4] Characteristically, Valentine embarked on a heavy programme of reading, from *Dialectical Materialism* and *Das Kapital* to *The Theory and Practice of Socialism,* so that she understood the political theory of her new party. Valentine may have needed a new religion to distract her from the cruel disappointment over her poetry, but more profoundly than this she still had her childhood longing to be a hero, a martyr for a good cause, a knight errant. Her Communism was not solely a matter of intellectual conviction, moral instinct or emotional response, but a combination of all three. It was deeply connected with her love of the land and respect for country people, and her awareness that the countryside was despoiled and its workers exploited under the existing system. She had also become, through her own experience and observation, a strong feminist, writing of the condition of women with natural sympathy and applied intelligence. To Valentine, Communism was an idealistic creed, which seemed to have infinite potential for changing existing oppressive systems of all kinds. Sylvia was equally radical and sincere, but too irreverent to espouse any cause over-earnestly, as Valentine invariably did. Both of them enjoyed playing the part to the full and confounding expectations of respectability.

In January 1935 Valentine wrote to the Communist Party HQ, offering the use of her 'small racing car' to the cause, for two days a month with herself as driver, to fetch, carry, or move comrades from place to place. She assured them it was a fast car, and could cover good distances. All letters to CPHQ were routinely opened and copied by MI5, who picked up on these new Party members immediately. A week later Colonel Sir Vernon Kell, the Director of MI5, wrote to the Chief Constable of Dorset, asking for more information on 'the man whose signature is enclosed and who uses the address 24 West Chaldon.'[5]

The hearing of the libel case in Dorchester made a good opportunity for observing him. Valentine had drily remarked that it was bound to be a costly procedure, especially as they 'were undoubtedly in the right',[6] but this was a self-fulfilling prophecy as with typical Ackland grandiosity they employed a full legal team, with KC, to defend them. Unfortunately, Llewelyn had been badly advised about phrasing the petition, and it was legally impossible to deny its defamatory nature. The verdict hinged on a technicality; the petition was 'privileged', as the judge instructed the jury, if the defendants were motivated by 'a sense of duty', but libellous if motivated by 'malice'. The prosecution suggested that Valentine and Sylvia were 'at loggerheads' with the vicarage because of the dog fight in which Sylvia was bitten, so the jury concluded that they were malicious and therefore guilty.[7]

In his summing up, the judge dwelt on how dreadful it was to have five of 'these unhappy girls' foisted onto the village.[8] Feuding was an inevitable result, but it should never have reached the legal stage; he awarded damages of £50 against Valentine and Sylvia, plus costs. The costs amounted to £733/15s/3d – a flabbergasting amount of money, more than twice Valentine's annual income, enough to buy a house. With Valentine's inherited anxieties about money, and her family's attitude towards her unremunerative work, it was galling for her to have to borrow from Ruth. The repayment of this enormous sum was a millstone; twenty years later Valentine triumphantly returned £100 which she still owed Sylvia (who, by then comfortably off, had completely forgotten the debt).

The whole drama was much enjoyed locally, not least by the police sergeant who reported on it to MI5. He explained about the suspicious car-offering letter-writer: 'the person is Miss Valentine Ackland, described as an Authoress, residing with a Miss Sylvia Townsend Warner … these two persons, who are close companions … were described by Counsel in the course of the case as "two literary ladies".' The court appearance gave him an opportunity to observe Valentine and make notes on her appearance:

> Age 28-35, 5'8"–9", slim build, smart appearance, sharp but regular features, pale complexion, brown or auburn hair which is Eton cropped, blue-grey eyes, eyelids slightly heavy, nose aquiline-medium, thin lips – slightly drooping at corners, good teeth … Refined speech, rather low voice, speech somewhat clipped. Dress – Short caracal coat and Princess Marina hat (Cossack type) with a small red and white feather in side. Dark skirt (medium length), silk stockings, shapely legs, Dk Shoes. Wears more than one ring on either hand. One large and noticeable ring on left hand. Wears wristwatch with broad band on left wrist.[9]

(This would not have pleased Valentine, as it added several years to her age and removed several inches from her height; she was proud of being almost six feet tall.)

About Sylvia, he merely remarked 'Miss Warner, I should imagine, is some years older than Miss Ackland.' Then there are details of their car, and 'for what it may be worth' a long examination of Valentine's firearms certificates for a rifle and pistol, which all seemed disappointingly correct – indeed, she'd asked him about altering them from Norfolk to Dorset.[10] This information would only increase MI5's interest.

The result of the court case upset both writers, if it didn't surprise them. Their own legal representation had been far more financially disastrous than the damages, and had singularly failed to represent their side of the story. They had been portrayed as malevolent dog-obsessed literary dabblers, rather than as principled women of conscience. This experience of the victory of the oppressor, and the injustice of the legal system, can only have strengthened their commitment to Communism.

'Intellectuals' were classified as bourgeoises by the Party, though Valentine and Sylvia were already to some extent de-classed by their bohemian choice of life as lesbians, artists, political radicals and working women. By living unconventionally, independent and hard up, they'd tried to give up their class distinctions and privileges. (They could not help retaining some obvious class indicators, however; their accents were positively grand, their dress and manner ineradicably posh, if eccentric, their educated cultural milieu unsheddable.) The Party's classification system was so rigid that Valentine once wrote to the *Daily Worker* pointing out that they were trying to create a classless society rather than perpetuate the existing system by constantly remarking on the comrades' backgrounds.

As new Party members, Valentine and Sylvia had to prove their commitment by inordinate amounts of letter-writing, envelope-stuffing, photostat-copying, marching and demonstrating, selling the *Daily Worker*, driving comrades about and putting them up. Their seriousness was also shown by lending their neighbours *Left Review* and circulating the books which they received as founder-members of the Left Book Club. Valentine also came up with an endearing scheme to leave typed recommendation-slips in public library books about current affairs, directing interested readers towards more radical volumes.

Self-abnegating service to the cause was decreed by the Party, but the writing skills of the new comrades were also put to good use. One strong appeal of Communism was the state support of art, as an expression of ideology and communication with the people. This agreed with Valentine's own deep conviction of the usefulness of poetry, the power of writing to change the world. Even if the political theorists had mass propaganda in mind, rather than inspiring literature, it was a welcome contrast to the 'moves sweetly' idea of poetry.

It was inevitable that Valentine would write about Communism, since all areas of her life connected so directly with her work. Much of her writing has a political aspect which has nothing to do with Party doctrine, but is instinctively political in the personal sense. Her nature poems often describe the place of the people in the landscape, workers in the country, acknowledging the hardship and dignity of their lives. As early as 1933 Valentine expressed the fear that England would become 'one wide suburb',[11] and the poems which celebrate nature, as they speak lyrically and wistfully of an already-disappearing rural England, or mark the seasons' changes and describe local landscapes, all manifest a strong awareness of the fragility of the environment and human responsibility towards it. Later, her work became more overtly poetry of protest – against war and oppressive regimes, including Stalin's – and poetry of witness, speaking for refugees, political prisoners, censored writers and the condemned. Writing revolutionary poetry opened the way for this later, more personal work, but during Valentine's Red period she developed a vigorous, authoritative voice which was fashionably of the moment.

The seriousness with which she took her new political allegiance brought a sense of purpose to this writing of Red poetry, a confirmation of the poet's vocation which could have wavered, after her loss of hope. This important new inspiration was balanced by other, less exciting, aspects of Party membership. Apart from the enormous amount of routine Party work Valentine and Sylvia undertook, and the seriousness with which they were writing, they were often overwhelmed by the number of visitors who came to stay in their remote and inconvenient cottage. Comrades such as Stephen Clark (later a fellow-volunteer in Spain), Edgell Rickword the activist and poet, Julius Lipton (who would later publish Valentine) and his wife Queenie, were extremely welcome but inevitably disruptive. Less welcome guests included George Brennan, an unemployed miner they took in briefly with proverbially hand-biting results. Eventually, Sylvia complained that their house should be re-named 'the Olde Communiste's Reste'.[12]

MI5 agents were, of course, on the alert, though with mixed results. Close monitoring of the suspects' post had produced nothing more suspicious (apart from their *Daily Worker* subscription) than poetry magazines, seed catalogues, department store bills, parcels from the London Library or various bookshops, and enormous supplies of the best coffee and cigarettes. In October 1935 Sir Vernon Kell renewed his enquiries to the Dorset Constabulary: had either of the two suspects been engaged in 'subversive activities of any kind' and were they 'in the habit of having visitors to their house'? He was also curious to find out 'whether you consider that either of these two appears to be in any way abnormal'?[13]

This possibility was presumably suggested by the initial gender-confusion about Valentine, but it also reveals a perceived link between sexual and political deviance, together with a deep suspicion of writers or artists, especially women. Like many of their Left-wing contemporaries in the cultural world – W H Auden, Nancy Cunard, Christopher Isherwood, C Day Lewis, George Orwell, J B Priestley, Paul Robeson, Stephen Spender, the list goes on – Valentine and Sylvia were under suspicion as much for their personalities as their politics.[14]

A local police sergeant again reported back, having made

> discreet enquiries respecting the two above mentioned Ladies, from the result I find they are still residing at 24 West Chaldon, near Dorchester, which is an old detached farm house situated about 200 yards from the roadway, their chief occupation appears to be the writing of stories believed [sic] for various newspapers, this applies more so to Miss Warner than Miss Ackland, they appear reserved in nature, taking no part in the village affairs and no subversive activities of any kind has [sic] come to my knowledge or taken place locally.[15]

(This does not tally with their own letters, some of which were copied by MI5, telling of their strenuous recruitment activities locally and frequent involvement in village events like the alternative Jubilee celebrations, which were given a revolutionary twist when villagers capered round the bonfire singing 'I'm Enery the Eighth I am' in a non-royalist manner.)[16]

He continued:

> There are very few visitors to the house, these consisting chiefly of the Powys family, who are also authors ... Miss Ackland is more on the active side than Miss Warner who is some years the elder, she drives an MG Sports Car, which I understand is registered in the name of Miss Warner, also spends a considerable time at shooting rabbits, for which she uses a rifle, and when at home she more often than not wears male clothing in preference to female attire. Miss Warner appears normal in habits. [– presumably meaning both clothing and behaviour. And finally:] I should also say they have some independent means.[17]

No doubt this confirmed MI5's worst fears.

Valentine's occupations did indeed include shooting rabbits (108 in the year), totting up days 'Devoid of Drink' (126) and annoying policemen.[18] With Sylvia, she supported striking Welsh miners by demonstrating at the pithead in Cwmfelinfach, in defiance of an enormous police presence. Here in Wales the police were distinctly nervous, but the following spring in London the comrades narrowly escaped a mounted police baton-charge at a peaceful political demonstration against a Fascist rally at the Albert Hall, which made clear where the authorities' sympathies lay. By then, support for the anti-Fascist movement in Britain was crystallising around one major issue; Sylvia always remembered Valentine 'on the pavement in Pall Mall, holding up her fist [clenched in the Communist salute] as the Arms for Spain demo went by.'[19] But their love still came before the Party. As Valentine defiantly wrote to Sylvia: 'I am already a traitor. I love you far more than anything else.'[20] Love – and her identity as Sylvia's lover – remained Valentine's priority, despite Party disapproval of personal relationships and individualism.

~

But in 1935 their relationship unexpectedly altered. Valentine was drinking heavily, though no one ever saw her actually drunk (presumably because she was in good training). Money was problematic, house-keeping exhausting, their political commitments never-ending; not surprisingly, Valentine was prone to violent depressions. And she was still smarting under the realisation that *Whether a Dove or Seagull* had failed to establish her as a major poet – and that she'd been ridiculous to imagine that it would. Always over-sensitive, she noticed that she was often treated as Sylvia's inferior – the 'wife' of the partnership, perhaps, despite appearances?

Valentine's approaching thirtieth birthday, as well as her drinking, no doubt contributed to her decision (if such it can be called) to seek other lovers besides Sylvia. Being back in Chaldon, the scene of previous adventures, could have contributed to this change in her behaviour, as well as her sense of being undervalued, even by Sylvia. She may also have been influenced by the inescapable ethos of 1930s Communism – free love, collectivism, lack of personal responsibility – despite her protestations against the Party line. And, was she again imitating a contemporary model of traditional masculinity, in which she perceived herself as the husband, Sylvia as the wife, and subsidiary lovers as mistresses or minor episodes? Within these roles, she remained faithful to Sylvia (apart from mild adultery) because Sylvia was recognised as the spouse with a permanent place in Valentine's life, while the others were merely 'light loves' of temporary duration who did not result in 'material or long term *mental* obligations'. Valentine expounded a dangerous doctrine justifying both physical and mental experiments in love: that 'both body and spirit (with the free consent of mind) can *without harm* exercise their skills in different, in various games.'[21]

In one area, Valentine was undisputed king, and she seems to have consciously used her sexual prowess to alter the power balance. This reminiscence from her diary twenty years later suggests that she re-established her authority in this way when she felt slighted by the influential critic William Empson, who ignored her in favour of Sylvia when he came to stay, accompanied by a girlfriend: 'I drank a great deal then AND made love to Ingeborg, of all people, to restore myself. Oddly enough, as it seemed to me then at any rate, it DID restore me

AND restore balance to the household too.'[22] At the time, Valentine recorded the episode in a series of laconic and barely legible diary entries: 'Ingeborg? ... Wrote poem 'After an argument' ... Ingeborg (Danced until 1am) ... came at 8 bringing me lilac ... gave me ring ... Gertrude came – about Ingeborg – silly old bitch.'[23] After the departure of Ingeborg and the chastened William, Valentine seemed to consider herself – as she had been with Bo – available for casual liaisons.

As Valentine's comment on Gertrude Powys indicates, she did not take kindly to remonstration. Sylvia was in a difficult position. Monogamy was not expected in their circle; to have another lover was, as Sylvia put it, 'a quite usual situation'.[24] And yet, there had been five years of exclusivity, they had both given up all former lovers, and Sylvia had admitted her preference for this. Valentine, too, had desired Sylvia's 'constancy'[25] and suffered sheepish retrospective jealousy about Sylvia's previous lovers. Later, Sylvia claimed that she 'never expected [Valentine] to forgo love-adventures',[26] but in 1935 it was an unpleasant shock. It wasn't Sylvia's style to take a lover herself to bring Valentine to order; she remained faithful (while decrying 'mere fidelity')[27] as a matter of self-respecting preference. She never criticised Valentine, never publicly complained, and maintained her pride with a wry worldliness. But in a revealing poem she once wrote 'How much more thoroughly / Than your love could, your faithlessness burns through me. / Now, only now, have you possessed me utterly.'[28]

From this time on, Sylvia treated Valentine's current amorous encounters with the same shrewd mixture of indulgent amusement and proprietorial pride, and even gave advice. These secondary lovers had a difficult habit of falling heavily for Valentine, showering her with gifts and promising eternal devotion. They were contained, dealt with smoothly, and when Valentine's passionate interest waned, despatched kindly but firmly; a process in which Sylvia assisted. (One such recalled being 'desperately upset' over her summary dismissal, but acquiescing quietly out of consideration for Sylvia.)[29] Valentine's affairs were, as Sylvia coolly remarked, 'vehement and sincere' though 'brief', but in many ways they hardly impinged on the monolithic structure of Sylvia and Valentine's partnership.[30] The adamantine impenetrability of their marriage must have seemed almost sinister to any 'mistress' who encountered its profound indifference to external influence.

Although later in her life Valentine was aware of the pain she'd caused to 'the series of people who loved me – Rodric, Myra, Lana, Whitty, Bo, Isobel, Francis ... Sydney, Betty, Garrow – even Oliver – and Katie – and later Janet, Evelyn, Elizabeth – I did damage to all these, and many simpler people too',[31] at the time this was not important to her. And she didn't even mention Sylvia in this list of broken hearts.

Writing of 1935 after Valentine's death, Sylvia remembered 'Ingeborg and Evelyn – but no matter to our love'.[32] These unwelcome revenants were the 'Ingeborg' of William Empson's visit, and 'Evelyn' Holahan, an American visitor to Chaldon. Evelyn was a tough New Yorker who lived in Greenwich Village and worked in an advertising agency; her accent and language amused Sylvia and she shared a commitment to anti-fascist politics. Like Ingeborg, one of Evelyn's attractions for Valentine (aside from availability) may have been her limited time in Chaldon; she left on good terms with both Valentine and Sylvia. Later she would become Valentine's implacable enemy.

Sylvia's acceptance of this new situation was complicated. Valentine's reputation as a lover and stories of her past exploits had always been a powerful aphrodisiac for them both, the preferred source of bedtime anecdote. And at some level, Sylvia colluded in her lover's new availability; if not exactly pimping for the Party, she wasn't above using Valentine's charms to attract prospective members.

Another American visitor to Chaldon, Betty Wade White, was cast this handsome bait when Sylvia was fishing for new recruits – though she can't have had any idea how it would be snapped up. Betty had met Sylvia in 1929, when Sylvia was on a triumphant writer's visit to New York as guest critic of the *Herald Tribune* and Betty was a young fan with literary aspirations. She was also extremely wealthy, an old-monied Episcopalian New Englander who valued her descent from Ann Bradstreet, the early settler known as America's first published woman poet. Her appearance was striking, with a full, pouting mouth; Sylvia mentions her 'aquamarine' eyes, Valentine her 'vine-tendril' hyacinthine hair.[33] She was Valentine's almost exact contemporary (born in June 1906) and, like Valentine, with a family keen on their 'good' social standing – though unlike Valentine she had not repudiated this background. Betty's mother believed in total control of her daughter, and used shameless emotional blackmail to manipulate her towards staying at home until she found someone to marry her.

Possibly it was an urge to liberate her from this fate, to save a soul for the bohemian, unconventional life which was her creed even before Communism, which had made Sylvia adopt Betty as her protégée. It was not an equal relationship; Betty confided and deferred, while Sylvia gave worldly advice and encouragement to Betty's efforts to remake herself. Perhaps Sylvia identified with the attempts to escape a dominant mother and establish an independent life, perhaps she felt a maternal instinct which competed with Mrs White's? Their unlikely friendship had survived long distance, and when Betty visited Chaldon Sylvia was gracious and affectionate towards her, encouraging Valentine to take her shooting and demonstrate the comrades' life. Although Valentine did not then exercise her self-appointed *droit de seigneur* on their guest, she certainly made an impression.

At the time Evelyn, Betty and other developments in the new situation were soon irrelevant. Valentine and Sylvia were more interested in Spain.

~

Spain was the great cause for the Left in 1936. Since the civil war had broken out between the elected socialist (Republican) government and the pro-royalist Fascist rebels commanded by General Franco, Britain had pursued a policy of non-intervention. This prevented arms sales and other support to the government forces while the Fascists (who represented landowners, the church and unreformed capitalism) were supplied with armaments by Hitler and Mussolini. To Valentine, the fight against Fascism was literally, as the leaflets put it, to 'Save Democracy, World Peace and British Freedom.'[34] Spain was a country she'd loved since being there with Bo, when she had seen its extremes of poverty and privilege. She was excited by the idea that the Spanish people were trying to remake their society by replacing the autocratic power of the church and aristocracy with a state system of greater equality. Their idealism was widely shared, as was belief in the slogan 'Culture is a weapon in the war against Fascism'.[35]

Valentine's first urge was to fight in Spain as a volunteer *miliciana*, honing her marksmanship on people rather than rabbits. British women did join the Brigades; the artist Felicia Browne was killed in action in 1936, rescuing a wounded comrade – 'killed in defence of democracy' as the newspaper reports said.[36] Valentine read of this, and saw Spanish propaganda photographs showing rifle-bearing women in dungarees drinking out of billy-cans; she yearned to be a 'woman warrior' if not a 'pretty Amazon'.[37] Sylvia had no intention of letting her go, and there was useful work to be done at home. (Sylvia had a leading role in several anti-Fascist organisations, and was expert at persuading well-known women to sign up.) The Party was also unwilling to endorse Valentine as a combatant; probably her writing skills were more relevant to the Party than her shooting – there was very little ammunition at the front.

To Valentine, consistently denied the chance of heroism, the potent notion that all workers were heroes was inspiring and she determined that she and Sylvia would contribute to the struggle in whatever way they could. They 'moved heaven and earth'[38] to get sent to Spain in some other capacity, and on 16 September Tom Wintringham (an impulsive fighting comrade) ordered them to Barcelona to work for British Medical Aid, attached to the Red Cross. Two days later they set off in the MG, drove through France despite repeated mechanical problems, and reached the Spanish border on 22 September.

They prudently left the car garaged at Cerbère, and took the train to Port-Bou, where the Spanish authorities refused them entry. For four hours, until the train returned, they were held under arrest at gunpoint. (This sort of reception, and worse, was a common experience for volunteers.) A second attempt the following day was less frightening but no more successful; although they met various contacts of Tom Wintringham's, the committee that issued permits again denied them entry. After two more days of waiting in France, an agent made contact and conducted them through the border, the essential permits were issued and they found themselves at last on the train for Barcelona.

The revolutionary new world in which they arrived was exciting and confusing in equal measure. Valentine observed equality, in which she so passionately believed, in action on the streets; clothes no longer demarcated the different classes, everyone was hatless, waiters addressed their customers informally and, best of all, women walked where they pleased. The atmosphere was carnivalesque yet intensely serious, vibrant with energy and suppressed violence. It was frighteningly chaotic. Everyone was armed, there was a warrant out for their escort's arrest, everyone stared at them. Many of the bomb-shattered buildings were collapsing and the streets barricaded. Their hotel (Lloret) was on the Ramblas, where radios blared out speeches interspersed with the *Internationale* all night, while cars – all requisitioned by one or other of the many feuding Left-wing parties – drove slowly up and down blowing their horns. The city was full of people; over a million refugees were supposed to have fled there, 'and it *looks* true', Valentine reported in her *Daily Worker* articles, *Uncensored Letters from Barcelona*.[39] There were food shortages, and permits were required to draw rations (of virtually anything), to move about, to use public transport, to escape arrest, to be out after curfew.

Valentine and Sylvia waited in queues, were interviewed by committees, protested their willingness and usefulness and were eventually granted the necessary permits, of which they were very proud. From the Partido Socialista Unificada de Cataluña (PSUC) they received a warrant establishing them as 'controladas por nuestro servicio' and then managed to obtain identity cards from both the Consell de Sanitat de Guerra and Primera Ambulancia Inglesia en España.[40] As Valentine wryly observed, street-sellers were doing a brisk trade in talc-cases 'for carrying about in one's pocket to keep all the passes'.[41] They wisely wore PSUC badges, as this was the umbrella party currently in control, though the rapid changes in government, explained quickly on their arrival, left them 'rather confused'.[42]

Valentine maintained allegiance to 'the United Socialist Party ... including "Labour", "Socialist", some radicals and the communists', and had no truck with what she called 'Anarchists or Trotsky-ists'.[43] She and Sylvia were not absolute innocents abroad; they knew there was inter-party fighting, and they heard atrocity stories – though they never witnessed sectarian violence. 'All this is history, anyway,' Valentine wrote, in her frank-and-honest reporter style, 'and you'll hear the whole story one day I hope. I don't know it yet.'[44] Much clenched-fist saluting seemed the safest option; shortly all British personnel were told to take off political insignia and wear Red Cross armbands with the Union Jack.

On their first visit to the hospital, Valentine reported the aftermath of a hand grenade accident; they heard the munitions truck explode, and shortly afterwards two lorries full of dead and wounded soldiers appeared, 'all young lads ... most of them with damaged faces and heads'[45] (just like Robert's plastic-surgery patients). Although Valentine wrote of this incident as an example of Republican bravery and medical efficiency, it was a distressing introduction to Barcelona.

The first days were spent in mundane tasks; food finding, shopping for the medical unit, shepherding new arrivals and looking after Hugh O'Donnell, their boss, who was seriously ill. Then their unit was allotted a villa in Sarria, an affluent suburb 'like a fantastic Hampstead'.[46] 86 Paseo Bonanova had been abandoned by a wealthy industrialist; it was large enough to become a hospital. Valentine and Sylvia's task was to search and cleanse the house, and as they surveyed the 'nightmare of bad taste'[47] still full of its erstwhile owner's personal possessions, they felt ill-at-ease. The place had been requisitioned for the people but – until the wounded arrived to justify the situation – it seemed awkward to be poking about in the cupboards; rather like looting Ruth's house.

Preparing the villa was a herculean task; trying to stock and provision it, move hospital equipment in and furniture out, then find two ambulances (with brakes, ideally), occupied Valentine and Sylvia completely. In an account not intended for publication, Valentine admitted that they were miserable, sometimes frightened, sorely tried by their colleagues, often in a frenzy of impatience. The entire male contingent was drunk for much of the time – and Valentine was not holding back herself. Asunción Lan, their cook-interpreter and minder, was distracted from her tasks by playing billiards all day, 'so for that day, at least, the flat was not cleaned.'[48] The ambulances which finally appeared were filthy and decrepit.

The worst incident occurred when they were fetched urgently to the Hotel Lloret because one of the English contingent had drunkenly emptied a chamber-pot out of the window onto the people sitting outside in the cafe below, and an angry mob had gathered to avenge the insult. Their colleague was shouting at the militia guard, but subsided when Valentine told him to 'Shut up, you fool – you'll be shot if you aren't careful!'[49] A hostile crowd waited silently outside the hotel, and Valentine and Sylvia were jostled and threatened by people inside the building until they barricaded themselves into a room with their compatriots. The situation was eventually defused by negotiation and the perpetrator deported unharmed, but it had been both ludicrous and unpleasant, like so much else in Barcelona.

In contrast, there was Asunción with her shrewd, cheerful affection for them, and Ramona Siles Garcia, a young *miliciana* who prided herself on her machine-gun skills and had been an ice-cream seller before the war. These two women exemplified the new Spain. A group of Ramona's fellow-soldiers from the Tom Mann Centuria of the International Brigade were important friends to Valentine and Sylvia in the confused socialising of the city. (The field postcards which reached Dorset from the Aragon Front told of the death or wounding in action of several of these comrades.)[50] Another fellow-volunteer, their comrade the Quaker Stephen Clark, remained a friend for life. The sheer chaos of a revolutionary government was difficult to bear for orderly English folk, but it was impossible not to admire the spirit

13. Comrades in Spain – Sylvia, Asunción and Valentine.

behind it. And there was one certainty which inspired Valentine, and which she never lost. 'Whatever wild stories are told me of these people's courage, I shall believe them always,' she wrote. 'It's easy to see that they are true.'[51]

Valentine understood that she was seeing theory in action, and if some of it was disquieting, much was inspiring. She knew that the carnage was not one-sided (although the Republicans were certainly getting the worst of it) and that there were Communists who tortured and murdered their enemies. But she and Sylvia had a large collection of official photographs, still hard to look at, showing the terrible injuries of air-raid casualties; women and children who were early victims of the Luftwaffe's new system of warfare on civilians. (In *Three Guineas* Virginia Woolf describes her own similar photographs, sombrely noting 'They are not pleasant photographs to look upon.')[52]

In Republican Spain, one response from these citizens of the front line was an outpouring of popular art – they sang Lorca's poetry in the streets, protested with music and painting, printed posters and leaflets of unsurpassed style and impact, and proclaimed their resistance even in the badges they wore on their hats. No wonder that, writing many years later about their contribution in Spain, Sylvia called it 'the proudest time of my life'. She remembered Valentine's 'impetuous chivalry ... her most glorious days, our highest demonstration of love spreading out to our fellows.'[53]

On this first trip Valentine and Sylvia were in Spain for less than a month; by 22 October 1936 they were back in Chaldon. Their experiences had made the time seem far longer, but although they'd been homesick in Spain they longed to return. Valentine's poem 'Badajoz to Chaldon, August 1936' expresses this tension memorably:

> Telephone wires cry in the wind
> and make song there. I stand in the misty night
> and listen. Hear voices from a far distance;
> hear sounds from further, outside the wires,
> than ever inside. Hear sounds from Spain.
> The mist muffles all but these, blankets, perhaps, the reply –
> But the wind plays the wires still, and the wires cry.[54]

~

As well as the poetry she was writing with such commitment, Valentine produced prose for the Party. She wrote regularly for *Left Review, Time and Tide,* the *Daily Worker* and other less overtly Left-wing journals, and also contributed to American publications and wrote frequent letters to mainstream newspapers – a public relations job she took seriously. Writing in the *Daily Worker* on 'Agricultural Workers' Plight' as 'Our Worker Correspondent' her tone is confident, easy, lightly ironical, man-to-man – and angry. This was the voice she developed to speak convincingly of the shame and despair many people felt about a government which did nothing effective to relieve the desperate condition of the unemployed while prevaricating over the threat of Fascism, in a weak attempt to preserve the status quo. Valentine wrote a series of articles on the dire situation of rural workers, emphasising the particular difficulties faced by women, with obvious empathy and authenticity. She was then commissioned to re-cast the articles as a book.

Country Conditions was published by Lawrence & Wishart in November 1936, the only prose book Valentine published during her lifetime. In the rush and excitement of the time she paid it scant attention, and because she was primarily a poet, the book did little to enhance her self-esteem. Yet it was a sustained piece of investigative journalism of which any professional could have been proud. Even today, it retains the power to move the reader, and although its specific details are social history now, the basic problem of rural poverty has not yet disappeared. It had a gratifyingly irritant effect on the establishment; *Country Life*, among others, printed a long review denying that the problem really existed – in most areas. More sympathetic critics praised it as a well-written polemic and a book that would do immense good.[55] (What Joan thought of this incursion into her territory can only be imagined.)

This publicity brought Valentine to the attention of the Party and another job followed. She was summoned to London on 24 November to drive a lorry to Spain, leading a convoy of two supply lorries since she knew the route. She was to carry important letters. The journey itself was an illegal act, the difficult drive over the mountain passes of the Pyrenees was now snowy and crossing the border – as they knew from experience – could be dangerous. Sylvia was forbidden to go too, and she was frantic. Valentine had been unwell with colitis; only a few days before Sylvia had written to the young enthusiast 'Let your love be, for once, a BRAKE on your actions.'[56] But now Valentine could not resist the opportunity to prove herself, even if Sylvia was excluded. Although the 'apparently very vital letters', Valentine reckoned, 'could really go with anyone,'[57] she felt her loyalty (and possibly her manhood?) was being tested. In a farewell letter, she told Sylvia she loved her more than anything, which made her a traitor to the Party – but in fact she passed the Party's test of her readiness to leave Sylvia behind. Sylvia wrote in reply 'If love could do it, you should not be cold, even on the worst of the Pyrenees.' She added 'How I can write these things and keep my reason, I don't know.'[58]

At the last minute, they were reprieved. Valentine became seriously ill, her temperature reached 103˚ and her bosses replaced her before she collapsed. Many years later she said that she was incapacitated at this inopportune moment because of her drinking, and there may be some truth in this. In Spain, she'd eaten little and drunk litres of strong black coffee with brandy, despite bleeding gastric ulcers. The diagnosis was 'colitis', a vague term covering various bowel disorders, any of which would have exacerbated by this diet, together with stress. Heavy drinking, combined with the trauma of parting from Sylvia and the prospect of the dangerous journey, could well have triggered a crisis. (Aside from the alcohol, Valentine's fear of the job could have manifested itself in physical form to get her out of it.) If Valentine felt any embarrassment, she did not show it, but was briskly matter-of-fact about her unreliable health. The cancellation was a disappointment but also a relief; her courage was part-proved. Sylvia was proud of her, but perhaps did not relish the alacrity she'd shown for solo heroics.

In 1937 Valentine was busier than ever on Party business, writing and reviewing for newspapers frequently but still finding time for poetry. She wrote several poems a week and sent them out within days of composition, noting publications tersely ('*Life and Letters Today* 3 poems at a guinea each.')[59] Her 'personal' poems had a more authoritative tone now:

Mirror

One portrait only that I would not part from
(in wreckage of house-move, rack of rent, and ruin),
one only gilt-framed master I admit
as ancestor and sacred ikon,
this, the joint throne where Time and I can sit.[60]

She could also be humorously self-deprecating, starting one poem 'What am I at, who cannot write about spring ...?' – she lists all the gloomy topics for poetry which she favours, and concludes 'What am I at / To write such lies, when fierce midsummer days / Are the weather of my mind, and suns are my days?'[61]

Yet, despite knowing herself blessed and happy, Valentine's joy in life, her ecstatic response to beauty and pleasure, alternated with a deep melancholy which could not be combated, the long shadow from childhood which always haunted her. She was thirty, and disappointed in herself. 'I have had for so long such a fine idea of myself ...' she wrote apologetically to Sylvia, 'that when I come to look at it now, at my age, I feel as though I must be laughed at for having ever hoped and intended so much.'[62] This is Valentine's sad inner voice speaking; there was nothing anyone could say to comfort her, no personal happiness or success could assuage her sense of loneliness and failure.

The chance of a return to Spain came later that year, with an invitation to attend the Writers' International Congress for the Defence of Culture, an event staged by the beleaguered Republican government. Since several of the cities to be visited in the proposed itinerary were under bombardment or in danger of being besieged, acceptance levels were not high. Valentine and Sylvia left on 1 July, travelling to Spain via Paris. As official British Delegates, their reception was very different from the previous chaos; wherever they went there were ceremonies of greeting, feasts and speeches in honour of these foreign guests who were brave enough to show their support for Spain. They were driven all over the Republican area, from Barcelona to Valencia and on to Madrid, to the front line at Guadalajara, then back to Madrid, Valencia, Barcelona.

Valentine's programme for the Congress is marked with ticks beside the names of friendly delegates. Valentine was listed first of the

British delegation, next to WH Auden (who didn't turn up); the list is not otherwise alphabetical. Their allies included 'writers in uniform' Ludwig Renn and André Malraux, poets Pablo Neruda, Octavio Paz and Langston Hughes (representing the important contribution of African-Americans). Aside from Sylvia, the best-known of what she called 'a depressingly puny and undistinguished British delegation'[63] was probably Stephen Spender, who took a violent dislike to Valentine and Sylvia, which was entirely reciprocated. He was offended by their zealous commitment to the Party, their love of Spain, their creativity, their femaleness and – worst of all – their indifference to his charm, and in his memoirs he caricatured them as a 'Lady Novelist' and 'Poetess' affectedly addressing each other as 'Comrade, darling'.[64] They loathed him for his contemptuous attitude to the whole event, exemplified by the suggestion (in his autobiography) that the Spaniards were deluded in imagining the Congress actually meant anything.

By contrast, Valentine was deeply struck by the people's conviction that the pen could be mightier than the sword. Wherever they went, the delegates were greeted by crowds of refugee women, who kissed their hands and begged them to tell their countries that the Spaniards were 'loyal *forever* to the Republic.'[65] Valentine wrote an account, *Invitation to Madrid,* which captures her response to the experience:

> 'Viva los Intellectuales!' was the greeting that astounded our ears from even the smallest, most isolated village we passed through on our long caravan of cars. It was profoundly moving, to be greeted so by these poor and ignorant and ruined people. It could not happen in my country ... But these people realise seriously that writers and artists can fight for them, and will fight, and that the sixty or so delegates could, if they would, wage a war that would literally shake the world towards their dearest dream of peace. They believed, too, that our coming was a pledge that we would fight. And it was a pledge![66]

Valentine kept this pledge for the rest of her life and never forgot meeting these refugees who believed in the power of the word. 'Viva los Intellectuales!' was, Sylvia observed, 'a strange sentiment to English ears'[67] and it inspired them both for their work to be considered a necessity of everyone's life, rather than an elite minority pastime.

The first night in Valencia there was an air-raid; a new experience for most of the delegates. They were all exhausted by the journey, by the opening meeting (at which Sylvia spoke) and the lengthy dinner at the hotel. Valentine was not ashamed to record that some of them were 'badly scared by the shock of bombardment and horror, the sight of destruction and death.'[68] They were all to see plenty more of it. In Madrid 'the darkness burst into flames again';[69] there were bombing raids by night and aerial battles in the sky by day, with rifle and grenade street-fighting on the outskirts of the city. The front line at Guadalajara, where the trees were stripped by machine-gun fire, was not unlike the First World War battlefields Valentine had once seen in France, except that the conflict was still going on. This sight, and the ruined villages and homeless refugees, provided a bitter foretaste of the next world war which was about to engulf them all.

But, as Sylvia remembered it, Spain did Valentine good, 'replaced her in herself'. The 'tall Englishwoman' was approved by the foreign delegates; 'the group of exiles, grave and sophisticated, accepted her as though she were one of themselves.'[70] Pablo Neruda gave her a lemon. Stephen Spender's caricature of 'literary ladies' (who make themselves ridiculous by taking the Spanish people seriously) appears somewhat mean-spirited beside the open-hearted sincerity of these other writers.

At the closing event of the Congress they heard La Pasionaria speak, and Pablo Casals played the Catalan national anthem (as he did after every concert he gave in exile through the long years of Franco's dictatorship). He asked the delegates if they believed Republican Spain was a civilised country? Considering this question, Valentine concluded that:

> the attitude of the working masses of Spain to the intellectual workers of all countries ... prove[s] conclusively where is the real future of culture and, by sharp and undeniable contrast, where is barbarism and gross intellectual darkness [by which she meant at home in Britain].[71]

On the way back through Paris they marched in the Bastille Day procession, and reached Chaldon on 16 July. They had been away less than three weeks.

Chapter Six:
Dark Entry

Shortly after their return from Spain, Valentine and Sylvia set about house-hunting. The damp and dilapidation of 24 West Chaldon were making their health, as well as their possessions, deteriorate. The well was contaminated (by dead rats) and the remote situation inconvenient, but not far enough from the frequently-rehearsed dramas of Chaldon. They just wanted something more comfortable. On 24 August 1937 they moved to a house within walking distance of Maiden Newton, an inland village on the other side of Dorchester which is bigger than Chaldon, with a railway station, post office and choice of shops (and pubs).

The house they chose is, of course, unusual; it stands alone, in the water-meadows between Maiden Newton and the next hamlet, Frome Vauchurch. It's built rising straight out of the River Frome, with a narrow deck cantilevered out over the water along the side of the house; light-ripples dance on the indoor ceilings. The garden is bordered all along one side by the river, with a fishing-place on the bank. Opposite, their view across the river was then open downland in a low curve up to the sky, uninhabited. (Later, a row of new bungalows would invade this horizon-line.) The river meanders towards the village in one direction, with a footpath leading there across the fields on the far bank. Their drive led – and still leads – to a narrow lane which crosses the river on a plain iron bridge.

The Victorian building is pleasantly unpretentious, easily habitable. There are enough rooms for them to have had a bedroom each, a spare room, an upstairs sitting-room for Valentine (where she worked) and a downstairs one for Sylvia, a dining-room, a spacious kitchen and the luxury of a downstairs lavatory. There's a verandah overlooking the front garden, and a conservatory on one side, which they called the long sun-parlour. It had running water and electricity, but these comforts were not the only reason they loved it. The river, of such central importance to the design of the house, was and still is a source of perpetual delight. That September Valentine began writing the river poems which would become one of the central themes in her work. 'By Grace of Water' is a quintessential example, opening 'Everywhere is the pattern of water.'[1] The house was always known as Frome Vauchurch (which they pronounced, naturally, as Froome Vowchurch). There were otters in the river, abundant fish, and swans came calling. Fishing immediately joined shooting as one of Valentine's great pleasures; she caught her first trout a few days after moving in.

Although increasingly uncomfortable about killing, Valentine was always proud of her skills and saw the destruction of rabbits as a necessary service to the countryside. She conquered her qualms, and the game was always for food – but when she and Sylvia kept rabbits during the war, they were quite unable to slaughter them, having made the mistake of giving them names. As Sylvia tartly observed 'It is providential that our humanity stops short with the animal creation, and that we can still contrive to cut and cook the cabbages we fondled as seedlings.'[2]

Hunting they hated because the ritualised slaughter was only for sport, not food; because of the cruelty involved; and on class grounds – aside from the damage periodically done to their beloved garden. The pointless destruction of otters by the Hunt caused them particular distress and anger, and they both sabotaged all kinds of hunting whenever possible. (Janet Machen remembered the three of them at Chaldon 'in the lane near the Manor House' where they 'scattered tacks to puncture the owners' tyres!' – probably as a revenge for landowning as well as hunting – 'Futile and very silly', she added.)[3] Sylvia believed she could make people fall off their horses just by looking at them (which she probably could) and kept a tally of injuries thus inflicted.

Valentine was avid to get back to the shooting in Spain, but she received a letter from Ramona which asked for help of a different kind:

> Valentine you ask me if there will be any job for you and I think you cannot do anything here but you will do some very good work for Spain in London. The idea is how you can arrange with the Party to get orphans from here Spain to London to care of them because we have thousands and we are short in food ... Comrade Valentine I am sure you will do your best ... My love with revolution greetings.[4]

In October 1937 Valentine went as a volunteer to Tythrop House orphanage, near Thame in Oxfordshire, preparing it to receive Basque children rescued from the destroyed town of Guernica. Sylvia visited only long enough to observe 'that tedious staff-room, all those idle quarrelling faces'.[5] Valentine was accompanied by Janet Machen, now twenty, who was a recruit to the cause. Her parents were strongly anti-Communist, and thought Janet quite mad, but she had Sylvia's resigned support. (Later, Janet felt she had been ruthlessly manipulated by both Valentine and Sylvia, especially when they abruptly left her in America during the early years of the war, but she still loved them both.) Her youth and enthusiasm were very necessary at Tythrop, which was grim.

Although the Georgian house itself was fine – Valentine admired its gracious proportions – the plumbing was broken, the hundred bedsteads bought for the children were rusted and filthy, and the blankets disgusting. Everything somehow had to be cleaned before the refugees arrived. Valentine's original ideas about providing 'some semblance of a home for them' was 'hampered by lack of everything we needed'.[6] When she went to collect the first consignment of five very small boys from the station, they immediately asked whether they could play football, and whether they could smoke? Valentine stopped the car to buy them cigarettes. She wrote that 'the desolation and forlorness [sic] of those children is something to remember for all time.'[7]

One of the boys who arrived later was incapable of speech and cried all the time, hiding in corners; to begin with the volunteers thought he was 'half-witted', then discovered that he had been trapped in a shell-hole for forty-eight hours during the bombardment of Bilbao, and seen both his parents killed as they ran to join him. There were already doubts about uprooting severely traumatised children from their own country, however dreadful the situation was there. But the camp, as Valentine called it, was full to capacity with these young refugees who had nowhere else to go.

It was also a difficult time for their carers, if to an infinitely lesser degree. At Tythrop, the volunteers suspected each other of being Fascist agents, and the food disagreed with Valentine. At home, she was depressed and bad-tempered; Sylvia wrote to her: 'In Madrid, I never felt a flutter of fear; and yet, sitting in our own kind house, under the shadow of your black moods I become an abject coward.'[8]

~

Now, in 1938, begins the disastrous love-affair which will almost destroy Valentine, and bring Sylvia close to madness. With hindsight it seems inevitable that Valentine's 'dozens and dozens and dozens' of infidelities would eventually cause trouble; Sylvia had already warned her: 'Be happy ... at any rate in the present instance. I might not always be the same.'[9] But there was no foretelling the scale of this catastrophe.

Since Betty Wade White had shown an interest in anti-Fascism (if not the Communist Party itself), she'd become a much closer friend, who vacillated between wanting to 'follow what S&V preach (and practice) politically'[10] or to get married and live a normal life, with lavish familial approval. This temptation accounted for some long silences while back in America, easily forgiven by Sylvia: 'If you don't write, I don't cease to think of you with love, be sure of that. But you write such charming lette-ers [sic] that when one does come I love you even more.'[11]

The fact that Betty had the contacts to raise thousands of dollars for the Spanish orphans or a Soap for Spain fund certainly worked in her favour, as did her frequent requests for advice and confessions about her troubled psyche. But, aside from the affectionate wish to help an unhappy young woman find herself, 'S&V's' multiple letters give the impression of an exercise of power just as manipulative as her mother's, a concerted campaign to recruit Betty to their way of thinking and radically re-make her life. (Janet had experienced a similar level of high-powered, high-minded character-moulding; she remembered Valentine's 'personal magnetism' but also the way she and Sylvia made *'use* of the personality'.)[12]

Retrospectively, Sylvia said that they had 'pitied' Betty, but this hardly covers the way in which both of them – but especially Sylvia – now cultivated and groomed her. They called her by her full adult 'Elizabeth' ('I know you are called Betty, but Elizabeth is your Chaldon name'), flattered her with letters hailing her as a fellow-intellectual, told her she was 'built on the same rig' as Sylvia, made her an intimate

14. Elizabeth Wade White's passport photograph and signature.

to every detail of their lives; Miss Green, Frankfort, their families, the Craskes. Sylvia's letters, in particular, woo her with extravagant promises of special favour; a privileged place within their relationship. Many years later Sylvia admitted, bitterly, 'Elizabeth was my doing.'[13]

S&V tried to pair Elizabeth off with various handsome young Communists, as alternative bridegrooms, but to no avail. More successfully, they encouraged her to take her own cottage in Chaldon to lodge Spanish refugees, and find various research projects as excuses to remain in England, despite the threat of European war. Sylvia even suggested she could stay with them for the duration:

> I cannot imagine any circumstances when the companionship of someone like yourself, steadfast and sensible and good-tempered and civilised, would not be a help and a stay and a comfort ... a real support to me![14]

And Valentine, whose initially stilted, almost dutiful, letters become ever-more enthusiastic, made an agreement that Elizabeth would take care of Sylvia if anything happened to Valentine (she was still hoping to return to Spain). All of which suggests that at this point Sylvia was the object of Elizabeth's affections, in a complicated emotional situation which S&V did not dislike.

During Elizabeth's visit to England in 1938, there was a jaunt to show her Winterton, where Valentine was always at her most swaggering. On 21 September Elizabeth recorded in her journal: 'I am hopelessly, helplessly, inarticulately and everlastingly in love.' (The inarticulacy didn't last, unfortunately for S&V.) But she did not expect this love to lead anywhere; it was an 'impossible dream and unapproachable star'.[15] Perhaps it was this realisation, as well as a wish to impress and please Sylvia, which led Elizabeth to make a disastrous attempt to join Quaker volunteers in Spain.

This adventure had been under discussion for a long time; her family were frantically opposed to the idea, while S&V were emphatically in favour. They apparently believed that experience as an aid worker there would make Elizabeth an individuated adult at last, and one of their own. Already they felt that their influence – or pressure – was showing. As Sylvia put it:

> Seeing you this year, seeing you so immensely strengthened and advanced and ripened, I could not but feel a certain glow in the thought that we may have had our part in your development; but it is the pride of the gardener, who sees the flowering tree.[16]

Unsurprisingly, Elizabeth had neither the stamina nor the commitment to make such a dangerous and uncomfortable journey alone. Although she wanted to please Sylvia and impress Valentine, and she had a perfectly genuine sympathy for the oppressed, she was used to a life of privilege and ease (as a Communist might have phrased it). After much waiting about in Paris, bolstered by encouraging and envious letters, with promises from Sylvia to come at once if required, Elizabeth's 'courage failed her'[17] over going to Spain and she was taken into the American Hospital with a nervous collapse. (This was more extreme than the attack of illness which prevented Valentine's solo journey, but comparable in its timing.) Elizabeth wrote home admitting that her mother had been right all along, that 'by upbringing and temperament' she was unsuited to the job, and that the doctor had said 'it would undoubtedly be fatal' for her to go.[18] Elizabeth certainly came to believe that she had narrowly escaped death, as well as psychological meltdown.

After this debacle, S&V picked up the pieces (no doubt uneasily aware that they had over-persuaded her to go), assuring Elizabeth that they still loved her, that she would 'always … be dear', that they could 'scarcely endure to wait to see' her.[19] Sylvia cabled:

> I WANT YOU HERE IMMEDIATELY OR SHALL I COME TO YOU SAY
> WHICH STOP SONNET ONE HUNDRED SIXTEEN SYLVIA[20]

(This refers to Shakespeare's sonnet 'Let me not to the marriage of true minds', with its pertinent lines 'love is not love / Which alters when it alteration finds.') They obviously felt responsible for Elizabeth's damaged psychological state, even anxious that she might kill herself if she thought she'd lost their affection by disappointing them.

Still smarting from her failure and humiliation, Elizabeth came for an extended stay, as Europe slithered further towards war. S&V encouraged her to defy her mother's orders to return immediately, and were almost excessively eager to demonstrate their unchanged love and approval: 'do not think we only love you when you are at your best. We love you without reservations', Sylvia assured her.[21] This was necessary, as Elizabeth was not an easy guest; she frequently 'plunged into injured gloom' but (as Sylvia tartly observed) 'at this time her sulks were still part of her fascination.'[22] When Elizabeth threatened to leave the house, Sylvia advised against 'flight' and added 'Valentine is very wise and very fond of you. If you can, open your heart to her. She will do it good.'[23] Possibly Elizabeth took this advice too literally, or acted on it unwisely; certainly, her relationship with Valentine changed.

'It was really only chance', Valentine wrote years later, 'made me fall in love, so dangerously, so stupidly, so unsuitably, so – apparently – irrevocably.'[24] Chance, proximity, and – perhaps – Sylvia's mistaken certainty that Betty's primary affection was for her, and would not change, even during an affair with Valentine?

S&V were aware of Elizabeth's lack of sexual experience and her longing to marry; her neuroses could be explained, in the popular psychology of the day, as sexual repression. Elizabeth had even told her mother about needing the sexual element of marriage, so it's unlikely she would have kept it secret from Sylvia, who she called her confessor. Whether Sylvia, having failed to supply any heterosexual lover, decided that Valentine could be the panacea Elizabeth needed, is a speculative interpretation of her remarkable letters, but not an unreasonable one. She had, on a previous occasion, given Valentine 'permission' for a love-affair with another (very) young protégée, on the basis that it would do her good, and Valentine would enjoy it. Possibly Sylvia allowed this affair in the same spirit; certainly she did not appear too upset by it, at first. Presumably with her consent, Valentine and Elizabeth went for a brief stay alone together in Chaldon, with predictable results.

If, for Valentine, this started as a diversion, it seemed very different to Elizabeth. As she described the progress of events to Valentine:

> all the old fears and mistakes have rounded upon me, first to defeat me from going to Spain, then to draw me very near to the edge of death. Then you came with a sharp sword and a gentle healing hand, and saved me ... The way is a difficult and beautiful one, my darling, help me to follow it truly, remembering the bridge and Rat's Barn [where they stayed] and the question, and all the lovely nights and days that now belong to us for ever.[25]

This letter ominously foretells Valentine's inevitable discovery that Elizabeth was not a 'light love' who would play by S&V's usual rules, or even acknowledge them. On the contrary, she would insist that the declaration on 'the bridge' and the consummation in Rat's Barn were life-changing encounters, surprising Valentine, to whom such incidents were not unusual. Despite the mental fragility Elizabeth had displayed under stress, she was an extraordinarily determined and powerful woman, and one of the very few not to be intimidated by Sylvia (possibly because she underestimated her).

With bohemian good manners, Sylvia accepted this new situation gracefully, and moved into the spare room so that Valentine could accommodate their guest more comfortably. Many years afterwards, she realised this had been a mistake. 'I was WRONG. I traduced my own unwavering love, I sullied our marriage. I hid my sacred distress from her when I should have been open and honoured it ... yet I did it to please.'[26]

The version of the story that Sylvia told herself at the time is preserved in her letters to Elizabeth, unwaveringly affectionate and even able to congratulate her on this marvellous opportunity to increase in adult wisdom. Later, after an agonising extended struggle during which her relationship with Valentine had been almost destroyed, Sylvia came to hate Elizabeth, and then she told the story in a different way, casting Elizabeth as a neurotic, monomaniac 'bitch'.[27]

Elizabeth's background had undoubtedly made her spoilt and demanding, but also desperate for love; according to her journals she would eagerly have married any of the young men her parents approved, if only any one of them had asked her. The strong sense of entitlement bred into her was by now matched with an equally strong rage that she had not got her due; despite her money, position and intellectual ambitions she was inexplicably unclaimed. Over thirty now, it was probably too late for the society wedding her family had expected, and the alternative life S&V represented offered a face-saving solution. So once Elizabeth had found a lover, she intended to keep them, to exercise her rights and demand anything that was being unreasonably withheld. Previous commitments were not to compete. In her letters to Valentine (relatively few of which survive) Elizabeth reveals herself in this unattractive light; Valentine's letters to her (very many of which survive) are equally self-justifying, blame-allotting, reproachful, and loving only in a possessive mode.

At the time, Sylvia was disturbed that her usual policy of collusion wasn't working; Valentine did not discuss her new lover. Elizabeth was still there at Christmas; Sylvia's Christmas poem to Valentine was about overhearing them making love. On their eighth anniversary, Valentine and Sylvia were sleeping separately, with Elizabeth in Sylvia's place.

For once, S&V had lost control of the situation. Elizabeth, in a post-mortem discussion many years later, stated that she'd believed sex led inexorably to marriage. She explained that her upbringing (and reading of great novels) had taught her this. If one of the lovers was already 'tied' to somebody else, they must gain freedom from the bondage of the old love, otherwise the new lovers must kiss and part. Elizabeth added righteously that she had been 'naively unaware of a pattern of morals and manners very different from this', which she described as 'eighteenth century'.[28] (In this terminology, Valentine's intention had been uncomplicated adultery, rather than divorce proceedings.) Elizabeth asserted that sexual love immediately gave her rights over Valentine, and turned Sylvia into the interloper, thus manipulating the situation so that Elizabeth retained the moral high ground – in her own estimation. She reminded Valentine:

> I was, when you took me in love in 1938, sexually very innocent and very passionate, revolted by promiscuity of any kind, terrified by the knowledge that I was a Lesbian, and deeply tired and lonely ... because I knew I must keep myself free and clear until I had found my own person.[29]

This omits to mention that Valentine was already somebody else's 'person' and that – even if she was behaving badly and playing dangerous games – she'd received Elizabeth's enthusiastic assent before she 'took' her.

Sylvia encapsulated the situation when she wrote: 'Valentine loved in the present. Elizabeth's love was pinned to a future conditional, to an amended Valentine she could safely call her own.'[30] But Elizabeth stayed on through the spring of 1939 while Valentine loved with increasing fervour and urgency, with a growing awareness that she was in an impossible situation. Sylvia was so unhappy she considered leaving; Valentine made her promise to stay. Valentine's work was not prospering; she had no time to write, and few poems of these months remain.

On her thirty-third birthday, Sylvia gave Valentine a manuscript book for poems; the next day Valentine wrote in it: 'E and I lying in love on a floor of bluebells.'[31] It was part of Sylvia's pain that there was no area of their shared life that Elizabeth did not touch; she knew Chaldon and Winterton, she met Ruth (and Joan) as well as Janet and her parents, she bought numerous Craskes, at Frome Vauchurch she fished in the river and gardened in the herb garden she'd discussed with Sylvia, she sent them expensive presents of books and wine. And, as Sylvia wryly observed, one of Elizabeth's unfair advantages was 'two large new ears';[32] certainly she was told Valentine's life-story in all its mythomanic splendour. Later, Elizabeth would use this intimate knowledge to S&V's disadvantage.

Spain was not forgotten in all this, and the news was bad. Barcelona fell in January 1939, Franco's troops entered Madrid on 27 March. The International Brigades had been disbanded and, despite their heroism and sacrifice, the Republicans were utterly defeated. Losses on both sides had been appalling. It was now that they learned, as Albert Camus wrote, that 'one can be right and still be beaten, that force can vanquish spirit, that there are times when courage is not its own reward.'[33] One of the survivors was the aristocratic Communist Ludwig Renn, who had been a friend to them in Spain. He came to Frome Vauchurch as an exile, straight from a French internment camp, where many of the International Brigades were refugees. Wounded, stateless and defeated, he cheered Sylvia up wonderfully. (Later, Valentine gave Ludwig some of her shirts, as his few clothes were in rags. Sylvia made use of this in a short story which calls Valentine by name, 'My Shirt is in Mexico'.)[34]

Elizabeth was now under intense pressure to return home, but Valentine couldn't bear the idea of being parted from her. A solution was offered by another Writers' Congress in Defence of Culture, in New York; S&V might not usually have accepted the invitation, but in the circumstances it was timely. The three of them travelled to New York together with Ludwig, who was funded by Elizabeth. Sylvia had last been there in 1929 when she enjoyed a great personal success (though unfortunately also met Elizabeth). In those pre-Valentine days she had been much feted and sought after, now she was in a very different mood. Outwardly, she gave no sign of her misery; William Maxwell, who edited her short stories at the *New Yorker*, only noticed 'she was dressed in black. Her voice had a slightly husky, intimate quality. Her conversation was so enchanting it made my head swim.'[35] He became her lifelong admirer. Another person Sylvia captivated on this trip was Paul Nordoff, the composer who set to music many of her and Valentine's poems, and collaborated with Sylvia on several major works.

Valentine was in no fit state to attend the Congress. What Sylvia called 'her fierce commanding young handwriting'[36] is often scrawled huge and drunken in her notebooks amid doodles and graffiti, oaths and rhymes. She wrote ditties about the delegates who disapproved of her: 'If only Christina Stead / were a little better bred,' or New York accents: 'Its irl / when its oil / its goil / when its girl.'[37] Sylvia performed her duties more soberly, but found the Congress 'small beer after Madrid'.[38] She endured a visit to Elizabeth's grand family home, where the other Whites were predictably horrified by Valentine; an obvious Lesbian, dressed as a man, drunk, making passes at the maids, smoking cigars and preaching Communism. Sylvia was uncomfortably aware that Elizabeth's mother saw her as 'the procuress of the situation.'[39]

Valentine was uncomfortable, too. Elizabeth was ever more proprietorial and arranged elaborate social events to show off her new acquisition, which it hated. But Elizabeth had always taken offence easily, and now she was extorting her due by anger or reproach. She was deeply disappointed by Valentine's reluctance to admit her claims, but was determined to convince her. Even at this late stage, Sylvia could return to her advisory role for the one-time protégée who had betrayed her so ruthlessly. Although she was consumed with misery, not only for her own ghastly situation but for Valentine's problem, presumably for Valentine's sake she wrote to 'Dearest Elizabeth':

> I know you are unhappy, and have been, and have reason for being unhappy. But it seems to me also that you have had times when you need not be unhappy, when you have been with Valentine, which is your happiness; and that you have not made the most of those times; because you have tried to make of them more than the most. That is to say you have tried to make a fine day into an insurance against bad weather, you have thought more of what it will be like when it is over than what it is like at the time. And things are only what they are at the time. There are no permanent moments. Whether the clock the calendar or the dead knell end

the moment it is a thing that must end. There are no roses that one can gather tomorrow.

And she signed her letter 'With my true love, Sylvia.'[40]

This excellent advice had no effect whatsoever. Elizabeth reproached Valentine later: 'if you had cared enough to want me entirely, we would have been together, forsaking all others, from the beginning, and no thing and no person, excepting our own two fierce characters, would ever have had a chance to come between us.'[41] From Elizabeth's viewpoint, Valentine's reluctance to leave Sylvia was both inexplicable and dishonest. An angry rhyme dashed off by Valentine gives an impression of the pressure Elizabeth exerted, and the response: 'Have you anything to bring me? / A heart to give or a song to sing me? / A vow to make – ever, forever? / Only *NEVER NEVER NEVER!* / If you've nothing then to give me / You shan't fuck me, you shan't wive me – / Excellent, I'm quit forever / Ever, Ever, Ever, *Ever!*'[42]

When the Congress was over, Valentine and Sylvia took a house for the summer with Elizabeth in Warren, Connecticut, scrupulously paying their share of the rent. This postponed their return to England, and Sylvia made the best of the situation with a dignified acquiescence. But at Warren, the devil was in the detail. Although set in lovely country which Elizabeth assiduously showed them (with her talent for dutiful, obvious sight-seeing), it was an inconvenient, ill-equipped house. Nevertheless, Sylvia assured her 'I am completely in love with the place' – though she also suggested many improvements to the incomplete domestic arrangements – and protested (too much?) 'how lovely everything is, and how happy we are, and how happy we will be. I can't begin to thank and praise you.'[43]

In the hot, thundery weather Valentine and Sylvia exhausted their energy on household tasks which Elizabeth left entirely to them. When she joined them, as Sylvia remembered with resentment, she always brought her own freshly-laundered clothes while they had no facilities to wash theirs. But this wasn't the real problem: in that 'hell-hole' Sylvia lay awake in torment all night listening to Elizabeth's dog obsessively scratching, and her 'monomaniac' monologue going 'on and on, railing, reproaching, analysing, accusing'.[44] This was the voice of misery, but Sylvia now believed that Elizabeth's love for Valentine was merely the desire for possession.

Valentine, who had seemed 'wicked and imperturbable' before, was now careworn and irritable. Once she threw a sandwich at Sylvia for being too conciliatory; 'it was well-aimed and thrown hard.' Elizabeth intervened with 'Well, that's no way to treat Sylvia,' so Sylvia knew her brave face had to be maintained, at the risk of greater humiliation for them all.[45] Janet had joined them in America now (thanks to Elizabeth's financial generosity) and she witnessed Sylvia's plight with robust outrage.

The emotional impasse was partly the result of Valentine's desire to write; she had a strong conviction that the events in her life were the seed which fertilised her creativity. Writing to Elizabeth long after, she explained this theory quite explicitly:

> You and I in conjunction (in my mind) acted the male part ... the rest of the process of bringing to birth was done by whatever it is that actually constructs such things as poems or pictures ... But – it would not have started at all if you and I had never met together.[46]

The idea of life-experiences providing the (pro-)creative force to make poetry could even become a motive for taking certain actions. Valentine wrote in self-justification 'I should not expect ever to write another poem, if I had not behaved just so.'[47] To suppress the emotion would have been to suppress the poem. This in turn meant that, logically, the most extreme and traumatic situations could be paradoxically good for Sylvia, if she was likely to write about them.

Valentine described her behaviour in America as 'lecherous, greedy and drunken' but her state of mind, by contrast, as 'very serious' about love, and poetry.[48] Certainly in her poetry there is a strong suggestion that she acknowledged, while writing, truths which could be refuted by her non-creative self. The love-poems to Elizabeth are equivocal, full of simultaneous love and foreboding. 'Warren, Connecticut 31.viii.39' begins 'For this a tree grew for fifty years,' but the living tree has perished, cut down for a transient fire 'That shudders its light on our faces and wavers and frightens / Itself with the shadows', and the final stanza ends 'For these brief shadows a fire was kindled / Months ago now, that you in love should stand here / And I beside you, warming ourselves at our fear.'[49]

The theme of fear is revisited in 'Dark Entry', a remarkable poem inspired by this curious name for a country road. After a verse considering naming, and the atmosphere of the place itself, 'Secretive as the landscape of your body, / Quiet and moody as a pool in the forest', they arrive. '"Dark Entry" says the map, and we drive through', but it is not as the name had made her imagine it.

> Dark Entry, like any other, is a track
> (Leads off the wide road, curls away and climbs
> Steeply and then runs down, runs down to nothing,
> And nothing is anywhere there from the beginning):
> You can even go up Dark Entry and get back.[50]

The sexual symbolism of this is obvious, and by no means positive; as a love poem it is too conflicted to be very encouraging. Valentine expresses her knowledge that she's travelling down a cul-de-sac which (despite its fascinating, though sinister, promise) is ordinary, leads nowhere, and even allows for the possibility of return.

Even in an overtly erotic poem to Elizabeth, like 'There is a silence of the body' (not one of Valentine's best efforts, partly because it uses almost comically crude extended penetrative imagery of 'sword and sheath'), there's more conflict than pleasure. The language suggests struggle – 'the two are inimical / they resist violently' – and pain: 'you are pierced and I am housed / the bright blade slides and the silken sheath is filled.'[51] These poems show a vivid awareness of conflicting emotions, an acceptance that this love is both dangerous and empty. Yet outside her poems, Valentine could ignore this.

When the summer tenancy at Warren ended, Valentine and Sylvia went, alone, to stay in a borrowed mountain cabin at Celo, North Carolina. Valentine was unwell, physically and emotionally exhausted, like Sylvia – and they were both desperately worried by the news of war in Europe. Nothing about their own situation was settled and, as Sylvia recalled, 'the shadow was driven inward, not away.'[52] She wrote of the outbreak of war in Valentine's notebook the bleak words: 'A war in Europe. A modern war.'[53] (Their knowledge of contemporary warfare was uncomfortably up to date; relatively few people had experienced a 'modern' air-raid or witnessed the results of Luftwaffe bombing, yet.)

Valentine wrote a lament for 'this epoch's funeral', beginning 'Autumn's the wind over this summer blowing'.[54] Everything was different now; they decided they must return to England. Before they left Celo, Sylvia was attacked by a swarm of wild bees as she walked alone; as she fled back to the cabin she lost consciousness. Valentine was always good in a crisis, calm and dependable; she knew what to do in this potentially fatal incident. Sylvia enjoyed having her undivided attention.

All the boats home were full of returning Europeans, so they had to wait in New York for a passage, where they saw Evelyn (their erstwhile Chaldon visitor) again. Elizabeth swiftly joined them there, so Sylvia was relegated to a single room once more. Valentine did not want to leave Elizabeth; their love-affair was physically so important to her that she could overlook the unhappy dramas that went with it. Elizabeth was determined that Valentine should remain in America for the duration of the war, for *ever*, and she begged her to stay. Valentine wavered, and might have surrendered if Elizabeth had not made an error of judgement; she suggested Valentine should apply for US citizenship, assuring her it would be safer to remain in America.

This misreading of her character enraged Valentine. If she had voluntarily travelled to the war-zone in Spain to support the anti-Fascist forces, was it likely that she'd seek safety now her own country was at war with Fascism? No doubt Valentine was genuinely offended, but it was also the excuse she so urgently needed. She moved to a different hotel with Sylvia, cancellation tickets duly appeared, and they took a brief and formal farewell of Elizabeth, who brought Evelyn with her.

Or, so Sylvia told the story years later. But her goodbye letter to Elizabeth suggests a more complicated scenario. Sylvia did not want Elizabeth to think she was

> conniving at a departure which must bring sorrow to two people, one loved so passionately and so long [Valentine, since 1930], the other loved profoundly, and for even longer [Elizabeth, since 1929]. I can only trust you to be magnanimous enough to believe that I have done nothing to bring this about ...

Evidently Sylvia still hoped to maintain her relationship with Elizabeth, and cared what Elizabeth thought of her. The letter suggests that Elizabeth had told Sylvia she'd previously been in love with *her* – Sylvia writes 'I knew you loved me, but did not guess how ...[so] it is no wonder our relationship remained as it did – a tender and trusting friendship.' Trusting might seem an ironical word to use, in the circumstances, but Sylvia made her meaning clear, in a way that is so different from her later attitude to Elizabeth that it's worth quoting at length:

> You say that when you fell in love with Valentine you betrayed my trust. You betrayed nothing. You acted naturally and properly, and as a person of sensibility and poetry should behave. There was no betrayal in that. In a way, there would have been betrayal if you had not acted as you did. For I have always urged you, as you remember, to take chances, to accept life, to enrich yourself by experience, to be wary of the cloistered virtue ... You acted as I expected you to act, as I felt you should act. So let there be no more thought of betrayal my dear, it is a false and belying word, and not appropriate to any one of us three.

You acted as I expected you to act, as I felt you should act – is this partly what the older Sylvia meant when she said that the Elizabeth affair had been her own fault? There was, clearly, more happening here than the adherence to a bohemian code by which Sylvia later explained her behaviour, although at the time she certainly invoked it:

> though what has happened now seems what ordinary people in their ordinary senses consider deplorable, and something to be overlooked, minimised, made up for, and put away as soon as possible, I hope that we are enough in our senses and far away enough from what is considered normal, to remember it in all its fullness, all its implications, and to remember it as something positive and constructive and vital.

Sylvia's letter continued, claiming that, despite her 'sharp and haunting regret' at seeing Elizabeth 'so pale, so sad, so tormented', she yet felt

> a deep pride and satisfaction mixed with that compassion for I see you also so profoundly enlarged and enriched that I cannot believe that when I sent the telegram to Paris telling you to come

> I did anything that I can ever feel sorry for ... I shall think of you thus, a fulfilled and experienced Elizabeth, however a sad one. But the Elizabeth I have always foreseen, and wanted to see –

And she ended 'My dear, I love you, and wish you well.'[55] Beyond magnanimity, this implies that even after the misery and humiliation of the time in America, Sylvia is still trying to present herself (to herself?) as master of the situation. She's never lost control, or been betrayed, her own creation has not turned on her and used all her lessons in alternative morality against *her*. Saving face, Sylvia maintains that Elizabeth is like them, a not-ordinary person of 'sensibility and poetry' whose actions are commendable, not the monomaniac bully who has tried to destroy her marriage. It's all really been *for* Sylvia, on her advice and loyal to her anti-normal philosophy of life.

This isn't to suggest that Sylvia was being hypocritical; she does not mention her own feelings, no doubt her sorrow – like Elizabeth's – was all part of living poetically. And, of course, she was taking Valentine away, leaving Elizabeth to enjoy her despair. As far as Sylvia knew, the affair was, in effect, over.

Simultaneously, Valentine was insisting that 'My whole heart, my mind, my body, all ache and beat with love for you, desire and love –'[56] and sending last-minute notes to Elizabeth by the *Aquitania's* pilot vessel. But they managed to leave. The urgent obligation to be in their own country when it was at war, a kind of deep-rooted gut patriotism that MI5 would never associate with the political Left, over-rode other desires.

Even after the trauma of America, Valentine and Sylvia were still together. The relationship which had already proved itself so resilient now seemed very frail, but with extraordinary tenacity, it survived. Partly, this must have been because of Sylvia's determined refusal to believe that she'd been betrayed, that Valentine and Elizabeth had done anything she didn't sanction. And partly, it was because she loved Valentine so completely, and Valentine loved her in return in a way which was never equalled with any of the other lovers, even Elizabeth.

During a storm, Valentine suddenly lurched across the cabin and fell into Sylvia's arms, swearing that everything would be well between them again. Valentine's old magic still worked for Sylvia; the one word that needed to be spoken had been said. Before dinner that evening, Valentine 'played the fruit-machine. And with a clatter it all fell out, she'd won the jackpot.'[57] The closing lines of Sylvia's extraordinary poem about the experience, 'In a foreign country', tell it all:

> Down, down to the innocence of legend it recedes –
> My sorrow, embossed with mountains, darkened with forests, laced
> With summer lightning, quilted with rivers and dirt roads –
> My sorrow, stately as a cope, vast as a basilica –
> My sorrow, embroidered all over with America,
> That at a word from you in mid-Atlantic I threw away.[58]

Chapter Seven:
For The Duration Interned

On their arrival at Frome Vauchurch in October 1939 Valentine and Sylvia were greeted with cries of 'Thank God you're safe at last!'[1] It was Mrs Keates (Sylvia's London cleaner), who'd been convinced that their ship would be torpedoed and sunk. With her entire family she was house-sitting in the comparative safety of Dorset, but these congenial evacuees – who delighted their hosts with their unconventional marital arrangements and limber Cockney – soon returned to London when no air-raids materialised.

The war had removed Valentine and Sylvia from an insoluble situation, and their return home offered the chance to repair their relationship – but Valentine was visibly miserable. She missed Elizabeth painfully, and – although their affair had been so unhappy – did not want to end it completely. Almost as soon as she was back, Valentine wrote to Elizabeth, demanding to know *'in what way, under what conditions, you would come to me'* and assuring her 'I did NOT choose to leave you *and I don't intend to lose you.'*[2] Elizabeth urged Valentine to come back to her immediately, and bring Sylvia if need be. This Valentine would not do; as she wrote in 'On not returning to America': 'Whether to do well for yourself and know it / Or diminish slowly and still be a poet – / Put a tick where it applies, and do not go to America.'[3] But Elizabeth persisted in her demands, and Valentine's letters to her gave no indication that the affair was really over, however miserable its continuance was making them both. Sylvia (who also still wrote affectionately to Elizabeth) waited for the sickness to run its course, supported by Valentine's Atlantic promise that all would be well – and Elizabeth's enforced absence.

Unfortunately they were not alone together; the Keates were replaced by two sergeants billeted in the house with their wives, some children, then other London friends and acquaintances. None stayed long, but all disrupted the household. Even Sylvia, with her tart humour, found their presence trying; there was nothing wrong with the evacuees, she explained, 'except that they were there'.[4] She and

Valentine found that the war altered life in Britain as dramatically as revolutionary government had transformed Barcelona. Privacy, self-determination and personal freedom were all sacrificed to the war effort.

As Communists, Valentine and Sylvia were not in a comfortable position. The Party had declared that this war would be an Imperialist struggle between capitalist powers, and demanded a 'People's Peace'. Accordingly Valentine and Sylvia left peace leaflets on tanks in army camps. Since the mid-1930s they had been involved in the peace movement locally, trying to recruit working-class members from the trade unions, not just the usual 'pretty pious, pretty respectable quakers, Fellowships of Reconciliation and so forth'[5] (as Sylvia explained to the comrades and, inadvertently, MI5). Even Valentine had wondered about the legality of their anti-war leaflets; those intercepted by the secret service in 1936, earnestly typed with much underlining, were indeed extremely subversive, so to distribute similar propaganda to soldiers during wartime was brave, if not foolhardy.

Many comrades had, like Sylvia, 'the profoundest doubts about this war' as a way to fight 'Nazidom',[6] but this position provoked enormous hostility, which was increased by Stalin's non-aggression pact with Hitler. In 1941 when Germany invaded Russia the official outlook changed abruptly, and wicked Reds suddenly became heroic comrades. Valentine and Sylvia were then able to collect for Soviet Aid and meet nothing but approval for the Soviet people's extraordinary resistance. It seemed bizarre, if gratifying, to hear the *Internationale* played after the film in the cinema while the audience stood respectfully. Still, Sylvia shrewdly commented that their neighbours believed they were dangerous fifth columnists because having 'had a strong impression that our views were uncongenial and reprehensible, now ... [they] feel convinced that we are, and always have been, blackshirts.'[7]

Doubts about the motives for the war, or its conduct, did not prevent Valentine and Sylvia from working to help people caught up in the machine, whether they were refugees, evacuees, or combatants. Valentine lamented that the destruction of youth was an inevitable result of war, as was the desecration of nature and the diminishment of personal liberty. She deplored all that was happening, but she and Sylvia treated the individuals involved with human sympathy.

Valentine took a pessimistic view of their chances of survival; Sylvia spoke words of reasoned encouragement, in a ritual that amused them both. Sylvia's strong sense of the ridiculous was a necessary antidote to the depressing atmosphere, and Valentine's humour did not fail her, though it became very black. They were grimly aware that despite (or because of) the most sincere efforts, their local defence was just as disorganised as Republican Barcelona, though in a different style. Air raid practice was 'like a knock about farce film done in slow motion',[8] despite the unquestionable bravery and good intentions of everyone involved.

During the early part of the war, Valentine wrote a cycle of poems, *War in Progress*, in a satirical Byronic style which suited her sardonic turn of mind, as well as her political outlook: 'America remains the only / Power uninvolved, and feels quite lonely,' or 'Above ground still? Fear not, there's one deep shelter / Open alike in Free and Fascist state, / Vast, private, silent and inviolate.' She lamented the despoilment of the countryside, refusing to accept as a necessary evil 'this mad mesh, this mess / Of barbed wire, of sandbags, of unhappiness', or 'the loved landscape blasted and savaged into strangeness / and all things dear destroyed, all love wasted and lost'. And 'Black-Out' records the depressing everyday detail which was common to everyone at that time: 'Darkness now / Comes by routine of cardboard shutter, rattle of curtain, / Comes like a sentence everyone's learnt to utter'.[9]

In June 1940, Sylvia and Valentine mourned the fall of Paris, the city they both loved which had been the symbol of resistance. That summer was particularly beautiful; they slept outside and heard the nightingales singing beside the river. But Elizabeth was still active; she hoped to come to England, despite wartime restrictions, though she thought Valentine should know that Evelyn had proposed to her. Elizabeth recounted that Evelyn had comforted her when she was in a state of collapse after Valentine's departure. When Evelyn declared that she was in love, Elizabeth replied 'But you must not be; I am in love with Valentine.'

Evelyn answered 'I know that, but let me do what I can for you.'[10]

Predictably enough, this bombshell goaded Valentine into her most extreme proposal yet; having previously only offered 'probable' fidelity, she now promised:

> I shall be faithful to you ... & I shall consider you as owning my pledged faith, & myself as owning your pledged faith; we shall *be each others'* property & possession. I will give you constancy of care and of protection. I will not leave you nor will I ever fail you, as lover, as husband, as companion. In return, you will give me constancy of love, of companionship and loyalty.

(Which would presumably mean resisting Evelyn, although Valentine doubted 'whether you can maintain your own standard of fidelity'.) She finished her long letter 'I love you – MINE.'

Valentine avoided 'committing the great offence of seeming to pledge what I cannot, yet, absolutely honestly promise you' by emphasising that this offer described her 'dear hopes' – and that this imaginary situation would be 'experimental'.[11] At the actual prospect of Elizabeth appearing in England (which was unlikely, but not impossible), Valentine's heart failed her. She advised Elizabeth not to, and Sylvia warned her against it too – citing the stress of wartime conditions, the misery of their last encounter and her own determination not to suffer in the same way again, in fact not to meet Elizabeth at all. It wasn't an experiment in which Sylvia was willing to participate; 'Valentine now knows how I feel',[12] she wrote to Elizabeth, revealingly.

Elizabeth wasn't given clearance to travel, in any case, but a different third person disrupted Valentine and Sylvia's life – Ruth, who was now isolated at The Hill House without her staff. Visiting was so difficult that Valentine felt obliged to stay indefinitely in Norfolk, leaving Frome Vauchurch in the care of the current evacuee-friend, Kit Dooley. Sylvia acquiesced, and arrived to find Ruth in her element, winning the war single-handed. ('Her tactics could teach Hitler quite a bit.')[13] The Norfolk coast was considered a likely invasion site, and the house by the dunes was soon requisitioned. Ruth was understandably upset, and played her part with high drama, exclaiming to anyone who would listen 'I've been seized!'[14]

Valentine and Sylvia had the unenviable job of helping Ruth pack up the entire house contents and move out. Since nothing had ever been tidied up or thrown away (Ruth's considerable energies being spent on organising other people) it was a gargantuan task to arrange the move. Sylvia was delighted to overhear Ruth, while sorting out a drawer, murmur 'Now, whose teeth can these be?'[15] Although Sylvia found Ruth utterly exasperating, she still thought her endlessly funny. Valentine's feelings about 'my mother, so charming and so generous and so maddening and so religious',[16] were complicated by love, and guilt.

'Yuletide at Home' was written at Winterton and captures the spirit of ghastly good cheer: 'At middle-age the Young return again, / Home-come for Yule ... Christmas coincident / With smiles and tears and dinner sharp at eight / Stretches its dogged length to merriment – / Aren't we all lucky to sit up so late?'[17] This appeared in the American *New Republic* which regularly published Valentine's poems during the 1940s. It paid well (and in dollars) and also printed a series of Valentine's *Letters from England* in which she adopted a more conventionally patriotic tone, praising British courage, humour and determination. It was a curious progression to move from those passionate reports from Spain, trying to awaken her country's conscience, to the task of enlisting American support now that her own nation was in the war zone.

Ruth was safely installed in another house in Winterton, and Valentine and Sylvia rented tiny Beach Cottage nearby. Here they received the news that an incendiary bomb had fallen on Frome Vauchurch, into the (luckily unoccupied) spare room. No one was hurt, though a featherbed and a bookcase they disliked were destroyed, but the havoc was 'indescribable'.[18] Kit Dooley put the fire out within ten minutes, but the mess was more recalcitrant. When they returned at the end of the year, feathers were still drifting ineradicably about the house.

Aside from these anxieties, Valentine and Sylvia were not very happy in Norfolk. The beloved sea was out of bounds, the sand-dunes had been mined and covered in barbed wire entanglements as a precaution against invasion. They witnessed the aftermath of an accident there; a shocked soldier running away from an explosion, carrying his comrade's blown-off foot. There were other kinds of horror too. Ruth exasperated them both beyond endurance. Sylvia's description indicates why:

> she emphasizes every other word so that the cat claws at the door screaming to get out, mirrors splinter, glasses leap from the

table, and the bedroom doors at quite the other end of the house rattle on their hinges. She also sticks like a gramophone record ... her attention strays and until it comes back again she will go on repeating the same adjective.[19]

Valentine could only remark that, far from sacrificing Sylvia on the family altar, 'on the contrary if anything is mincemeat as a result of being there it is the altar.'[20]

At some point during 1940, Valentine took a 'cure' for alcoholism, which worked only briefly. Ruth might well have driven anyone to drink, if they could come by it during the war, but Valentine considered her alcoholism to be more acute than mere stress-induced excess. Her judgement about the scale of the problem is confused by her guilt about it; clearly she was drunk sometimes, as her notebooks testify, but she was never publicly inebriated or unable to function. Sylvia did not consider her a heavy drinker (though Sylvia was no abstainer herself). But what worried Valentine was that she drank secretly – or at least, alone in her room. The cause of her guilt was perhaps the need to do something surreptitiously, in private, which she was unable to stop – an addiction to a bad habit, as much as a physical craving. Sylvia was quite unembarrassed to write in her diary that she'd got drunk on cherry brandy, or over-indulged with a guest, but for her this was social drinking, a relaxing pleasure. Valentine did not drink to relax, or to lose control, but to overcome internal controls which prevented her from functioning as she wished. Since she had no other means to do so, alcohol continued to be essential to her.

In a letter to Evelyn, written from Winterton in 1940, Valentine refers to problems keeping 'integrity of mind (sanity, I suppose)' in the current situation of 'lack of sleep, lack of liberty, increased tension & so on' while under 'attack from outside', when her 'own life shelters a Fifth Column.' By this she implies Evelyn's 'treachery' in transferring her allegiance to Elizabeth. And Valentine insists that she has 'a right to know' how things stand in their 'triple-alliance'. This claiming of ownership of Evelyn, as well as Elizabeth, demonstrates another aspect of Valentine's sexual voracity, perhaps; a seigneurial sense of feudal dues owed by past lovers. Evelyn's furious, chilly reply, typed on headed paper from her workplace, denied any such three-way alliance, or any 'intentions' towards Elizabeth, and mocked Valentine's apparent doubts that 'the only person in this world whom [Elizabeth] truly loves is yourself and that her one consuming desire is to be with you again.' And she added 'if it does not happen, I assure you it will be tragic for her', leaving Valentine the impression that Elizabeth was 'in a definite danger.'[21] (No wonder Evelyn, as well as Valentine, was drinking heavily.)

~

When Valentine and Sylvia were able to return home to Frome Vauchurch – after deciding that their presence in Winterton was not helping Ruth – they found that much had changed. Bombs fell nearby, planes fought overhead. War mentality had overcome Dorset, idiots were in the ascendant, but Valentine and Sylvia were no use to anybody. *Los Intellectuales* were not to be mobilized in this country. The daily practicalities of living were becoming ever more time-consuming and boring. Yet the purgatory of Winterton had cleansed them of the American episode. On Valentine's Day 1941, Valentine could write to Sylvia that their relationship had suffered nothing worse than a scratch on the surface of a record and 'because the record is so lovely and well-completed we shall not notice the scratch.'[22]

So, despite outside circumstances, they were happier. And there was the consolation of the river: 'Bright bar of sun on water, striking across my ceiling, / turning like spiralled rod of glass on a French clock, or silver / hurry of mercury from the dentist's bottle ... / Who sees this, on a winter morning of war, and does not tremble / with the same unchosen joy as the sun and the water?'[23]

The summer of 1941 was again beautiful, gardens in the most glorious flower, the countryside poignantly lovely. Valentine and Sylvia volunteered for night fire-watching duty, and walked the lanes making owl-calls on their whistles (the emergency blasts Sylvia had already practised 'very quietly in the toilet').[24] They also took a YMCA van delivering cigarettes and chocolate to soldiers posted along the Isle of Purbeck coastline; beautiful scenery which, as Sylvia observed, 'holiday-makers would give their eyes to be in' but 'of course they [the soldiers] are bored to perishing point.'[25]

Valentine dreaded the effects of war on the national psyche, as well as on the land itself. She feared that, rather than necessary discipline to ensure 'singleness of aim' there was now a 'superstitious and tyrannical insistence upon absolute obedience and conformity ... a descent, yet again, into darkness.'[26] Enforced conformity was a frightening prospect for Valentine, so visibly gender *non*-conformist. She knew that Fascists had murdered the poet Federico Garcia Lorca because he was homosexual, more than for his political beliefs. She knew that the Nazis were exterminating 'others like me.'[27] But it seemed that the different might not fare too well under a war government in Britain, either.

MI5 were particularly worried by the employment of Communists during wartime, and they did not lose sight of Valentine and Sylvia. Valentine signed on, with resignation, at the Territorial Army HQ in Dorchester, as a general typist. Although her typing was certainly excellent, this hardly seems like a good use of her talents, especially after the experience gained in Spain. Valentine laughed at herself for having imagined that the unintelligible knitting-patterns she was set to type out were coded messages. Equally mistakenly, MI5 imagined that a telegram she sent to Elizabeth about buying Craskes was a coded message, and spent much effort tracing innocent people named Craske, and considering the import of 'SOLOMON SEVEN VERSES SEVEN EIGHT' at the end of the message. The biblical text turned out to read: 'Thy stature is like to a palm tree and thy breasts to clusters of grapes. I said I will go up to the palm tree, I will take hold of the boughs thereof now'. The MI5 report comments: 'the biblical quotation is of an unusual character – and possibly rather unpleasant.'[28]

As a clerk (and later secretary) Valentine avoided notice, rather than seeking a more glamorous or even heroic role by joining the women's forces, wearing uniform, and doing work – such as driving – which had previously been reserved for men. This uncharacteristic failure to indulge in gender disruption suggests ambivalence about the war itself, initially, as well as internal reservations about her own probable reception in a more conventional field of operations than Republican Spain. (She did, later, try and find a job with the Auxiliary Fire Service, which had women's teams, but without success.) Joan, by contrast, had a high-ranking job in the Red Cross which gave her considerable power over others and gained her an MBE.

In the same spirit of self-mockery as the knitting-pattern codes, Valentine joked that she would make a model censor because she 'was always perfectly shameless about reading letters not meant for her, and ... was ideally suited for the work by never having much inclination to answer letters back.'[29] MI5 were, of course, reading *her* letters perfectly shamelessly and reported anxiously, after she'd moved to the Civil Defence Office later in the war, that 'she is not a person who should be employed on highly confidential work' (and also asked 'to hear whether Miss Ackland comes to your notice, in connection with the Communist Party at Dorchester.')[30] Since Valentine was still young enough to be classed as a 'mobile grade' of unmarried female, she could in theory be drafted anywhere in the country. Sylvia, too, had to report for local war work; as she irately observed, if she'd had a husband that would have been of sufficient 'national importance'[31] to exempt her, but their relationship was, of course, unrecognised.

Sylvia found work lecturing, through the Workers Educational Association, to widely differing audiences; soldiers, evacuees, women in the forces (who, Sylvia noticed, had 'all the disadvantages of being soldiers and none of the fun').[32] MI5 were strongly against allowing her to 'be virtually free to circulate and talk amongst troops at their station', although one officer thought it might be permissible 'provided the authorities are aware that she is a Party member ... [and have] one or two of her lectures monitored.' His colleague objected:

> I do not consider this young woman is at all suitable as a lecturer to the troops. Miss Warner has been known to us for nearly six years as an active participant in Left Wing movements, and there is no reason to believe she has changed her views. If she were in one of the women's Auxiliary Services, I should have to place her under observation ... [it is] manifestly absurd that any person who would have to figure on the Special Observation List should be employed in this way.[33]

Nevertheless, Sylvia was able to share her unorthodox views on subjects such as Matriarchy, Utopia, Thomas Hood's 'The Song of the Shirt' or Jewry's Bachelor Deity – to the chagrin of the secret service and the great enjoyment of her listeners.

Writing was not officially an occupation at all. This was one of the worst blows for Valentine, the loss of her self-image as a poet, the further erosion of that sense of special vocation which had always sustained her. 'Is it wrong and stupid to be depressed that a fate so common as daily work should embrace even Valentine?' she wrote in her diary. 'I've been *too long free*, that's the truth! To conform, to catch morning trains, to stand in corridors, to call Colonels "Sir", to reason patiently, even respectfully, with fools ... I find all this most difficult.'[34] And she wrote, in 'Protective Custody': 'Into the war the poet is taken, / Made one of, a comrade; returned / Swift to a life he had slowly forsaken / And for the duration interned.'[35]

It was Valentine's superiors she found difficult; her co-workers treated her well; with 'chivalry',[36] she said. Since she had no experience of clerical work, but had aberrant class origins, Valentine was relieved to find her colleagues were protective and kindly. No doubt this reflected her own consideration and politeness towards them; her Communist convictions and experiences in Spain had convinced her that class divisions were iniquitous. Not many of her bosses shared this view – for many, one of the worst things about the war was the class upheaval it caused. But congenial workmates in the typing pool couldn't disguise the fact that – like them – Valentine was wasting her time and sacrificing her freedom to no good purpose.

Sylvia, by contrast, had a good war in her way. Her enjoyment of human foible and keen sense of the ridiculous stood her in good stead, as did her use of her colleagues in the Women's Voluntary Service as excellent copy; 'county hags' with their 'high bred passions' raging.[37] And from her office, Valentine contributed 'keen passions and rivalries which toss all of us as tho' we were the Balkan states'.[38] At home, they were busy planting subsistence vegetables in the garden and breeding their inedible rabbits. Valentine dug a trench which inexplicably contributed to the war effort; Sylvia experimented with new recipes for their 'mingy and monotonous' ration.[39] She was – extraordinarily – working on a novel, *The Corner That Held Them*, and often retired to Marxist contemplation of her medieval nunnery.

Valentine did not have a large project into which she could escape in her imagination. She also had a source of private pain. Many of the long letters she was still exchanging with Elizabeth dissected the course of their affair, and their current emotional condition. Of her defection to Evelyn, Elizabeth explained that she was not 'stoic or hermit enough' to live celibate forever, but she also admitted that she knew 'how deeply wounded in sexual pride and sense of possession' Valentine would be.[40] Valentine was certainly enraged; she was particularly upset that Elizabeth had – at Evelyn's request – taken off a ring she had promised to wear forever, that as well as setting up house together they had established a business partnership (White & Holahan, Books) and exchanged 'assertions of permanency'.[41] In her letters Elizabeth relayed all this with a wealth of detail which drove Valentine into a frenzy of jealousy, while continuing to assert undying love and to imply that Valentine was very immoral. (Valentine was moved to respond: 'in taking it upon yourself to represent Morality as against Immorality, you are putting yourself into a false position ... Your code is different from mine ... Don't so heavily assume that you are Puritan and White and I am therefore Sardanapolitan and Black!')[42]

What Elizabeth never did was tell Valentine that it was unreasonable to expect lifelong constancy after they had parted, especially while Valentine had a continuing relationship with Sylvia; that would have been to admit that the affair was over. It was far more effective to keep up a dialogue, examining and re-examining their past emotions, and keeping present emotions engaged. Deeply disillusioned, Valentine wrote to her:

> One must recognise oneself in the eyes of the person who says 'I love you' ... This is not egoism nor is it any kind of conceit; it applies equally to either person and is the essential of loving and being loved. There must be a true and recognisable Image. In our case, if it ever were true, it is now awry as anything in a distorting mirror.[43]

But she continued writing. She let Elizabeth know that she considered herself bound by no vows of fidelity, and during the war she had several affairs (with colleagues at the office, among others). Valentine defended her promiscuity in a long letter which Elizabeth cannot have been pleased to receive:

> It is possible and I am certain it is good, to enjoy physical contacts, pleasure and delight without any obligation beyond the natural

155

courtesy of mutual gratitude and acceptance ... There is NO INHERENT MORAL BADNESS in being able to enjoy without regret! ... it is blasphemy only to recognise [desire / the flame of life] in its tremendous, apocalyptic appearances ... the business of man is to kindle from that flame *every time it touches him*.[44]

Although Elizabeth was not content to be merely a 'light love', according to this (somewhat exhausting) philosophy Valentine was unlikely to settle down to monogamy with Sylvia. Elizabeth still hoped.

As the war dragged on into 1942, civilian morale sank. It was a bitter, snowy winter and Valentine had a painful and persistent ear infection. Rations were getting short, so their stores of hay and paraffin were being stolen, and vegetables mysteriously vanished from the garden. At the end of January Valentine was given compassionate leave from her job at the Territorial Army HQ on health grounds. She and Sylvia were encompassed in their old intimacy, and had time to enjoy it. Sylvia was delighted when Valentine was observed by the baffled occupants of a grand car as she bowed ceremoniously three times to a magpie (an unusual superstition). Valentine pointed out to *her* that anyone who looked in through the kitchen window might think them eccentric to be stroking Thomas the cat with their forks.

Valentine's leave wasn't permanent, so they searched for more congenial work which would fulfil her wartime obligations locally (otherwise she could be called up). Despite much negotiation with the Fire Service, only office-based work seemed available. In March she began a job with Civil Defence in Dorchester which she found 'beyond words bewildering'.[45] Sylvia hoped it might be less tedious; she was in the same building on WVS days and they could travel in and lunch together sometimes. There were other compensations, too; a uniform of sorts: 'a fine topcoat and a rather rakish beret' with

> a very noble pair of trousers (called SLACKS when they're female!) and a funny little jacket which is cut with a riotous swagger at the back and which has capacious pockets ... they don't supply anything for one to wear on top of the trousers or underneath 'em either, which is strange when you consider the high level of our public morals.[46]

As a job, Valentine initially found it

> pleasantly various ... I do the usual work of typing, taking down letters, telephoning and so on, but in addition I handle equipment and issue [gas masks and first aid equipment]... and deal with the VERY odd, assorted people who are our Wardens, First Aiders, Firemen and so on.[47]

There was an invasion scare on the Dorset coast, and they were told that in the event their house would be requisitioned as a machine-gun post because of its proximity to the bridge over the river. If this happened, not much would survive, so they packed up their most precious possessions to be sent to safety with Nora at Little Zeal – from their 'fortress of books'[48] sending Havelock Ellis, Krafft-Ebing and the literature of their life.

The local home guard now recruited an unofficial women's troop, with hand-grenade practices and rifle-training. This prompted one of Valentine's best-known poems, 'Teaching to Shoot', a wry commentary on the contradictions of war and love which expresses her feelings for Sylvia, and their characters, with extraordinary poignance:

> When we were first together as lover and beloved
> We had nothing to learn; together we improved
> On all the world's wide learning, and bettered it, and loved.
>
> Now you stand on the summer lawn and I am to show you
> First how to raise the gun to shoulder, bow head, stare quickly,
> and fire;
> Then how to struggle with the clumsy bolt (outdated), withdraw,
> return, and again – fire.
>
> As the evening darkens, even this summer evening, and the trees
> Bend down under the night-wind and the leaves rush in a flaming
> fire,
> I am to show you how to bend your body, take step lightly –
> and I hold your arm
> (Thin and sleek and cool as a willow-wand fresh in my hand),
> And in your hand you clasp fervently this dirty lump, this
> grenade...[49]

15. 'Everywhere is the pattern of water' – Sylvia fording the river, 1940s.

As 1942 drew towards winter, Valentine's health again deteriorated; she succumbed to every infection in the office, and found recovery slow. Sylvia looked after her as best she could and thought – as always – of less fortunate comrades. 'I am haunted,' she wrote,

> with the companionship of innumerable people in Europe who also nurse some loved one dependent on them, and have nothing for them, nothing beyond the barest coarse husks and hedge-brews. I feel as though I should be deformed for the rest of my life with this inequity of man's making to which willy-nilly I consent and willy-nilly profit by.[50]

This imaginative empathy with the suffering of individuals was inevitably painful. Sylvia alleviated her distress (and privileged guilt) through practical efforts to help those within her reach. Valentine, with her private, inward-looking and contemplative nature, did less and worried more; she looked on horrors which she was too sensitive to witness but powerless to prevent.

During these war years, outwardly Valentine's life became very routine; a pattern of commuting by train to work in the office throughout the week, recuperating on Sundays, working in the garden and the house, and participating in the endless tedium of merely subsisting in wartime conditions. Inwardly, however, she was beginning to lose her ability to function as a poet – or a person. She well knew that her circumstances were relatively easy, but that did not help her to endure boredom, the petty tyranny of little Hitlers, and a regime which was obviously undermining her health. When she was free, the ecstasy which natural beauty had always given her, the pleasures of the river, weather and seasons, were almost unbearable by contrast.

The decline in Valentine's mental health was disguised to most people (including her employers) by the breakdown of her physical health under the stress. But Sylvia knew of it, though she says they did not mention Valentine's 'mental sickness'.[51] There was always a bodily illness on her sicknotes: flu, ear infections, arthritis, infectious hepatitis, gastro-enteritis. Later Valentine blamed her alcoholism for this breakdown, but it was symptom as well as cause. The root of Valentine's agony was unerringly named by Sylvia: 'To be a poet was her deepest concern, her deepest obligation; to abdicate would be to sin against her light.'[52] Sylvia believed that Valentine's situation was frustrating 'the process of poetry',[53] thus her deepest self was being denied, her truest identity lost. In a poem of 1944, 'Did I feel like a poet long ago?', Valentine concludes: 'Where's the lost poet now, say! Oh take me a rifle / And show me the way.'[54]

Yet, as always with Valentine, there was another side to the story. Despite her despair and her sense of losing herself, Valentine could still write poems like 'Winter Illness' which shows technical control, delight in language, and a sense of calm contentment:

> Birds sail across the blue square,
> Diagonally across the window-boundaried air;
> Winter birds, no thread-needle flight of swallows there,
> The steady sombre passage of rooks outward or homeward bound,
> The pigeons' hasty passing, the lovely dart and dive,
> Swirl, flounce, and set-aside,
> Splash-water, the crossed and lively flight
> Of seagulls over the river;
> And best of all, in chequered and patterned cover,
> Shaken out, drawn back, folded, and spread again over
> All my window of sky, there fly the plover.[55]

As time passed, Valentine became more reconciled to Elizabeth's defection; once she accepted that the affair was over, she could begin some sort of recovery. Although there were still the long emotionally-charged letters, still the reproaches and justifications, Valentine began to write of their love-affair in the past tense: 'what went wrong with us', and to tell Elizabeth 'It is probably *better* that we never meet again.' She didn't want Elizabeth to risk 'what you have so properly & sensibly made for yourself [with Evelyn]' and was even able to assure her:

> I do not hate you at all. (Naturally I do not "hate" Evelyn either. I used to feel a spirited kind of rage with her which would have been very happily used up if I had been able to throw her into the river … that kind of nonsense fades out and time just obliterates it…)[56]

Although Valentine wrote 'it is still a considerable pain to me to probe like this into a wound which so nearly did not start to heal', she accepted that it *was* now healing. And she explained, disarmingly, that she continued to want Elizabeth's letters 'because a heart loves to think that it is beloved and, I suppose, I have not wanted to let that go'.[57]

~

Early in 1944, Dorset was declared a closed area; all non-residents had to depart (to the relief of some inhabitants) and residents were not allowed to leave. Bombing of the south coast intensified, and destruction extended even to Chaldon. Miss Green was hit by a random bomber dumping its remaining cargo after a raid. By extraordinary good luck, their tenants the Pitmans heard the Dorchester All Clear sounding, and were out of the cottage before it was hit. They were unharmed, but there was nothing left of the house. Sylvia reflected bitterly that the freak destruction had spared the workers' cottages (owned by the wealthy local estate) in their disgraceful condition 'with scarcely a bug shaken out of them'.[58] Apart from the financial loss of the property, this was not a good omen. Although they had outgrown Miss Green, it was their honeymoon cottage, the place of their first love, and for it to be physically obliterated seemed significant. Despite its symbolism, they bore the shock of the loss philosophically; so many others had lost so much more.

In April Valentine wrote her first *Poems of Release*, on sick-leave yet again. Sylvia had a new part-time job (as well as her WVS work and lecturing) as the local doctor's dispenser and assistant. Dr Lander was a humane man with whom she discussed Valentine's condition. His repeated insistence that she was too ill to return to work (this time because of severe gastric pain which might be gallstones or 'nervous colitis') eventually led to her discharge as unfit. Whether the symptoms were the result of years of alcohol abuse, stress-related, or psychosomatic, would be difficult to establish – most probably a combination of causes. But it seems clear that, while Valentine's health problems were very real, they always paralleled her inner struggles with the shadows of her childhood; the fear of being unloved, exiled, forgotten.

Dr Lander allowed Sylvia to give her 'essential' job full-time to Valentine (pre-empting her redeployment at some other unsuitable work), so she was still making an official contribution to the war-effort.

Valentine was a good dispenser, methodical and punctilious, proud of her medical forebears. It seemed she could at last make a positive contribution in a small local way. The actual work was harder and more responsible than her clerical jobs, but it wasn't time-wasting and soul-destroying. It was also closer to home, far more varied and flexible, and far more congenial than office politics in Dorchester. Under this new regime Valentine began to recover; Sylvia rejoiced that her stratagem had succeeded.

Valentine wrote her a love-poem which, with its title 'Poem in Middle Age', and its theme of refusing to drink the waters of Lethe (which bring the dead forgetfulness), stands as a tribute to the longevity of their partnership, and her ambitions for its perpetuity:

> Do not touch the slowly flowing water;
> If you die before me do not drink
> One drop of it, but lie on the cold bank ...
> Refuse to touch the water until you see me come, my Love,
> And we stoop down together.[59]

It's remarkable that she managed to write such a personal poem at all. The ban on the area had been lifted, and Dorset was again invaded by evacuees. Sylvia was overwhelmed with the work of finding shelter and food for unfortunate people fleeing from the Blitz. She left a funny account of her words of comfort to them and her fellow WVS ladies:

> nobody need be ashamed of lice nowadays ... Londoners seldom like porridge, pubs open at six, nettle-stings are not the same as nettle-rash, fish and chips will come out in a van, lost prams shall be traced, those are *our* planes, Londoners can't be expected to go to bed before eleven, cows don't bite ...[60]

Characteristically, Sylvia was appalled at the degrading slave-market system whereby evacuees were exhibited for their hosts to select them; she had chosen a woman and her daughter, and felt they might never forgive her. (It would be ghastly having strangers in the house again.) Valentine's response to the influx was also droll. She wrote to a friend:

> Sylvia says that my solicitude for my visitors, care for them and sympathy with them is so obvious that it evokes panic in their private breasts. Visitors, I reply, should not have breasts and when they have that sort of visitor never keeps them private. But the last thing I want to do is cause panic.[61]

In 1945 the interminable-seeming war in Europe ended. Valentine wrote in her diary on May Day: 'I was sure we would all collapse, perhaps die of joy – Instead, it feels as if we had all died of fatigue and impacted rage before the joy came'.[62] These feelings were shared by many, for differing reasons. Nothing would ever be the same; there could be no return to the England which had existed before the war. And yet, paradoxically, there was not *enough* change as a result of this titanic upheaval. The revolutionary moment had passed, the class structure and gender inequality that had existed before the war were to be firmly reinstated (despite the landslide election of a Labour government). Communism was being eradicated by the Allies in Europe, even where Communists had formed the backbone of resistance to the Nazis. American influence in Britain was already ushering in the Cold War world view. As if this wasn't enough, the full horror of the Nazi regime and the scale of the Holocaust was becoming known.

> I hear them coming again. If I tell you to listen
> I shall have to wake you and you, in sleep outpoured
> Beside me, will wake and dismiss me to perdition
> With a brief pat, a kiss, a comforting word.
>
> I hear them returning, I tell you, whether in dream or waking
> It's too late to know.[63]

On a personal level, the discomforts and privations of everyday life showed no signs of improvement yet; it would be a long time before the yearned-for trip abroad, or regular expeditions to London, would be possible. Then there were disasters which, though minor in the context of the devastation of Europe, were still part of it. All the family furniture from The Hill House, put into storage by the Army, had been destroyed. Powdered milk had been stored above it so that when the roof leaked everything was covered with a cheese-like substance, and rotted. The house, too, was damaged beyond repair:

They had destroyed the grape-vines, the lovely lilac-grove by the small pond; they had gutted the bluebell wood and made their latrines in the Aldborough Garden where the daffodil and narcissus bulbs were, and the Star of Bethlehem flowers. They had gutted the house too, and smashed as much of the glass as they could, and broken down the little foolish parapets and defaced the walls and torn up the wood of the stairs and the drawing-room floor. Like any other victim under the rule of the Military State, the house was blinded, deafened, witless and starved. And so it died finally.[64]

Although nothing could replace Winterton in her personal iconography, Valentine was now able to secure Frome Vauchurch as their permanent home. She and Sylvia were alarmed when the owner of the house gave them notice. After their long tenancy, they were appalled at the thought of leaving their beloved river and the house built out over the water. Following much negotiation, they eventually acquired the freehold (in Valentine's name, with Ruth's money). Later, they also bought the field next door, Cornum, which protected them from building encroachment there (though not across the river, where the bungalows later appeared). They hadn't felt insecure in their previous tenancy, but it was a relief that the house was now permanently theirs.

When she was forty, in 1946, Valentine was able to interpret her life in two completely opposing ways. On the positive side, she lived with an exceptional woman in a beautiful place where she could write poetry; they were safe, they had survived. She wrote in her diary: 'I don't believe that anyone who has ever lived has known greater happiness from sight and sound and sensation than I have known.'[65] Much about her situation was idyllic, and life would become easier as day-to-day wartime restrictions were gradually lifted. Valentine was once again able – in her best frame of mind – to think of herself as a poet, among a community of poets. On the other hand, she was disappointed in the public aspect of her career; although she regularly saw her work published in magazines, there was no likelihood of a book at this time of paper shortages and wartime publishing schedules.

Her novel, *A Start in Life,* which Valentine called her 'Norfolk story' and tinkered over for years, was shaping itself into a project that would never be finished. It's a curious work, written from the heart, that suffers from an impossibly episodic plot which references early picaresque novels but doesn't develop them. Johnny, the alter ego hero, is a youth whose 'innocent' but homoerotic relationship with an older man has led to a chain of events in which he murders his father. Sent to reform school, Johnny runs away and becomes the lover (and unofficial husband) of a beautiful fairground girl, Tansy. Accepted by the gypsy gang, Johnny is initiated into their way of life as they tour Norfolk, encountering various adventures along the way, always on the run from the police. Valentine clearly identified with the honourable father-killer who is exiled from mainstream society but adopted by an alternative culture to live differently, dedicated to freedom and love. The work offers interesting insights into her imaginative world and her nostalgia for a lost pastoral England.

Also weighing on the negative side was the aftermath of severe mental anguish, and poor physical health for her age. The war had taken its toll, as had the hard living of Valentine's youth; now the damp situation of the house made her arthritis increasingly troublesome. She was still drinking heavily – though with DD intervals – and both she and Sylvia smoked incessantly. Sylvia admitted that Valentine looked 'lifeless and almost plain'.[66] Her family was extremely trying, which Sylvia believed had a bad effect on Valentine's health. Joan was still Joan. Ruth took up an enormous amount of time and energy, which Valentine gave gladly; but Ruth, infuriatingly, barely noticed her efforts. Sylvia described a visit, complete with verbatim conversation and eventual loss of temper:

> Valentine's mother has been staying with us, with the usual devastating effect on Valentine's health. She *always* comes in May – for Valentine's birthday, with the result that it is only by the skin of our teeth that Valentine survives to be a year older. I think the word 'trite' must have been invented for her. This is the kind of conversation we have.
> R: And who do you say she is?
> V: She is Mary Tompkins. She lives with her brother John on the Dorchester Road.
> R: Oh. She lives on the Dorchester Road?

V: Yes.

R: With her brother John?

V   Yes.

R: And he's her brother?

V: Yes, he's her brother. She's his sister. They live together on
      the Dorchester Road.

R: On the *Dorchester* Road?

V: Yes. The Dorchester Road.

R: And she's his sister.

V: ......

R: How delightful!

Really it's like this. Only worse. Much worse.[67]

Sylvia herself was, at fifty-two, fitter than Valentine. She was still working on *The Corner That Held Them,* eagerly awaited by her publisher, and also had a commission for a guide book about Somerset. In the spring they went there on the first holiday they'd taken since the start of the war, using carefully-hoarded petrol to drive about with unaccustomed freedom, revelling in exploration. Sylvia's regular short story contributions were not bringing in as much money as they once had (and certainly not the large sums they would later) but her editors were still keen. The greatest concern for her was Nora, prickly as ever; Sylvia was concerned that her mental health was declining.

Everyone's psychological insecurities had been exacerbated by America's use of the atomic bomb, among its many and unknown effects. Valentine wrote a poem, 'August 6th', memorialising Hiroshima, which effectively evokes the surreal evil and madness of the event:

When out of the clear sky, the bright
Sky over Japan, they tumbled the death of light,
For a moment, it's said, there was brilliance sword-sharp,
A dazzle of white, and then dark.

Into that cavernous blackness, as home to hell,
Agonies crowded; and high above in the swell
Of the gentle tide of the sky, lucid and fair,
Men floated serenely as angels disporting there.[68]

Chapter Eight:
Lazarus Risen

Valentine's main preoccupation, apart from her work, was now the state of her soul. Spiritual matters had always been important to her, but she believed that at forty the soul should begin to take precedence over the body. This long-held idea was the result of her meditations on death and her reading of philosophy and religious books (not only Christian or Western). She thought the soul might be immortal only if it was strong enough to survive without the body, and that it could be strengthened in readiness for this separation by spiritual exercise. The quest for enlightenment led Valentine to write some of her most impressive poems about journeying through her inner landscape: 'Journey from Winter', 'Being Alive', 'Whether the lost thing found'.

It also led to an interior debate, a struggle for supremacy between soul and body. Valentine's maniacally religious upbringing and brief but intense foray into Catholicism had presented this duality as oppositional, always. Now Valentine felt the conflicting demands of these two sides of her self, and explored the dichotomy in a series of poems which cast 'Lord Body' as the poor Ape with its brutish desires, the soul as the 'Dearest Child' exiled from heaven or the 'lost lady [who] lies asleep.'[1] The poet could simultaneously express fellow-feeling for the primitive, instinctive body and intellectual sympathy with the exiled, imprisoned soul. (This also connects with Valentine's personification of her heart – the organ of love – as 'Master' or 'Lord' of the body: 'from where in the tossing ship my heart had slept, / At your call roused up the sleeping Lord.')[2] From now on, domination of the Ape would be fought for between the heart and the soul.

Although Valentine found her meditations in some ways painful, the consolations of philosophy were very real to her. This beautiful contemplative poem epitomises the profound comfort she discovered:

Whether the lost thing found, the exile reaching coast
Late and at last, a wide ocean crossed
And foothold on soil once more:

Which, soul does not know for sure, but feels
Sometimes this, and sometimes as if she were still
Alien, a stateless creature, one without knowledge of home;
Until on an evening, perhaps, when the west wind steals
Like the ghost of summers past over the greying hill,
Suddenly soul awakes, and knows she has come
To the place that's her own.

And now in welcome the sky
Lights star after star on high, and the world sails on,
Stately, a ship into darkness going, tall on the seas
Of calm and eternal night;
And all on board her are safe and bound for home.[3]

~

At the end of 1946, Valentine took a new full-time job as secretary-dispenser to Dr Basil Gaster in Evershot, the next village. This was an eminently practical move to relieve financial anxieties using the marketable skill provided by her wartime enforced employment with Dr Lander, but it did not improve her self-image as poet. She noted sadly:

> When one is not working at trades union rates, nor even receiving a regular wage, but merely going on from day to day laboriously laying up treasure in heaven, it is natural enough to exaggerate a little here and there in one's private account of hours worked and output achieved.[4]

Her humour, however, remained intact. A marginal scribble in one of her poetry notebooks reads: 'Female handkerchiefs – male noses bigger? more blown? Or males grander – more powerful? Soc. for Prov. lgr. Hank for Women? Soc. for Enc. Women's Larger Noses.'[5] Less intentional but equally typical is the shopping list (which summarises an entire biography's-worth of character drawing):

> *coffee tip parking shrimps bullets petrol.*[6]

Throughout 1947 Valentine continued her slow exploration of religious matters, though not in any conventional sense. She veered between being 'Devoid of Drink' or (to judge from her handwriting) thoroughly drunk. During the summer she kept her demons at bay, but in the autumn she and Sylvia went on holiday to Dublin where the easy availability of alcohol, as well as butter and eggs, contributed to her relapse. On their return Valentine was drinking heavily again. Then she had a life-changing experience. There was nothing outwardly dramatic about this; it was, typically, an entirely private happening.

On 7 October, Valentine went to bed as near drunk as she ever was, and experienced a terrifying sensation, 'as if Eternity were opening all around me; and it was black as Hell.' She cried out in panic 'Is God there?' but received no sense of an answering presence, nothing except 'emptiness and the rushing, swirling dark'.[7] In despair, she made an oath that she would not drink again, swearing it by the nothingness she had addressed as God. This was a Faustian act of drunken bravado, a gesture of nihilism she was never able to explain afterwards. Her words were not even received by the total silence; she knew 'there was nothing to receive anything.'[8]

Valentine fell into bed, slept, woke with the inevitable hangover. She felt unwell all day, but by evening she noticed a change in herself. Inexplicably, she was freed from the shackles of her addiction, not only in the physical sense that she no longer craved alcohol, but also in the emotional sense that the need for it had vanished. She was healed, psychologically, and – as she put it – 'walking in tranquillity and perfect confidence'.[9] This sudden transformation was permanent and complete; for many years she drank no alcohol at all. She did not use the experience as proof for the existence of God, she didn't even tell Sylvia about it at the time, but she derived from it a spiritual confidence which enabled her to write poems of calm joy.

Sylvia steadfastly refused to notice any difference in Valentine 'beyond a corking or uncorking of bottles'.[10] She herself continued to drink enthusiastically and unapologetically; she enjoyed wine with her meals, gin before and brandy after, she drank whisky if she felt cold and champagne when celebrating. The difference between them was, no doubt, Sylvia's uncomplicated attitude to pleasure, her lack of guilt and less obsessive personality. However much she enjoyed, or needed, a glass of wine, she never developed a problematic relationship with it.

But Valentine's complete refusal of all alcohol – though necessary to her – meant that there was one more pleasure they could no longer share.

Very soon after, in December 1947, Sylvia faced a crisis. She was summoned to stay with her mother after Nora had fallen downstairs and it was suspected that she'd suffered a stroke. To her daughter, senility seemed more of a problem, but Sylvia managed to cope with Nora's repetitive dottiness fairly well, until it changed suddenly and alarmingly into a more aggressive form of dementia. Valentine abandoned the cats to a neighbour and drove to Devon, to find Sylvia alone with a frighteningly mad mother. Sylvia had promised that Nora would never have to leave Little Zeal (the house built by her second husband for her first), but this situation was unforeseen.

Valentine persuaded Sylvia that in these circumstances they must take Nora to a place of safety. This was the outside voice of reason which Sylvia needed to condone her action. On Christmas Eve, she moved Nora to the Windermere Nursing Home in Paignton. (Sylvia remarked of its Torquay Baronial interior decor: 'Even after a fortnight of the vagaries of a disordered mind ... this made an impression on me.')[11] It was an unhappy Christmas, inevitably, but Valentine's stalwart advice prevented Sylvia from sacrificing her own independent life by staying with Nora – as was generally expected – when it would do no good. Privately, Sylvia admitted some pangs of conscience, but she was determined that 'go down quick into the pit I will not.'[12]

~

In early 1948, Valentine experienced a sense of rejuvenation which she celebrated in 'The New Spring': 'What is this season which cannot be spring? / ... only winter's cold should be my weather. And yet ...'[13] This feeling of rebirth was an emergence from the depression which had dogged her, an almost-forgotten sense of possibility. Unfortunately it only increased her internal conflict. Even as ideas about the immortality of the spirit were absorbing Valentine, she was experiencing physical desires unusually sharply. Her diary is full of philosophical and religious speculations, prayers and meditations on the nature of God. Much of this all too clearly relates to the guilt-inducing self-examinations of her childhood religious indoctrination by Ruth. She considered that 'in matters large or small refusing to admit a desire or preference' was laudable, and aimed to 'resist the dissipation of time and having stupid desires.'[14] These renunciations were required over small temptations; she felt more confident over resisting 'the desire for having an MG car or a holiday or a lover'.[15] This confidence was entirely misplaced.

Less than a month later Valentine recorded sending a telegram inviting Nancy Cunard to visit for two nights while Sylvia was away 'and only', she added candidly, 'because I want to go to bed with her.' Valentine questioned her own needs and whether she should give in to her desires, and concluded:

> I want bed. I want skill and sophistication and pleasure. I want to experience that peculiar and especial fusing with another living person. I want to please and be pleased ... for love of life, love of delight, delight in lust and for the sense of renewal and of success that comes from being in bed with someone experienced and equally glad to be there.[16]

(Sylvia apparently did not spring to mind as a possible candidate, even when she was at home.) This ruthless yet self-indulgent examination prompted her to admit: 'the intensity of what I have felt today scares me about seeing Elizabeth.'[17] For the end of the war meant the possibility of transatlantic travel again.

Even in this 'trance of desire'[18] Valentine asserted that she was still on her quest for God: 'I remember that I have experienced awe, exaltation and apprehension of the spirit – of immortality – of God – directly from delight in bed'. She concluded cheerfully 'any rising of the sap, any spring season in the heart or body, makes me directly alive to God'.[19] This somewhat unorthodox view was not one Valentine could always maintain in her poetry, which explored the divergence between the physical and spiritual, rather than their convergence. In 'Lord Body' she laments having to dethrone the body 'Because the rightful Heir, the prince of the blood, has come; / Even so, because I have been proud to own you, / I weep as the time draws near to turn you from your home.'[20] In the original draft she asks 'Forgive me' and in the margin is scrawled the word 'ingratitude'.[21] This suggests that her farewell to the supremacy of the body is ambivalent, and reluctant.

In a series of poems about the resurrection of Lazarus, Valentine continued to explore these preoccupations:

> Roll the stone back and enter in:
> When I unwrap the winding-sheet
> Where shall I start?
> Somewhere the coil ended and can begin –
> At head, or feet,
> Or over the heart?[22]

And Valentine questioned, of the two women present at the awakening, 'On whom did his eyes first dwell / When the cloth was wound from his head?'[23] She saw herself as the reborn Lazarus-figure returned from the dead, but to Sylvia the unwelcome revenant was Elizabeth.

Valentine was simultaneously writing poems which asserted the supremacy of the spirit, beautiful meditations on time and eternity. Yet even here, her conclusion about the importance of the moment – now – could be read as an argument for immediate action:

> To Now, which is all we have, eternities deliver
> Each one of us this present from the anonymous giver.[24]

Sylvia had, in Valentine's eyes, such a pure character that she had no need to worry about the state of her soul; it was perfectly robust. She was sometimes interested in Valentine's current reading, but always from the human angle, the art inspired or the ritual practised. Her distance from this hugely important aspect of Valentine's life perhaps contributed to the estrangement Valentine was feeling when she wrote: 'This I have longed for beyond all count of cost / And yet know nothing of, know only what I have lost / In turning from you, my dearest love of old, / Love more beloved than any, love more true.'[25]

On her birthday in 1948 Valentine wrote a poem to Sylvia, as she always did, 'I wait through the year's long days for a sign of your favour', which, as this first line indicates, suggests a growing intellectual distance between them, finally overcome by great love in the triumphant ending: 'I stood so, at the year's end, to-day, and suddenly saw you, / Crossing the time-emptied square to bring me your favour.'[26]

For their nineteenth anniversary on 12 January 1949, Valentine's poem to Sylvia was again double-edged, describing various 'ones' who had been loved, apart from the 'one alone' who 'stayed in all weather / Stayed through the long years, stays forever.' (A compliment of a kind.)

16. 'One love stays forever' – Sylvia as she was in Chaldon in the 1930s.

The most significant of these others was 'Treasured in case, one day or another' she might 'return, and a song flow from her.'[27] In her poetry, Valentine was warning Sylvia that Elizabeth was occupying her mind, and might re-enter their life. To 'Living near the Asylum' she added a note of the distance to New York, 3040 miles, emphasising the last line 'The old grief back again.'[28] Sylvia recognised the recurrent sickness, but she may not have realised its imminence.

In February, they went on holiday to Italy, where Sylvia was very happy 'hand-in-hand with Valentine'. She noted prophetically: 'If ever I should write to you to complain of my lot, remind me that in the February of 1949 I went with Valentine to Italy.'[29]

But Elizabeth was coming to England, as she had been planning since at least 1942, sometimes imagining a poignant last encounter to say farewell, sometimes a final settling of unfinished business with Evelyn as witness. Now she wrote to Valentine demanding a meeting. In their correspondence, Valentine had told her repeatedly that it would be better not to see each other again: 'we well might feel the old violence of passion and desire but ... It would be wrong, I think, to allow it. You have hated and abused me; I have hated and abused you ... it would not be seemly to make love when we cannot be in love together.' Elizabeth's idea of bringing Evelyn as a kind of second in their duel because, she said, 'I have developed a sort of animal instinct of self-preservation by now', Valentine described as 'grotesque'. She told Elizabeth 'you have this crazy situation in mind – a kind of Browning Last Ride Together'.[30] And yet, now that Elizabeth was actually coming to England, Valentine was tempted to see her again – all the more so because she knew the probable consequences. Elizabeth was absolutely determined, she insisted that the meeting must happen, and Valentine could not refuse.

Not long before, Valentine had written in her diary: 'I had a clear understanding just now of the ruinous waste I have made in my life – in my life and so many other people's too'. She listed the names of all these lovers she had damaged, adding (as in the Catholic confession's admission of sins) 'and many more I have forgotten.' From them, Valentine acknowledged, 'I had so much love and grace. And I laid it all in ruins.'[31] Yet she was apparently powerless to stop herself doing it all over again.

In April Elizabeth came to Dorset and stayed in Evershot, close to the surgery where Valentine worked. They met in Yeovil, for a somewhat constrained formal tea together; afterwards Valentine drove Elizabeth back to her hotel. Alone in her room, Elizabeth gave Valentine a ring, they kissed, 'at once the old love flowed back.'[32] The resumption of the situation they'd been in ten years before was instant and absolute. When Elizabeth said 'I do not believe we could ever live together'[33] Valentine only replied, with apparent regret, that she did not know. Elizabeth departed, in accordance with her busy visitor's schedule, leaving Valentine and Sylvia in an altered world.

Valentine described her love as 'a violent desire to possess' with a 'profound obligation' to love; she added that Elizabeth could bore and irritate her, and that she could 'obviously' have killed her. And yet 'at a touch all that is blown away.'[34] Even under the spell of erotic obsession, Valentine knew that Sylvia was her real love. She compared the two women and concluded:

> I never feel E. is my *equal*, although I know she excels me in learning, shrewdness, courage of some kinds and uprightness, but I always feel that S. and I are peers – are the same degree of person, in spite of all the obvious superiority she has over me, and most other people in achievement and scholarship ...[35]

But Valentine was currently interested in the physical, in which Elizabeth's superiority to everyone else was an indefinable quality, evident only to Valentine. Sylvia knew there was no arguing with lust.

In another Lazarus poem, Valentine abandoned her meditations on the body/soul divide, and refigured death as life without sex. Here, the soul's dismay at being reincarnated in the earthly body is swiftly overcome by physical ecstasy; 'resurrection' is a resumption of sexuality. 'Did Lazarus weep, my Love, as I have wept, / ... Because he had forgotten while he slept / The ecstasy of touch and sound and sight, / ... As I in my death-sleep forgot the light / Until I resurrected to your eyes?'[36] Valentine also translated a series of Meleager's erotic 'Heliodora' poems, addressed to Elizabeth, which reveal her state very clearly: 'Memory returns, / Lame from the last fray, scarred still from his burns: / But Heliodora smiles, walks to the door, and turns ...'[37]

Sylvia, despite Valentine's hints, had not seen the resumption of the affair as a foregone conclusion. Possibly she'd considered Elizabeth safely paired-off with Evelyn, and thought that Valentine's continuing preoccupation with her was merely habitual self-dramatising. But now her attention was certainly riveted to Valentine, as of old. Later, Valentine mentioned this pleasing result of her infidelity: 'just after the war', she wrote:

> I drowned in this loneliness. [Sylvia] turned into a shadow, she went from me and I drowned. I came agonisingly to life ... because

of Elizabeth and Sylvia's (to me sudden) return to love of me ... or, more justly, to awareness of me as still being there; for I do not think she ever ceased from loving me.[38]

Sylvia might have been gratified to know that she was, in one sense, the person whose notice Valentine was trying to attract.

Sylvia recorded in righteous anger that Elizabeth's visit had never been – as she'd imagined – intended as an 'epilogue, but was deliberately the search for a second act.'[39] Elizabeth denied that she'd had any such intention; she told Valentine that it would never work for them to live together because of the 'vast differences' and 'dangerous likenesses' in their temperaments. She did, however, claim to have a 'purely romantic and quite irresponsible knowledge that you were my own person, my beloved and destined love forever.' Although it was 'very wrong', Elizabeth decided 'I must, whatever the cost, come and find you and look at you and touch your hand and hear your voice once more in my life.' Though rather more than hand-touching took place, Elizabeth insisted that the most she'd expected was 'to meet in love and remembrance and depart in peace.'[40] Despite her fondness for quasi-biblical language (which Valentine could also use in moments of emotional fervour), Elizabeth was impressive when she spoke of the power of her love. Even Sylvia did not deny that Elizabeth really did love Valentine.

Elizabeth explained her distressingly prompt transfer of affections to Evelyn in a way which soothed Valentine's wounded pride: she had perceived Evelyn as a 'link' provided by Valentine, through whom they maintained contact. Thus the rival became instead a viceroy, and betrayal was transformed into being faithful in a fashion. Valentine now saw Elizabeth as a new lover, not the same person who had quarrelled with her so bitterly before, not 'the one who had been spoiled' but a 'redeemed, transfigured love'.[41] And so the outstanding problems between them were resolved, Sylvia and Evelyn relegated to the background, Elizabeth in the ascendant again. She arranged to come back on 10 May, and stay at the King's Arms in Dorchester. After that, she was due to return to America, where her mother was seriously ill.

Valentine duly met Elizabeth in Dorchester for lunch, but then stayed with her there for three days while Sylvia waited alone at Frome Vauchurch with no word. According to Valentine's somewhat incoherent diary:

> On the first night everything happened; we were completely and irrevocably restored to each other ... Everything happened – I do not know how anyone can believe man to be mortal, who has experienced how instantly, in joy, he becomes a god![42]

Valentine was carried away by the force of her exaltation, and made promises to Elizabeth – that they would live together always, that Elizabeth would be her wife rather than her mistress, and so on – which she was not in a position to keep easily, having already made them to Sylvia.

On her return home Valentine, 'melancholy and remote',[43] formally told Sylvia that she was in love with Elizabeth, and intended to live with her. In her shock and misery, Sylvia did not immediately grasp that Valentine expected her to live with them *à trois*, in a retired wife position. When she understood, Sylvia vehemently refused such 'falsehood and degradation'.[44] She determined to leave Valentine, if Elizabeth did indeed come back to take her place.

Without Elizabeth, Valentine pined, didn't eat, talked in her sleep. Sylvia was desperate with unhappiness, but Valentine appeared not to notice; her mind was elsewhere, convinced that God approved of her new love and the omens were good. But letters from Elizabeth did not augur so well. Claiming that her relationship with Evelyn was close to 'disintegration', she was pressuring Valentine to 'implement my promise of taking her to live with me; and I both long to, for I love her and am in love with her, and yet I feel I cannot conceive of life without always being in close, household companionship with Sylvia.'[45] Valentine's wishes, as well as her obligations, were impossible to reconcile.

One (rather drastic) solution presented itself when Valentine's doctor referred her to a cancer specialist for an opinion on her breast pain. Valentine told Elizabeth immediately 'because somehow she *must* be prevented from cutting adrift from her home.'[46] It was to be kept secret from Sylvia, but Elizabeth promptly told Evelyn, although Valentine had specifically asked her not to. (Her discovery of this would cause Valentine painful disillusionment later.) Sylvia accompanied her to Sherborne for the consultation, unaware of the doctor's suspicions – though she noticed how much thinner Valentine was looking and exclaimed 'My serpent, you have cast your skin.'[47] It was the kind of remark to delight Valentine. (She adored snakes, handled them fearlessly, and felt akin to them; her phobia was for moths, which always horrified her.)

The weight-loss was caused by love, not cancer; the diagnosis was mastitis, for which testosterone was prescribed (perhaps superfluously). Valentine emerged 'pale and swaying', saying 'I'm feeling such thankfulness.' Sylvia considered her 'heroic'[48] to have kept the secret – and perhaps it would have been superhuman to continue keeping it altogether. Privately, Valentine admitted some remorse at her own joy, when she knew that

> Sylvia most of all, and Elizabeth in her peculiar trouble and distance from me, are both suffering sharply from the present dreadful situation in our lives – and poor Evelyn too, the greatest loser of all, or at least the poorest and most desolate.[49]

Since death was not to rescue Valentine, she had to tell Elizabeth that she couldn't live without Sylvia, although she wanted Elizabeth too. The working out of any arrangement was postponed, because Elizabeth's mother was dying and she could not, in any case, leave her. During this strange respite, Sylvia experienced her anguish in an apparently uninterrupted life, a beautiful summer. It was a time of conflicted emotions for Valentine:

> The June rain falls tonight, gentle as moths against the pane,
> Sorrow within the room burns a beseeching flame;
> The night's tears long to come in, they return again and again,
> Wooing with soft anonymous pity a grief that has no name.[50]

Valentine's spiritual conflict had resolved itself, temporarily, into a convenient belief that body and soul are equal before God. In 'A solitary thought' she stresses the illogicality of denial: 'They give me permission to fodder the brute and water him at need, / But please him, never, nor free, to feed on happiness.'[51]

On 4 July, Valentine received a cable with news of Mrs White's death. Planning for the future began more urgently, with letters making conditions and suggesting terms which made Sylvia compare Elizabeth to a debt-collector. Now Valentine was appalled at the prospect before her. She wrote:

> Sylvia is so deeply dear to me, so completely integrated, that we are practically incapable of sense or sense of life when we are apart ... we are 'oned' and the thought of being about to live a day-to-day life away from her is completely staggering; it makes me dizzy – I cannot comprehend it.

Apart from terror for herself, Valentine was now aware of Sylvia's suffering: 'the sight, and knowledge in my heart and mind and *bones* of her desolation and woe and shock appals me so that I am really stricken in my heart and cannot endure it'.[52]

(Sylvia had resolved that she was not going to pretend any more. Elizabeth wrote *her* a letter with

> a sprig of rosemary in it, to match an embellished sentence about friendship ... I carried this out onto the deck ... and dropped it in the river. I discarded, with that rosemary sprig, any further attempt to 'keep in' with Elizabeth, to remain on respectable terms with her, to perpetuate whitewash ... I threw away caution, priggishness and hypocrisy ... I had ... sided with myself.)[53]

But an overriding sense of urgency enabled Valentine to carry on, despite the pain she was inflicting and sharing. 'Sometimes' she wrote miserably,

> I feel *almost* sure I have gone fatally wrong ... but *is* it evil and destroying, to find again the youth and pleasure, the bright shining pleasure of being beloved, of giving and taking that happiness, of being resurrected to that life again, once more, before it is too late?[54]

On the last day of June they went to Chaldon, to inspect the bombed ruins of Miss Green for the first time, and mourn 'that lost roof-tree'.[55] Their destroyed first home was a painfully obvious parallel to the ruined landscape of their love. Valentine climbed about the wild garden, while Sylvia stood in what had been the living-room, looking down at the broken hearth. When Sylvia wept at the sight of their thorn-tree, Valentine felt heartbroken, but she insisted their faith was inviolate:

> it is much more than anything done or left undone, made or broken by *me*. What I thought and felt and resolved, listening to the inn sign creaking that October night, was thought and felt and vowed once and for all. It is eternal, as the thorn tree is – as we are.[56]

Sylvia reached the same conclusion, and she wrote Valentine an extraordinary letter, the antithesis of Elizabeth's conditional bargaining. Sylvia repudiated all that she'd previously done to assist Valentine in her affair with Elizabeth; although intended to please, it had made her guilty of dishonouring their love. While accepting that Valentine did love Elizabeth, and that their physical relationship had rejuvenated Valentine, she proudly claimed the unique status of her own love:

> When you were walking about the garden of Miss Green I stood looking at the remains of the hearth, asking myself what it was that you lit with the first fire. Not only our perfection of bodily love, not only our intensity of joy in each other, not only our innocence, our paradisal innocence; ... something rarer, and yet more durable, some especial virtue, some blessing that had been given. And then I knew. The word, I suppose, is trust. From the moment you spoke from the other side of the wall and I came in to you, we have been sure of each other, as sure as fish are of water, as birds are of air. We are each other's element.
>
> That is why we make each other's heaven in hell's despite. And that is why, when I saw the blackthorn, I burst into tears. It was not grief, or regret, or comparison of then or now. I wept from illumination, I wept with acceptance. I accept. I take you back again in my heart, you are as much mine as I am yours. Not only can I have no doubt of your love for me, I have no doubt of my love for you, no doubt that it is right, no doubt that you demand it and require it. We are each other's element, we are what we live by, and such a love is beyond every other consideration. Yes, I will go to Pen Mill if you ask me. Yes, I will come back. Yes, if you ask

me I will go away again, and I will come back when you ask me. But going, and returning, and whatever I do and wherever I go, I will unwaveringly and sternly and completely hold you in my love, and hold your love for me, and follow no other intention but that we may completely live and love together again. Any other way, I wrong you.[57]

Valentine wrote in answer:

Everything you say to me is true ... I am thankful you could write it, thankful we went to Miss Green and she replaced us in the positions she first devised for us ... I understand, accept, agree...[58]

But nothing apparently changed, yet. Pen Mill, in Sylvia's letter, was the hotel in Yeovil where she intended to stay during Elizabeth's visit to England – for now her residence had shrunk to a visit, a trial run. Obviously beset with doubts, Elizabeth was writing Valentine 'dreadful'[59] letters of reproach, talking of the prior claims of her bereaved father and Evelyn but suggesting that their relationship might continue on an occasional basis – which Valentine condemned as 'half-heartedness in the face of a decision'.[60] When she accused Valentine, via Evelyn, of neurotic fits of cruelty, Valentine replied with denial, and the sad admission: 'in the unexpected ecstasy of a returning spring, I believed everything ... it was silly.'[61]

Although Sylvia had tried to ensure that Valentine didn't misinterpret her 'mannerly love' as 'autumnal complaisance',[62] she was still Valentine's confidante. When Valentine told her that Evelyn was drinking too much and threatening suicide, Sylvia immediately asked 'If Evelyn kills herself for love of Eliz: will Eliz: feel that this gives her an everlasting claim on Valentine?' Valentine replied 'Quite certainly.'[63]

Sylvia accepted the arrangement which was eventually negotiated – that Elizabeth would stay with Valentine at Frome Vauchurch for the month of September – indeed, she encouraged Valentine to accept it, on the understanding that Sylvia would quit the house. Perhaps she did not believe that Valentine would actually consent to Elizabeth sleeping in their bed, using their house and garden and – for Sylvia – defiling everything they shared. (Sylvia imagined her sound and smell filling the house, her gaze touching their possessions.) Perhaps she hoped that by externalising what Valentine was doing, once the situation was made visible Valentine would understand and repudiate it. But Valentine was beyond sense; she could not bring herself to stop Elizabeth, there seemed no choice.

Valentine and Sylvia tidied the house and put away treasured possessions as though they were expecting tenants. It gave Sylvia little pleasure to know that Valentine was dreading September; as they made the preparations Sylvia feared for her own sanity. She dreamed of 'this baleful Elizabeth' with loathing and terror, as 'a frightful never-quite-forgotten sore re-opening in my flesh'.[64] (The once-loved protégée had shape-shifted into a hideous self-inflicted plague.) Sylvia had trusted in Valentine's return to her in mid-Atlantic; to doubt it now brought even this fearless woman close to destruction. Yet, with an instinct for eventually recovering Valentine, she refused to accept mitigation and also – most crucially – refused to stop loving Valentine, or allow her love to be denied.

On the last day of August she 'made the adulterous bed',[65] said farewell to her cats and her garden, and Valentine drove her to the hotel in Yeovil. It was a plain, decent place, serving the generous inept English food Sylvia abhorred. Valentine begged Sylvia to rescue her from Elizabeth if she seemed in danger of being taken away. They were brave until 'the horrified, incredulous embrace of parting'.[66] Sylvia had a list in her diary headed PRACTICAL CONSIDERATIONS, such as 'Do GH [*Good Housekeeping*] article without fail',[67] and she set to work.

Valentine already knew that her love-affair was foundering. She had written to Elizabeth: 'I was wrong in thinking that our situation could keep its quality of "panache" unblemished, *unreduced* … I have proved myself wrong, and that must be admitted.'[68] Now, she found the reality of separation from Sylvia unbearable (as Sylvia no doubt intended). Valentine had hoped to soothe Sylvia's anguish with attentions: letters written and services rendered, flowers and presents bestowed. The reality was that Sylvia supported *her*, writing daily letters of comfort and reassurance to her 'perplexed love' – but lamenting in her diary 'She lives and loves innocently with Eliz: because I am shaken with fears and doubts, ravished with physical and mental jealousy, and steadily murder myself in concealing it.'[69]

(So, even after her decision to side with herself, Sylvia was still in a way enabling the affair by hiding her devastation from Valentine.)

Valentine complained to Sylvia, perhaps genuinely, that time passed very slowly and tediously away from her. Scrupulously avoiding the vulgarity of outright criticism, Valentine intimated when Elizabeth was quiet, reasonable, and even helped in the house, or when she was angry, demanding to know where she stood, insisting Valentine must apply for a US visa. Sylvia once remarked that it was bizarre to be Valentine's Chief of Staff in this campaign, but Valentine told Sylvia that it was *with the Sylvia in herself* that she loved Elizabeth.[70] (And perhaps Sylvia had loved Betty, before, with the Valentine in *her*self?)

Throughout September, Valentine visited Sylvia at Yeovil as though *they* were the ones having a clandestine affair. She snatched Sylvia for secret visits home when Elizabeth was out, and met her for assignations. It was the classic adulterer's split life for Valentine; although she was undoubtedly in pain about Sylvia, she wasn't too upset to enjoy Elizabeth's presence, and take full advantage of it. Writing to Elizabeth afterwards, she reminisced: 'We have been happy, we have been most happy. I look at myself and remember that you have loved to look at me; I look at you in my memory and know that I love you forever.'[71]

As the month progressed, Valentine confided to Sylvia her hope that Elizabeth would enjoy her time there, and depart without recriminations. But Elizabeth was upset by furious letters from Evelyn, who (according to Elizabeth) wanted to fight a duel with Valentine, or preferably just shoot her. She did not tell Valentine that – worse – Evelyn had actually criticised not only her 'selfish histrionics' but also the 'spectacle' of her masculinity: '… how grotesque it is for a woman to try to act like a man. All the wedding-ring, collar-and-tie, strutting and talking, business is pathetic and grotesque'[72] (although she'd fallen for it in her time). If, by calling her the Dorset Sappho and ridiculing her butchness, Evelyn intended to undermine Valentine's attraction for Elizabeth, she didn't succeed. All the same, her letters sent Elizabeth into black moods, which Valentine treated with generous doses of benzedrine.

Despite this, Elizabeth remained discontented. She talked of 'all I have sacrificed' and 'the least I might expect' in night-long monologues which she described (to Sylvia's amusement) as 'getting down to fundamentals'.[73] Valentine was utterly exhausted by all this, and told the ever-sympathetic Sylvia of 'that kind of monster that she [Elizabeth] carries in her'.[74] While Sylvia deplored the fact that Elizabeth expected Valentine 'to do the garden as well as cook, house-keep, sweep, dust, work every morning at Gaster's, take her for drives, make love all night and listen to her wasted life all day',[75] she must have rejoiced in their domestic discord. And Valentine had written nothing during this time, of course.

~

One of the distractions Valentine provided for Sylvia at Yeovil was a memoir: *For Sylvia: An Honest Account*. Valentine was an obsessive writer of autobiographies, and several versions exist of essentially the same book, as well as variant treatments in fragmentary states, and shorter pieces. Each has a different dominant motif: one long memoir takes Lob, the spirit of the English country, as its unifying theme. *For Sylvia* makes alcoholism – and guilt of all sorts – its subject. In the autobiographical writings with a different emphasis, though the plot is the same, the author's personality appears differently too. The book was posthumously published in 1985, and widely praised for its eloquence, emotional honesty, and muscular prose. (Sylvia described Valentine's autobiographical writing as 'almost insolently good'.)[76]

For Sylvia was written quickly, while Valentine was awaiting Elizabeth's arrival, and thought she might have cancer. Its strength, candour and dark humour are utterly characteristic – as is the guilt theme, for which alcoholism is cited as the reason. But her extremes of self-disgust must be read in the context of that time, for much of her other life-writing doesn't mention alcohol – or guilt – at all. It's as though she wanted to create a smokescreen for her unfaithfulness by revealing another kind of bad behaviour, hitherto secret. Since Sylvia can hardly have been unaware of Valentine's drinking (and was apparently unconcerned), in writing of her self-disgust about her alcohol addiction, was Valentine also obliquely referring to her other addictive habits, including her promiscuity? As Ruth's daughter, her sense of guilt and self-abasement was highly developed, but when she confessed, she relied on Sylvia's forgiveness and absolution for all her sins.

Sylvia was perturbed by the memoir, but she didn't waste time in assuring Valentine that she was exaggerating her drink problem (now resolved, anyway), or ascertaining exactly how much she *used* to drink. Instead, she deprecated Valentine's equally addictive habit of 'violent self-reproach', and questioned her entire reading of her life. 'If you could read your autobiography with the pure eyes of all-seeing Jove you would be thankful that you have been so good,' Sylvia reasoned, 'that you have kept such integrity and sensibility and been *Inébranlable* [the Ackland motto again] through such black gusts of tempest, and so quick to feel the sun and light and relish versing on the morrow of tempests.'[77] Thus Sylvia insisted that her Valentine was intrinsically good, while Elizabeth assured hers that she was not.

On 29 September, Valentine took Elizabeth to London, to say goodbye, and Sylvia went back home. When Valentine returned the following day, she looked so tired that Sylvia was alarmed. The reunion was hard, for Valentine seemed absent in spirit, unable to acknowledge Sylvia's presence. 'I think she is very ill – and that I have nothing to cure her with,'[78] Sylvia lamented. Valentine's sickness was, indeed, painful; she was insanely obsessed with Elizabeth, but made miserable by her. She knew the agony of grief she was causing Sylvia, but lacked the strength to stop it. They went on holiday to Norfolk in October (an unusual attempt to spare themselves) and stayed at an unfortunately-named Warren Farm.

Their misery was not private even there: they saw Joan, and Sylvia had 'never felt her more accursed'. She was disturbed when Valentine told her that the fear and pity always previously inspired by Joan – 'this creature who hated and tormented her' – had mysteriously vanished. Sylvia instantly knew the terrible reason why; Elizabeth was another Joan, and Valentine 'could not serve two such obligations'.[79] (And perhaps Valentine's desperate struggle to redeem Elizabeth's love, make it new and erase the disgrace of having 'hated and abused' each other, was in part connected with her perennial failure to make things right with Joan.)

Valentine began to write again; she continued the Norfolk story, which was always a refuge for her, and wrote a series of 'poems of loss'.

This one uses the character of the Norfolk coast to describe her state of mind:

> There is not very much to say: the sand says it
> night and day, night and day:
> blown against grasses, the skeleton of spray
> rattles and speaks; the dry sand says it.
>
> This thing that we strive to say, the timeless sand
> speaks to the grasses, to the grasses
> prattles its hopeless wisdom, 'Nothing passes –'
> Speechless, I hold your silence in my hand.[80]

After a fortnight, they returned unwillingly home. Valentine alternated between being politely stern and distant, and breaking down so completely that Sylvia feared for her. Elizabeth wrote to demand all or nothing, Valentine temporised, a year's trial co-habiting was suggested, then the offer withdrawn, counter-proposals made, repeated month-long visits considered and then rejected. 'We are in such a fix,' Sylvia said.[81]

Valentine had despaired of Elizabeth; she was unsurprised when Elizabeth told her that she'd immediately resumed her sexual relationship with Evelyn, although Evelyn had resisted this at first. (Sylvia, characteristically, was horrified on *Evelyn's* behalf, writing that Elizabeth was 'stealing from Evelyn Evelyn's poor desperate mongrel attempt to restore personal honour. Unfaithfulness too – but it is the rape of Evelyn that shocks me most.')[82] Valentine, by contrast, was so disillusioned that she answered Elizabeth's disclosures with world-weary indifference: 'If you can find comfort with Evelyn, obviously only the part of me which is most idealistic ... can possibly disapprove ... If your body consents, take comfort with another's body and thank God that you can.' In a reversal of their previous roles, Valentine made it clear that *she* was shut off from 'lesser joys'. 'I accept abstinence; I can never accept deprivation,' she wrote.[83] (Her abstinence did not remain complete, according to Sylvia, who noted in March the following year that they slept in the same bed, embraced, and 'once or twice I have been more than that to her ... or rather, she has needed more than that, and taken it.')[84]

By November, Valentine had to admit that things had gone badly wrong with the affair; she knew that Elizabeth was bitterly disappointed and considered it 'insufficient and incomplete'.[85] Sylvia had never seen Valentine in such anguish, now as bad as her own. Elizabeth was writing to Sylvia again, 'asserting over and over again a jointure in Valentine',[86] but to Valentine she wrote that she had 'risked everything and failed'.[87] Valentine wrote a poem to Sylvia, 'Weather Forecast', beginning 'Oh my darling, how the skies do rain down tears' which, after describing the inundation, concludes:

> I see the vast horizon of our grief,
> Burdened with rainclouds of our gathering years.[88]

Chapter Nine:
Lord Body

As the new decade began, in 1950, Valentine was still in wild mental confusion. Also physically unwell, she needed X-rays of her back, and further treatment for her breast problems. Sylvia thought this ill-health was due to stress about Elizabeth, who was threatening another trip to England. If she did come back, Sylvia was horrified to learn that Valentine was prepared to return to 'the slavery she repudiated'.[1] The same crisis could repeat itself indefinitely.

On 12 February, Sylvia heard from Nora's nursing home that her mother was ill. (Visiting recently, Sylvia had been heart-rent when Nora compared her own madness with Swift's.) Next day Valentine drove her to Torquay, but they arrived to find that Nora had died in her sleep. In this situation, Valentine managed to forget her own absorbing drama; she cherished Sylvia tenderly, made efficient arrangements, was tactful and understanding about Sylvia's grief, and relief. Sylvia's inheritance from Nora altered her position; with Little Zeal (and an income) her options – including the ability to leave – greatly increased.

Elizabeth arranged to meet Valentine for a few days in March. There was now no question of another stay at Frome Vauchurch. Sylvia begged Valentine not to 'tear everything open again before anything has settled to heal.'[2] At the last moment, she suggested that they should escape to Paris together instead. Valentine refused, even though she'd once asked Sylvia to rescue her if need be. (This refusal was one of Valentine's most disastrous choices.) She retreated into her delusion, assuring Sylvia she loved them both so much that all would be well. Sylvia determined that she herself would stop hoping, and accept a life-in-death without Valentine.

In London, Valentine had a happy reunion with Elizabeth; they went straight to their hotel and made love. But the following day Elizabeth was so sulky and reproachful that Valentine felt hated, not loved. Even though Valentine realised that their love was over, they 'lay together' again, in exactly the sex-without-love scenario she had once condemned. By trying to show Valentine how much she was suffering, Elizabeth revealed herself in a way which was incompatible with Valentine's ideal. This had already happened in those long letters, but not conclusively face to face. Valentine realised 'I loved, I still love, my fancy, nothing else. It is not love of her.'[3]

During the sleepless night, she told Elizabeth 'such a blight had come from our love-making ... it was proven to be wicked,' and that they could never be lovers again, 'renouncing desire'. It was a seminal decision, the dark opposite to the affirmation of love with Sylvia at Miss Green. 'She did not then mind very much,' Valentine recalled a few months later. 'And now she has completely "made over" the whole story, so that plainly I deserted her without any reason except that I was "unable to accept her complete sacrifice and self-abandonment." And so on.'[4]

When she regained the haven of Frome Vauchurch, Valentine greeted Sylvia with the words 'It is at an end.' Sylvia instantly believed this, though experience had taught her that they still had to undergo 'a bitter assorting of old circumstances to a new order'. She was moved when Valentine told her 'I took you with me ... You were a touchstone';[5] her love had proved steadfast and resilient under unspeakable stress.

In June 1950 Valentine wrote a 'Poem for Sylvia' celebrating 'this sudden restoration of ourselves to each other'.[6] It was a particularly beautiful summer; the landscape itself seemed to be reflecting their reprieve, the weather was like a benediction:

> ... Our years have marched like may,
> Like blossoming hedges of may that this spring has watched,
> Seeing their white processional over the hills.
> The festival ranks were ranged about us; the sun
> Trumpeted light and the circus of sky was filled
> With the flourish and show of the scent and the light and the
> bounty;
> By day and by moonlight the splendid rejoicing went on.[7]

Outside poetry, there were still difficulties. Elizabeth telephoned so often, threatening nervous breakdown or suicide, that Valentine took to making herself unavailable by leaving the phone off the hook. But Elizabeth had no intention of making a clean break or going quietly;

Sylvia wrote bitterly 'we shall never escape her, she will hang on like a corpse until we are rotten too.'[8] And Valentine told Sylvia: 'Sometimes I cannot understand why I have done it. I begin to rack my brains for a reason.'[9]

Thus began the long post-mortem which would continue, especially for Valentine, for many years. Sylvia summed up Valentine's gains: 'a repossession of me, of our love and life together, and a catharsis ... a sense of homecoming to her undivided self.'[10] Valentine did her utmost to show Sylvia that they were indeed 'one again – and ready to renew and flourish and love better than before.'[11] She devised outings, picnics to celebrate the first strawberries or drives to see bluebells; she brought Sylvia flowers, jewellery, poems; she made gifts of speech, saying how much happier she was. And she certainly needed to make up to Sylvia, for a great deal.

Although she was happier, Valentine had one area of anxiety. She wrote in her diary: 'I have had strange and singular experiences, practically nothing of which has been *used* yet – and I have only written a few, almost inarticulate poems in the first pure days'.[12] Valentine's feeling that her love for Elizabeth had been sterile and unhealthy was confirmed by the fact that this inundation of raw material had produced a poor creative harvest. (In her diary she exaggerated, as ever: she was writing poems, though not with the facility and productivity of earlier years.)

This worry about her work was exacerbated by a piece of tactlessness; what Valentine described as one of Sylvia's 'blind spots'. The American writer Marchette Chute came to visit; after much discussion of Sylvia's writing, she politely asked about Valentine's work too, and Sylvia replied that she worked for the local doctor. 'I felt bitterly belittled,' Valentine wrote. 'I do not *dare* to announce to myself that I am only a writer as earlier generations of women were tatters and cross-stitchers ... I cannot reconcile myself, yet, to accepting it as a hobby.'[13] This contrasted sharply with Elizabeth's exaggerated reverence for Valentine as a poet; 'I found that I treasured this most deeply,' Valentine reminisced, '– I *adored* to feel myself admired.'[14]

Valentine now tried to be as Sylvia wished her. When their much-beloved cat Thomas, last of the Frankfort kittens, had to be put down,

Valentine shot him herself, out of Sylvia's sight, and buried him by the river. The timing of his death was significant, as though he'd waited for Valentine's return, but it marked a distance from their youthful, unsullied love. They found a young Siamese kitten, Niou, born on the day of Tom's death, who would grow into a cat of great sensibility, important to them both.

But Valentine's family were still causing problems. Ruth had deeply wounded and antagonised Sylvia by her enthusiastic acceptance of Elizabeth and encouragement of Valentine in that direction. Elizabeth still wooed Ruth with expensive presents and expansive lunches, with the result that Valentine had a constant struggle to maintain her version of events. She patiently reiterated that Sylvia had *not* spoilt a happy romance, that she had *not* returned to Sylvia out of pity, and so on. Staying with Ruth at Winterton, Valentine 'felt a frightful, dismal conviction that she would drink again' because of 'old associations, fatigue, and Ruth's incessant offering of bottles.'[15]

In early September 1950, Valentine left her job with Dr Gaster, to make way for a radical change in their life. (She remained, however, an unofficial local medic; for years afterwards people would come to her for prescriptions, which Dorchester chemists willingly fulfilled. She also dispensed traditional remedies, it's said, combining therapies like a thoroughly modern wise-woman.) With Sylvia, she escaped on holiday to France, where Sylvia was delighted by the speed and brio of Valentine's driving, and intensely pleased by all they saw. Valentine enjoyed herself more tentatively, partly because the practical responsibilities were all hers, but also because her violent emotional extremes were now modified. On their return she noted that her pleasures were more muted: 'less vivid, less wonderful – but instead of being disappointed I am *glad*, now –'.[16]

Their winter plans had been made; on 27 October they moved to Norfolk for an extended stay. The house they rented in Salthouse was isolated on the shingle beach close to the sea, separated from the village by saltmarshes. Great Eye Folly was an inspired choice; living there reminded them of the other remote places – Miss Green, Frankfort, West Chaldon – where they had been self-sufficient, before the comforts of Frome Vauchurch. Valentine was kept busy collecting driftwood for the solid fuel boiler which heated sea-water, fettling the lamps and candles, catching rainwater to cook in, buying Malvern water to drink, rescuing oiled birds on the beach or watching seals, dolphins and passing ships. They were always alert for the tides and the weather, involved with the elements more intimately than they had been since Chaldon.

Sylvia wrote of 'the extreme happiness of our life here', and among her record of blizzards, gales and floods noted again 'we are deeply happy'.[17] This was a rough but effective treatment for their condition; relying entirely on their own resources, they were constantly occupied but always together. This off-grid existence was like a retreat, or a nature cure, and it worked, for both of them – at least for a while.

Into this strange idyll came angry letters from Elizabeth, accusing Valentine of escaping reality. (Elizabeth was now too close for comfort, not only back in England but actually *living* in Oxford to research her ancestor Anne Bradstreet.) Valentine told Sylvia that Elizabeth would 'never let go of her grudge'[18] and was deeply distressed to realise 'the black morass of bitterness in her heart for me – and *because* of me'.[19] She still felt love for Elizabeth, but knew it was false 'except when it is an assault of desire and that is usually, now, confined to the simplest category, scarcely at all widening into the country of imagination and poetry.'[20]

Valentine's life in that country was slowly reviving. In Norfolk, she was writing more poetry, and Sylvia was 'deeply impressed' by this work in which she recognised 'a new quality'. These first and last stanzas of 'Salthouse, New Year's Eve' illustrate Sylvia's analysis approving 'more statement, compacter clauses and more artifice of syntax'[21] (a critique which demonstrates the disadvantages of writing for her):

> The cold stands tall as a tower to the stone-white moon,
> It rises from darkness out of the prostrate sea;
> And dead the shore sleeps, now as the slow earth turns
> From pretence of a past year to pretence of new ...
>
> So stand we here, and the round earth heels over,
> Bearing the living sea, leaving the moon;
> Heavy with night and winter, the earth turns over,
> Her children borne safe on her breast towards the sun.[22]

In her notebooks Valentine wrote observations of nature which are accurate and evocative of that harsh but beautiful coast; of pools in the marshes 'like cast down armour, like knights left lying on the field of battle'; of plover flying at nightfall, 'their far-off cry, from the centre of the flock, as if it were a *cry from the heart*.' Weather is wonderfully described: 'The matador wind flings his cloak of cloud', and 'now the sea chills to pewter'.[23] Among these notes inspired by the place are poems about her own state: 'Do not let me bear about a dead child / The Prince who should be born of me,'[24] one such fragment starts; this unborn offspring is her soul, but also perhaps her poetry, and the aborted yet still unburied affair.

Valentine was also thinking about her own fertility, and trying to repudiate her troubled paternal heritage:

> My hand and the pen: my wrist and the white silk cuff
> Broad round the narrow bones and the fragile skin –
> My father's hand, my father's father's wrist,
> His great-grandfather's pattern and texture of stuff –
> Very long ago, they say, something caused all this to begin,
> And my child ... I have no child. It's been long enough.[25]

This illustrates Valentine's sense of herself as her father's son, in the male line of her forebears, and yet capable of child-bearing, with choice. It also raises the valid question of what kind of heredity a child of hers would have. Recalling the loss of Tamar, soon after writing this poem, Valentine wrote, with one of her flashes of wisdom, 'it most deeply grieved me – but *now is now* and no one can be *childless* in this world so full of children.'[26]

Valentine treated the numerous children she knew with calm respect and empathy; the contact she'd always maintained with her own child-self made communication with them easy for her. Those she taught to shoot, fish, box, drive, type, name flowers, stars, birds, insects, and animals, all remember her with strong affection. She had no sentimentality about having children, no self-pity about being without them. Tamar was a specific loss, not a generalised lack. Even the idea of having children *with* Sylvia she could treat flippantly; she wrote about their imagined offspring 'I wish we had been able to raise a brood of them, they would have been HEAVEN. Like [the cats] Niou and Kaoru!'[27]

Her poems, Valentine's real posterity, enjoyed more public success while they were at Great Eye Folly. Several of her poems were broadcast on the radio, over the winter season. Sylvia thought they were 'admirably'[28] performed (by Phoebe Waterfield) but Valentine was intensely disappointed, as usual, by the response of those she knew. She lamented: 'I hoped *someone would hear a poem of mine and* HEAR IT', and calculated all the people who had failed to listen – including Elizabeth. Then she bewailed her inability to enjoy her successes ('and what small successes at that').[29] The insecurity and lack of confidence which Joan had fostered so well always deprived Valentine of the elusive 'proof' of being a poet. No achievement could convince Valentine – her damage was too profound – and the failure of others to understand her work, or compliment her on it, was always seen as proof of its inadequacy rather than their indifference.

Sylvia was writing short stories again, too, although the sale of Little Zeal reduced financial pressures. Ruth's health problems distracted them from work; her heart was bad, and Valentine wanted to move closer, permanently. Despite all Ruth's infuriating characteristics, Valentine had the self-knowledge to prophecy: 'I should not be able to stand up on my feet when she is dead.'[30] But they found nowhere suitable nearby, only what Sylvia called 'great gaunt rectories with contaminated water-supplies and poltergeists'.[31] Ruth came to Salthouse for New Year, determinedly keeping her tradition, and after her visit they collapsed 'into miserable guilt and lethargy though we couldn't as usual see *what* we had done to make everything so harsh and calamitous.'[32]

Sylvia observed that Joan exploited Ruth's undeniable age, and possible illness, to manipulate Valentine; 'I resent this extremely.'[33] Another awkwardness was Ruth's increasingly unreliable interpretation of events; she told everyone that Valentine had been awarded the OBE for the brilliance with which she'd organised Civil Defence throughout Dorset. Valentine grimly corrected this misapprehension: 'I was a clerk at 30/- [shillings] a week and opened doors for gentlemen I learnt to call sir.'[34] But she was still mortified, especially when Ruth was interviewed in a radio programme about war work.

In March, the spring tide and strong winds brought the sea up over the saltmarshes, and Valentine drove Sylvia and Niou to safety with waves lapping the car wheels. By now, having to evacuate the house was just another adventure; they were inured to life on the edge. They left the strange house sadly at the end of their tenancy, and returned to their other life in the house by the river.

~

Back at home, Valentine and Sylvia settled into a domestic pattern suited to their (still) emotionally-convalescent state. They drove out to look at the sunset, or walk in a particular wood or see a special view, treating the Dorset landscape like a foreign country. Valentine noted the wildflowers, birds and butterflies appearing in their turn. Every few months they went to London (staying in Joan's flat in her absence), where they dined at Bertorelli or Savarin and went to exhibitions, theatre or opera, with a sense of occasion. At home, there was pleasure in sowing and harvesting the garden, and Valentine planted willow-trees. They listened to the radio with attention – mainly classical music (Valentine's favourite Reynaldo Hahn song was 'L'Heure Exquise') but also the detective series *Matt Dillon*, for which Valentine would ritualistically light a cigar.

In June 1951 Valentine was seriously ill with measles and a congested lung: she lay semi-conscious, breathing from an oxygen cylinder, while Sylvia was distraught. 'I depend so entirely on her for my strength and wits that with her away in this stupor I am abject,'[35] she wrote. A fortnight later Valentine was able to put on her trousers, proudly recording that she had been 'officially ill for a month'.[36] Her health was not good; at the age of forty-five her arthritis was so bad she wore a sacro-iliac belt, she had severe breast pain and testosterone treatment had disrupted her periods, she had lost all her teeth (as many people did during the war) and suffered from migraine, colitis, and repeated infections. She felt that finishing the affair with Elizabeth meant the end of the primacy of physical life for her – although when she'd thought this at forty, Lord Body had refused to submit. Now, her renunciation had added poignance because the 'last' affair, the great physical resurrection, had ended so badly.

Valentine attempted to accept the signs of ageing, but this only increased her preoccupation with death. 'All joy and pleasure is coloured by remembrance of death – of loss and termination,'[37] she wrote. This had made sensation more intense when she was younger. Now, reflections on her own mortality led her to try and alter her personality to one she deemed more appropriate to her advanced years. (What Sylvia thought of her lover's self-imposed ancientry at twelve years her junior can only be imagined.) Valentine tried to bid farewell to the lover part of herself, but this brought the poet under threat, too. The close correlation she had made between the two roles meant that the poet's persona would be seriously diminished by the loss of the lover – a dilemma Valentine pondered.

Apart from her life-work of poetry, Valentine was now jobless. She had been offered secretarial work by a young widow, but Sylvia vetoed

17. Frome Vauchurch, the river front and deck overhanging the water.

the idea – perhaps understandably. She suggested that Valentine should act as *her* secretary instead, unpaid, so that she could write more. Valentine was deeply offended by this idea (partly because she already performed many of those tasks), but typically she vowed to do more, spend less, never complain. Her self-esteem was so low that she considered drinking again, for the sake of her writing: 'When I was thoroughly sodden I wrote with a kind of stumbling, blind felicity ... Now I am merely good – and DUMB.'[38]

This crisis of confidence made her wonder whether it was more important to write the poem or have it read – when even asking the question showed she was 'deep in the mire'.[39] Valentine could be dryly humorous about her depression, noting 'The aftermath of renunciation is always, I suspect, dusty.'[40] But at times she felt her poetic self, as well as her 'lover' self, in jeopardy, and she wrote simply: '*I feel myself destroyed.*'[41]

Sylvia didn't always notice Valentine's darkness; she saw her fortitude about pain as beyond stoicism, 'part of nature's flow of rivers lakes and seasons'.[42] And gloom was not all-encircling; Sylvia still enjoyed Valentine's ironic humour. When their neighbour's little girl presented them with the plastic eggcup she'd been awarded as second prize in a pipe-cleaner model competition, it emerged that she'd actually entered their model (made to demonstrate the technique to her).

'Did you say *second* prize?' Valentine demanded.[43]

But Sylvia did notice that Valentine was intent on Doing Good Works, in which she could 'smell desolation'.[44] Sylvia's attention was distracted by her new novel *The Flint Anchor*, a sustained feat of imagination which meant that 'everything that isn't in the book has only an interposed existence.'[45] Her preoccupation, and its cause, didn't escape Valentine who sometimes found it 'a very hard thing to bear' in contrast with her own creative problems of dearth. She admitted 'a black envy wells up in my throat, and I find it difficult not to take umbrage and think that she is – as children say – "being superior"'.[46]

There were pleasure jaunts; a driving holiday in Northumberland and a visit to the Festival of Britain in the summer. But they were still plagued by Elizabeth's attentions. Sylvia was disarmed by Valentine's admission that 'from time to time I enjoy it',[47] and she knew that

Valentine was steadfastly refusing invitations to meet. Privately, Valentine was tormented by a growing realisation of the pain she had caused Sylvia; having been able to ignore it at the time, its enormity shocked her now. She wrote 'It makes my heart bleed as though newly broken by my own desperate will ... I have loosed the harpies about my head, and they fly blackly round the room, and the noise of their wings drowns the noise of the sad weather outside.'[48] Yet, as Sylvia observed over the continuing exchange of letters, 'they can and must want to go on with it. A passion is very little killed that dies so hard.'[49]

Valentine was capable of cynicism about her own motives, and one of the relatively few poems she completed early in 1952 is a sardonic reflection on her internal struggles:

> It would be most foolish, surely,
> After such long struggles, so much hard fighting,
> This anonymous afternoon to surrender at discretion –
> It would be foolish, surely?
> Especially as I am alone now,
> Never in forty years have been deeper sunk
> In loneliness: so that to summon her,
> Or her, or any of them, would be
> Intolerable effort, surely, intolerable indiscretion;
> Since they are all dismissed, and suitably
> Rewarded – or if not suitably,
> At least rewarded by someone other than me.
>
> It would be most foolish, and it should not be.
> Watch the sun set, instead; watch the clouds
> Run over and spill long rivulets of gold upon the hill.
> Watch, watch! Stand at the window!
> Ignore the bed.
> Ignore the imaginary footstep on the stair.
> Watch the sun sink, but do not think of night,
> Except as a preliminary to the return of light.
> And be still, be very solitary and still;
> For the footstep on the stair has stopped – was never there.
> Do not open the door; do not open
> Any door. All is locked for the night. All is secure.[50]

Even outside her poems, Valentine was tempted to meet Elizabeth. She had to remind herself that if the affair resumed it might cause 'sufficient upset to endanger' Sylvia's novel.[51] The supremacy of Lord Body was by no means over for Valentine (now or possibly ever). Chatting at a drinks party in the 1950s Jean Larson noticed Valentine catch sight of an unknown woman with piercing blue eyes, draw herself up to her full height and stride over to her, being suave and charming. 'Oh, no,' Sylvia exclaimed. 'Valentine's smitten again!'[52]

~

In April 1952 Sylvia became seriously ill in her turn; eventually shingles or chickenpox was diagnosed. Valentine was not well herself, suffering from heavy irregular bleeding for which a fibroid operation was suggested. But she was frantic over Sylvia, 'so indescribably dear to me', and nursed her devotedly – despite inward suspicions that '[I have] an unfortunate bedside manner: perhaps too "thoughtful".'[53]

When Sylvia was beginning to recover, after ten days in bed, another group of Valentine's poems was broadcast. True to her vows of self-abnegation, she told no-one about it in advance, and thus avoided any disappointment. Her own comments still contain a ghostly whisper of humour:

> It was read by a hesitant young woman with uncertain vowels; she treated it as if she were moving cautiously about in a junk-shop, unsure of what – if anything there – might be valuable; and handling each line as if it might come unstuck in her fingers. But even so, it sounded more workmanlike than the previous 'moderns' that were read, and I think it had more content to it: I think, almost, one might have suspected it of having an intended meaning.[54]

In May they went on a recuperative holiday to Cornwall. On their return, Sylvia received from Paul Nordoff records of his song-cycle *Lost Summer*; music written to the words of her private poems about the Elizabeth affair. Sylvia listened to the records alone, and was so moved that she claimed the tragedy was 'justified ... for this music has come out of it' – although she admitted that, unfortunately, for Valentine there was 'no such foison'.[55]

The following week on a particularly splendid day Valentine put on her panama hat and a lavender tie to celebrate the return of summer. Sylvia played the music to her and, when she wept, commented blandly 'alas, that it had to grieve her so.'[56] In fact, Valentine was so distraught by this experience that she thought longingly of suicide 'and knew the urgency Judas felt as he hurried out to the field and how thankfully he handled the rope and put it about his throat.'[57]

In a fictionalised account, Valentine wrote: 'If only I, too, from that ruin and loss, that anguish, that despair, might have put out some flower, one flower, after everything else had fallen away.' She contrasted how Sylvia with her 'clear untarnished intellect' had 'remained potent ... never spoken while the tempest raged,' but kept her words 'safe and dry, kept them as seeds for a new sowing.' The harvest had been so great that even 'this sad little musician' had produced from it, so 'our disaster had become his fortune!' Worst of all, in the end Valentine / the narrator 'accepted the justice of her sentence ... my seed has rotted, his has flourished.'[58] And she considered herself creatively dead – although the experience had in fact produced this remarkable, intense prose.

Valentine had undeniably put Sylvia through agony, but this was a thorough revenge. It confirmed all Valentine's deepest anxieties; her jealousy of Sylvia's artistic collaborations since *Whether a Dove or Seagull*, her current lack of artistic potency compared with Sylvia's almost exaggerated fecundity, and her perceived inability to make artistic offspring with Sylvia (or indeed any other kind). Valentine knew her own part in this distribution of roles; she was Judas, the betrayer with a kiss, who was 'mute, so he could not even echo the Word.'[59] She could not now – or ever again – complain of anything Sylvia might chose to say or do, not even the cold-blooded pragmatism of publicly revealing their personal tragedy for the sake of making art (something Valentine would certainly have done herself). Experiencing the depths of shame, she wanted to kill herself. But this would have been the ultimate betrayal, a dereliction of duty which Valentine could never execute while Sylvia lived.

Instead, on 27 May she set off to meet Elizabeth, looking elegant and animated – to Sylvia's chagrin. After the initial awkwardness over their parting two years before, Valentine slipped back into the old familiarity. When Elizabeth spent too long repairing her make-up, Valentine called impatiently 'You've been almost a quarter of an hour ...' and was rewarded with a most unsettling Heliodora smile. Soon Elizabeth was telling her 'I love you with all my life, for ever and for ever', and when Valentine accidentally touched her shoulder they 'fused like two thin wires in a short-circuit ...'[60] Surprisingly, however, the current was switched off in time.

Elizabeth told Valentine 'I love you far outside time or life; and there is nothing else at all that I care about.' Valentine thought Elizabeth's looks had deteriorated, but she still felt 'violent lust' when they kissed goodbye; 'in that second of time I fell like a shooting-star, and almost I could hear the sound of my falling and my fire.' Yet she knew this was a delusion of love, 'only because she loved me and the blood ran fast in my veins ... I enjoyed that familiar, that *young* sensation of desire – even the anguish it caused me'.[61] This pleasurable pain soon returned; Valentine recorded:

> My mind and body *raged* with desire ... I had to get up and roam the house and go out of doors, into the misty morning, filled with birds and the scent of syringa – which of course did no good to me at all![62]

Sylvia was alarmed, but she had reached the stage of merely hoping for ignorance. This approach tempted Valentine; her policy of truth-telling had caused too much pain, and Elizabeth's expectations were now reduced. Valentine wrote humorously of her inner voice, a

> modern devil, who knows a bit of psychology and rattles it off at appropriate moments: 'But how *silly*, and how *dangerous*, this is! See how ill you are becoming; how lethargic, how fat, how bored – how violent inside your private mind ... *You can't work as you are* – for pity's sake go ahead and take the girl! What harm could it do? She longs for it; you long for it: there's not much time left for either of you – and here she *is* and it's summer, and no one need be a penny the wiser ... How CAN it be "wrong" or "bad" when it is so beautiful and bright?'

Valentine could only resist this temptation by remembering Sylvia's misery, 'a sombre talisman enough, ... for that is done and I did it and it cannot be undone.'[63] So although this desire continued to trouble Valentine for some years yet, she resisted her devil successfully. Elizabeth persisted in giving what Valentine unkindly but accurately described as her 'noble widow performance',[64] and returned some of Valentine's presents to her – a wounding gesture. Valentine felt sorry for Elizabeth, but now realised how carefully she had planned her campaign and manoeuvred for ultimate success. In 'Postscript to Fable', Valentine describes the spider Arachne making her web for the prey again and again only to find that despite all her cunning, 'All she's caught is a sort of inedible bee: / All she's caught, poor Arachne, is me.'[65]

Valentine had always made the connection between her passion and her poetry. It was an obvious correlation: she was violently in love with Sylvia – she wrote love poems; she was full of political fervour – she declared it; she felt deep joy in the natural world – she expressed it in pastoral poetry; she was on a spiritual quest – she described it. The events of her life provided raw material for her poetry, but not in terms of 'plot'; often her poems were about an internal experience, or one in which the poet was merely a witness. But the emotion created by her experience was necessary to power the creative process; it was energy. So experience (whether physical, mental, spiritual or ideally a combination), and the resulting sensation and emotion were absolutely essential fuel to fire the poetic machine. There had never been a shortage before.

Although Valentine did write poems to Elizabeth (and more poems about herself and Sylvia during the affair), it had not provided the inspiration she expected. This was partly, no doubt, because almost daily letters to Elizabeth leached creative energy, and insistent psychoanalysing in reply impeded the poetic process. There was no fallow time enabling the mind to operate unobserved, unencumbered by expectation and without conscious consideration. The inner life incessantly externalised by immediate exhumation and postmortem of every idea pre-empted any possibility of seed-setting, growth and harvest.

The affair with Elizabeth is important in relation to Valentine's work not because it was creative, but because it demonstrates the fundamental link in her mind between sexual energy and poetry. The imagery of potency and sterility which she used about *Lost Summer* demonstrates that to her, potency was the poet's right. Because sexual and poetic power were virtually synonymous to her, she would have to engage in an intense struggle to recast her poetic persona, and find her power source elsewhere, after ceasing to embody the lover. Without this identity, her creative self was frighteningly reduced while she endeavoured to reinvent herself, until she discovered a different source of potency within her poetic self. 'Poem in a Bad Year' was written while this transformation was in progress, and exhorts the poet: 'Wherever we find ourselves, let us walk as we walked in the Kingdom – / All exile must end at last in restoration / If only the Princes remember their true estate.'[66]

In August 1952, Valentine sent off some poems to the Hand and Flower Press, a small poetry publisher, noting: 'I could not but think them good of their kind.'[67] The press agreed, offering to publish a selection of her poems.

This success was encouraging but not financially rewarding. Valentine wrote in her diary: 'I wish I might have a job.'[68] With Vera Hickson, provider of Niou, she had started visiting auctions and buying small antiques. She had a good eye for unusual pieces and was skilled at restoration. A few days after wishing, she wrote:

> Today it occurred to me that it might be possible to open a small shop, in the long sun-parlour; in which to sell oddments such as stuff bought in recent sales ... this is such an ODD plan for me to have, that it may be an answer...[69]

It was. Sylvia enthusiastically encouraged the idea, embroidering a tartan silk box with 'Souvenir de Balmoral' in black jet beads as a kitsch contribution. (Elizabeth's returned presents went in too.) Valentine whistled about her work, and proudly recorded the progress of the Not-Shop, as it was known until official permission arrived.

The venture was, perhaps surprisingly, a financial success. In business, Valentine was able to be disciplined about money in a way which eluded her personally; she never ran up debt. Since she was not greedy about profit, the shop gained the reputation of being reasonably-priced; since she had a tray of curios for a shilling each, there was no embarrassment about going there and not finding anything cheap enough. In buying, Valentine was fair and so was often offered interesting things – although she sometimes bought junk because she felt sorry for people. Financial acumen was only part of the business. More importantly, Valentine also had idiosyncratic taste, and a sense of objects as individual things, relics of people and containers of their love. She became expert at buying on behalf of customers, interpreting their taste with flair, and her shop was especially popular with collectors of dolls' houses and miniature objects, fairings and lustreware, swordsticks and musical boxes. Sylvia recalled: 'It was ... her loving attention to other people's wishes and tastes which made the shop a pleasure to her as much as to others.'[70]

Valentine had always been a dexterous mender and cleaner of guns, clocks, lighters and small mechanisms in general, and now transferred these skills to become a meticulous restorer. Although she sent out lists and sold through the post, Valentine also had plenty of local business. Roger Peers, previously curator of the Dorset County Museum, recalled first meeting her when two elderly ladies asked his advice about selling their Roman antiques and he called Valentine in for an opinion. He was impressed by Valentine's authority and knowledge of obscure detail, the products of an ever-interested enthusiasm.

Sylvia adored the buying-trips which took them across the country, combining business with pleasure. Locally, Valentine went as far as Exeter, but they drove on extended tours down through Devon and Cornwall, to Presteigne and Leintwardine in Wales, to the North Country and Scotland, meeting eccentric characters and finding strange and beautiful old objects. Sylvia was proud of Valentine's expertise, which she used in her Mr Edom stories. Sometimes, when Valentine became very busy, Sylvia resented the shop and its distractions. More often it was a relief because it solved Valentine's financial problems and gave her a dignified profession. Valentine had a certain personal status within this world – as she realised when she was invited to join one of the illegal rings of dealers she had observed operating at auctions. (She didn't.) But important as the shop became, Valentine still regarded her principal work as poetry.

The shop brought them much pleasure, however. The treasure trove Valentine amassed became a sight to be visited, together with its notorious proprietors. It brought them a much wider range of acquaintances locally, most importantly the artist Reynolds Stone and his wife Janet, and the Pinney family of Bettiscombe Manor, bohemian aristocrats much given to entertaining and bringing their guests to marvel. Thus the shop's customers included Vivienne Graham Green, Peggy Ashcroft, Frances Cornford, Kathleen Raine, Enid Bagnold and the like. Its style is hinted at by the tale of their beautiful young friend Jean Larson, who noticed a plate illustrated with a winged figure appearing to a surprised woman. She pounced on it with Catholic delight, exclaiming: 'Oh! The Annunciation!'

'No, darling,' Valentine drawled. 'Cinderella.'[71]

At the end of 1952 Sylvia acquired a new, expensive car, a grey Wolseley. Remarkably, this did not go unnoticed by MI5, still alert for signs of subversive behaviour. In November Sir Percy Sillitoe (now head of MI5) had asked the Chief Constable of Dorset to provide 'an up to date report on these two women who in the past have been of particular interest to us.' In December, the report duly arrived:

> The two ladies in question live in a rather isolated position just outside the village of Maiden Newton, and they keep very much to themselves. There is no evidence whatever of their having disclosed Communist sympathies ... It is known, however, that both persons are great readers and that they do possess some literature appertaining to Socialism. This has only very recently come to light and it may or may not be significant ...

Detective Sergeant Parsons, who signed the report, was evidently sceptical about the Red threat posed by the two literary ladies, despite his disclosure of their reading habits – an activity always viewed with suspicion by police states. He concluded 'Miss ACKLAND has within the past few weeks acquired a new Wolsley [sic] saloon, Reg. No. F.P.R. 219, grey colour.'[72]

Valentine was delighted with the car. She wrote:

> [driving] is a skill of mine – perhaps my only unfailing and always satisfactory accomplishment – and dear my Love understands this and has given me this beautiful instrument to play on ... as she gave me a matchless instrument for another skill I had ...[73]

This skill, in Valentine's vocabulary, was slipping into the past tense. Early in 1953 she wrote of being 'for so long incapacitated from making love', adding 'even now it is a fiendish agony to me'.[74] Whether poor health (including arthritis) or psychological pain now so seriously impeded this most crucial enactment of her identity, other skills – such as driving – became more important as symbols of self. Writing poetry, the most vital of these attributes, was also the most invisible and difficult to quantify. Analysing her creative health, Valentine claimed 'I have worked as hard and as long and as steadfastly as most people, I think,' but she also accused herself of 'indolence and non-application', and as a result felt 'profoundly, incurably, guilty'.[75]

When *Whether a Dove or Seagull* was credited only to Sylvia, or when one of Valentine's poems was in *The Countryman* and Sylvia tactlessly remarked how much the magazine had recently deteriorated, Valentine felt humiliated. One of her short stories, 'Beyond Thy Dust', was read by John Neville on the radio, and she did not remind Sylvia that it was on. Sylvia inevitably forgot to listen (as she had previously forgotten a broadcast of poems), and Valentine believed she was embarrassed by the inadequacy of the work. Reading Sylvia's diaries in full, this does not appear to be true; she genuinely admired Valentine's writing, although she did not think her fiction particularly commercial. This contradiction dogged Valentine; she was ambitious, but her best work was unconventional and not easily categorised. Many of her published (or broadcast) fiction pieces were 'realistic' ghost stories: Valentine's scarier speculations on death and its aftermath delivered in the ordinary, manly voice of a Somerset Maugham or J B Priestley, and now similarly dated. Her more experimental stories – less plot-driven and in more poetic prose, or in her muscular semi-autobiographical style – have aged better. This was a way of being paid to practise her craft (like writing reviews and non-fiction essays), but it did not compare with her real work.

Her poetry – where her true talent lies – was Valentine's most widely-published form of work, but even here, writing as a lesbian in her own voice inevitably made her an outsider. Despite her desire for wider recognition, for an audience, Valentine knew that her identity as a poet did not, finally, depend on publication. Indeed, she realised that this could sometimes impede poetry, lamenting 'If only I could write – if *only* I could write – if *only* I had never published anything, never had that sickness of ambition – never done *anything* but write and love.'[76] In November, the Hand and Flower Press cancelled the publication of her book, because the press was closing down.

~

Early in 1953, great floods in East Anglia destroyed Great Eye Folly, 'that matchless, lonely, solitary castle'[77] – yet another beloved building gone. Other certainties were crumbling; Valentine allowed her Party membership to lapse. Her letters to the Party explaining her decision were duly intercepted and logged by MI5. However, their report that year still insisted 'we have no information to suggest she has relinquished her Communist sympathies.'[78] (The same conclusion was reached about Sylvia, and the files on both women remained open.)

Although she still called herself a Marxist during the 1950s, Valentine no longer supported the Party because Stalin's human rights abuses had disillusioned her with Soviet communism, and although she broke the news of 'Uncle Joe's' death gently to Sylvia, Valentine accepted that the revolution in Russia had failed. Sylvia dismissed evil rumours about Stalin as anti-Soviet propaganda, and equated any disappointment at the shortfall between ideal and actuality as a treacherous move to the Right. Thus, clinging staunchly to similar political beliefs sent them in opposing directions.

For Valentine, political awareness was instinctively a personal issue; she did not separate ethical considerations from practical politics. When she read in the news of 'Craig and Bentley', on trial for murdering a policeman, she recognised that their guilt was a communal sin because, brought up in this society, they were both

> absolutely incapable of knowing right from wrong – or indeed, of knowing *right* at all. I know beyond doubt that their state is largely the fault of my generation. Not entirely, but we have a plain, and a considerable, share in their guilt. We could have known better, and we would not.[79]

Valentine explored this theme in her poetry of the 1950s in a highly individual way, which combined her thinking on political and spiritual themes (pre-figuring protest poetry against war and environmental destruction in the next decade). The same acceptance of communal responsibility appears again in 'For all that takes place under this dome of the sky':

> ... For the badger, the otter, the fox – for all here
> Hunted and driven over their own ground, the land
> That is theirs, so small a portion of it under the sky:
> For this and for these who will now dare
> Speak one word of excuse or call mercy with a prayer?

She repudiates the idea that if 'We keep our eyes closed, our minds blank, not to know / What black deed we do', we will be able to 'Win some kind of forgiveness, some shabby salvation ...' The climax of the poem offers little hope for the continuity of the natural world, but none at all for humankind:

> And the flood rises and the flood rises and the blood flows and
> the blood flows;
> And we turn on each other, father on son and brother on brother;
> And the flood rises and the blood flows –
> And carelessly, every summer, blooms and burns and falls the
> rose.[80]

Valentine's repeated use of flood images as a metaphor for world destruction gives her words a curiously contemporary ring, foreshadowing the extreme climate catastrophes of the next century.

Within her poetry (when she could write it) Valentine was at her most confident; even her despair is asserted with vital energy. But in her daily life, things were more confused. There were moments of intense enjoyment: shooting with an expensive new air-pistol, improvising a Siamese cats' national anthem, or meeting Sylvia by 'romantic and fortunate chance'[81] when shopping in Dorchester. Set against these pleasures were problems. About Elizabeth, Valentine now admitted she had been self-deceptive to believe that a renewal of their affair could be anything but disastrous – 'for evidently I knew.'[82] But meeting again in May 1953, she was astonished at the 'paroxysm of desire' which she felt when they touched. Sadly, she told Elizabeth 'I shall always love you, and always want you.' Elizabeth answered that Valentine was 'the centre and meaning and whole life of my life.' But Valentine understood at last that while, as she put it, 'I MUST not have her', the real tragedy was that she could never have *her*. Her desire was for an imaginary woman, 'the not-impossible she', not the forceful, intelligent American, who was always disillusioned in her turn by the actual Valentine.[83] Even so, for years afterwards, Elizabeth insisted on occasional meetings, which gave the ex-lovers little pleasure while unnerving their respective partners.

Ruth was another factor oppressing Valentine; was it manipulation or genuine forgetfulness that made her write a long letter complaining about having been ill all alone when Valentine had, in fact, driven instantly to nurse her? Even the mildest remonstrance sent her into a rage, in which she would accuse Valentine and Sylvia of 'living for nothing but pleasure, holidays and a grand car'. Sylvia acidly remarked: 'we outrage her if we go away for a holiday, we insult her if we have a visitor, and we trample on her if we live quiet and happy by ourselves.'[84] But what was an irritant to Sylvia upset Valentine in a different degree. In August 1954, Sylvia was seriously worried to witness a crisis of nerves when Valentine shook visibly. Valentine attributed this to reading about Nazi atrocities, but Sylvia thought it was an overdose of Winterton duties.

In her mind, Valentine was sometimes back in the state of loneliness and alienation she had known as an excluded child sitting in the cold and dark on the kitchen stairs at Brook Street. That summer, she wrote despairingly:

> I cannot write. I cannot feel. I cannot unfreeze from the clench of my loss – I have lost my Love and I have lost the poet I thought I was. I am without any light or hope at all. I am done for. I am done for.[85]

In her diary she quoted 'Accept the cold content', the poem about suicide she had written in 1949, when she felt she had lost Sylvia, with a note that it was a true statement of how she felt when she touched 'the bottom of the pit'.[86] The last stanza reads:

> Deep in your cold content, sleep in the comfort
> Of the unchanging winter of her frown;
> And in the quiet embrace of darkness lying
> Confide your soul, and lay your body down.[87]

Chapter Ten:
Saint and Rogue

In the autumn of 1954 Valentine bought herself a puppy: a black poodle she named Candace. Sylvia observed, correctly, that the dog was 'to be tried as a medicine against her melancholy',[1] but she was not pleased. There was much argument, until Valentine decided that she had not 'asserted' herself enough, and did so, telling Sylvia irately that she 'would not have any more talk about it.'[2] This was an error. Sylvia knew that Valentine felt a desperate need for a pet as company, to love her unconditionally, and most of all to need her: areas of Sylvia's responsibility. She therefore hated the dog, resented its presence and – being Sylvia – never relented. Candy was, predictably, a neurotic dog who chased the cats, couldn't be house-trained properly and howled if Valentine went out (when Sylvia would silence the dog by squirting a water-pistol down her throat). Sylvia made Valentine sleep in the spare room because Candy disturbed her.

When the new cat Kaoru had first arrived, they'd slept apart for practical reasons, and Valentine hated it. She felt dislocated and cold, woke 'bereft' in a 'miasma of unwantedness' and suspected that this was 'the thin-end-of-the-wedge'; if not, 'how dangerous it must be to let the nights mount up against us – and how fearful a thing to do, how fearful, at this late stage.' Sadly, Valentine had then concluded that she had no right 'to ask for any restoration' (although she lamented 'my loss of the fire I loved so much. It kindles in me suddenly ... always for my love, never now for anyone or anything but the one.')[3] Now the separate bedrooms situation was repeated, without hope of remission.

In happier moments, Valentine believed that her love for Sylvia was a reciprocated grand passion, and felt that their difficulties were superficial. She might regret 'having won no name for myself by which to praise her', she might wonder whether 'my divided or two-sided sex perhaps makes it more difficult for her to feel secure and sheltered', but in the end she felt 'sure (MOST steadfastly sure) that no one had ever been loved more absolutely, nor loved with more intense, watchful, new-springing admiration and *pleasure* – for I love her in all ways at once.' Valentine believed that they had both been enriched by their experiences of 'many emotions (of sorrow and grief and bitterness, but also of most intense and happy love, of trust and – also, for her also of apparent betrayal – and of *endurance*, compliance, respect and honour).'[4]

The problem that had now arisen between them was loss of communication; Valentine thought her own silence was because 'the mind goes through menopause too.' When she was depressed, in her 'black grave', she could not 'get near my Love – not even near enough to smile at her and see her eyes, much less to speak and be answered'. Valentine could not understand why they both felt so isolated: 'It is not lack of love –' she mused, 'but it may be lack of love-making.' In one of her darkest moments, Valentine wrote:

> that it should be like *this*, after twenty-five years, after such ecstacy such fire of love ... My love for her, I thought in my pride and youth would wrap her and shelter her and keep her safe and warm and to her life's end secure ... and now I know that I blight her.[5]

On Christmas Eve 1954, Valentine contemplated suicide again, in despair because she couldn't tell Sylvia how much she loved her, and believed Sylvia would be better off without her. Early in 1955, she wrote 'This is the coldest winter', which in the last stanza expresses her bleak situation with great clarity:

> Who has returned alive from exile, who has told
> News of the north? None, for that bitter dark
> Turns all to stone and silence. I know I bear its mark –
> A stone heart carried in a breast stone cold.[6]

Read in conjunction with 'Accept the cold content', this offers a painful understanding of her cold and lightless mental world. The absolute isolation of the depressed person (as well as their unlucky lover) is conveyed in a final Lazarus poem:

> 'If she were to rise out of the cold earth,' I said,
> 'I would know her again: if like Lazarus dead
>   She came in her bandaging grave-clothes and walked to my side
>   I would hold her against me again as I held her my bride,
>   Nor think, if we shared it together, her grave an unwelcoming bed.'

I said – But who can explain me the truth of this day
When she came home, alive still, returned from a brief time away,
And I in the moment of greeting found nothing to say
Of the love in my heart, but wound her with words cold as clay?
Who can call her to rise from this grave I have made, bid her
come to my side, bid her stay?[7]

It's a paradox that here, even out of loneliness and despair Valentine makes living poetry. To live in Now – a necessary and desirable poetic attribute for Valentine – means attempting to create from all areas of experience. Solace, perhaps even healing, came from the world around her, and poetry inspired by the natural world never failed her, although it might come rarely or slowly. The river, which in July 1955 flooded and flowed through the house, was still a source. She writes that 'The recurrent pattern of water drawn on the world / Is image of all that we know, all re-discovered / After long search – the word, the secret, the way.'[8]

In the last resort, whatever her inmost despair, Valentine knew that in the making of poetry was her salvation. Her voice never deserted her, however much she feared its loss, and she remained faithful to her vocation to speak.

O flame do not die –
The leaping tongue, the kindling eye,
And that hearth fire which is our home,
The heart that watched for you to come:
All wasted, all extinguished lie
If in this night you die.[9]

12 January 1956 was the twenty-fifth anniversary of Valentine and Sylvia's marriage vow. Valentine wrote: 'so it is in some sense a silver wedding anniversary ("in some sense" is a decency-bit to acknowledge convention! It is quite as real as any other marriage – and far more real than many silver weddings.)'[10] Painfully demonstrating their disharmony, Valentine gave Sylvia her present on the 11th, insisting they were celebrating the night of the 11th-12th. Sylvia stuck to the 12th, averring it had been the 12th-13th. Valentine was technically wrong and since they had celebrated on the 12th for the last twenty-four years, inexplicably so. However, Sylvia was delighted with the antique silver

heart and diamond ring of some grandeur which Valentine gave her. With unusual restraint, Valentine did not mention her latest project.

~

As she approached fifty, Valentine's spiritual search was leading her towards Catholicism. Its main attraction for her was the mass, which she saw as a ritual means to gain instant access to the spiritual universe. A trip to Rome in the autumn had perhaps influenced her, as various friends may have done. Her old lover Bo had moved nearby and (after some years of not speaking) was now a frequent companion to Valentine (who always remembered 'when she was so very dear'),[11] and still a devout Catholic. A new friend, Bill (Jane) Long, accompanied Valentine and Sylvia on a January trip to Wales in her Baby Austin. Sylvia liked Bill's impulsiveness, which encouraged Valentine to be even less cautious. Sylvia was now translating Proust, on which she concentrated to the virtual exclusion of everything else. At home, Valentine felt that Sylvia had ceased to see her properly, an annihilation similar to that which she experienced after the war, when the resumption of the Elizabeth affair had regained Sylvia's attention.

At some level Valentine may have felt that another crisis was required, but her resurgent spiritual needs were perfectly genuine. She'd once again taken the path of sexual abstinence (usually) in the aftermath of Elizabeth, but this was problematic, because she had always so specifically associated the physical with the spiritual. The beauty and pleasure of the physical world, apprehended and experienced with both mind and body, had given her access to her spiritual self through sexual love, as well as other forms of pleasure in beauty. Thus the soul / body dichotomy was not always true in her experience, and by forsaking sex Valentine had closed off a direct pathway into the spiritual realm. She needed to find alternative routes.

Valentine also required this change as part of the reinvention of her poetic identity. (One of her favourite metaphysical poets, John Donne, had moved from writing of profane to sacred love and produced some of his greatest poetry after this conversion.) She had already begun to re-formulate her view of the poet as 'the preacher, the teacher' with certain special duties of witness and spiritual mediation. The poet, to her, was a warrior on behalf of the silenced, one of Shelley's 'legislators of mankind', and to obtain spiritual authority fitted her view of poetry as a vocation. Valentine once said of Sylvia: 'she has power to create, the nearest to pure holiness anyone can ever reach', which parallels Gertrude Stein's descriptions of herself as a 'saint' – a perception elucidated by Judy Grahn: 'Artists bear the same focus of leadership and shamanistic interpretation of the cosmos to human perceptions, in our age, as saints did for their societies in the Middle Ages.'[12] So Valentine wanted to be, in this sense, a shaman, even a priest.

To have this power, spiritual rather than temporal, would be a new source of potency, not wholly separate from that which Valentine had wielded as a lover but reached by a different path. A letter from Elizabeth gave Valentine a startling insight into her own desires: on reading the words 'the long habit of reaching out for your guidance, and even authority ... is still strongly instinctive with me', she was 'very nearly swept back into the maelstrom again.' Sitting at her desk with her head in her hands Valentine discovered:

> I am passionately ambitious for power ... over a human being ... I violently desire to command and be obeyed. I feel that delicate, most delicious flush of warmth ... even just from writing these words ...

She realised that Elizabeth had recognised and exploited this to gain power over *her* 'by that desperate abandonment she could bring about; by her fighting back with such stubbornness, and then collapsing ...' (This was outside the dynamic of Valentine's equal relationship with Sylvia.) Valentine was tempted to use this love of power, and its potential for igniting her passion, but regretfully decided to 'try to forget how exquisitely exciting the sensation is.'[13] Yet to become a philosopher-priest, a sage and holy guide, would be a way to wield this power and generate emotional energy, though in a different guise. (It would also be an appropriation of another traditionally masculine role.)

Catholicism thus offered Valentine the possibility of renewing her work, and restoring her identity as a poet, by transforming her negative lack of physical love into a positive power generator. The church was a romantic idea for Valentine, and her adventure into Catholicism can be seen as another great affair, the last perverse mistress to be loved in secret, wooed and eventually won. It was another severe trial of Sylvia's love, whether Valentine was recalling her attention or testing what sacrifices she would make.

Until now, Valentine had shared Sylvia's abhorrence of Catholicism (through personal experience rather than instinct); her need to do this must have been very pressing. She debated for months over many problematic aspects of the church's teachings and its reactionary politics, weighed against her desire for the ancient ritual, and for confession of her heavy sins (although she did not believe in absolution). She knew that if she re-converted, Sylvia would be appalled and a 'gulf' would open because of her 'contempt for anyone who "submits" intellectually.'[14] Valentine understood that Sylvia could simultaneously have race-loyalty towards the Church of England (and love its liturgy) and yet hate all organised religion so much that 'to see Sylvia attacking someone who is "professionally" religious ... is a TERRIFYING sight.' And Valentine had seen 'never-really-thought-about-it-before' people simply demolished.[15] Thus Catholicism would be a double insult, both to Sylvia's instinct and intellect. Valentine feared that Sylvia would believe she had betrayed their shared allegiance to 'the Voltaire, Anatole France school ... the shrewd, pertinent, disillusioned wise ones who write like angels and have been our masters and guides all our lives.'[16]

Nevertheless, Valentine told Sylvia she wanted to live as a Catholic. Her response was far worse than Valentine's worst imaginings. She was extremely shocked, having no prior idea of Valentine's plans, utterly horrified, and quite unable to understand how a person of Valentine's intellect could succumb to hocus-pocus. She was also deeply disillusioned, 'much more so than about Elizabeth because this was quite out of the range of her comprehension.'[17] What distressed Sylvia most was the retrospective damage done; by claiming that she'd *always* been a Catholic Valentine re-wrote the past as well as the present. During the affair with Elizabeth, Valentine had been all too true to her lover-poet self; even in the depths of despair Sylvia had recognised quintessential Valentine. But this sudden shift of focus changed her into an unrecognisable person, utterly alien, and antagonistic to the radical values they had always shared.

Valentine's poet-priest persona was a figure that Sylvia would always refuse to recognise. She once wrote to Valentine: 'There is hardly a hairsbreadth between Saint and Rogue, and you could be either.'[18] This contradiction had delighted Sylvia; at any sign of over-saintliness she would protest ('Please never give up your naughtinesses. It would impoverish my days.')[19] But now Valentine was planning to retire the Rogue forever. Sylvia said that Valentine was 'disclosed as someone different from the person she thought',[20] and her most profound certainties were shaken.

Unfortunately, the local priest delighted in minor legalities; Valentine was 'lapsed' so to be re-admitted to the church required various formalities, all apparently devised to outrage Sylvia. Valentine had to contact her long-ago husband Richard Turpin, who politely told her that he'd left the church and never bothered to complete the annulment – so they were presumably still married in the eyes of the church. Valentine therefore needed a letter from the Bishop for permission to live apart from her husband – a ludicrous situation which was deeply insulting to her partner of twenty-five years. Sylvia naturally speculated on whether she herself would be a sin, or invisible? (Neither a good option.) She thought Valentine would probably be told to leave her. Yet if this church which deplored homosexuality ignored their union, it could only be because between women it didn't count. Despite all this, Valentine persevered, and was received back into communion with the Catholic church, to the great interest of the local Catholic community.

The price Valentine paid for this was higher than she had foreseen. Sylvia could not absorb this shock as she had so many others, and she would not try. In terms of seeing how far Valentine could go, this was too far. Valentine understood that Sylvia saw her as 'a weakling ... a renegade ... a betrayer of national history as well as a betrayer of the free mind'. Valentine described their difference as merely 'a tract of country we cannot walk about in together'[21] but the problem was that there were now so few footpaths they could follow through the landscape where they had once wandered at will. They could hardly even discuss their irreconcilable points of view because, as Sylvia said, 'analysis is out of the question: we are not analysing the same thing.'[22]

As a convert, Valentine had no childhood memories of Catholicism, neither bad experiences nor boredom to inoculate against its pageant.

Her first experience of it had been as a young adult, associating it with the sinful glamour of people she wished to emulate. Although she'd been disillusioned by the church's censorship of books, and had personally experienced its appalling misogyny and medieval patriarchalism, she still (it's evident from her diaries) kept a romantic ideal of saintly heroism, knights crusader, quests for the holy grail, and so on. Most of all, she wished to participate in the 'communion of the saints', the timeless community of all Catholics, which brought her into the great company of so many artists and poets.

For Sylvia, there were many less positive associations of Catholicism. She had been brought up – however distantly – within the Anglican tradition of distrusting all papists as superstitious, disloyal idolaters. (It was different for foreigners.) On a more intellectual level, she was bound to abhor the church's treatment of women (thinking of marriage, contraception and abortion, not to mention witch-hunts) and its historical record: the Inquisition, the Crusades, pogroms, missions to the heathen. Then there was the recent collusion with Fascism, the lack of papal resistance to Nazism, the post-war rapacity. During the Spanish Civil War the church was with Franco, and many British and Irish Catholics had volunteered to fight for the Fascists simply for that reason. No wonder Sylvia found it incomprehensible that Valentine could join them.

Valentine was deeply saddened by the increasing distance between them, but she obstinately believed that she had done a good thing, and that only Sylvia's desolation was keeping her from being completely happy. 'Loving is my whole life,' Valentine wrote, '... this one, this all-important thing: that I love Sylvia and live in love.'[23] Yet it didn't apparently occur to her to try and spare Sylvia this pain. Nor did Sylvia consider compromise; in her diary she wrote virulent anti-Catholic remarks almost daily with bitter satisfaction. Her pleasure in Valentine was spoilt. The statement 'I admired her long legs – the legs of a nymph,' would now be qualified: 'and thought how shocking it is they should be crumpled *in a pew*.'[24] All the anger she had somehow contained over Elizabeth now spilled out.

Time did not improve the confrontation about Catholicism. Valentine took her new duties (fasting, penances after confession, holy days of obligation) very seriously – as with her rigorous Communism, there was an element here of playing the part to the full – but she longed for Sylvia to assent, and share them. Instead, Valentine knew that Sylvia, far from being reconciled,

> hates and loathes and fears and condemns it. She is hanging on to the last remnants of concealment, and when they fray away she will have to admit to herself that she scorns and condemns me: and that will break her heart ...

Valentine was distressed when Sylvia complained that she often 'spoke roughly', but she felt that Sylvia 'flinched' at her, which *made* her speak roughly. Valentine would gladly have died for Sylvia, but she suspected Sylvia of believing herself to have '*spent her life for nothing*: grown old in serving me, and I have crossed over into the enemy's camp.'[25]

Sylvia contemplated changing her will, giving Valentine only a life-interest, in case she spent her inheritance on building a church. She objected to being personally implicated; she hated 'the accumulation of alien books and new come objects' on Valentine's dressing-table with 'poor Tib's photograph still staring out among them.'[26] (Tib was Sylvia's private nickname.) Valentine's early rising to go to mass, her fasting and Friday fish-eating, her constant typing of devotional writings and her enforced acquaintance with the Catholic Ladies' Guild, Sylvia loathed; it reminded her of the preoccupation with Elizabeth. She mourned 'Another than EWW has taken her away – silently, invisibly.'[27]

When Bill Long converted (the first of many to follow Valentine), Sylvia was horrified to be asked if she'd do the same? But perhaps what she most abhorred was the Catholic emphasis on self-denial, guilt and good works, all reminiscent of Ruth. Sylvia perceived this as bad for Valentine's mental health, no cure for melancholy but a stifler of mirth and extortioner of arid duties. She saw Valentine as 'never happy, never free from care and abstract frettings and self-tormentings of her religion.'[28] These abominations were what Valentine perversely most enjoyed.

Sometimes, Sylvia could convince herself that the whole strange masquerade was typical of 'my alarming and distracting and sheltering and supporting and protean only Love'[29] – part of Valentine's mystery. When they were abroad, she attended mass with an anthropologist's pleasure. And she had not lost her complete reliance on Valentine;

when they were crashed into by a motorbike, she recorded her 'admiration for Valentine who, pale as the death she had averted, telephoned, was interviewed, remembered, never failed anyone.'[30] She believed Valentine's assurances ('I can't, don't doubt her love for me') but felt distanced ('At moments she reaches out to me and is surprised and happy to find I am still here').[31]

There were times when it was possible to communicate, even about Catholicism. When Sylvia wrote telling Valentine how much she had always admired her for quitting the church in her youth, although Valentine might now regret it, Valentine answered,

> OF COURSE I look back on my action then with respect and approbation. Then, as now, I could not and would not abide blackmail and bullying ... not for a moment do I reprobate the young creature (hard now to know its sex at that stage) who stalked out of the Confessional metaphorically clutching Ulysses ... *and* who told the old priest where to put it ...

Valentine abjured Sylvia not to think she had 'ever turned against the things Molly-Ackland, Molly-Turpin, Valentine Ackland did ... I love you, you see; *all the me's love you*.' (As she'd always insisted: 'all my goodness and all my badness loves you.')[32]

Trying to comfort Sylvia, Valentine compared Catholicism to a pair of old stays, or a Wolseley instead of an MG – comfortable and convenient at her age. But Sylvia never really moved from her 'O what a noble mind is here o'erthrown' stance. Valentine wrote compassionately of Sylvia's almost phobic anti-Catholicism, but she guessed her reaction was connected in some way with the Elizabeth episode. She even asked Sylvia to consider whether her grief and rage were to do with it. She did not ask whether Sylvia felt guilt and anger that Valentine had sought for spiritual inspiration outside their joint life, or jealousy and rejection over her renunciation of sexuality for religion. Without answers to these difficult questions, Valentine was determined to cherish Sylvia as she always had done; to bring her breakfast in bed, open her wine, fill her lighter, buy her flowers, type for her, point out the stars and the weather, drive her about, show her a comet or the Northern Lights like giving her a present. And of course Valentine wrote her poems.

For their January anniversary of 1957, she wrote Sylvia one of her 'occasional' poems, beginning 'If we had no books to read, if we could not draw music out of the air', which insists that they can always reassure each other of the existence of 'swans in the world', free to 'launch away into air / And their wings will sound through the darkness as they fly.'[33] Less encouraging for Sylvia was this awkward attempt to reconcile the conflicting areas of Valentine's life:

> I stand committed now
> To the trees and the wood of the trees:
> To beauty and love and longing and loss,
> To the sweetness shown in your brow,
> Known in your hand's touch, at your glance – All these,
> And the incomprehensible fatality of Holy Cross.[34]

~

There was another catastrophe during 1956 – the coming of the atomic age to Dorset – which utterly united Valentine and Sylvia. Plans were unveiled for an atomic research station to be sited on the vast tract of wild land which formed the inland view from the Five Maries at Chaldon, Hardy's 'Egdon Heath'. The heath was, in Hardy's phrase, 'an ancient permanence',[35] untouched land of great beauty and immeasurable environmental importance, a wilderness which had been central to the Wessex identity since time immemorial. 'Winfrith' (known, like Sellafield, by the name of an unfortunate nearby village) was initiated with such secrecy that local people guessed it must be a military installation. It was to be on an enormous scale, effectively ruining the heath.

Protest was muted. The local press didn't mention any possible disadvantages (or danger) from a nuclear reactor, nor did they suggest that the huge resource of the unspoilt heath might bring any possible benefits to the local community. According to the *Dorset Echo* 'the general feeling is one of welcome to the research station plan, as a source of revenue to the neighbouring villages.' There was uninformed enthusiasm for 'a new industrial future.'[36]

It was left to Valentine to write about the dangers of a nuclear reactor; true to her Communist journalistic training, and her disillusionment, she knew that money would be the major issue. She emphasised that the county would be no richer. Even Hardy's connection with the heath she transformed into possible loss of touristic income, if 'the landscape of his genius' were to be destroyed. She questioned whether the reactor could be 'beneficial' and introduced the concept of 'loss' for the county and 'the whole Kingdom'.[37] But she and other protestors were simply outgunned by powerful interests who were, conveniently, operating in a society which believed that progress inevitably meant improvement.

The enquiry, held in 1957, was a formality, although Valentine and Sylvia both attended it. The government scientists, local landowners and expert witnesses overcame local opposition with a mixture of bullying, persuasion and lavish but unspecific visions of financial gain. The nuclear reactor, with its many outbuildings and security walls and carparks and workers' accommodation blocks, was duly built, and the sinister structure dominated views of what was once the heath.

The irrevocable despoilment of the heath, at uncounted cost to local people's health and happiness, influenced Valentine's work. Exile as a state of mind had long been a preoccupation, as had the plight of wartime refugees, but now she saw dispossession and disconnection from the land as a result of the despoilation of nature. Human damage to the environment could expel people from their natural place in the landscape. It was a literal loss of Eden. Her poem 'Summer' begins 'I saw our mother, Eve, walk down the lane, / And she alone as the sweet evening light / Came like a scent from the tall blossoming hedge.' But the idyll is soon disrupted, for the figure of Eve is accursed: 'And such deep loneliness went with her, I could feel / The living things in field and hedgerow flinch ...' The poet senses the same inheritance:

> ... on my heart too
> The shadow fell, for I in the long line
> Of her lost children am, and I must go
> Alone as she does, and cast my blighting too
> As she does hers, over the living world.[38]

This poem was written in 1962; as well as describing the human condition, with its inheritance of sorrow, it carries a recognition of the danger humanity presents to the natural world, and the deathly price of dissociating from it.

In 1957 a small book of Valentine's poems came out, but it was not exactly the renewal she'd hoped for. Sylvia, belatedly realising some of Valentine's anguish about her work, copied into her own diary, chose, typed out and had privately printed *Twenty-Eight Poems by Valentine Ackland*. A carefully-chosen selection, the inclusion at the end of several weaker religious poems could suggest that Sylvia wanted Valentine to read something into the ordering of her work – or simply that Sylvia hoped to please her. The little book is well-designed and set, like a poetry pamphlet, but Valentine had reservations about it. These Sylvia put down to her 'melancholy doctrine of abnegation and embracing crosses',[39] but perhaps Valentine had noticed the chronological decline in Sylvia's selection. There was also her hesitance about self-publishing, and the old history of disappointments.

Valentine had been deeply upset the previous year when the American journal *Partisan Review* published an anthology, *Modern Writing*, which contained a story of hers. This was a prestigious publication, she was introduced as an exciting writer and the story, 'Urn Burial', was strong. But, as usual, all Valentine's pleasure was spoiled by the non-reaction of her friends, especially Bo, who forgot to read it. The regularity with which this happened suggests that Valentine was impossibly sensitive to the lack of interest most non-readers feel in a writer's work, but also that she had a highly-developed wrecking-mechanism which prevented her from enjoying even well-deserved success. She was determined not to re-enact the same scene over *Twenty-Eight Poems*, but her muted response disappointed Sylvia.

'Urn Burial' takes its title from one of Valentine's favourite works by one of her most beloved writers, Sir Thomas Browne; it's linked to Norfolk, death, and philosophical speculation. But the story is written in a curt, almost satirical style, and its subject matter is a triangular relationship between three women. It's set in New England, and is angrily critical of rich American manners. Although not explicitly stated, the nature of the women's relationship is clear; Dulcie, the visiting Englishwoman, is Janey's ex-lover, Sara is her partner of the last seventeen years. As a ghastly social encounter it contains some comedy, but the moral of the story is that it would have been better not to meet again. Dulcie is a wise, world-weary character who controls the situation and maintains power over Janey: an off-putting glimpse of Valentine's 'sage' persona.

Valentine felt oppressed that her poetry had not returned to her, even though she had this new sacred source of inspiration. She wrote to Sylvia 'It breaks my heart that I cannot write poetry now. You thought you had married, if not a poet, at least someone who could catch feathers'.[40] (This image, of poetry as feathers falling, was important to Valentine.) But it was an illusory sense of loss; Catholicism had not recreated the sudden vivid inspirations of youth, but there was no loss of power in her poetic voice, so English, lyrical and melancholy.

It had always been one of Valentine's gifts to relate the spiritual state to the material world in a completely integrated and convincing way, ever since poems like 'Space is invisible waves' in *Whether a Dove or Seagull*, but now that capacity was increasing. She understood the profound communication of which pastoral poetry is capable; in Kathleen Raine's words:

> Meanings, moods, the whole scale of our inner experience, finds in nature the 'correspondences' through which we may know our boundless selves. Nature is the common, universal language understood by all.[41]

'All Souls' Night', with its contemplative atmosphere and echoes of Sappho, is one of these poems which effortlessly finds the correspondence of mood in nature:

> In the warm November dark, when rain had ceased from falling,
> I went from the house at midnight, and stepped out of light
> Into the shallow green cavern of night and a cloudy moonlight.
> How tall and tranquil and silent stood the trees;
> The last fallen leaves of the poplar lay on the grass like flowers,
> And like flowers in the sky shone the gentle Pleiades.[42]

'Every autumn a wind', a longer poem, moves further into the mystical, metaphysical world of her imagination, indicating that Valentine found the natural world a source of poetic emotion, as well as a means of expressing it. The last stanza begins 'And love wells within me and spills over the world ...' and describes 'that beyond which folds / About us, warm as life, and is our life, and holds / Our days and deaths and births within its sheltering folds.'[43]

In a rare piece of writing explicitly about the link between poetry and religion, Valentine's authentic prose voice sounds confident and clear, stating the connection she felt between creative imagination and an awareness of the spiritual dimension:

> Of course I have always known there are two different ways of viewing Truth: the flat and the 3-dimensional.
>
> 'Do you really *believe* in the Assumption?' (But it isn't a query there, properly; it is an exclamation-mark.)
>
> In Flatland, of course I do not believe it. I *cannot*: in Flatland nothing happens that cannot be seen to happen, touched and smelt and heard to happen. Nothing happens that doesn't appear to be able to happen FLAT, so to speak.
>
> No poet can live long in Flatland.
>
> Yes: I do not 'believe' in the Assumption: but I know it happened – or what is the right word? Most words, now, are Flatland words. In one of the Coptic accounts of the Death of the Virgin and of her Assumption, it says that she 'prayed in the language of Heaven' and in the language of Heaven she lives – perhaps, in the language of Heaven, one says that she is ...
>
> Fortunately all poems are in the language of Heaven, and pictures are painted in it too, very often, and music is in the language of Heaven: and some of the things I handle now and then are certainly the furniture and trappings of Heaven.[44]

In the spring of 1958, Valentine and Sylvia had another intensely happy holiday in France, driving through Provence. Sylvia was delighted by the food, the blossom, the nightingales; Valentine by the flagrant Catholicism and her hope that Sylvia might be 'drawn into the Ark'.[45] Indeed, Sylvia was not so antagonistic (either because they were on holiday, or because she expected foreigners to be papists), but she was determined not to be tempted by 'the devil rattling a pair of church doors'.[46] On their return, hostilities on this topic were resumed.

Ruth was increasingly demanding, and Valentine had to visit her frequently – then came the appalling suggestion that Ruth should move closer, perhaps to Dorchester. This was averted, doubtless at some cost to Valentine, but the problem continued. Joan was also unwell, suffering in her personal life and embattled at work; she was prone to quarrel violently with Ruth and require Valentine to act as a go-between. Sylvia knew that Valentine's natural love for Ruth would never be enough for this 'vampire' mother, that Valentine was spread too thin. 'I sometimes think Joan plus Ruth is eating her away,' she commented – adding, inevitably, 'and religion has denuded her of all the protective enamel she used to have, the power of switching her mind elsewhere.'[47]

Valentine was now needed by Joan to go on convalescent boating weekends in Norfolk, to cheer her up and support her. Sylvia found this sibling duty rather ironical, considering their history, and said so. Valentine tried to reassure her: 'Don't think I have forgotten that Joan has a deep enmity towards me ... Nor do I forget that she has done me much damage'.[48] But Sylvia felt that Valentine's strong sense of duty was being exploited and it was doing her no good, physically or emotionally. When Valentine cracked a kneecap, she was still expected to drive Ruth and Joan to their respective homes and get herself back to Dorset, opening all the gates en route, as they were both too frail to get out of the car.

The emotional onslaught was even worse. Joan emanated 'murderous, just-below-the-surface hatred',[49] and she still knew exactly how to upset Valentine. They hadn't met face to face for some time when Valentine's support was first summoned. Joan stared at Valentine markedly throughout dinner, and eventually burst out in 'mock exasperation'; 'Haven't you ever Been Through anything? You haven't got a *line* on your face!' Joan had a fairly accurate idea of what Valentine had Been Through – much of it inflicted by Joan – but Valentine had enough self-protection to answer flippantly. Afterwards, though, she worried that she had a 'bland visage' or looked smug or had a characterless face; as ever, Joan knew just how to undermine her confidence.[50]

Actually, although Valentine was young-looking for her age, she was no Dorian Gray. In her early fifties she still looked 'so young, so stately, so elegant, with scarcely a grey hair or a wrinkle', that biased Sylvia thought she looked 'scarcely a day older'[51] than she had in 1930.

18. 'She has done me much damage' – Valentine's sister Joan, in wartime uniform.

Her greatest concern was her weight, which tended to fluctuate as the result of trying to regain a youthful figure which had been sometimes anorexically underweight; when Valentine periodically lost a stone it was in pursuit of her serpentine looks. She disliked having photographs taken now, and few exist of her in later life. But she still wore her hair short, and her diaries – in which she so much enjoyed describing dapper clothes – often mention new corduroy trousers, coloured shirts and ties, panama hats and linen jackets.

Of growing older, Valentine wrote that she felt 'the pathos, and not the tragedy. And I'm afraid tragedy is really my line.' With the same self-deprecating humour, she joked that she thought of ageing 'in terms of consolations like cakes or pocket-knives or books on Doing Something'.[52]

Despite her comparatively youthful appearance, Valentine's health was not good in general; she was getting bad headaches and had a drooping eyelid. She suspected some of her symptoms might be

19. Valentine's lighter with integral personal ashtray, chrome and
    crocodile leather.

caused by 'over-smoking'. There was now a growing awareness of the link between smoking and cancer, and Valentine considered this in the light of Robert's death, her own breast cancer scare, and Ruth's 'gay histories of cancers she has known'.[53] But she wrote defiantly:

> observation has taught me to think [it] regrettably likely that I shall die of something: and statisticians perhaps could calculate whether I am more likely to die from cancer of the lungs or from the effects of war – direct or indirect. And he may calculate that the former is the greater risk. But, sir, I do enjoy smoking and so far, participating in two major and one minor war, I have not enjoyed myself at all.[54]

So she smoked on.

Gradually, the pattern established by Valentine's new regime became familiar, if not accepted. Sylvia's vitriolic diary entries subsided into complaints about Valentine's 'incessant chattering' and the co-religionists 'who pullulate round her like worms in a wound'.[55] The moments when Sylvia saw Valentine unexpectedly in a London station and 'a current of love arched' between them, or when Valentine said 'Goodnight, darling' and Sylvia was 'encompassed with a realisation that she really does love me, that I exist for her',[56] were actually frequent, but ever-surprising. Their love was still vigorous, in fact, but it could feel submerged under the accretions of their different interests.

Sylvia now recognised that Valentine had gained something from her conversion, but not something Sylvia liked. She observed, of Valentine giving advice:

> Her wisdom and diagnosis were extremely impressive. I admire thoroughness, grasp, professionalism of faith. I ought, therefore, to feel reconciled. But I don't. Like the devils, I admire and tremble at this enormous and growing distance between us.[57]

This new role of priest-like guide increased Valentine's self-esteem (and sense of power), but it simultaneously distracted her from her work and took up her time in writing innumerable letters, giving support and advising people. Being a Catholic – like being a Communist – was a full-time job.

Sylvia apparently believed that Valentine regretted their involvement in Spain, whereas in fact she enjoyed surprising her co-religionists with stories about it – making clear which side she'd been on. When she saw Valentine recounting one of their Civil War adventures, 'standing there so tall and handsome', Sylvia remembered 'the sound and the smell and the truth and enthusiasm of those days', and concluded 'she has stifled more than she thinks.'[58]

But even five years later, a book about the International Brigades inspired Valentine to write a poem beginning 'Reading the book about Spain my heart cried out "Comrades!"'[59] – hardly the viewpoint of a renegade. 'Bliss was it in that dawn to be alive,' she quoted, envisaging the International Brigades as a 'failed attempt'[60] for humankind to ascend to the next, higher order of being. Valentine knew that ideals had been sullied, but 'their faith stayed with them because they rushed past it to death', while 'our hope cast down its eyes.' She denied that the failure of a political ideal in practice invalidates the ideal itself. 'Only one thing is left us, the thing we meant all along ... / Love is the final word, as love is the centre and first.'[61]

If Valentine felt morally bound to condemn Franco's repressive regime (despite its adherence to Catholicism), she was equally opposed to the censorship and persecution of artists in the Soviet Union. That regime's hypocritical insistence of the importance of artists and intellectuals she compared to a worn-out record still being played repeatedly:

> I suppose it has become like the Blue Danube for our mothers! Most of us – the ageing soi-disant Intellectuals – soften and twitter and break into happy tears when we hear it – remembering the heavenly waltzes of our gaudy youth, clasped in the Bear's arms.[62]

Sylvia still dismissed bad reports of the regime as propaganda, so this was a constant source of friction, for which again she blamed religion.

Although Valentine had apparently committed herself to Catholicism, she privately admitted to a higher preoccupation. She felt that everything she did apart from writing was 'filling-in', but writing was not always possible. 'I never had a reliable talent,' she wrote, 'but what I had was all I had.'[63] Yet when Valentine did write, she was producing some beautiful poetry. This short lyric from 1959 is classically simple, restrained and well-judged:

> While I slept we crossed the line between May and June;
> The morning came, gently walking down from the hill,
> And by the time I stirred it was full day
> And she had brought summer with her into my room.[64]

Chapter Eleven:
The Good Englishman

Whatever their causes of dissension, in an emergency Valentine and Sylvia could 'call themselves together',[1] back into a complete unity. In September 1959, Valentine had to undergo a small operation to remove an infected fragment of tooth-root from her jaw. Sylvia was intensely anxious because of her blood-pressure, bad reaction to anaesthetics, and certain expectation of death. She had the operation in Weymouth; Sylvia stayed at a nearby hotel with Janet, and everything went well. While caring for each other, Valentine and Sylvia were able to ignore the differences which had come between them, and regain their true estimation of one another.

One of the occasional rhyming poems Valentine wrote for Sylvia in later life explicitly sets out to advise us by their example: 'I have tried very hard to write / a poem about love which might / explain to those who sift our dust / when we have gone what rite they must / perform .../ if they would make their love as we/ made ours: out of a moment's chance / a timeless immortality.' She compares their age with the eternity of their love: 'winter is walking, and in me / the cold last season fastens too – / but Oh my Love! I look at you / and all the heaven of summer see', and asks 'How can we tell the way to make / Love last forever?' The final stanza provides the answer, and Valentine's deepest beliefs (if not her best poetry):

> The fire we kindled on the hearth
> on our first morning still in earth
> burns and is one with all the fire
> the world holds in its heart. Desire
> (we'll tell them) only that your love
> shall burn so brightly through your day
> that when night comes the fire will stay
> and love and truth immortal prove.[2]

Valentine's deeply concerned love for Sylvia gave her many anxieties, particularly about ageing. In Valentine's view old age began at sixty, and thoughts of it at forty; by this reckoning at nearly seventy Sylvia was ancient already. Possibly Valentine emphasised her own ageing in order to minimise Sylvia's; certainly she was over-preoccupied with death (as she had been ever since her father's sudden, shocking disappearance into its void). She suffered from many simultaneous but not mutually exclusive fears; she obsessively dreaded the possibility that Sylvia might pre-decease her, bequeathing the prospect of a lonely old age; but this terror co-existed with the dread that *she* might die first, leaving Sylvia alone without comfort or protection.

These worries were not irrational or easily dismissed, but Valentine experienced them intensely at an age when death, for either of them, would have been untimely, and there was no particular reason to expect it. She was unable to stop herself from dwelling on the unknowable variables of the future; although she'd been able to survive actual painful events by 'closing the aperture of my sensations to its very smallest diameter',[3] she could not do the same with her imagination. (To repress that would, of course, have been a denial of her vocation.)

In 1960 these problems were emphasised when Valentine's health was again a cause for such concern that religio-political dissension was put aside. Her headaches and eye problems were finally diagnosed as temporal arteriosis, a disorder of the artery supplying blood to the eye. (It seemed Robert's dire predictions of sex-induced blindness might belatedly be proved right.) In March Valentine began cortizone treatment, which usually worked efficiently on the condition. She remained on the drug for three months without improvement, and a diagnostic operation seemed inevitable. With her characteristic mixture of courage and pessimism, Valentine learnt Braille. Sylvia was most concerned about what would happen to a blind Valentine later, without her? She wasn't entirely reassured when Valentine told her about a new order of nuns in Somerset for 'handicapped religeuses'.[4]

When cortizone and witch magic had both failed, as her sight was at risk Valentine agreed to the operation. She was not a good patient (although she could be physically brave, even stoical) because hospital was a torment like the office for her, without any privacy or quiet for reading. When she was unexpectedly kept in hospital for two days before the operation, to get her blood-pressure down, Sylvia thought it would probably have the opposite effect. The operation was finally performed on 4 August, when an inch-long section of artery was removed, revealing a blockage caused by a clot, rather than arteritis; an alternative route had maintained the blood supply to the eye.

Sylvia saw Valentine afterwards; 'she lay propped up, her head bandaged to one side, delicate fronds of hair rising above the bandage, like an exquisitely elegant Byronic brigand.' The 'keen-sighted falcon' of Sylvia's private mythology was preserved, and in illness she could again recognise the handsome, wicked lover of the past. Even the scar on Valentine's temple pleased Sylvia: 'it stands up, like a comet. I had imagined it horizontal.'[5]

For the fortnight of convalescence, Sylvia's diary was free from anti-Catholic comment, but as Valentine recovered antagonism re-emerged. Even then, Sylvia too retained her vision. After an acrimonious discussion in which Valentine demanded why Sylvia could accept Flat-earthers but not Catholics, Sylvia told her the mass was 'unassimilable ... so punctual, so strictly limited.' Valentine answered, 'it is everywhere, but only complete in the Mass itself, which is the rainbow, though rainbow elements exist in every drop of dew, in every splash of water.' Sylvia privately rejoiced that Valentine was 'such a poet'.[6]

The more poetic aspects of Valentine's metaphysical interests (rather than their expression through organised religion) always pleased Sylvia. Valentine's hair-raisingly accurate tarot-readings and her belief that she had second sight, usually in premonitory dreams, complemented Sylvia's convictions about her own witchcraft and ghost-sightings. She was proud of Valentine's propensity to see strange things; prehistoric people climbing their earthwork, ape-like creatures crouching on Durdle Door, her dead father conversing with her in the new car. These supernatural occurrences were no more than Sylvia would expect from so extraordinary a person, part of the poet's sensibility.

Feeling considerably better, if not exactly well, Valentine longed to go North, to cross 'the sea or a frontier or at least the Trent'.[7] But Ruth was ill in a nursing home, Nancy Cunard was incarcerated in a lunatic asylum; both needed visiting. It was not until they'd fulfilled all the obligations of family and friendship that they managed an antiques-hunting holiday in November. Ruth's declining health spared them her traditional New Year visitation, but it was a subdued time. Sylvia was still deeply engaged on her Proust translation, which was not discussed with Valentine, whose preoccupations are summed up by her rare poems. *Poems of Loss* or *Poems of Darkness*, a series written in 1960, are concerned with her ability – or lack of it – to write, and her sadness about estrangement from Sylvia.

'Undone?' is an unusual poem, which suggests that god-given poetry *is* her religion – or perhaps his religion, as the (auto)biographical subject takes the masculine form: 'Forty-five years ago he held a pen in his hand / And wrote on lined paper, as he is doing to-night: / At nine years old, poems were answers to a Royal command, / The angels who brought them ordered "Take pen, and write –".' But inevitably the poet is 'Now ageing and ill, confused by sorrow and failure' and can only manage 'one tentative word'. The poem ends with a question: 'Does he call on a last-minute saviour, / The one he obeyed in his boyhood...?'[8]

And, in an apparently effortless lyric, Valentine recorded a clash with Sylvia which still carries the charge of the painful moment it captures:

> After you had spoken you went away,
> Because you had no more to say, because nothing remained
> To be done or undone; and after you had spoken
> I stood in my silent room while the silence explained
> Succinctly that once and for all our hearts had broken.[9]

One cause of tension was Valentine's increasing commitment to the church; far from being a 'bad Catholic' she was becoming a devout one. She had entered the probation period – a fairy-tale year and a day – to become an Oblate of the Order of St Benedict, a minor official position within the Benedictine hierarchy which involved taking modified vows and saying the Office of the Order every day. This dedication to the monastic ideal seemed to Valentine a source of inner strength; to Sylvia it was incomprehensible. It also involved regular retreats at Buckfast Abbey, to her intense irritation. Valentine also may have become a member of Opus Dei, a 'secret' organisation within the church which focused on good works but also generated sinister rumours, not unlike the Freemasons, and was said to have right-wing affiliations, especially

20. The poet in her boyhood – Molly dressed for riding, aged 9, in 1915.

in Spain. Some of the other Catholics with whom she associated were certainly in Opus Dei, and to Valentine its message of work in God's name would have been attractive. But, having publicly identified herself as a Republican during the Spanish Civil War, she'd have been an unlikely recruit.

A happy time with Sylvia was spent in Paris as guests of an American friend, Franklin Brewer, who entertained them in great splendour. Indeed, there was much everyday happiness, but never settled weather. Valentine was still beset by family; Joan developed facial shingles and was hospitalised with a suppurated palate, while Ruth was staying with the Apsley relations, too ill to return home. It was now two years since she had lived alone, and that time had been spent in nursing-homes, hotels and at Apsley, where her niece Betty handled her far better than her daughters could. To prevent her moving closer, Valentine visited assiduously. Sylvia's outlook was too partisan to be entirely helpful; of the birthday visit to Ruth she remarked '248 bloody miles to be sucked by a vampire.'[10]

Ruth was obviously failing, though she sang 'gallantly' in a family chorus. On 4 June Valentine was summoned urgently. Ruth was still conscious when she arrived, and Betty said 'Molly has come.' Ruth recognised her daughter and said her last words to her: 'My darling! Wonderful – wonderful –.' Valentine always remembered her delighted greeting, and the way 'her eyes filled with tears and the most indescribably beautiful smile of purest joy lighted her face.' (The kind of response Valentine always hoped for when she entered a room.) At this moment of extremity, with all their previous problems supremely irrelevant – and Joan absent on *her* sick-bed – Ruth and Valentine were at last able to love each other without constraint.

Valentine then experienced a transformative moment, when she felt the need to

> turn, with all my sins and offences and negligences [towards Ruth] and put them all into the embrace of her love: *to be forgiven* ... And I did ... and knew for the first time in my conscious life the feeling of relationship between mother and child ... This was so pure, so kind, so strong ... that I walked in joy, though with grief as strong and pure beside the joy...[11]

Ruth died, with Valentine beside her, in the small hours of 6 June, 'like the fall of a feather.'[12] She was eighty-five, and her life had become untenable, but Valentine's sense of loss was immense. Her bereavement, in all its complexity of sorrow, was far more profound than all the years of mutual irritation and moral blackmail would have suggested. She suffered bitterly, but accepted the redemptive joy of their final acknowledgement of love.

Joan, who had been unable to reach Ruth's death-bed, had no such comfort. She replaced her mother as Apsley's permanent invalid, complaining to Valentine that she was at death's door too, no better, unable to sleep or eat. When Betty seized the chance to telephone privately from a neighbour's, she explained that Joan was in fact eating, sleeping and recovering perfectly well. By July she'd improved enough to be received into the Catholic church, with Valentine as her godmother; an event which Sylvia understandably deplored.

The task of clearing Ruth's house still fell to Valentine and Sylvia, however, and it was unpleasant. Untouched for so long, and not in a good state before, the house had become very sordid within. On the same sad visit they buried Ruth's ashes, and visited Valentine's old ally and one-time maid Trina, who no longer knew her.

Their own home, though tidier, was now under threat from a new road which would cut through their own field, Cornum, near the house. This re-awakened Valentine's quest for another Frankfort, a new happiness. Although the thought of leaving her garden upset Sylvia very much she did not mention her reluctance, so at intervals Valentine would enthusiastically discover ruins with neglected gardens which needed rescuing, and Sylvia would look round politely and decline. The by-pass was never built, but it remained a worrying possibility.

As the result of much pious fasting, Valentine was thinner. Early in 1962, Sylvia was delighted that she was 'so elegant and thin again'[13] but rather unfairly disliked the means. She was unsympathetic to the faintings and stomach-pangs fasting caused, refusing 'to condole pure-heartedly with sufferings provoked by being *silly*'.[14] Sylvia also abhorred the causes of Valentine's depression. On the first anniversary of Ruth's death, Valentine wrote apologising 'for my present affliction of seeming so *black*'.[15] (Unsympathetically, Sylvia was surprised that after a year Valentine still 'grieved on'.)[16] Sylvia noted sadly 'music could mend it, but so could adequate sleep, a mind less voluntarily subjected to senses of duty, of obligation – above all, religious obligation to this worthless punctuality and formality. But it seems that I can't.'[17] Yet on a holiday to Orta – where Sylvia could accept Italian Catholic fervour at Easter – they were again extremely happy together. Their regular buying trips were also a mutual pleasure; away from home, Valentine's religious timetable was less rigorous and it was easier for Sylvia to forget her grudge.

Despite its recurring problems, life at Frome Vauchurch was not unremittingly dour; the pendulum swung both ways. Sylvia was immensely proud of Valentine's achievement with the shop, writing a blurb for it which began, 'Eight years ago VA set up a Small Antiques business ... Her monthly catalogues now go to a mailing list of customers in Britain, the Dominions and the USA and she sends ... 300 parcels p.a. [per annum].'[18] Although Valentine was sometimes gloomy, her paroxysms of darkness were reserved for her diary; she still had her ironic humour, a gift for repartee which Sylvia relished, and a manner of living which didn't lack frivolity. She enjoyed luxuries such as good clothes, a new gun, expensive scent and – especially – books and records, as well as new gadgets like a tape-recorder.

VALENTINE ACKLAND

FROME VAUCHURCH, MAIDEN NEWTON, DORCHESTER, DORSET
(Maiden Newton 276)

Stock includes Glass, China, Brass and Copper, Textiles, Lace, Books, Prints and Frames, Pewter, and a few specimens of Antique Furniture. There are collections of Oddments all priced at 2/6 and 1/-. Prices are plainly marked and invariably very moderate.

TO REACH THE SHOP : Take the first turning on the left going through Maiden Newton from Dorchester (road signposted Frome Vauchurch). The house is on the right, just before you cross the iron bridge over the river. There is a name-plate on the gate and a drive leading to the house, which stands about 100 yards from the road.

The house was bitterly cold in winter; its Chaldon-trained occupants were impervious to all but severe weather, rarely bothering to close doors and relying on log fires for warmth. The water inside the house regularly froze. With great suspicion, Valentine eventually tried an electric blanket (a present from a chilly guest) and called through to Sylvia 'I am in *heaven*.'[19] Converted thus far, they still eschewed central heating and carpets (and, of course, television) and an ordinary fridge was adequate for Valentine's ice-cream making. Sylvia was pleased to see her sitting by the fire 'looking like a gentleman of leisure and cultured affluence' or building a 'testudodrome' in the garden for a colony of affectionate tortoises.[20]

Candace was one of Valentine's self-indulgences Sylvia could never approve, but Valentine cherished the little dog for its dependence. When Candy suddenly attacked her while she was driving, this uncharacteristic outburst was explained by a brain tumour diagnosis. Valentine coped with increasingly unpredictable behaviour, until the dog had to be put down. Sylvia saw to this, as Valentine was completely unable to deal with it; another failure added to her list of private disasters.

Valentine replaced Candace immediately, despite Sylvia's opposition, 'because I am alone so much now – and at night'.[21] Fidele, although the same breed, was a more appealing dog who won Sylvia's favour by good behaviour towards the cats. But Fiddle (as she inevitably became known) soon died, during a spaying operation. In the car returning from the vet Valentine could not stop herself from 'wailing aloud like a lunatic'. Sylvia was sympathetic; Valentine had felt her 'closed' to the loss of Candy.[22] Fougere, the replacement poodle, was more like Candace and Sylvia never took to her as she had to the short-lived Fidele. Her Niou was best-beloved; Valentine went fishing most evenings for trout for the old cat.

~

Valentine read several newspapers daily and cut out stories of human rights abuses; articles on war and genocide or the torture and execution of political prisoners, and photographs of these horrors. Although this seemed to her an essential way of keeping contact with people in darkness and witnessing their dispossession, it was not calculated to cheer. Valentine's efforts to comprehend the suffering of the world brought her too much pain for her mental welfare; already struggling with depression, at times this self-imposed task brought her close to despair.

But Valentine kept the faith; she still believed in poetry. 'Hope of Poetry', though bleakly cold, is a poem with a positive conclusion and a conviction of poetry's importance which reaches far beyond Valentine's individual situation. It opens:

> Sometimes in the bleakest days of winter, after the turn of the
> year,
> ... You may see the unbelievable, tender green of a plant
> There risen from the stripped and anguished earth, there shining
> like a flame –

This is the flame of hope, 'and even the jack-boot treading / Cannot quench this tongue of bright fire from the heart of the world.'[23] Much of the dark imagery used here – black uniforms, jack-boots, beatings – reflects Valentine's political preoccupations. Her thoughts had moved from political systems, so inevitably flawed, to the predicament of the suffering individual – and all sentient beings.

Valentine hoped that poetry could make a difference, in the 1960s as in the 1930s, merely by its existence as a place of peace and freedom, an alternative mode of being which was mightier than the forces of darkness. She understood Virginia Woolf's claim that 'as a woman my country is the whole world', and remained passionately committed to witnessing the wrongs of that world and speaking for those denied a voice. Anything which roused her to protest, she would write about, from a race lynching in America's southern states to a judicial hanging in Britain, torture in Russia or nuclear testing in China. (Valentine told Sylvia she believed all nuclear weapons were evil, and she supported unilateral disarmament.) Her abhorrence of war was not party-biased; she was equally against China's invasion of Tibet and America's war in Vietnam. She and Sylvia were still having 'lacerating' conversations about Soviet Russia.[24] In this second stanza of 'After a conversation about Pasternak', Valentine expresses her fury at Sylvia's silence, and that of the other pro-Soviet intellectuals who would only protest against right-wing abuses:

Lap them around, who in one half of the world lie already dead.
March in protest, boycott, fight for the coloured, the maltreated;
March in protest, boycott, rage till the rich are unseated;
But for one half of the prisoners in the world – lap them in lead.[25]

This conviction that she had an obligation to speak though her poetry partly explains the despair Valentine felt when she could not write; it was a dereliction of duty. Many of her poems fall into the time-honoured category of poems on the theme of being unable to write. This potentially (unintentionally) comic theme in fact makes use of inner tensions to generate creative energy, just as the tensions within love, or the urgency of political protest, could be inspirational. Valentine wanted to remain able to write, to be ready. 'When you are ready, you will be summoned,' UA Fanthorpe writes,

> as the great Russian poet Anna Akhmatova was. During the Stalinist terror, she was waiting in a line outside the Leningrad prison where her son was detained. 'A woman with blue lips standing beside me ... whispered in my ear (in those days we all spoke in a whisper) – Can you put this into words? And I said – I can.' We all have to be ready for that moment when the woman with the blue lips turns to us.[26]

Valentine knew herself to be one of a community of poets who can, and therefore must, put it into words.

Her urgent sense of poetic mission did not only cover the poetry of witness. Love poetry was still of paramount importance to her, including the poems to Sylvia about ageing and loss. In a letter Valentine described herself as a 'stony mountain' beneath which was 'a river running fast and clear.' She assured Sylvia 'it is the same water of love which you have seen flowing through green meadows; but for the present time it is in darkness and underground. But it is still living water.'[27] Valentine was enabled, when she was writing poetry, to bring this living water up into the light. Her poetic vision was based on a certainty of enduring love, which she celebrated in poems as diverse as the Dylan Thomas-influenced 'I lay beside you and the long-legged years went free as foals'[28] or the 'Epithalamium for Death' in which the use of sexual double-entendre (the orgasm / death parallel so often employed as a conceit by the Metaphysical poets) makes the poem's end surprisingly witty and tender: 'we must stand together, lie together, together reach our dying; / With no hindrance, then, to the consummation of our ritual down-lying, / But a smooth coming together so that forever we are made the one-alone.'[29]

It was the depth of their love which gave Valentine and Sylvia such an ability to hurt one another, and its strength that underpinned all their work. Valentine wrote of it:

> love grown old has its own magnificence, its own *panache*. I think of the thorn tree, of the hedgerow oaks in Norfolk, bent and stunted and tree-roots exposed – in winter gales they have a great and moving beauty. I hope my Love may know that between us we have grown a love into a tree like that.[30]

It was their thirty-third anniversary on 12 January 1963. There was a great cold all over the country, deep snow fell at Christmas and lay on the ground for many weeks; Frome Vauchurch was cut off. Extreme weather was usually a pleasure (apart from anxiety for the birds) but many local people now suspected that the snow was radioactive, and felt uneasy. Valentine slipped on the ice and hurt her back badly – she could not be taken to hospital until a fortnight later, when the damage was improving. These cumulative incidents made her feel more physically fragile, more embattled. Snow lasted until Valentine's Day, when a sudden thaw made the river rise alarmingly. Spring followed fast, and Valentine brought Sylvia the first narcissus. ('Shut your eyes. Smell.')[31]

Valentine's health was progressively but inexplicably worse. Her ankles were so swollen that a fellow-sufferer remarked 'I see you've got dropsy too.'[32] She was prescribed Stilboestrol, a synthetic oestrogen about which she had grave doubts (such HRT-type drugs were later implicated in the onset of breast cancer). At length her doctor produced a diagnosis: TB of the pericardium, a serious condition requiring major surgery. Sylvia – perhaps having become accustomed to Valentine's mediocre health – was very shocked at the news, although she knew 'It is what love entails, it is what we accepted so long ago when she gave herself, her own worth then not knowing.'[33] Valentine herself was curiously unruffled, almost relieved that all her immoveable symptoms had coalesced into a recognisable disease.

She closed the shop, and sent out a letter to her customers, carefully phrased 'because', she explained to Sylvia, 'I must avoid being any sex.' (Presumably many of her mail order customers were unaware of her official gender, and she did not want to enlighten them.) 'Valentine Ackland regrets that owing to illness the shop will be closed for about two months; after that time it is hoped to send out a celebratory list.'[34]

A visit to a Harley Street specialist – still Valentine's instinctive reaction – brought a different diagnosis; heart problems, thrombosis and over-active thyroid. She was admitted to the Brompton Hospital for blood-thinning treatment with Warfarin, while Sylvia booked into a hotel. The hospital trauma was re-enacted; Sylvia thought that Valentine looked 'like a wild animal caged in a fairground',[35] and got her moved to a private room. In solitude Valentine began to improve; after ten days she was home. Thyroid and heart pills kept the condition under control, and after a check-up two months later Valentine cabled home 'All perfectly well returning triumphant.'[36]

In July Niou died, and Sylvia was so distressed that Valentine thought 'never, now, would the loss of me be the loss of so complete a love.'[37] (She was wrong.) Sylvia praised her for comforting, providing, carrying Sylvia through. In September they had a 'perfectly happy' holiday in Florence.[38] On their return, they got a new cat, Quiddity, predictably loathed by Kaoru. Valentine was visited by a policeman who inspected her gun-licence and suggested she should give up firearms; her response was to buy a new rifle which had been a 'Severe Temptation'.[39] She celebrated Sylvia's seventieth birthday by shooting rats, and her collection of guns remained undisturbed in the umbrella stand. Whether this police visit was connected with previous MI5 surveillance requests, or merely a local initiative, is unclear.

At Christmas, Valentine and Sylvia sent cards to women political prisoners (in Greece, rather than Russia) and anonymously paid the accounts of hard-pressed neighbours in the village shops, as they did every year. Ruth's death had left Valentine well-off, and she used her inheritance – as Sylvia used hers from Nora, and her increasing income from writing – more often in generosity to friends and neighbours than in purchasing Severe Temptations. Valentine gave Sylvia, as always, a typed booklet of poems written during the year, 'the first one so moving I could not speak of it until the next day.'[40] But 1964 started sadly with the death of Quiddity in the river. Sybil Chase, the neighbour who found him, was to become an important part of their lives; she gardened, sometimes helped in the house and converted to Catholicism with her son Rob, another of Valentine's numerous godchildren.

Sylvia was now deeply absorbed in another major new project: the biography of T H White, author of the bestselling *The Sword in the Stone*. Once she'd accepted the commission, Sylvia plunged into it with her usual total immersion. There were vast quantities of material, some of which was lodged in Dorchester Museum, there were visits to his friends and his Alderney house – and there was Sylvia's tactlessness. Returning from a visit to David Garnett, who was editing White's letters, Sylvia blithely remarked 'It is lovely to collaborate with someone – someone congenial – it is the purest of human pleasures!' As he was a proprietorial ex-lover of Sylvia's, who had trouble in recognising the validity of any subsequent relationships, or lesbian relationships at all, this was an unwise remark. But Valentine merely lamented 'So far have I gone from her habitation'.[41]

Their new cat also had an obsession with White (T H rather than Elizabeth Wade). Valentine wrote in a letter: 'Pericles has developed a habit of chewing up papers. With the house full of priceless mss by T H White our lives are *haggard* and we live in a state of perpetual terror.'[42] One curious thing about the biography, which was published in 1967 to enormous acclaim, is the inescapable parallel portrait of Valentine which haunts its pages. She had much in common with this White – age (he was nine days older), alcoholism, homosexuality, love of fast cars and speed, passionate devotion to birds, animals and their symbolism, delight in shooting and fishing, intense sensitivity to suffering. But significant characteristics were not shared – his paedophilia, sado-masochism, lifelong singleness, bestseller status and, of course, gender – among them.

Sylvia wrote with perceptive compassion about White's shyness, his drinking, his difficulties with writing poetry, his homosexuality, pacifism, fear of blindness, interest in Catholicism, loneliness and so on; acute insights clearly informed by her intimate knowledge of Valentine. She also treated his unpublished work, or self-published poetry, as equal in importance for him, to his unexpected bestseller. Among many examples of this simultaneous delineation of character, these two suffice: 'Skilled killing was a part of White's compartmented character' and 'He turned to [animals] as a renewal and enlargement of his being.'[43] White was perhaps made comprehensible to Sylvia through Valentine, or perhaps their shared complexities irresistibly reminded Sylvia of her.

Having to take White's Catholic leanings seriously perhaps made Sylvia less antagonistic; and a new friend, Peg Manisty, did much to mollify her too. Peg was a great addition to Valentine's life, and was loved by Sylvia also. She was a Catholic, and after seeing a letter from her in *The Tablet* Valentine wrote to her suggesting they might be related. Peg had seen Valentine's poetry in the same place, and replied that they were 'certainly connected'; Valentine's maternal great-grandfather, Sir Henry Manisty, was Peg's great-great uncle. (Valentine saw these Scots forebears who were judges and barristers as book-reading ancestors; once in her Macrory grandmother's house little Molly found a cheque in a drawer, made out to her grandfather from Charles Dickens.)

Valentine – who wrote tens of thousands of letters in the course of her life – gradually adopted this new cousin-several-times-removed as her chief correspondent. Sylvia could bear Peg's religion better because it was impossible to dismiss her intellect; she was a lawyer in the Family Division of the High Court. Over the next few years Sylvia and Valentine often spent Christmas together with Peg in hotels; like Janet, Peg was a great source of youth and cousinly support.

~

In 1965 Valentine was fifty-nine. On the eve of her birthday she reviewed her life and 'unspeakably melancholy state' regarding writing. Thinking about her current DD life, she wrote:

> When I feel a shadowy return of the craving, I wonder whether I lost my only outlet into poetry then? But since then I have written

my best poems, I think – but fewer and fewer – and I lost my power of love-passion then, too. Or was it because of EWW and that appalling catastrophe? Or did poetry leave me when I returned to the Faith? Or – what?[44]

This analysis is accurate about the poetry; Valentine was writing less, but producing some of her best work. The easy access to creativity which alcohol had provided was now lacking, but devoid of drink she had greater authority and control. This paradoxical relationship between art and alcohol – the fuel which fires both pyrotechnics and creative burn-out – was never resolved for Valentine. She drew back from self-destruction, but sacrificed Bacchic inspiration – and missed it.

The idea that the Elizabeth affair had damaged the source of her poetry (rather than enhancing it as expected) was obviously related to the suspicion that Catholicism was not compatible with poetry either. These great outpourings of sexual or spiritual passion had not resulted in a flood of poetry, but had blocked or diverted the source. Valentine was beginning to suspect that her poetic self exercised a separate artistic integrity in responding differently to 'true' or 'false' emotions. The one completely true emotion which never ceased to be a source of poetry was her own sorrow about creative dearth, which was an eternal subject.

The American writer William Maxwell was stunned by the violent imagery and vivid rendering of a poet's dumbness in Valentine's poem 'I remember the story of a poet long ago…' in which the poet is blinded and maimed for some forgotten offence, 'But I remember him now, almost every day, / Stumbling over my silent, lightless way.'[45]

The conclusion Valentine reached on this birthday eve was a courageous though sad one:

> I will not commit the easy blasphemy of the defeated – I will not deny my belief that I had sometimes a power to write poems, and always … ALWAYS have had as my most passionate desire and longing … this 'creative stop' is the cause (as I know quite well) of my illness, of my gradual but to me so obvious decay and loss of powers.

This 'very complete but, as always with me, very unimportant martyrdom'[46] was a mystery to Valentine's friends. Some were completely unaware she was a poet. Others, such as Jean Larson, found her a constructive and encouraging critic of their own poetry, entirely supportive and accepting of their wish to write. But those who tried to encourage Valentine had a difficult task. Bo was too brutal: 'You could write them all out of court! ... I *often* wonder *why* you don't get more published – You could so *easily* if you tried –'. Janet Stone was too inquisitive: 'Do you write things under another NAME? Why don't you write? Because you live with Sylvia? I *do* wonder why – I mean, I know you *have* ...'[47]

Valentine's most important reader, Sylvia, was a staunch and genuine admirer of her work – but Sylvia was often too immersed in her own writing to notice Valentine's. Because of the long ago disaster of *Whether a Dove or Seagull*, Sylvia never helped her to conventional publication, but Valentine feared that friends presumed she did. (In Malcolm Elwin's 1947 miscellany of English writing, *The Pleasure Ground*, Valentine and Sylvia were both included; one of Valentine's poems was called 'After a conversation with Sylvia', which perhaps added to this impression.) Valentine was not envious of Sylvia's talent, or her remarkable powers of concentration; on the contrary, she was immensely proud of Sylvia and facilitated her work. But, by her own admission, Valentine did sometimes envy Sylvia's success, particularly the status her position gave her. When she was writing, Valentine felt she was a poet among a community, but socially she had been made to feel aware of a hierarchy in which she was not even placed. Although some fellow-artists – Edmund Blunden, Ralph Vaughan Williams, even C Day Lewis – managed to treat Valentine in a civilised manner, others – such as William Empson – treated her like a paid companion. Even during the visits of friends like William Maxwell, she was careful not to take centre stage.

Those who knew her well describe Valentine as particularly witty, compassionate and good company. One visitor wrote to Sylvia:

> I loved Valentine. There is something quite amazingly attractive about her, physically and then when she speaks and looks at you.

I felt her spirit almost possessing me, as when I meet someone great. She was so kind …[48]

This was not the immediate impression she gave to some acquaintances. Forbidding, calm to the point of sternness, distantly polite, some people found her positively frightening. But this exterior armour was swiftly shed, and Valentine was held in high regard by a vast cross-section of people. This was important to her, and explains the significance of the Catholic community which seemed so importunate to Sylvia, but convinced Valentine she was needed.

Valentine's anxiety to be of service was exacerbated by her conception of her duties as an Oblate; on the renewal of her vows she reviewed her work-load for an average day. Her examination of conscience found the saying of office and prayers, visiting a church, all 'the Opus Dei part', 'very thin', but in combination with the household chores, looking after the animals, driving out to shop and buy stock, doing the shop letters, parcels and accounts, sorting, restoring and pricing her antiques, there was no time left to pause, let alone write. Although she had eaten 'sparingly', she concluded she'd had too much, smoked excessively and thought about appearance, possessions, money and pleasure too much.[49] No wonder Sylvia was exasperated.

A happier side of the desire to serve was Valentine's loving care for Sylvia, which went far beyond bringing her breakfast in bed or turning her bed down at night. In the first few lines of this simple occasional poem she expresses some of that concern and tenderness: 'Out of the cold, / The winter of growing old, / Come in, my Love, and shelter from the cold.'[50]

Continuing poor health kept Valentine taking a pharmaceutical cocktail including benzedrine, preludin, amytal and valium. When she came off the drugs experimentally, she was amazed by the improvement in wits, memory and mood. Sylvia was also frequently unwell, with recurring bouts of pleurodynia, an unpleasant virus affecting the lungs. Going away was often beneficial to their health, and hopes for their trip to Cornwall in 1966 were particularly high.

Valentine had rented Bosanko Cottage for three weeks as an anniversary present for Sylvia. It was an isolated and beautiful place near Truro, a National Trust property without modernisation which reminded them of Miss Green. They hoped to recapture something of that early bliss; Sylvia had brought her paintbox ready for three weeks of promised leisure; Valentine was secretly hoping for 'the thing which suddenly brings her back to me, as we were at Chaldon, at Frankfort, in Paris'.[51] They lit fires and unpacked and cooked; Sylvia noted with delight that Bosanko already smelled of them: 'coffee, garlic, woodsmoke and Fougère soap'.[52] Valentine revelled in their 'romantic solitude'.[53]

But on the first morning, a face appeared at the window, a ghost from the past; it was Rachel Braden, of that first visit to Chaldon. She was visiting England from Canada; finding that they were away from home she'd taken the train to Truro and booked to stay there for two weeks so she could visit them often. Valentine might have been pleased to see her again, at Frome Vauchurch, but not here. The whole idea of Bosanko was quiet, seclusion, a rediscovery of each other. They were both 'dreadfully daunted'[54] at the disruption to the imagined idyll.

Foreboding became despair. Hard frosts made the house unbearably cold, even for those inured to the rigours of Frome Vauchurch; Valentine and Sylvia decamped to a hotel. They enjoyed the warmth and luxury there, confident that the pipes were being unfrozen. But next day they heard that nothing could be done until the thaw came; there was no option but to leave. Sylvia wept with disappointment as they were packing, then she was frightened when Valentine unintentionally said 'Goodbye' to her as she kissed her. Valentine interpreted this as a farewell to her hopes, for she believed that at Bosanko they had begun to recapture their carefree love. Sylvia knew it was 'the promised broken fulfilment she farewelled', but she remembered it later as 'An omen. For Bosanko was a recall of Miss Green.'[55]

Valentine was sixty in May 1966; the end of 'Middle Age',[56] she thought. She worried about becoming like Ruth, ever more demanding and reproachful, with Sylvia taking over Valentine's old role of 'holding her off' and managing not to show the slightest interest beyond a polite astonishment that anyone could make so much fuss and inflict it on ME.'[57] After the brief mirage of Bosanko, they'd relapsed into the same fretful anxious co-habitation, interspersed with habitual pleasures. Valentine was hurt when Sylvia forgot to tell her about a re-issue of Lolly Willowes, but had intimate discussions with her priest about feeling 'frozen out';[58] exactly the kind of indiscretion Sylvia dreaded.

The enormously high expectations Valentine had of their relationship were never reduced, however much she might lament its disappointments. Although she saw other marriages with little communication or apparent love, continuing from inertia rather than enthusiasm, this was not the standard she could accept. Valentine longed for the kind of loving intimacy she and Sylvia had known early in their relationship; she recalled their life at Chaldon or Frankfort as an era of romantic passion which she hoped to recapture. But sometimes she felt they had lost an essential element of this relationship; not youth, idealism or being 'in love' so much as being able to understand each other – although there were still times when they spoke the same private language.

Valentine's gift for writing which captured the moment, the exact transient mood, often reproduced bad moments particularly vividly, as in 'Night Poem II', with its last couplet encapsulating the inability to communicate even when love is present:

> I am charged so full with grief that no words will come:
> I look at you – love lurches towards my lips – and I am dumb.[59]

But she could do the same with happier emotions, too; 'A not-poem about love, written during a sleepless night' begins ecstatically:

> I kneel at your feet, I kiss your hands, I am your lover.
> I love you more than water, more than I love the swans
> Cruising along the river beside our house;
> More than I loved the summers, the abundant years.[60]

A comparison of the two poems suggests that Valentine's emotional responses remained, as always, extreme.

~

'Hold on. This is not as bad as you think', Sylvia wrote to Janet in June 1966. 'Valentine had a car-crash on Tuesday ... I supposed Valentine was dead.' But it wasn't as bad as that; Sylvia was right. 'It was a head-on collision in a narrow lane' – and Valentine drove fast – but 'she had just slowed for a squirrel', then sounded her horn as she approached a bend. When another car appeared Valentine 'drew into the side to let it pass ... next thing she knew was a violent crash.' At the impact, she flung herself sideways to protect Fougere, and struck her head on the dashboard. Her nose ('her lovely nose') was broken, and her knee, again; she had head injuries which left her face so swollen she could hardly see, and sustained multiple cuts and bruises. The other (female) driver berated Valentine as she lay bleeding in the wreckage, none of the people who encountered the crash gave any practical help, and the ambulance didn't arrive for an hour.

Sylvia, alerted by Valentine's intended host, arrived at Dorchester hospital just as Valentine was brought in, covered in blood. The casualty department surprised them with a brutal and callous attitude which was unexpected. After being ignored for long periods, then eventually X-rayed, Valentine was released from the ordeal and sent home without treatment, 'thus, as she said, escaping death twice in one day.'[61]

In the aftermath of the accident, it was difficult to establish exactly what had happened. Possibly one of the cars skidded in mud; probably Valentine's steering-column broke as she turned the wheel sharply left (the steering-wheel was broken off). The car had just been serviced by a nice but 'hopeless' mechanic, who had already caused serious problems by misfitting a part, so mechanical failure or malfunction may have contributed – although Valentine was fanatical about motor maintenance, returning the car to the garage if it had the slightest rattle or creak, and would probably have noticed anything amiss.

Valentine had no recollection of making an error of judgement or losing control; with her scrupulous honesty she would have readily confessed, like the young motorcyclist who had once ridden into them, 'It was all my fault.'[62] However, she was on a prescription drug cocktail which might well have affected her reactions. Her honesty about being unsure how it had happened was as good as an admission of guilt, since the other people involved were less scrupulous – as well as lacking in the basic humanity to assist an injured person in a crash. But their passenger had been slightly injured too, and they brought a case against Valentine for dangerous driving.

Valentine's pride was hurt, though she was comforted by the flowers and messages sent by their friends and neighbours. As soon as she was able, she drove out, first in a hire car, then in their new car (the old one was a write-off). She wrote calmly and rationally to friends, telling of the accident as a misfortune rather than a calamity, and took the precaution of recording the police interview with her, without their knowledge. At the trial, things went badly. Valentine's defence was a reasonable one that her car had probably skidded, considering the mud on its back wheels. Her lawyer was completely unprepared for the other car's passenger to swear that the dog had caused the accident (no one had mentioned Fou before). The 'total inattention of the two redfaced yokel magistrates'[63] enraged Sylvia, so she was unsurprised by the result. Valentine's licence was endorsed.

It was an ordeal to go into Dorchester again with well-meaning people commiserating about 'what the papers said'. Valentine noticed her reflection in a shop window, walking along as Robert had, 'erect and head slightly to one side and HELD there,'[64] and recognised her father's stance against adversity. Dr Hollis, who respected her stoicism, remarked of the court system, 'You can't win unless you lie.'

'I wish I HAD,' Valentine replied.

'But you couldn't, could you?' he said, with insight.[65]

Valentine did not allow herself to be intimidated by this outcome; she continued to drive often, and fast. She and Sylvia went on a successful driving holiday to Scotland in October. The shock and trauma emerged only once, when Valentine's car was parked in the King's Arms car park and she fell down beside it, repeatedly crying out 'No one helps me.' Sylvia realised that this cry of abandonment emenated from 'the long session of bleeding unattended on the Mappowder lane ... horribly shaken.'[66] But the day after this crisis of nerves, Valentine drove out as usual.

Her main comfort, the church, was changing, withdrawing the absolute continuity which had been its great attraction for her. In the upheavals of Vatican II's reformation, Latin mass was to be withdrawn (and was already becoming difficult to find), the old ritual was reduced, and mystery was replaced by accessibility. This was enormously unpopular and against the wishes of the vast majority of its members, but the church was not a democracy. Valentine had taken vows of obedience, but without the Latin mass she felt spiritually 'homeless', though she struggled to overcome her doubts. One of her greatest difficulties, in common with many co-religionists, was the banality of the new English liturgy, which she found 'unspeakably illiterate and vulgar'.[67] In an attempt to modernise, the ancient ritual had been rendered bland, unpoetic and correspondingly unmagical. This committee-penned compromise of a liturgy was a torment to Valentine; the beginning of the end of her Catholicism.

Sylvia was restored to Valentine by finishing *T H White*, the last of *her* infidelities. Yet Sylvia still lived a double life, simultaneously in everyday existence and constant regret for the lost past. Driving over the remains of Winfrith Heath she remarked 'The smell of the Heath is unchanged, everything else gone ... "Into my heart an air that kills from that far country blows".'[68] When Valentine attempted to recover that land of lost content Sylvia merely replied 'one cannot go back to the lost and gone.'[69] Sometimes, though, they did: in the 'shining glory' of Christmas 1966 at Painswick with Peg, or the following Christmas by the sea in Cornwall when Valentine wrote 'My heart broke within me for love and joy and relief and longing.'[70]

They were also completely united in protesting about the war in Vietnam and the escalating nuclear arms race. Valentine's poem 'Vietnam (or any of the other wars)' is an anti-war poem which parallels 'the rain-bringing wind in summer' with 'the long grieving / Of all hearts, of all souls' in a poignant lament.[71] Another aspect of protest is humorously examined in 'On a Calendar of Anti-War Poems' (a present from Elizabeth) which opens:

> 'Waddyou think of the anti-war pomes?'
> Asked the American, the good American ...
> 'They are very bad poems,' replied the Englishman,
> The good Englishman who felt this impolite and ungrateful ...

But it ends with a chilling reminder of the war dead:

> From the dyed-red ground still parched in spite of the constant
> Spillings of blood upon it, a voice spoke ...
> 'Will you remember?'[72]

'June 17th 1967 China explodes the H-bomb', an angry political poem, traces the 'sin' of nuclear proliferation to the 'desire / to be a little safer than the others', and lays the blame not on armies but 'the men with cheque-books / With interests, with friends behind the scenes, / Men with long sight who see and do not shrink'.[73] Despite their political differences, Valentine and Sylvia were early members of the Campaign for Nuclear Disarmament and Amnesty International – whose letter-writing campaigns appealed to them both.

The year of the anti-war calendar, 1968, was a good one for Valentine poetically, in inverse proportion to everything else. In January old Kaoru died, but Valentine decided not to replace him until her ill-health had been investigated. She again suspected she had breast cancer, as she was suffering severe pain despite taking codeine and valium. Peg bought them a kitten anyway; Titus was an instant success with the resident Pericles. But this could not alleviate Valentine's nervous state, which the doctor believed to be the cause of her pain. She was in misery about the new-fangled church; Sylvia considered her to be as obsessive as she had been over Elizabeth in 1949, when she had experienced similar pain before. Sylvia knew Valentine's propensity for self-torment, and they discussed the possibility that her pain was psychosomatic. Ironically, twelve years ago Sylvia would have been delighted if Valentine had quit the church, but now she hoped she would stay in, otherwise she would be destitute – and it was too late for Sylvia, anyway.

In March, Valentine's doctor referred her to a cancer specialist. She and Sylvia both suspected the worst. Sylvia wrote, about the possibility of survival:

> Of course it can be done – sometimes. But how much depends on the slope of character, I wonder? I would have considerable confidence in myself, with levity to aid me. But her slope has for so long been tending downwards, pressed downwards by one calamity or another.[74]

This analysis is confirmed by Valentine's words to her, after the local consultant did indeed suspect cancer. 'Don't grieve,' she said, lying beside Sylvia in bed. 'I have had a very happy life.'[75]

A London specialist with a reassuring title was booked, but Valentine had to visit him alone, because on the morning of the appointment Sylvia collapsed. Sylvia was appalled ('I totally failed her')[76] but Valentine was effectively distracted from her own troubles. She returned to find Sylvia with a temperature of 103°, only able to discern Valentine through a veil of delirium and hardly to hear her bad news. When she was better, Sylvia marvelled that having cancer did not visibly change Valentine: 'She looked so handsome, so suave ... strange that she should drive as masterly as ever.'[77]

After the usual delays and distressing postponements, Valentine had a partial mastectomy at Guy's Hospital on 10 April. She then stayed at Peg's house in Sussex while she underwent radium treatments. So many sympathisers told her about their own, or their friends', successful mastectomies that she joked 'it seems we are a nation of Amazons.'[78] This solidarity from all sorts of people encouraged Valentine; she was touched to be greeted by an acquaintance in Dorchester 'that trousered woman who loves Fou ... She put her hand on my shoulder and called me her friend and said she was so glad to see me again.' Despite the trouser-wearer's evident poverty she said 'I'm going to stand you a present, mate!' and bought Valentine a punnet of strawberries.[79] Such kindly gestures, both from fellow trouser-wearers and others, confirmed Valentine's lifelong faith in the potential of ordinary people to transform the earth.

By August, she was strong enough to bring Sylvia her supper in bed. And she was writing. 'I have written a little clutch of poems lately,' she told Peg, 'which – if it could go on – would make up for everything, *everything*'.[80] Her poems now had an urgency, a passion, which combined the ease and vigour of her youthful work with a mature, profound voice. 'Poem in the Chinese Manner' extends Valentine's private symbolism of feathers as poems to include other poets as yet unborn, suggesting a kind of eternal life not only in her own poems but in the very fact of poetry's existence:

> Every year for twenty years I have planted young willows:
> The river is never without an admirer as it flows past our house.
> Every year since my tenth in the world I have picked up a
> dropped feather,
> Saying, 'This is a poem to be; it fell from the flying Bird'.
> But the Bird only rarely perches: the willows live only briefly.
> No matter: when I am gone the river will flow, not missing
> admirers,
> And the Bird will let fall single feathers, and sometimes alight.[81]

Chapter Twelve:
How Wild and Strange A Live Man Is

In the great sense of creative inspiration, as well as in smaller matters, Valentine's illness released her into a happier life. Paradoxically, the possibility of death – which she'd always feared so much – brought freedom from many of her other shadows. She could write, with an overwhelmingly urgent reason to do so. Her extreme unhappiness about the Catholic church was modified by an increasing interest in Quaker practice. Best of all, she and Sylvia were again aware of the reality of their love, and restored to celebration of it in the everyday. Despite the pain of recognising the profundity of their bond as they faced possible parting, this outpouring of love brought them unexpected happiness.

By the autumn of 1968, Valentine knew she was not cured. On 19 December she was back in hospital for another operation, this time a full mastectomy. She wrote to Sylvia beforehand 'We are bound, by very love, to be undaunted ... your love has never failed and never will, life or death, hell or high water'. (She also asked Sylvia's forgiveness for 'any excursions in search of my own right way.')[1] Sylvia's reply was a gift, written to assure Valentine of the utter success of her lifelong attempt to love completely, and that all her 'excursions' were forgiven:

> I have never doubted your love, nor my own ... that glorious span of thirty-eight years of love and trust and happiness – care and courage too – will shine on us and protect us. I have always believed in you. Even when you sent me scented shells, I believed in them. You are my faith, I will live and die in it. If I have to live on alone, I will live and die in it ... my heart's thanks for all you have given me, all your understanding, your support, your tenderness, your courage, your trust. And your Beauty, outside and in, and your delightfulness. Never has any woman been so well and truly loved as I.[2]

This was Valentine's absolution, confirmation and redemption in a single document, her 'greatest treasure',[3] as she wrote on the back.

Sylvia stayed at the Goring Hotel over Christmas and New Year, visiting Valentine daily, remaining all day and reading to her, chatting or sitting in silence, holding hands. (She was just seventy-six.) On 10 January 1969 they returned home, in time for their thirty-ninth anniversary. Spring was early, and Valentine was able to pick garden flowers in the mild weather. In February and March, check-ups revealed 'nothing amiss'.[4] Valentine wrote a laconic little rhyme, 'Reflections as I pack to go to London', which encapsulates her style: 'How nice it would be / If I were not me / But someone quite other – / Much less of a bother.'[5]

On these visits to London, they went to the theatre (*Brief Lives*), shopped at Liberty and Aquascutum, had tea at Fortnum's and dinner at Overton's (oysters and champagne). Sylvia noted: 'For an hour or so [at dinner] recaptured our early London', and Valentine wrote: 'we *really were* happy.'[6] Sylvia persuaded Valentine to drink champagne on most days – she was no longer afraid her addiction might return – or take a little Charmes-Chambertin with the grouse.

The Quakers were a great comfort now, assuring Valentine she was held in the light. Their non-hierarchical inclusive practices were radical by comparison to the Catholic tradition and their political affiliations – pacifist and pro-CND – were more congenial to Valentine. They were also the first religious group to discuss homosexuality publicly (other than as a sin) and had recently concluded that there were no good reasons to exclude homosexuals from their community – again, in strong contrast to the official Catholic line. All this appealed to Valentine and – best of all – Sylvia accompanied her to Quaker meeting, spoke at it, and found the ethos agreeable. So at last they were able to unite publicly in spiritual exercise.

The Society of Friends had replaced the Catholic church for Valentine, though she wrote to Peg that she felt herself 'unchangeably Catholic, but with a far wider embrace'.[7] (Another Catholic told me 'Valentine was driven out by the noise. She was a quiet person.')[8] A priest warned her that if she could no longer accept the church's infallibility, she was out of communion with it. Since she neither believed in the doctrine of Infallibility, the Immaculate Conception, the Supremacy of Catholicism, or the Mass as the only real Presence, she was far out indeed. When she had declined to see the chaplain at Guy's Hospital, her loss of faith had suddenly become clear. Her only concern was for her many godchildren and those who had, frankly, converted only because of her; she did not wish to influence them now. But she was one among many who found the post-Vatican II regime intolerable, and quit the Catholic church to become Orthodox, High Anglican, Copt or whatever shade of Christianity they felt best maintained the original faith. Valentine began the process of joining the Quakers officially.

During the summer, Valentine endured increasing pain in her shoulder, which became so bad that she lost consciousness when it was manipulated for X-ray. It was some time before lung cancer was suggested as the probable reason for this. As Valentine told Elizabeth, with grim understatement, 'I'm perhaps in trouble again.'[9] Stilboestrol was again prescribed to try and stop the spread of the cancer, with a battery of other drugs.

In the terse rhyme 'June 1969' Valentine wrote:

> Behind the window of my eyes
> A Someone sits
> And views from there without surprise
> The falling bits
> Of that fine world I did devise
> With my well wits.[10]

Valentine still drove into Dorchester for shopping, and kept her antiques shop going to some extent (aided by Sylvia), but she usually rested in the afternoon and often had supper in bed. With great sensitivity, Sylvia still let Valentine bring breakfast to her in bed and maintain some of her essential jobs in the house, privately realising 'how lost I shall be without her.'[11] Although they talked about Valentine's death neither of them yet accepted it as inevitable. Valentine hoped and prayed for a reprieve and Sylvia, in her desperation, asked Jean Larson to intercede for her at Lourdes, in the hope of any miracle, even a Catholic one.

Her situation gave Valentine her sharpest poet's eye, and she made good use of it. Her *Poems in Pain* are small masterpieces of the English lyric tradition, with the resignation and sadness of a folk tale. 'The Crow' is less of a ballad, more modern in style, and it snatches the suggestion of immortality from an image which is apparently of carrion death:

The crow that for several days has lain dead on the green
                                          haystack-cover
Knew strange resurrection to-day as the June storms began
                                          to gather:
The southerly wind sang in the telephone wires and his shabby
                                black plumage started to quiver,
And as I passed by I saw the bird's wing feathers
Rise for an instant, as if he had learned how to rise, and to live
                                 for ever.[12]

Valentine was now very ill, and deeply disillusioned with her treatment. A medical miracle was not forthcoming on a September visit to London, when Valentine recorded 'very bad report and outlook'.[13] But at another Overton's dinner, Sylvia wrote, 'she looked so handsome and so grandly the host that I forgot the present and was back in our glorious, glorified beginnings – almost.'[14] A week later the specialist wanted Valentine to return to London in order to go into hospital for tests and an overhaul of the drug regime. Valentine refused.

As she pointed out to her friend Dr Hollins, she could no longer reach London, except in an ambulance. The proposed tests would be torture, and it was hardly worthwhile for somebody with her life-expectancy to endure it. To Valentine's amazement, the doctor agreed. When she told him she would prefer to die quickly than continue in her present state, he wept. He agreed to change her medication to palliative drugs, and to help her when the time came – but he wanted to try one new hormone treatment, which could cause great improvement or sudden death. 'Suddenly is good,'[15] Valentine said. To Sylvia, the doctor spoke of Valentine's fortitude, adding that she was an example to all who knew her.

Valentine was now facing the crisis she had always feared, even when she and Sylvia were first in love and she wanted them to kill themselves 'so that we'd get it over because the knowledge of it then was too much to bear.' Now, she found the pain of leaving Sylvia 'immeasurably worse', but she was determined to spare her what she could.[16] Valentine's attacks of 'timor mortis' were kept to herself. Now that the time had actually come, Valentine's courage was, as she intended, exemplary.

To Elizabeth she wrote 'Such a situation has its peculiar nastiness for the victim, but I'm quite aware – too poignantly aware – that it wounds most bitterly those it is not engaged in killing.'[17] Elizabeth saw Valentine once in Dorchester to say a final farewell; Valentine commended her calm and gentle behaviour and asked her to stay away which, to her credit, she did.

Valentine continued to write even when it was physically difficult. She typed letters to close friends in the last months of her life, and she also wrote in her poetry notebooks. The handwriting is shaky and obviously cost the writer, but the poems are still impressive. Some are fragmentary or broken off, and since there was no process of revision or later selection these unfinished poems were not included in *Journey from Winter*. Although they couldn't form part of a critical overview of her finished work, it is relevant to an understanding of Valentine as a poet to realise with what confidence and fluency she was still writing. A poem about the craziness of noise concludes: 'Like the beautiful voice of the sea, this rare coming silence / Has rhythm to ear. To a listener homesick and dying / It sounds of the sea – it sounds of the beautiful sea.'[18]

'Sunt Lumina', written late in September 1969, is a long loosely-structured poem, inspired by Sylvia running upstairs to show Valentine the sun dancing: 'And the spark leaps from his dark words: / And the beautiful things in the world are lights / The love, the love, the *love* we hold in our heart / All loves are one, one love is all loves – sunt lumina.'[19] The last words of poetry Valentine wrote make an uncompleted poem which is, like 'Sunt Lumina', written by the instinctive poet in Valentine, entirely unrevised and written straight down without corrections, under heavy medication. It's a record of her strong poetic vision in the last weeks of her life:

> Absorbed, one thinks of the deep sleep of the stones,
> High on the beach where only the storm tide or spring tide
> Drives spray upon them, they sleep
> In the dun-colour, dull-colour as if they could not waken,
> Ever again and yet they come from the sea
> And the sea owns them – and the sea reaches out to touch –
> Blessed, thrice-blessed sea! Light kindles in pebbles,
> Fire flashes from sea and the ocean[20]

The poem breaks off. 'The stone has its soul too' was a theme Valentine had considered for a long time, with its references to the Quaker concept of inner light in everything. But here it has been absorbed into an image of immortality deep in the poet's psyche, and worked into a metaphor for her own spiritual state, with grace and simplicity.

Valentine's life as a poet had prepared her to die as one too, and her work was a source of immense strength to her – and to Sylvia. The relationship between poetry and death was always hugely influential on Valentine's work, and that of so many other poets, as David Constantine brilliantly interprets:

> The whole achieved poem is a deed of life, in the face, in the teeth of death. Poetics is the devising of strategies, a reflection on the practice of a deed of life against all death in life, against the numerous forms of living death, and against the fact and reality of death itself.[21]

This offers the final key to Valentine's lifelong quest to be a poet, not just as a celebration of her ecstatic response to being alive, or in search of continuance in this world (a future existence in poetry), but as a death-defying act.

In her last poems, she goes beyond the bounds of this enactment, whose determined practice throughout her life in the end freed her to write of her own death with acceptance, to assent to its inevitability and – by completely possessing life – to suggest the mysterious possibility of continuance within that spiritual world which poetry touches.

~

Throughout September and early October, Valentine and Sylvia lived quietly, enjoying the gentle seasonal pleasures of raspberry-picking, drinking coffee in the sunshine, playing with the cats. They went to meeting, and saw friends who gave what help they could. Sylvia noted with approval that Vivenne Graham Green stayed 'an exemplary five minutes',[22] but she was displeased with Bo, who cheeringly patted Valentine on the chest with excruciating but politely-disguised results. Sylvia discouraged emotional visits. She protected Valentine's stoical reserve, her wish to die 'in the high Roman fashion ... in control of the situation and her proud self.'[23] Alone together, they could weep when the swans flew over, and talk about Miss Green: 'its windows still shine, though a bomb destroyed it.'[24] Valentine read aloud to Sylvia. Sylvia wrote poems for Valentine. They talked about the London of their youth, their long lives together, and their belief that death would not separate them perpetually.

To Peg, Valentine wrote 'DON'T count on Christmas';[25] towards the end of October she was so much worse that Sylvia gave up all hope. She wrote to Janet: 'it is so very hard for her to farewell a life she so passionately lived, to hear the swans fly over and see the leaves colour and know it is for the last time.'[26] On 4 November, the Catholic priest came offering extreme unction; Sylvia thought the holy oils might be of comfort, but Valentine refused them. Each wanted to console the other, but Valentine was clearly not willing to make a death-bed return to the faith even with Sylvia's tacit permission. She did not need it now.

The last entry in Valentine's diary (apart from notes on medication) is a joke from Anatole France, one of the 'guides' she and Sylvia had always acknowledged:

> An old marchioness ... was visited during her last sickness by the priest ... who wanted to prepare her to die. 'Is that really necessary?' she asked. 'I see everybody else manage it perfectly well the first time.'[27]

The polite lover Valentine dictated a final note to Elizabeth (but found someone other than Sylvia to write it), ending: 'please do not worry about me; all is well.'[28] The political Valentine was still interested in the anti-Vietnam War speeches from a rally which were broadcast on the radio and 'revived her to the excitement of reality.'[29] Sylvia reminded herself that Valentine had told her of Niou liking to sit by the river because the sound of water made dying easier, and that the same river still flowed beneath the bedroom window.

Sylvia was helped with nursing Valentine by their friend Sybil and another neighbour who was a retired nurse. Dr Hollins was as good as his word, and provided the merciful drugs which removed anxiety as well as pain. Sylvia held Valentine's hand and sat by the bed, reading poetry and reciting their marriage vows during periods of unconsciousness, talking of happy times past when Valentine roused a little. As Valentine approached death Sylvia waited with her, noting 'The stormy morning: the flash of sunrising, the tall rainbow so upright. Breathing like a tree creaking.'[30] Early on 9 November Valentine died. She was sixty-three and, as she'd undoubtedly have recorded in her diary, wearing her red silk pyjamas.

~

Non omnis moriar was the epitaph Valentine had chosen many years before, from Horace's *Odes*, which can be translated as 'I shall not altogether die' or 'Not all of me shall perish', but also carries the sense 'I shall not die to all.' Horace was referring to poetic immortality, which Valentine was no doubt invoking too, as well as the other kinds.

Sylvia laid out Valentine's body herself, comparing her 'tragic calm beauty'[31] to the dead Christ, and grieving over it in a queer pietà. She put rosemary and white cyclamen from the garden into Valentine's folded hands, and ensured that everything was done properly. The morning after Valentine's death Sylvia found a 'strong brown and white flight feather' on the floor beside her writing-chair, and 'knew at once it was from her.'[32] This was the first of many signs and messages which Sylvia connected with Valentine, interpreting them as a means of communication while she herself was still 'in the cellular prison of time.'[33]

Valentine, once so anxious about death, had left instructions about her funeral designed to give Sylvia minimal inconvenience, adding 'none of this is of much importance'. She and Sylvia had originally planned to be buried together at Frome Vauchurch 'in our own place', but since the by-pass scare they worried that 'the ground will be invaded'. So Valentine was cremated – another non-Catholic choice – and her ashes (after spending a few nights in their oak box beside Sylvia) were buried in East Chaldon churchyard, 'that happy place'. This was Valentine's request, provided they could be buried together, but she added 'I do not in the least mind being buried here, or anywhere, without any priest or clergyman attending.'[34] But the vicar of Chaldon obliged, and read the old burial service to Sylvia's satisfaction, with the epistle Valentine had requested, 'For the trumpet shall sound ...' Sylvia put the ashes in the ground herself – 'such good earth' – and laid a

'knot of rosemary and married myrtle on the top.' (For the cremation, Sylvia's flowers from the garden were 'beech boughs, rosemary, lad's love, fern, bay … and a breast knot of thyme.')[35] The plain well-lettered memorial stone carried both their names, Valentine's dates with a space for Sylvia's to be added later, and the all-important epitaph.

Sylvia did not imagine she would survive long without Valentine. She began the task of settling Valentine's will, which was characteristically long, detailed and imaginative, with a carefully-considered list of bequests to her friends, ex-lovers, godchildren, kind neighbours. Jewellery, antiques and books went to those who would value them, religious objects to Catholics, heirlooms to family, gold sovereigns or diamonds to those who were hard up. ('She can sell this: it is valuable … I would LIKE her to have the money.') No one whose life had touched Valentine's was forgotten; there were many bequests such as 'Maureen who is in Clark the Chemists shop: my Voigtlander camera, with thanks for her kindness to me for so many years.'[36] Aside from these small personal gifts, which were subject to her approval, Valentine's estate was left, of course, to Sylvia.

In the emotional agony of her situation Sylvia found comfort (as she always had before) in the source of her pain – Valentine. Their love, and her pride in that love, sheltered her through grief, guilt, retrospective jealousy, desperate pity, all the changing weathers of bereavement. 'I am a part of her she left behind,'[37] Sylvia wrote, and the desire that Valentine's life with her should be properly acknowledged, and they should be remembered together, became the focus of her life.

Sylvia responded to her bereavement as a writer, despite her cry that 'when Valentine died, all the words fell off like leaves after a frost.'[38] She used the power of the word to make Valentine's death into a tragic tale, and to record her own extremity in perceptive detail. The journal of her devastating grief makes painful reading, but this state has rarely been observed and described so accurately.

For Sylvia, the inner landscape which she inhabited with Valentine was more vividly alive than the outer world. She read and re-read their long exchange of letters and poems, and in her mind continued the dialogue with Valentine. Friends came and went, she accepted lifts to meeting, she cleaned and sorted and made parcels, but within she was back in the vulnerable and exciting position of the newly-in-love, all in all to each other.

> The bell rang fiercely. I jumped up to open the front door. It stood open, and Candy was prancing on the doorstep. Half-fainting, I stood on the doorstep and shut my eyes to call in my shattered senses. Then I heard her calling, 'I'm sorry to be back unexpectedly. But I couldn't wait.' It was her voice. And then I was in her embrace, and my arms clasped her, the smooth strength of her body: her actual bodily presence. She had brought the whole of herself back to me, all our years of bodily love and worship. 'With my body I thee worship.'

Sylvia called these visitations in dreams and visions 'The Practice of the Presence of Valentine', paraphrasing the title of a devotional book in which the presence in question is God's.[39]

The obsessional dreaming of Valentine by night and thinking of her by day was enormously important for Sylvia, as continued contact. The visitations she experienced were not only a phenomenon of the immediate aftermath of losing Valentine, they occurred until

Sylvia's death (though less frequently as time went by). In 1972, Sylvia wrote:

> I woke in my sleep and there she was beside me in actuality of being: not remembered, not evoked, not a sense of presence. *Actual.*
>
> I was sitting in the kitchen & she standing beside me, in a cotton shirt and grey trousers, looking down on me, with love, intimately, ordinarily, with her look of tantalising a little, her easy amorous look. She was within touch of my hand. I looked at her, & felt the whole force of my love for her, its amazement, a delighted awe, entrancement, rapture. We were familiar, ourselves to ourselves. I was withheld from speaking. I looked, I gave myself. I loved with my whole being. No words occurred to me. I knew I must not try to touch her and I was wholly an embrace of her. And then without ending it was at an end.[40]

This was not unusual; Sylvia dreamed of Valentine buying her violets, coming to collect her in a taxi, driving them about in a beautiful landscape, holding restored Tamar, coming to find Sylvia or waiting for her at the station. She never recorded dreaming of Valentine ill – her dreams are of physical delight in Valentine's height, looks, strength, warmth – her overwhelming feeling in them is of great joy and safety. Listening to Beethoven in 'the long room which is so much hers, I suddenly felt that if I could sit down beside her that would be all the immortality I would need: to sit down beside her and flow back into her keeping.'[41]

Sylvia's grief went through the inevitable tropes of bereavement. A strong perception of the physical loss of Valentine led her to a poignant compassion for human mortality which produced some tenderly moving private poems, including a 'Lullaby for Valentine'. The remaining relics of Valentine's life were dear to Sylvia by their physical connection; she wrote:

> her corduroy trousers overwhelmed me with a sense of our plighted happiness – how blessed are the shepherds – so soft, so supple, so often washed and worn again – as familiar as a pelt ... I won't send them away. I will be Queen Victoria.[42]

She was proud of Valentine's sartorial style, and wrote appreciatively of 'her *shirts*, their colours: the scarlet silk, the grey and silver brocade, the cobalt blue canvas-cloth, the willow-green silk'.[43]

In her physical dispossession, Sylvia was comforted by Valentine's own staunch beliefs, and she recalled some words she'd heard at Quaker meeting: 'We remember those we loved in their bodies, which we loved, in which they loved us. This is the mystery of the incarnation.'[44] Sylvia attended meeting occasionally for the rest of her life.

A sense of Valentine's life as completed led Sylvia to re-examine it as a whole, and this searching remembrance led to 'agonies of remorse',[45] as well as retrospective joy. It was a kind of sustenance to recall details of their time together, and admire Valentine's virtues: 'she was so brave, so true to life ... it was she who taught me to love truly and honestly.'[46] Sylvia regretted the sadnesses and disappointments of Valentine's life: the loss of Tamar, the neglect of her poetry, her later melancholy, their estrangement over Catholicism. She lamented her own failings, both real and imaginary, and suffered anew the painful times. Of Valentine's miserable affair with Elizabeth, she demanded 'O WHY was I so restrained and undemanding? What mightn't a good YELL have done?'[47]

Sylvia sometimes felt pointless guilt for outliving her lover. She knew Valentine had escaped 'the misery of the survivor' but mourned that she had borne 'the agony, the concern, the hopeless yearning to stay and comfort, of the dying one.'[48] But she expected to die soon herself; she said of a friend who had died nine months after her husband – 'She couldn't have grieved more than I do.'[49] This expectation was an intense relief to Sylvia; she was unafraid of dying because she felt sure she would be 'companioned' by Valentine. But, perhaps partly because Valentine remained so present in her mind, Sylvia survived over eight years more, until 1978. In 1975 she wrote disbelievingly 'How *can* I have survived so long without her?'[50]

(Though in 1976, on Valentine's Day, when she re-read her diary for February 1969 with its account of Valentine's suffering Sylvia thought, fleetingly, 'I am happier now', she quickly dismissed this as 'A false thought.' Yet how could she not be, now that her lover's pain was over?)

Valentine seemed to Sylvia to be profoundly connected still with everything which surrounded her; she wrote: 'All her trees wait for her still ... I feel the sun, the light. They are all hers ... she wears the turning globe.' Everything had its link with Valentine, even the weather: 'A day like my Love, fathomlessly gentle, warm, fostering', and the landscape: 'the curve of the downs was exactly like the curve of her reposing nakedness.'[52] This was a continuation of Valentine's deep sense of connection with nature in her poetry.

The remainder of Sylvia's life was an act of remembrance for Valentine. She lived on at Frome Vauchurch in essentially the same pattern of days; writing was her main occupation, together with the productive pleasures of gardening and cooking, the solace of her cats and the support of books, with the important companionship of friends and correspondents. Her greatest pleasure was to talk of Valentine and hear her praised; new friends and old were told the chronicles of their life together. Sylvia re-read all their letters and poems to one another, and planned to publish the letters, with a linking narrative. She employed a young friend, the Pinney's daughter Susanna ('Soo'), to type the letters, and this project created another major account of their joint life. In 1998, a shorter version edited by Susanna Pinney was published as *I'll Stand by You: The Letters of Sylvia Townsend Warner & Valentine Ackland.*

Sylvia also created other memorials; she was determined that they should be 'remembered together'.[53] Various bequests were made in memory of Valentine, always in their joint names, in perpetuity. A significant number of Craskes went to the Britten-Pears gallery at Aldeburgh, where they are now usually credited as the Sylvia Townsend Warner Collection. Their Spanish Civil War memorabilia – those crucial multiple identity-cards, among other heady reminders of the moment – though given to St Anthony's College, Oxford, in-explicably ended up in the Bodleian, minus dedication, despite the terms of the bequest.

An important collection of Valentine's twentieth century poetry books was left to the Arts Council Poetry Library (now the National Poetry Library, in London's Southbank Centre). Again, this has now lapsed from being titled in their joint names to being known as just the Sylvia Townsend Warner Bequest – rather oddly, as Sylvia was very much alive to oversee the donation. Luckily, as Valentine had stipulated – perhaps foreseeing the short memories of institutions – a bookplate

The Gift of Valentine Ackland & Sylvia Townsend Warner

designed by Reynolds Stone was put inside every book to proclaim it *The Gift of Valentine Ackland & Sylvia Townsend Warner.* (The NPL has redeemed itself in other ways, hosting an exhibition highlighting the bequest as a core of the collection, and other events.)

Most importantly of all, Sylvia ensured that Valentine's papers would be preserved with her own, in the Warner-Ackland Archive – which has now, like the rest of her memorials, reverted to being called after Sylvia alone.

Soon after Valentine's death, Sylvia printed a companion pamphlet to the *Twenty-Eight Poems* which had disappointed her in 1957. *Later Poems of Valentine Ackland* is a short selection but contains some of her best work. (Unfortunately, it also contains a poem which isn't Valentine's at all; 'where the hills make a home hollow', is actually by Mary Casey, née Powys, who – as Sylvia explained – 'was an admirer of [Valentine's] poems, was perhaps influenced by them, which might account for a resemblance of handling which misled me.')[54] It was designed as a memorial volume, with Valentine's dates on the cover.

Then in 1973 *The Nature of the Moment*, a handsome hardback volume of a substantial sixty-two pages with eighty-five poems, was published by Sylvia's old poetry publishers Chatto & Windus. Sylvia selected the poems, after her editor Norah Smallwood proposed the book; Valentine's first mainstream poetry publication since *Whether a Dove or Seagull* thirty-nine years before. It's an assured collection which establishes the author as a poet of strong individuality with a pure lyric voice, passionate yet melancholy. Reviews were respectful, but the book was neither currently fashionable nor of period interest, as yet. Sylvia's pleasure was tinged with bitter regret that it had not appeared within Valentine's lifetime. No doubt the positive but muted reviews would have disappointed her, she would have agonised over whether Chatto were only doing it to please Sylvia, and been freshly amazed over people's indifference to poetry – but it would still have been a significant publication.

The book's biographical note, written by Sylvia, reveals Valentine's gender more than the author's photograph does, and speaks of her 'lyrical disposition' and 'implacable regard for truth'. It concludes: 'she wrote on, faithful to a lifelong ambition to write the kind of poetry which would convey truth and the moment with plain-dealing integrity'. In Sylvia's drafts and notes, there is more vivid detail: 'Extremely observant, open to impressions: driven by the obligation to catch the moment, frame it, set it down, pure. A life of obligation, terror and frustration ... reckless trust.'[55] She wrote a brief, unfinished biography of Valentine, describing her early work as: 'sardonic, impatient, in despair, in desire, in love with life, in dread of death, they are all young poems'.[56] But to Sylvia, the character of their creator never really changed.

Contemplating Sylvia's work and her own, Valentine wrote: 'I think it may be that in Sylvia's work I have sometimes some seed of myself sown.'[57] Her characteristic modest hesitation is contrasted by the equally characteristic dual imagery of growing to harvest or sexual impregnation. Both readings are appropriate to Valentine's role as she saw it. She believed in her sacred trust to nurture Sylvia's genius, to tend that garden in a domestic sense, and be a helpmeet. (This role would often be seen as wifely, but their relationship confounded those who tried to assign them binary male / female roles, perceiving Valentine as the masculine partner. This marriage did not conform to heterosexual expectations.) Valentine had no problem in simultaneously holding a strong belief in her powers of poetic potency, and her ability to fecundate creativity, which here encompasses the fertilization of Sylvia's work. This also reflects her view that insemination is only the first stage in a long process towards the birth of a living creation.

Sylvia's writings confirm this assessment of Valentine's contribution to her work. Living in such close intellectual proximity, it was inevitable that there would be much cross-fertilization of ideas, a shared imaginative landscape, mutual influence in many areas. Certain examples of Valentine's presence in Sylvia's work are illuminating about them both. Often Valentine was a source of story, a literal initiator, and Sylvia wrote in her diary some phrase such as 'Began a short story on what Valentine told me.'[58] Of the Mr Edom antique shop series ('So much a part of living with Valentine, and made her laugh'), Sylvia wrote explicitly, 'Every line of them refers back to her, or was fed by her'.[59] After writing 'The Music at Long Verney', Sylvia realised that it sprang from Valentine, though more obliquely, and wrote, 'My Love, everything I have flows from you.'[60]

Aside from these invisible presences, Valentine also appears as a character; before her death Sylvia often evoked a Valentine-figure in her work. The host in *The Cat's Cradle Book* ('I had never seen a handsomer young man'),[61] who speaks cat, quotes Havelock Ellis and dispenses asparagus, is an easily recognisable portrait. A character actually called Valentine appears in 'My Shirt is in Mexico', the sartorial story with an unusually upbeat ending mentioned in Chapter Six. There are Valentine elements in not immediately-recognisable characters, such as the tall, boxing Sophia Willoughby in *Summer Will Show*. Just as the characteristics of Valentine are sometimes fragmented and partial, so the other references to her are not always in the expected context. Thus in 'A Scent of Roses', the 'incantation of Thurne', a description of Norfolk, is, Sylvia explained, 'a love-poem to my Love.'[62]

These are encoded messages to Valentine, references to their private language, and invocations of her, which increased in intensity after Valentine's death, although Sylvia had always configured her lover in her writing (even in works such as her biography of T H White in which Valentine's presence is uninvited). To write of her after her death gave Sylvia comfort, the sense she described as 'My mind, my consciousness, safe in her arms.'[63] The great series of tales upon which Sylvia then embarked, *Kingdoms of Elfin*, was a tribute to Valentine. These short stories contain countless references to her which any reader familiar with their life cannot fail to notice. Since Sylvia was aware that, with the publication of their letters, her diary, Valentine's memoirs and other personal documents, the key to her code would be, increasingly, in the public domain, it was clearly her intention to share these references with her future readers. Thus much of her work, even that written before Valentine's death, is a kind of time-capsule, the buried references to Valentine ready to emerge in a 'more rational age'.[64] This is surely an example of Sylvia's disruptive humour, as well as a memorial to her transgressive love.

The Five Black Swans, one of the early tales of Elfin, illustrates how the presence of Valentine was conjured. The eponymous swans were special birds in Valentine's iconography; black swans signalled death, and refer to her poem 'Sleep', with its weird lines: 'And by her death I ambushed / Alone the wild black swan.'[65] (These lines haunted Sylvia, and she believed them to refer to her own death.) Valentine herself is evoked in the story as her alter ego Thomas the Rhymer, the poet of legend who could speak only truth, who is seen by Tiphaine, Queen of Elfhame: 'there, lolling on the grass was a handsome man – so handsome that she checked her horse's pace to have a completer look at him'. When they become lovers, 'from then on it was as though she lived to music', and he gives her a yellow snail shell. Tiphaine, although by far the older, outlives her human lover, and the tale is a meditation on Thomas' talents and his tragic mortalness. When Tiphaine eventually dies, many centuries later, her last words are 'Thomas – O Thomas, my love.'[66] (Sylvia's identification with Tiphaine was strangely prescient, for she died on the death-date she gave her character, May Day.) This fairytale version of their particular situation and relationship is rendered into a work of universal application on love, loss, inequalities of various sorts and the longevity of love. The story is merely one example of how Sylvia practised the presence of Valentine, as part of her strategy to keep her lover alive. It was undoubtedly her intention that Valentine's centrality in her work, as well as in her life, would be acknowledged.[67]

Further Poems of Valentine Ackland, another posthumous collection, was published in 1978 by Welmont Publishing, a small press owned by their old comrade Julius Lipton. He believed that Valentine would eventually be honoured 'as the great English poet which she no doubt is',[68] and the book was intended to confirm that assessment. Sylvia's last diary entry, for 8 January 1978, reads 'Poems to Julius', and this reflects her commitment to Valentine's work which continued unabated until the end of her own life.

When Sylvia died, aged eighty-four, she was more than ready to rejoin Valentine; 'And so to where I wait, come gently on' (the last line of William Allingham's poem 'No funeral gloom') is frequently quoted in her diary. She was buried with Valentine at Chaldon, as she desired. William Maxwell, who corresponded with her about Valentine with unfailing tact and compassion, wrote just before Sylvia died to tell her what he thought awaited her, and she would have recognised his reference to the last of Strauss's *Four Last Songs*, 'At Sunset':

> You know I am not religious, but I do have this talent for knowing what is in wrapped packages. If asked to testify in court I would have said that when Valentine drove Emmy and you and me to a high heath so that we could hear the skylarks, no skylarks were heard. But either there or somewhere, I have heard them. Their song coming out of a cloud. In a dazzling brightness that made me squint my eyes. Inside this particular package is just that: a skylark in a cloud, giving directions to another bird, and then suddenly there are two skylarks singing in a dazzling brightness brimming with joy. I think of them continually.[69]

~

In the list of bequests which accompanied Valentine's will, she mentioned her manuscripts separately. 'I do not know about the mass of papers I may leave,' she wrote. 'Poems – if they can be stored away in some place where they won't decay, it may be that one day they will emerge and come to life.' Valentine could envisage this resurrection taking place 'if anyone has time and patience to find them.'[70] Sylvia's creation of their joint archive ensured that this possibility could become reality. The poems and other writings, stored safely away in the archive, have indeed been able to emerge and come to life for researchers with the time and patience to find them.

Of the poems in *Whether a Dove or Seagull*, Valentine wrote to Sylvia in 1934: 'I can imagine someone like me getting them out of the LL [London Library] and reading them – with something – in even 75 years' time.'[71] The readers she imagined in 2009 (and later in the twenty-first century) can indeed feel 'something' when they read the poems of Valentine Ackland, both in that first book and later ones. As it turned out, her work was not forgotten but – as she hoped – re-discovered.

In 2008 a full retrospective of Valentine's work, *Journey from Winter: Selected Poems*, which I edited, was published by the Fyfield

Books imprint of Carcanet Press, one of Britain's largest and most established poetry publishers. As well as several hundred poems, ordered chronologically, it includes critical biographical sections which set Valentine's work in the context of her life. This book introduced Valentine's poetry to new readers, and made many previously unpublished poems available for the first time.

In the same year, the National Poetry Library at the Southbank Centre hosted Liz Mathews' exhibition and artist's residency, *Journey from Winter*, which set Valentine's own poetry and texts from the bequest in a library-wide installation that included the books

24. *Stele* (detail) by Liz Mathews, shown in the National Poetry Library, London.

what shall we do to speak?
guns have deafened us, bombs have made us dumb—
Have they?
Ask the refugees, the starved, the frozen, the weak—
Here they come!

25. A manuscript poem by Valentine, written on the endpaper of a book
   in the National Poetry Library bequest.

themselves. There were exhibition talks by the artist and a *Live Poetry*
celebration of Sylvia and Valentine with Claire Harman and myself.

More recently, in 2015 the V&A's LGBTQ History Month 'Friday Late'
was entitled *Queer and Now*; I discussed Valentine's life, work and
contemporary relevance with curator Dr Amy Mechowski at an over-
subscribed event called *I am a Citizen of these Cities: Bearing Queer
Witness to the 20th Century*.

With the great resurgence of interest in modernism and mid-
century style, literature included, Valentine's writing has taken its place
among her contemporaries as a body of work unlike any other, with
its unique gender-outsider voice, its combination of English lyricism
and revolutionary fervour, ecstasy and despair, spiritual consolation
and erotic power. Many of her political poems and poems of witness
can now be read as within a tradition of Communist or anti-war
or environmental protest poems, but they were new and ground-
breaking in their own time. Her life touched the twentieth century at
key points, and she bore witness to her time with a distinctive voice
and persona, a queer eye. And she is one of those poets who is actively
present in every poem; for 'a bloody little minor poet'[72] Valentine's
voice has an individuality that's all her own.

But although Valentine's work is now the subject of doctoral theses
and appears regularly in studies of twentieth century literature and
poetry anthologies, her gender non-conformism is just as frequently
referenced; she's known as the lover of Sylvia Townsend Warner, or
a cross-dresser whose sartorial style made her 'clearly identifiable as

lesbian',[73] rather than simply as a poet. These were the three great themes in Valentine's life; her love for Sylvia, the expression of her gender-transgressive identity, and her commitment to writing poetry. So there is a certain poetic justice (as well as an irony which Valentine would have appreciated) if her reputation as a poet is sometimes subsumed by stories of her flamboyant life as a lover and gender rebel. Despite her self-identification as a poet above all else, Valentine would never compromise her non-gender-conformist appearance or her primary role as Sylvia's lover. Her work was sometimes sacrificed to these aspects of her life – although they were also, paradoxically, essential elements of her poetic persona.

In 1935 Valentine told her Communist friend (and later, publisher) Julius Lipton that it was 'a thousand times more difficult for a woman poet to get a hearing.'[74] She did not speculate by how many thousands that thousand would need to be multiplied for a woman poet who was also a cross-dressed lesbian. Valentine's extremely visible gender transgressions damaged her career in ways which should not be underestimated. Just because prejudice isn't precisely quantifiable, as Sarah Shulman has observed, it is futile to pretend it doesn't exist.[75] The blacklist in which Valentine half-believed was a reality, in the form of the secret MI5 file marking them both as Communists, but also focusing on Valentine's 'abnormality'. On several occasions (as when a young friend's husband insisted she must stop associating with Valentine and Sylvia) Communism was a useful social euphemism for lesbianism.

As a couple they were, not uniquely but still very unusually, 'out' (in that their relationship was undisguised, and celebrated in print) so to some extent this prejudice applied to them both, of course. Valentine felt that Sylvia never received the recognition her genius deserved, and greeted the critical success of the T H White biography as belated appreciation of her gifts. When Sylvia was at last made a Fellow of the Royal Society of Literature in 1967, they joked that presumably the selection process for this 'first public acknowledgement'[76] was alphabetical.

But there is a curious sense in which Valentine took the blame for the couple's relationship, as though her gender-disruption made *her* the lesbian of the two, but Sylvia not. When Valentine is identified merely as 'Sylvia Townsend Warner's lesbian companion'[77] (by literary diarist Frances Partridge, brought to tea when staying with their friends Janet and Reynolds Stone), there's an implication that the nameless companion is the lesbian, not Sylvia. This fits with the sexist idea that the perceived 'woman' of the couple – the femme in a butch/femme relationship – is asexual, merely the vessel for the desires of others; she could just as easily be with a 'real' man, the choice isn't really hers, her sexuality is passive. (Not a perception easy to reconcile with Sylvia's forceful personality.)

Early on in my researches people regularly assured me that Sylvia 'wasn't a lesbian' or 'just loved Valentine', as though protecting Sylvia from a slur on her character. Though the world has moved on somewhat since then, as Sylvia hoped it might, there's still sometimes a curious reluctance to admit the full extent of her sexuality. Perhaps this is, again, from a wish to protect her reputation? During their own lifetime, Valentine was occasionally treated with disdain (which she usually attributed to other causes, such as her lack of recognition in comparison with Sylvia) – witness Robert Frost's disgust, Stephen Spender's mockery, or her recollection that 'Bill Empson treated me like a paid companion.'[78] Contempt and aversion could be expressed openly, even among bohemians, and anti-lesbian prejudice was widespread. Even now, fifty years after her death, Valentine's gender non-conformism can still be portrayed as grotesque or intrinsically comic, from a heteronormative position of implicit superiority.[79]

Thus Valentine's cross-dressed appearance and her public identity as Sylvia's lesbian lover were real barriers to her acceptance as a writer in her own lifetime. For anyone with doubts about this, it's instructive to re-imagine Valentine's life as the Ackland's only son – however obvious the exercise may seem. After a public school and university education (Harrow and Oxford, perhaps) young Ackland would have trained for a career traditional to the family, the Bar or medicine. His youthful sexual experiences with women would have been seen as healthily normal, and Robert might even have encouraged them. Ruth's religious influence would have been greatly reduced; Joan's bullying given far less scope, if any. This boy wouldn't have needed to marry in order to escape home; he'd have enjoyed a lavish allowance, as well as the means to make his own living in a profession. His early attempts to write poetry would have been taken seriously – probably hailed as genius by the family – and his literary career established through traditional routes, starting at university. He could have fought in Spain, if he chose; all his freedoms and choices would have been infinitely greater throughout his life. Marrying a woman twelve years older might have been unusual, but his infidelity to her – or any wife – would have seemed absolutely standard, not worth remark. None of this was so for an Ackland daughter.

Valentine's private relationship with Sylvia, though it was her greatest source of inspiration, also had its price. As Sylvia's lover, Valentine had undertaken what might be considered a full-time job. Sylvia's capacities were so vast that her friends were always functioning at the top end of their capabilities in order to keep up with her at all, but Valentine did this – emotionally and intellectually, as well as conversationally – on a daily basis. And she had to maintain her own myth, the self-created Valentine she'd imagined and Sylvia had recognised. Although all this relationship was Valentine's privilege and delight, it also brought responsibilities which consumed much time and energy, as she privately admitted:

> I have served her and loved her without ever changing ... I have given her all I had to give ... It would not be true to say that I have *given up* this or that for her ... But it is true that I have often, consciously, made way or not taken or thrown overboard for her sake – and, of course, for my own sake, because I have loved her so much more than anything else, always.[80]

If Valentine contributed to Sylvia's work in important ways, Sylvia's imprint is on Valentine's work too, in mutual cross-fertilization. This may not have helped Valentine's individual career, as their poems were too often compared as though in perpetual competition, rather than read in terms of similarities, contrasts, echoes and patterns of influence – as a conversation, indeed. Confusions about their poems continue, with Valentine's work attributed to Sylvia and vice versa – which is easily done, as Sylvia copied out Valentine's poems into her own notebooks, and prepared them for publication, while Valentine typed most of Sylvia's for her. (And let's not forget that Sylvia herself mis-attributed a poem to Valentine in a posthumous collection.)[81]

During Valentine's lifetime, one woman poet per thousand was more than enough for most people, and Sylvia's existing reputation had already used up their household quota. It's a sad paradox, that with all Sylvia's belief in Valentine's poetry and attempts to encourage her writing, it was partly Sylvia's success that made it difficult for Valentine's work to be 'read on its own merits'.[82] Also entirely contrary to Sylvia's intentions, after the publication of *Whether a Dove or Seagull* (and the ensuing 'for Ackland see Warner' debacle) Valentine lost confidence. And their decision to live in country seclusion, although it brought them many pleasures and enhanced their privacy, inevitably isolated them from the London literary life which would have brought them both more exposure. Both often expressed homesickness for 'Darling London'[83] and Valentine used to worry that Sylvia missed this world (though she wasn't exactly short of literary contacts, with an address-book running from Louis Aragon to Leonard Woolf). But their self-sufficiency was particularly injurious to Valentine's career, as she had no agent, regular publisher, or group of associated poets.

Some of these circumstances obviously contributed to Valentine's limited recognition as a poet in her lifetime – but so of course did the lack of the elusive but essential luck every writer needs. In a mysterious parallel to that lack was the damage to her own psyche, the aftermath of abuse and childhood trauma which resulted in depression and alcoholism. Extremes of despair and ecstasy may have powered Valentine's creativity, but they also led to her dependence on alcohol and other addictions as emotional props. Considering all these disadvantages, as well as those paradoxically conferred by Valentine's status as Sylvia's lover and a trouser-wearing lesbian, her life's determination to be a poet begins to seem almost crazily heroic.

Yet Valentine's dogged, habitual attempts to work created another problem: the dissipation of her writing energies in unfinished prose projects, multiple memoirs, daily diaries, and incessant letter-writing. But this apparently unproductive effort was not, after all, wasted; the autobiographical prose writing – mythomanic, guilt-ridden, self-deceptive, scaldingly honest – tells so much about Valentine and Sylvia's lives; not only the outward events, but the 'thinking; this sitting in a chair day in, day out, with a cigarette and a sheet of paper and a pen and an ink pot.'[84]

The evidence of her writing is sometimes conflicting, but in Valentine's last instructions regarding her manuscripts she made a special note about her diaries – that although they could be kept, Sylvia should not read them, 'because I had a habit of writing to relieve my own tensions, and they are misleading. They *are* misleading, for my life with Sylvia has been wholly blessed and intensely, profoundly happy and rich: no one has had a more blessed life than I.'[85] Looking back, Valentine claimed that expressing the pain of her troubled psyche was merely a bad habit, not a glimpse of a sadder self; that the lover who experienced ecstatic joy was her true identity. This was the story she wanted to tell, at the end – and there is no reason to believe that it's less accurate than any of the other versions.

And Valentine expected these life-writings to be read, later – if not by Sylvia, by others. Sylvia ensured that these many narratives of Valentine's inner life, with all their contradictions and alternative interpretations, would survive, to give readers the illusion of meeting a complex, mercurial human being. Reflecting in her diary about their love-letters being read (when the letters were being typed for eventual publication) Sylvia wrote: 'Strange to think of Valentine now real [to the reader] ... an intimate, without intermediacy of acquaintance. It pleases me, so.'[86]

~

Here, the late Valentine interjects a final disruptive word, reminding us that nobody is neatly categorisable as they may seem after death; that we can best understand each other's strangeness by knowing our own.

When you look at me, after I have died,
And note the tidy hair, the sleeping head,
Closed eyes and quiet hands – Do not decide
Too readily that I was so. Instead,
Look at your own heart while you may, and see
How wild and strange a live man is, and so remember me.[87]

A Personal Note:
The Quest for Valentine

A J A Symons, the first modern biographer (author of *The Quest for Corvo*) wrote at the end of his remarkable book: 'every one of the works which had been left and lost in obscurity ... had been collected together by sympathetic hands and ... alone of all living men, I had read every line of every one.'[1] Although I couldn't possibly make the same grandiose claim about Valentine, it did sometimes feel like that; as though I (whatever my gender) was researching a very obscure, self-destructive queer writer most of whose work nobody else had ever read.

When I began to research Valentine and Sylvia during the late 1990s, I was in my thirties; some years earlier my mother had asked me if I knew about them, but I didn't, really. I'd tried one of Sylvia's novels at school – possibly *Mr Fortune's Maggot* – when I was too young for it, and never gone back. I didn't realise Valentine was a writer, too, and I didn't appreciate that my mother thought I'd be interested in Valentine as a fellow gender transgressor. But after my mother's death in 1998 I found her white-creased green-spined Virago copy of Sylvia's *Diary*, and I remembered what she'd said.

I read the book on holiday and afterwards it stayed in my mind as vividly as swimming in the Atlantic. I wept reading it on the beach, I read long sections of it aloud to Liz, I turned the corner down on almost every page. It was by then some years since Claire Harman's award-winning biography of Sylvia Townsend Warner had been published, which I read with fascination as soon as we got home (she also edited Sylvia's *Diary* and *Poems*, of course). Like so many others who have discovered Valentine and Sylvia's life and work, it soon became hard to imagine the time before I knew about them. When I was commissioned to write a series on lesbian writers and artists for *Diva* magazine, Valentine and Sylvia were obvious candidates for one of the articles.

I visited the archive in the Dorchester Museum to find photographs for the magazine, curator Dr Morine Krisdottir kindly showed me round, and I realised the unusual nature of the collection, the fascination of the material. It was moving and exciting to touch the actual manuscripts and diaries, to decipher the handwriting which I'd later read so easily, to feel that the writers were not so very long ago or far away after all. The idea of writing properly about Valentine was irresistible. I was lucky enough to interest a publisher in the proposal, and was commissioned to write the first biography of Valentine.

My luck continued. Susanna Pinney, then the Literary Executor of the Estate, interviewed me and (despite the fact that I hadn't written a full-length biography before) decided that I could do the job. She most helpfully gave me the necessary permissions, authorised the biography, and gave me open access to the archive, even allowing me to take some of the contents away to study at home.

Every Sunday afternoon, Liz and I would drive from London to Dorchester in our rusty, trusty Citroën 2CV, through the New Forest and along that familiar clogged westward road. To begin with, we stayed at the King's Arms, which was apparently unchanged since Valentine and Sylvia's day, sacred ground but now slightly seedy. (This was before the days of internet sites for cheap stays.) Then we discovered a small boutique hotel on the High Street, Westwood House, which was really too expensive for us but on Sunday nights had special offers, and would upgrade guests to the best available room. The rooms were all named after Dorset villages, so we paid for Mappowder, the small basement at the front, and were usually given Plush, which was the lavish bridal suite. ('You wouldn't believe how people shag in this hotel!' Sylvia, the nice owner, once remarked to us, rather meaningfully. We told her it was even worse at the King's Arms.)

She was from Maiden Newton, and knew all about Valentine and Sylvia, after whom she was named. She had the gossip from their cleaner and other villagers, among whom they were still remembered with amazement, and also the rumours from her Ladies' Bridge Club, which were lurid but inaccurate. But this helped me to understand why some women flatly refused to speak to me about Valentine and Sylvia, or claimed to have hardly known them at all, never been to their house, or have complete amnesia about them.

All day on Monday, we worked in the museum. I researched in the Archive, Liz helped me and also volunteered in the scheme to create a digital catalogue, and other museum backstage projects like moving the Hardy archive. We often had lunch in a pub with some of our co-workers, or picnicked in a flowery graveyard when the weather was fine. Then on Monday evening we drove back to London, ready to open our contemporary ceramics gallery-shop on Tuesday morning, where I managed the gallery while Liz worked in the studio as a potter. In between visitors, I worked on the material we'd gathered in Dorchester.

There was also much visiting of important places to be done; we drank scrumpy at *The Sailor's Return* in Chaldon, swam in the sea at Burton Bradstock, rode the varnished grey fairground horses on a deserted Weymouth sea front, tramped Chesil Beach and Maiden Castle, looked across the river at Frome Vauchurch and saw two garden chairs set by the water, empty, as though their owners had just stepped into the long sun parlour for a moment. There was a trip

26. The garden at Frome Vauchurch.

to the offices of the *Dorset Echo*, in a surreal industrial park, where the enormous archive volumes smelling of mildew were brought out with great ceremony on trolleys like the British Library's. And there was the frightful January stay at Chydyok, kindly loaned by Janet Machen, who allowed favoured people to stay there, but only went herself in summer.

I remember meeting Janet for the first time at the King's Arms in Dorchester; she was immediately friendly in a fierce and astute way which I associated with her cousin Sylvia. She asked me at once if I was 'on Valentine's side' and, as I said yes, added 'but I can see you are!' This didn't mean she wanted a hagiography; she was sometimes intensely critical of both Valentine and Sylvia, but at the same time loyal within that code of truth-telling which again I recognised from Sylvia's letters. She wrote to me: 'there is a great deal of ground, isn't there that you have to cover and slowly this elusive beautiful person will take shape.'[2] Janet was old, then, so old that when she showed me photographs of herself in the 1930s she would say 'That's me' pointing at the robust young woman in the past, before telling some eye-popping anecdote. Of the photograph of herself sitting beside Valentine on the door steps, she said 'Valentine looks so innocent, doesn't she, but all the time she was lightly stroking the inside of my arm – like this – with the very tips of her fingers.' I've never looked at a photo of Valentine in quite the same way since.

Janet's eyesight was no longer good, but she still drove a very muddy white car with great determination. We once saw her whisk through the narrow carriage archway into the King's Arms car park like a Georgian coachman driving to an inch, or perhaps like Valentine – who taught her to drive – speeding through hazards with aplomb.

Over the course of several years, Janet helped enormously by talking freely and sensitively of these two women she'd known so intimately and so long. She also gave me Valentine's poetry books, letters and mementoes, always with a purpose. In her house, the beautiful barn conversion at Margaret Marsh, she showed us some of the jewellery Valentine had given to Elizabeth, which Elizabeth had in turn given to her, including a gold ring inlaid with deep blue enamel round the raised gold letters AMOR VINCIT OMNIA, and their names engraved on the

27. Janet Machen with Valentine in Chaldon.

inside. It was a particularly Sylvia touch, I thought, for Janet to then go off in the car to collect a friend from the station, leaving us to put everything away, lock up and be gone before she got back.

When Valentine's selected poems were published in my edition, Janet sent me a thank you card (of Chydyok) with Valentine's lighter – a characteristically elaborate chrome and leather device also containing a kind of portable ashtray, which seemed a suitable reward, though not as great as Janet's slightly unnerving earlier remark 'They'd have liked you. Oh, yes, they'd have liked *you* all right'.

Peg Manisty I met only once, helpfully introduced by Susanna Pinney. Soo, Liz and I drove down to Sussex together, to the Catholic residential home in a beautiful country house where Peg lived in her old age. It was an only partially-successful visit, as it took a long time to get there in the vintage 2CV, and when we arrived Peg – though she looked elegant – was vague, not absolutely confused but extremely absent-minded in a *grande dame* manner. I put my recording-machine away. But then, when we were just chatting rather than interviewing, she began to talk about the way Valentine always dressed like a man, remembering her vividly, talking about her love of motorcars. I was touched when, more than once, she called me 'dear boy' and inexplicably but charmingly said, as we parted, 'You'll win all the prizes.'

Marianna Clark, wife of Stephen, Valentine and Sylvia's dear friend, was also a delight to interview (and not at all vague). When I telephoned her to ask about her memories of their long friendship, she took the occasion very seriously and answered all my questions with formal care. Then conversation and her reciprocal curiosity got the better of us, and hours later we were still asking each other what we thought about God, ghosts, childhood experiences ... one of the pleasures of the task. I'd been introduced to her by Roger Peers, the retired curator of Dorchester Museum, who knew everyone and helped me to contact them, as well as showing me his books from the library at Frome Vauchurch. Many other people – far too many to write about here – helped. Very few hindered. I was amazed by the number of people who entrusted me with memorabilia, gave me signed books, issued introductions, tips, asides, directions, recipes, warnings, wishes.

Jean Larson generously gave me her copy of Valentine's *Twenty-Eight Poems*, with Sylvia's dedication, lent me her many letters from Valentine and Sylvia from the 1950s and '60s (mostly about the antiques shop, as she used to go to auctions and sales for Valentine), and later gave me Valentine's letters – all now in the archive. Jean often talked about Valentine and Sylvia's support for her when she was in need of friends but on one visit, after particularly reminiscing about the fun they'd all had together, she suddenly cried 'I wish those days were come again!'

As I write now, it's over twenty years since as a young writer I first began to find out about Valentine Ackland. My subject (if I can call Valentine something so prosaic) has inevitably become part of my life, as her poems can become part of all her readers' lives, if they so choose. Like many writers who research a subject over an extended time, I have sometimes felt resistant to over-identification with the one topic, like an unwilling portrait-painter eternally condemned to revise the same likeness, for their sins. (And, as Sybille Bedford reminds us, 'a biographer is an artist under oath'.)[3] But in fact, I've been lucky that my other writing – of fiction, plays and poetry – has co-existed with this long-gestated biography; my work has benefited in so many different ways – with unexpected opportunities and travels and meetings and picnics interrupted by dogs who were over-excited because 'they'm just been to church to have their pictures took' – none of which would have happened without the quest for Valentine.

When the original biography was due for delivery, the publisher had folded, unable to honour their contracts, so their forthcoming titles never did come out. Instead, I wrote on Valentine for Carcanet Press in *Journey from Winter*, and for *The Guardian* on her centenary in 2006, for various magazines and academic journals, Edwin Mellen Press's *Critical Essays on Sylvia Townsend Warner* and so on. And I talked about her life and work a great deal too, on BBC radio (*Woman's Hour* and *From the Ban to the Booker*), in the Southbank Centre's *Literature and Spoken Word Programme* at the National Poetry Library, in libraries and at book festivals, at gay literary salons, and club nights. Many of these occasions were made memorable for me by the enthusiasm of the audience, often young gay people hearing about Valentine for the first time. BBC Radio 4 commissioned me to write a play, *Comrade Ackland and I*, which – like Sylvia's riffs on fragments of history – iconoclastically imagines the possibility that she could have used witchcraft to stop Valentine driving to Spain. And in 2020 The Society of Authors awarded me an Authors' Foundation grant for this biography. Research is never wasted, as they say.

(This is my retrospective version, of course. At the time, I was bereft to lose the book whose arrival was so imminent, taken by surprise, shocked, baulked, angry. Very few people understood the cost of writing such a biography – in time, commitment, intellectual investment, emotional energy, imaginative endeavour, physical labour, not to mention financial outlay. I felt unequal to explaining, and for a while I didn't talk about it. My disappointment, if such a setback can be contained in the word, was complicated by a kind of awkward sympathy for Valentine, invisibled again, together with illogical guilt and personal chagrin over my lost opportunity to celebrate gender transgression. It was a long time before I could face the prospect of engaging with it all again.)

Many lives were interconnected with Valentine's while she lived, and there are people alive now who still remember her with fondness, gratitude, dislike or fury. But also many of the people who told me about Valentine are now dead, and her life doesn't seem relatively close anymore, but from a distant era. The world has changed radically in a few decades, from one similar to that Valentine and Sylvia inhabited to a sometimes almost unrecognisable place, with the explosion of technology and AI, the floods and fires of climate crisis, the growth of political extremism and nationalism, the financial disasters of late capitalism, the spread of pandemics and the accelerated destruction of the natural world.

In Dorchester, then, there were places still much as they had been when Valentine and Sylvia shopped there; in the Judge Jefferies tea room, as Liz observed, they clearly hadn't changed the solid oak loo-seats since the war, creating a literary heritage experience of a whole new kind. I bought a classic pair of driving-gloves in the leather and basket shop that had been there forever, and a hat in the gentleman's outfitters on the High Street where Sylvia bought clothes for Valentine (if she hadn't sent to London for them). Staying in the town a feeling of familiarity – entirely spurious, but real – and of moving in a different time, inevitably developed. Although that was in the twenty-first century, just, Dorchester now seems to have caught up with this new millennium. Proper coffee, cool places to eat, unwelcome chain stores; a different ethos.

It is in the countryside, the English landscape, that it's still most possible to experience a sense of being in the same place as these writers, and in some inexplicable way step out of time for a moment. Despite all the changes, the incessant new road-building and house-developing, and the appalling impoverishments of climate change, by the coast or on the downs we can still glimpse a view very like the one Valentine and Sylvia saw. May blossom, sun on water, the Pleiades in the night sky or the rain on the leaves – are there in the poems, and still there in the world. When Valentine wrote about them she was claiming a kind of immortality in nature, aside from that in memory and poetry. But as her century recedes further into the past, connections are most often

28. 'A view very like the one that Valentine and Sylvia saw' – on the
    Dorset coast.

made through her poetry. Now she has become one of 'the poets', that great company it was always her ambition to join, we readers of today know her – as she did her 'friends and protectors' – through her own words.

To return to Symons, his finale continued: 'Nothing was left to be discovered: the Quest was ended …' which no biographer in their senses would claim now. Much is surely left to be discovered, re-interpreted, and re-discovered. But, for me, I hope the quest is ended, if not the connection. He concluded his 'experiment in biography' with the words 'Hail, strange tormented spirit, in whatever hell or heaven has been allotted for your ever-lasting rest!'[4]

Valentine, true to her great obsession with these matters, imagined where her own ghost would walk, and (while resisting any Symons-like temptation to address the biographee directly) in the same realm of fantasy I allow myself to imagine the two lovers, still strolling together in spirit through the landscapes which were most precious to them:

> … when I am dead for sure my ghost will haunt there [Frankfort] loving and grieving – there, and along the Drove at Chaldon, where my love stood beside the thorn tree and vowed her troth to me. Because of that vow and because of our life together, I do not think that she will leave me alone, even when I am a ghost; and if she will walk with me, we will be happy – as we always have been, even in despair, together.[5]

Acknowledgements

The Society of Authors awarded me an Authors' Foundation Grant towards the research and writing costs of this biography for which I am most grateful.

I am also very grateful to the current Literary Executor of the Valentine Ackland and Sylvia Townsend Warner Literary Estate, Tanya Stobbs – and her predecessor Susanna Pinney – for their kind permissions to quote from the works, and for their support and encouragement of this book. The Elizabeth Wade White Papers in the New York Public Library are quoted by kind permission of Peter H Judd, who most helpfully sent me scanned copies of the originals during the Covid-19 crisis when it wasn't possible to travel to see them, thus enabling me to work from the virtual documents themselves; copyright acknowledgement for this is also due to the New York Public Library. MI5 files from the National Archive are quoted with the necessary acknowledgement that this work contains public sector information licensed under the Open Government Licence v3.0.

I'd like to thank everyone who has lent or given me books and other Valentiniana; so many people have contributed in various ways, over a long time.

At the start, Dr Clare Rowntree helped me to understand the (characteristically extensive) VA medical evidence, Ray Russell of Tartarus Press alerted me to a missing provenance, Dr Julianne Lambert at the Bodleian Library excavated hard-to-find documents and Anna Greening, Archivist of Queen's College, Harley Street, provided Valentine's school record. Dr Morine Krisdottir was the knowledgeable Curator of the Warner/Ackland Archive when I was working there. Sylv and Tone (then) of Westwood House Hotel in Dorchester were generous with their hospitality, like many others in Dorset. And special thanks to these people who spent substantial time talking to me about Valentine and Sylvia, now sadly all 'the late' – Janet Machen Pollock, Jean Larson, Margaret (Peg) Manisty, Roger Peers, Marianna Clark. I owe Claire Harman thanks for her interest in this book and of course for all her pioneering work on STW. I've also enjoyed interesting Ackland talks with Ailsa Granne, one of the first generation of scholars to study Ackland and Warner since *Journey from Winter* was published, who so generously acknowledged it in her PhD thesis, (which I'm delighted is to be published as a scholarly monograph by Routledge).

Special thanks to my wonderful agent, Ann Evans at Jonathan Clowes, and to other generous encouragers of my work: Nikki and Charlotte Diamond; Maureen Duffy; the Davids (Hass and Mitchell); Maggie Ford, Jeremy Hooker; Mimi Khalvati; Julie Lydall and Elin Høyland; Flora MacDonald; Dan Mathews; Joyce Mitchell (O Shenandoah); Jane, Pip and Clare Rowntree; Mary Stewart; Katie Webb; among so many other friends and family, especially my first supporters – my grandmother, Muriel Worsdell, and my mother, Caroline Bingham.

And most of all to Liz Mathews: I'd dedicate the book to her, with love and thanks, but she's too much a part of it, a contributor and enabler in life and art, without whose strength and enthusiasm this book wouldn't be here and neither would I.

Picture Credits

Author's collection: 1, 7, 21
EWW papers: 14, 27
Liz Mathews: 2, 3, 17, 19, 22, 23, 24, 25, 26, 28
STW/VA Archive: 4, 5, 6, 8, 9, 10, 11, 12, 13, 15, 16, 18, 20.

Notes

All references to Valentine Ackland (VA) and Sylvia Townsend Warner (STW)'s diaries, papers, memoirs, typescripts, shopping lists and letters to one another are from the original documents in the Warner-Ackland Archive, now in the Dorset History Centre, Dorchester, unless otherwise stated. I've used dates to identify them. I've included page references for VA's poems in *Journey from Winter*, but not for her only published memoir *For Sylvia*, as I worked from the typescript version in the archive, which has slight variants from the edited printed book. The same applies to STW's linking Narratives for the letters published in *I'll Stand by You*; I have included page numbers for the start of each Narrative in the book for the reader's convenience, but there will be minor variants from the printed versions ('mere' for 'more', and so on).

~

MI5 NA refers to declassified MI5 documents in the National Archives, Catalogue ref: KV/2/2337, 2338.

Bodleian refers to STW and VA's Spanish Civil War Papers, John Johnson Collection, Bodleian Library, Oxford: two box files of loose papers and memorabilia including newspaper cuttings, leaflets, photos and identity cards and passes, which were uncatalogued when I found them.

EWW Papers refers to the Elizabeth Wade White Papers in the New York Public Library. Peter Haring Judd kindly gave me access to electronic versions of the originals when it wasn't possible to travel to New York in 2020, so in most cases I was able to work from these rather than his transcriptions in *The Akeing Heart*, where some of them are published with slight variants. I should also explain that some of the most important letters exchanged between Elizabeth (EWW) and VA were copied and kept in VA's diaries, which enabled me to include excerpts from them in *Journey from Winter* before the EWW Papers were available; see introduction to *News of the North*. A box of memorabilia and documents relating to them both, which was given to Janet Machen by EWW, and then to me, also contains copies of some letters.

EoL – Michael Steinman (ed), *The Element of Lavishness: Letters of Sylvia Townsend Warner & William Maxwell* (Washington DC: Counterpoint, 2001).

ISBY – Susanna Pinney (ed), *I'll Stand by You: The Letters of Sylvia Townsend Warner & Valentine Ackland* (London: Pimlico, 1998).

JfW – Frances Bingham (ed), *Journey from Winter: Selected Poems of Valentine Ackland* (Manchester: Carcanet, 2008).

Letters – William Maxwell (ed), *Sylvia Townsend Warner Letters* (London: Chatto & Windus, 1982).

NM – Valentine Ackland, *The Nature of the Moment* (London: Chatto & Windus, 1973).

STW Poems – Claire Harman (ed), *Sylvia Townsend Warner: New Collected Poems* (Manchester: Carcanet, 2008).

TAH – Peter Haring Judd, *The Akeing Heart: Letters between Sylvia Townsend Warner, Valentine Ackland & Elizabeth Wade White* (Reading: Handheld Press, 2018).

TNP – Wendy Mulford, *This Narrow Place. Sylvia Townsend Warner and Valentine Ackland: Life, Letters and Politics, 1930–1951* (London: Pandora Press, 1988).

See the Select Bibliography, after the Notes, for details of relevant books.

~

Introduction: It Is Urgent You Understand

1. *'Of course'* – VA diary, 19 March 1966.
2. 'life ...' – Virginia Woolf, *Orlando* (London: The Hogarth Press, 1928), p240.
3. 'It is growing dusk' – VA diary, 29 November 1953.
4. 'written at about' – VA ms note on typescript of poem, 'Accept the cold content', August 1949. *The Sea Change* was an opera libretto STW wrote for Paul Nordoff, at an unhappy time.
5. 'Reading my own works' – VA poem, 1941, *JfW* p132.

Chapter 1: Becoming Valentine

1. 'unheard-of then' – VA memoir *1924–25*.
2. 'It was an extraordinary place' – VA memoir *For Sylvia*.
3. 'like a tiger' – ibid.
4. 'steadfastly' to 'that comes' – ibid.
5. 'nice, normal people' – ibid.
6. 'Will you please' – ibid.
7. 'Married Dick' – VA diary, 9 July 1925.
8. 'It comes off' – VA memoir *1924–25*.
9. 'I suppose I do' to 'any other situation' – VA memoir *For Sylvia*.
10. 'What is all this' / rest of dialogue – VA memoir *For Sylvia*; *1924–25*.
11. 'O Shenandoah' – VA memoir *1924–25* (from the American folksong).
12. 'I haven't kissed' – ibid.
13. 'a mixture of cringe' – STW diary, 14 March 1932.
14. 'She told me' – VA memoir *For Sylvia*.
15. 'I will' – ibid.
16. 'Why CAN'T' – VA letter to Peg Manisty, nd, c 1967.
17. 'My husband' – VA memoir *For Sylvia*.
18. 'There' – ibid.
19. 'I'm fainting' – ibid.
20. 'the ordinary' – ibid.
21. 'possibly' – ibid.
22. 'a privately-adventurous' – VA memoir *1940*.
23. 'My mind' – VA memoir *For Sylvia*.
24. 'We did not' – ibid.
25. 'I did not understand' – VA diary, 2 November 1958.
26. 'under a haystack' – VA memoir *For Sylvia*.
27. 'commonplace cause' to 'beloved' – VA diary, 2 November 1958.
28. 'nervous injury' – VA memoir *For Sylvia*.
29. 'I fought' – VA memoir *1924–25*.
30. 'sickened' – VA memoir *For Sylvia*.
31. 'every chance' – ibid.
32. 'Physically revolted' – ibid.
33. 'moult away' – ibid.
34. 'embarked together' – ibid.
35. 'We made a list' – ibid.
36. 'Let who will' – VA rhyme for Valentine's Day 1935.
37. 'Why don't more people' – VA letter to Peg Manisty, nd, c 1966.

38. 'deeply / Bo is a' – VA diary, 5 January 1925.

39. 'She looks like an angel' – VA memoir *1924–25*.

40. 'slowly and so' – ibid.

41. 'Well' – ibid.

42. 'considerate' – VA memoir *For Sylvia*.

43. 'Bo made love' – VA memoir *1924–25*.

44. 'dedicated' – ibid.

45. 'I am/ I WILL' – ibid.

46. 'My beautiful / Let a gale' – ibid.

47. 'Spain' – VA diary, 28 May 1925.

48. 'light love' – VA diary, 10 December 1946

49. 'I was naturally' – VA memoir *For Sylvia*.

50. 'walked' – from VA poem 'Who walked around Mecklenburgh Square', 2 October 1940.

51. 'All right / Never' – VA memoir *For Sylvia*.

52. 'told him' – VA letter to STW, 12 October 1957.

53. 'the strange ambiguity' – STW diary, 3 January 1931 Although in *TAH* this miscarriage is referred to as an 'abortion' (p30), there is no evidence to suggest it was an intentional termination of pregnancy. Valentine's diary at the time and later recollections all refer to it as an accident, and it seems unlikely that her searingly honest autobiographical writing would suppress the fact if she'd undergone a then-illegal operation.

54. 'stately and happy' – STW diary, 18 January 1970.

55. 'Breakfast' – STW diary, 13 January 1931.

Chapter 2: An Essential Part Of Me

1. 'Come to tea' – VA poem 'They said to me "Come to tea and meet a poet ..."', 2 March 1966.

2. 'Is this your eldest' – STW diary, 20 February 1928.

3. 'almost all the strokes' – STW diary, 30 December 1930.

4. 'that amiable' – STW diary, 4 April 1954.

5. 'rude' – STW diary, 11 October 1930.

6. 'And I' – VA poem 'Space is invisible waves', *JfW* p67.

7. 'viola' – STW diary, 11 August 1939.

8. 'eager / sit to' – VA diary, 18 July 1928 (referring to Frau Reiss, later the photographer of Marlene Dietrich).

9. 'monstrously expensive' – VA diary, 13 June 1928.

10. 'An erudite' – VA poem series *Limerick Diary* 1928.

11. 'Nancy Cunard' – ibid.

12. 'Tonight' – ibid. 'Mais, ça c'est le destin', VA's comment on the man being expected to pay the bill, translates as 'That's fate', or 'That's just how it is'.

13. 'Really' – ibid.
14. 'God!' – VA diary, 10 June 1928.
15. 'has all this' – VA diary, 11 July 1928.
16. 'For I' – VA diary, 7 July 1928, quoting Shakespeare, Sonnet 147.
17. 'Don't be afraid' – VA diary, 12 June 1928.
18. 'the hallucinated' – VA diary, 20 February 1954.
19. 'it is always' – VA diary, 10 June 1928.
20. 'I never played' – VA poem 'I loved you with a fleshly love' (*Poems of Dorothy* 4).
21. 'Night ends' – VA poem 'See you tomorrow night', *JfW* p70.
22. 'Nothing better' – VA diary, 18 July 1928.
23. '*Of course*' – VA diary, 20 December 1928.
24. 'lovers ashamed' – VA poem 'Lesbian', 1928. A related poem, 'Lesbian love', has been mis-attributed to STW in the past, as she copied it out into her own diary later, but it is in VA's hand in her ms notebook of 1928, and clearly relates to her diary entries about the subject made at the same time.
25. 'for which' – VA memoir *1922 Lana*.
26. 'the first' – ibid.
27. 'extremely well-dressed' – ibid.
28. 'not done' – VA diary, 30 October 1957.
29. 'Don't you know' – VA memoir *1922 Lana*.
30. 'recognised the face' – VA diary, 30 October 1957.
31. 'wild confusion' – VA memoir *For Sylvia*.
32. 'Darling' – VA memoir *1922*.
33. 'like you / Do not' – ibid.
34. 'We lay awake' – VA memoir *1922 Lana*.
35. 'that there was a considerable' – VA memoir *Partial Explanation of 1922–26*.
36. 'That less-than-month' – VA diary, 30 October 1957.
37. 'it was a miracle' – VA memoir *1922 Lana*.
38. 'to separate lives' – ibid.
39. 'a pretty' – ibid.
40. 'horribly' – ibid.
41. 'venom-speaking' – VA diary, 25 August 1930.
42. 'tormented' – VA diary, 30 November 1961.
43. 'Joan' – VA diary, 1 February 1952.
44. 'I was terrified' – VA, memoir 1940.
45. 'I am fated' – VA diary, 30 November 1961.
46. 'the shadow' – VA diary, 31 October 1957.
47. 'an Idiot' – VA diary, 31 October 1957.

48. 'a long / she would be so much' – VA memoir *1920–21 Myra*.
49. 'During those two months' – VA memoir *Partial Explanation of 1922–26*.
50. 'My sister' – VA diary, 27 December 1952.
51. 'great, continuing' – VA diary, 30 November 1961.
52. 'one to embrace' – VA diary, 31 October 1957.
53. 'She *is* harm' – STW diary, 15 March 1968.
54. 'just a little' – VA memoir *1922 Lana*.
55. 'the very things' – ibid.
56. 'there was always' – ibid.
57. 'all right' – ibid.
58. 'apparently some people' – VA memoir *1922*.
59. 'souvenir' – VA memoir *1922 Lana*
60. 'too vulgar' – ibid.
61. 'She was sensitive' – VA memoir *For Sylvia*.
62. 'I had been abroad' – VA memoir *1922–1923*.
63. 'completely unable' – VA memoir *1940*.
64. 'I can't speak' – VA diary, 30 October 1957.
65. 'the most horrible thing / How can it' – ibid.
66. 'the worst, filthiest' – VA memoir *For Sylvia*.
67. 'in the News' – ibid.
68. 'My father' – ibid.
69. 'almost unhinged' – ibid.
70. 'would have understood' – VA memoir *1922 Lana*.
71. 'treacle of manliness' – VA, *Attempt to Explain 1921–26*.
72. 'gross attentions' – VA memoir *1922 Lana*.
73. 'I was innocent' – ibid.
74. 'Girls' – ibid.
75. 'Since she did not' – STW letter to William Maxwell, 1 January 1966, *EoL* p160.
76. 'But he did not know' – VA diary, 30 October 1957.
77. 'almost beyond help' – VA memoir *1922–1923*.
78. 'didn't quite fit in' – VA memoir *1922 Lana*.
79. 'very much astray' – VA memoir *1922–1923*.
80. 'It's quite alright' – STW diary, 7 July 1953.
81. 'flattened herself' – VA memoir *1922–1923*.
82. 'with appalling realism' – VA memoir *Deaths in the Family*.
83. 'barely sane' – ibid.
84. 'accepted the whole' – VA memoir *For Sylvia*.
85. 'frantic grief' – VA memoir *Deaths in the Family*.

Chapter 3: Valentine's Trousers

1. 'lesbians could wear' – VA diary, 9 August 1931.

2. 'a man trapped' – Lilian Faderman (ed), *Chloe Plus Olivia. An Anthology of Lesbian Literature from the Seventeenth Century to the Present* (London: Penguin, 1994), p139.

3. 'the sex' – STW letter to VA, 6 September 1949. See, for example, VA's poem 'Undone' (quoted in Chapter 11); STW's 'she was in my bed, clasping me' (diary, 18 October 1949). Judith Halberstam's *Female Masculinity* (Durham NC: Duke University Press, 1998) remains one of the best books to clarify the issues involved here and examine many of the misapprehensions surrounding the complex relationship between lesbianism and masculinity and the processes by which 'dysfunction and dysphoria actually become part and parcel of this complicated and fully actualised sexual identity [for the stone butch]', p139. (A 'stone butch' is a lesbian who, in Valentine's parlance, is actively and exclusively 'the lover rather than the beloved'.)

4. 'charming woman' – VA diary, 16 June 1962.

5. 'dear, dear car' – VA travel diary, 27 September 1953.

6. 'high heels' – Janet Machen, conversation with author, 7 December 2003.

7. 'imprisonment' – VA diary, 26 September 1932.

8. 'eccentric' – VA diary, 19 July 1930.

9. 'How lovely!' – VA diary, 1 June 1931.

10. 'strange romantic' – VA memoir *For Sylvia*.

11. 'picked up' – VA draft letter to Alyse Gregory in poem-book nd, c 1947.

12. 'I was wax' to 'shopkeeper' – ibid.

13. 'mutilated' – STW letter to William Maxwell, 9 April 1971, *EoL* p220.

14. 'my handsome' – STW diary, 3 January 1963.

15. 'deplored' – VA diary, 13 July 1931.

16. 'haunted' – VA letter to STW, 2 January 1931.

17. 'If I could' – VA diary, 1 June 1931.

18. 'dozens' – Janet Machen conversation with author, 7 December 2003.

19. Also see VA's poem 'The Cottage at Night', *JfW* p113.

20. 'soft, too-gentle' – VA diary, 10 January 1930.

21. 'The Lonely / who... will be' – VA poem 'The Lonely Woman', *JfW* p74; VA poem 'Private Arthur Lesley Ramsay', *JfW* (extract in introduction to *WDS*) p20.

22. 'pigskin shoes' – STW diary, 25 May 1970.

23. 'I am very grateful' – VA diary, 4 May 1930 (transcription of STW letter).

24. 'pleasing minor verse' – VA diary, 7 May 1930.

25. 'As for poetry' – VA diary, 27 May 1930 (transcription of STW letter).

26. 'decided to die' – VA diary, 23 May 1930.

27. 'made it all / I have' – VA diary, 27 May 1930; 2 June 1930.

28. 'They fled there' – VA diary, 7 July 1930.

29. 'Letter from Sylvia' – VA diary, 7 July 1930, 12 July 1930.

30. 'Even then' – STW diary, 26 August 1972.

31. 'I long for' – VA diary, 12 July 1930.

32. 'made love/ I have always' – VA diary, 5 June 1930.

33. 'the intensity of passion' – ibid.

34. 'blessed night' – ibid.

35. 'she might be / God knows' – VA diary, 24 July 1930; 22 July 1930.

36. 'Her poems' – VA diary, 12 July 1930.

37. 'What a perfect' – VA diary, 2 August 1930.

38. 'Sylvia's clothes' – VA diary, 3 August 1930.

39. 'I shall not any longer' – VA diary, 4 August 1930.

40. 'I wish I did not want' – VA diary, 5 August 1930.

41. 'I love you' – ibid.

42. 'I love it' – VA diary, 6 August 1930.

43. 'I should have liked' – ibid.

44. 'Because I am' – Claire Harman, *Sylvia Townsend Warner: A Biography* (London: Chatto & Windus, 1989), p66 (told to Hilary Spurling by Madge Garland). David Jones (author of *In Parenthesis*) 'once hissed' at Sylvia that he 'would like to see her burned at the stake', VA wrote in a letter to Peg Manisty, nd c 1965.

45. 'Look after yourself' – VA diary, 19 August 1930.

46. 'I sat reading' – VA poem 'The Cottage at Night', 27 August 1930, *JfW* p113.

47. 'tangible proof' – VA diary, 19 August 1930.

48. 'Watching her hand' – STW Narrative 1, *ISBY* p5.

49. 'Now I can' – VA diary, 25 September 1930.

50. 'She looked / her hands / joy' – VA diary, 27, 28 September 1930; STW letter to VA, 3 November 1930.

51. 'What do you think' – VA diary, 29 September 1930.

52. 'a duck cooking' – VA memoir *For Sylvia*.

53. 'embellished with' – STW diary, 5 October 1930.

54. 'the composed' – STW, Narrative 1, *ISBY* p5.

55. 'I was born / Scotland' – VA letters to Peg Manisty, nd.

56. 'so horribly feared' – VA diary, 25 February 1951.

57. 'My father's father' – VA letter to Barbara Whittaker, nd.

58. 'I have a really sinister' – VA letter to STW, 10 February 1959.

59. 'These are very deep' – VA's intense admiration of (and identification with) her father, combined with his neglect/indulgence of her as a child, his ignoring of Joan's behaviour and his final rejection, left her with conflicted emotions towards him – and, my informant implied, herself.

60. 'very delicate' – VA memoir *1940*.

61. 'spiritual masturbation' – VA fictional autobiographical fragment, untitled, opens 'In 1906'.

62. 'I do not remember' – VA diary, 13 January 1957.

63. 'friends and protectors' – VA diary, 31 October 1957.

64. 'I see that my' – VA diary, 26 December 1951.

65. 'my parents' – VA memoir *Attempt to Explain 1921–1926*.

66. 'backward / very good indeed' – VA's school reports, Queen's College Archive.

67. 'attached one or two / Molly's' – VA memoir *Attempt to Explain 1921–1926*.

68. 'Steady on' – VA memoir *Ham, or Royalties I have known about*.

69. 'there were' – ibid.

70. 'fear and rapture' – VA memoir *1940*.

Chapter 4: Sylvia's Lover

1. 'her heart' – William Maxwell, *Letters*, cover blurb.

2. 'rough music' – *Dorset Echo*, 18 January 1935.

3. 'Valentine shook' – STW diary, 11 October 1930.

4. 'Sometimes I think' – ibid. In *For Sylvia* Valentine also recalls her statement as 'I sometimes think I am utterly unloved'.

5. 'Well / Do you / found love' – STW diary, 7 January, 28 March 1970; Narrative 1, *ISBY*, p5.

6. 'Our lives' – VA memoir *For Sylvia*.

7. 'a bridal / more of a strain' – STW diary, 12 October 1930.

8. 'life rising up in me' – STW diary, 13 October 1930.

9. 'one orange' – STW diary, 16 October 1930.

10. 'Oh, strip off' – STW letter to VA, 16 October 1930.

11. 'the sure rightness' – VA letter to STW, 15 October 1930.

12. 'Her wit' – VA diary, 14 October 1930.

13. 'Everything smiled' – VA diary, nd [30?] October 1930.

14. 'How to house' – STW diary, 19 January 1931.

15. 'lonely, mysterious creature' – STW letter to VA, 4 October 1952.

16. 'a very young, fastidious' – STW diary, 18 October 1930.

17. 'my more than music / true sky / light / like God / resignation' – STW poems 'I watch the mirror's grace', 'What weather with you now', *JfW* p83, p92; STW letter to VA, I June 1933; STW diary, 20 July 1932; STW letter to VA, 22 January 1931.

18. 'I see the vital importance' – VA diary, 19 July 1931.

19. 'Perhaps you had better' – VA letter to STW, 5 January 1931.

20. 'how romantic' – STW letter to VA, 21 August 1931.

21. 'in the future' – STW letter to VA, 15 September 1931.

22. 'Do you remember' – STW letter to VA, 4 October 1952.
23. 'when Bo' – STW diary, 25 May 1970.
24. 'I cannot bear' – VA diary, 23 October 1930.
25. 'I feel such a swine' – VA diary, 1 November 1930.
26. 'a little ironically' – VA diary, 3 November 1930. 'My Old Dutch' is a well-known music hall song about long-term marital happiness.
27. 'everything / I do not want' – VA letter to Bo Foster, quoted to STW, 24 March 1931.
28. 'It was not an easy' – STW diary, 31 October 1930.
29. 'like being in a liner' – STW diary, 29 October 1930.
30. 'Nothing is changed' – VA diary, 24 October 1930.
31. 'Miss Maaalie's / his Lordship' – STW, Narrative 2 & 4, *ISBY* pp24, 92.
32. 'vowed and prayed' – STW diary, 7 November 1930.
33. 'We are both of us' – STW letter to VA, 3 November 1930.
34. 'Call up the Devil' – VA poem, 9 December 1933.
35. 'bubble bubble' – VA diary, date removed, late October 1930.
36. 'without a waver' – STW diary, 10 July 1931.
37. 'The eyes' – VA poem 'The eyes of body', *JfW* p46. (I had to read this poem on *Woman's Hour*, rather early in the morning for such exploits on BBC Radio 4.)
38. 'I looked at all' – VA diary (written again in STW's hand), 12 January 1931.
39. 'God spoke' – ibid.
40. 'I have been teased' – VA diary, 20 July 1931.
41. 'had known for certain' – STW diary, 20 July 1931.
42. 'Well, at any rate' – STW, Narrative 4, *ISBY* p92.
43. 'You see' – STW diary, 18 June 1931.
44. 'What must we do' – VA poem, 16 October 1932, *JfW* p45.
45. 'The clock plods on' – VA poem, 16 October 1930, *JfW* p41.
46. 'The moment' – VA diary, 25–26 November 1933.
47. 'if I am not' – STW letter to VA, 26 March 1931.
48. 'with intent' – VA diary, 11 January 1953.
49. 'sudden and intense/ so nice' – VA letter to STW, 29 March 1931.
50. 'I found this' – STW letter to VA, 19 September 1932.
51. 'the brandy' – VA diary, 18 July 1931.
52. 'If Charles' – ibid.
53. 'with refusing' – STW letter to VA, 4 October 1952.
54. 'I have seen' – VA letter to STW, 17 August 1931.
55. 'But what violent' – VA letter to STW, dated 'Friday' [21 August 1931].
56. 'I was just / And as soon' – STW letter to VA, 21 August 1931.
57. 'O Miss' – STW diary, 12 January 1931.
58. 'new sort / recurring cry' – STW diary, 16 October 1931, November 1930.

59. 'hideous nauseating' – VA diary, 2 March 1932.

60. 'a bloody little' – VA diary, 16 October 1932.

61. 'I have' – VA diary, 15 October 1932.

62. 'Most days' – VA diary, 21 October 1932; emphasis in the original.

63. 'imprisonment / Balls / which did she prefer / Hurry up' – VA diary, 26 September, 27 February, 28 September, 3 October, all 1932.

64. 'writing the beginning' – VA diary, 11 December 1932.

65. 'Let it be' – VA diary, 11 October 1932.

66. '^{2}/$_3$ in favour / *Honi soit*' – VA diary, 21 October 1932.

67. 'the perfect house' – VA memoir *For Sylvia*.

68. 'I was picking' – ibid.

69. 'expensive/ Sylvia' – STW letter to Llewelyn Powys, 24 March 1934, *Letters* p30.

70. 'No one has ever' – VA diary, 26 November 1933.

71. 'Last night' – VA diary, 20 December 1933.

72. 'this kind paradise' – STW, Narrative 5, *ISBY* p112.

73. 'simple-hearted' – VA diary, 31 July 1933.

74. 'I was simply' – VA diary, 25 May 1950.

75. 'Probably' – STW, Narrative 5, *ISBY* p112.

76. 'a remarkable / two good / good technician' – *Poetry, New York Herald Tribune* reviews preserved in VA diary, 1933.

77. 'moves sweetly / Miss Warner' – transcribed in VA diary, 1933.

78. The confusion caused by the authorship puzzle is persistent; for one instance of many, in Margaret Reynolds' excellent *The Sappho Companion* (London: Chatto & Windus, 2000) VA's poem 'The clock plods on' is attributed to 'Sylvia Townsend Warner and Valentine Ackland', as though the poets wrote together like Michael Field – which would pose many interpretative problems.

79. 'if *you* could have' – Robert Frost letter to Louis Untermeyer, 23 February 1933, in *The Letters of Robert Frost to Louis Untermeyer* (London: Jonathan Cape, 1964), quoted in Claire Harman's *STW* p133.

80. 'I still wish' – VA diary, 8 February 1933.

81. 'behaving most' – VA diary, 3 March 1934.

82. 'I bitterly resent' – VA diary, 31 January 1934.

83. 'N.B. *About my poems*' – VA diary, 21 September 1934, emphasis in original.

84. 'Poesy' – VA diary, nd March 1934, quoting John Clare's 'Decay A Ballad'.

85. 'Oh, yes' – VA poem, 'Sylvia makes the best cakes', 1934.

86. All poems in *WDS*, reprinted in *JfW* pp25–105.

87. NPL Special Collections.

Chapter 5: Comrade, Darling

1. 'the house' – STW *The Cat's Cradle Book*, London: Chatto & Windus, 1960, p39 (its first publication, in the US, was in 1940).
2. 'should be treated' – *Dorset Echo*, 18 January 1935.
3. 'outgrown Eden' – STW biographical essay on VA c 1973.
4. 'at that date' – STW 1975 interview by Val Warner and Michael Schmidt, *PN Review 23*, 1981, p35.
5. 'the man' – 11 January 1935 MI5 NA.
6. 'were undoubtedly' – VA memoir *For Sylvia*.
7. 'privileged / loggerheads' – *Dorset Echo,* 19 January 1935.
8. 'these unhappy girls' – ibid.
9. 'the person is / Age' – MI5 NA.
10. 'Miss Warner' – ibid.
11. 'one wide suburb' – VA diary, 23 December 1933.
12. 'the Olde' – STW letter to Queenie Lipton, 29 May 1936, quoted in *TNP* p83.
13. 'subversive activities / whether you consider' – Colonel Sir Vernon Kell letter to Chief Constable Major Peel Yates, 8 October 1935, MI5 NA.
14. For further mind-boggling details, see James Smith's fascinating *British Writers and MI5 Surveillance 1930–1960* (Cambridge: Cambridge University Press, 2013).
15. 'discreet enquiries' – 11 October 1935, from Sergeant 26, Arthur Young, Dorset Constabulary, Wool, MI5 NA.
16. 'I'm Enery' – VA letter to Tom Wintringham, 11 May 1935, MI5 NA.
17. 'There are very few visitors' – 11 October 1935, report from Sergeant 26, Arthur Young, Dorset Constabulary, Wool, MI5 NA.
18. '108 / Devoid of Drink / 126' – VA diary, 14 November 1935.
19. 'on the pavement' – STW diary, 24 June 1970.
20. 'I am already' – VA letter to STW, 24 November 1936.
21. 'light loves / material / both body' – VA diary, 10 December 1946, emphasis in original.
22. 'I drank' – VA diary, 22 May 1955.
23. 'Ingeborg' – VA diary, 22 May 1935.
24. 'a quite usual' – STW, Narrative 8, *ISBY* p162.
25. 'constancy' – VA letter to STW, 30 November 1930.
26. 'never expected' – STW, Narrative 8, *ISBY* p162.
27. 'mere fidelity' – ibid.
28. 'How much more' – STW poem, 'How this despair enjoys me', [August 1928], *STW Poems* p148.
29. 'desperately upset' – author interview 2001.
30. 'vehement / brief' – STW Narrative 8, *ISBY* p163.
31. 'the series of people' – VA diary, 15 November 1948.

32. 'Ingeborg and Evelyn' – STW diary, 12 September 1970.

33. 'aquamarine / vine-tendril' – STW diary, 30 January 1950; VA diary, 30 May 1952.

34. 'Save Democracy' – leaflets, Bodleian.

35. 'Culture' – ibid.

36. 'killed in defence' – newspaper cutting, Bodleian.

37. 'woman warrior' – ibid.

38. 'moved heaven' – VA typescript *To Spain in September 1936.*

39. 'and it *looks*' – VA typescript *Uncensored Letters from Barcelona 1936.*

40. 'controladas' – ID cards and warrant, Bodleian

41. 'for carrying'– VA typescript *Uncensored Letters from Barcelona 1936.*

42. 'rather confused' – VA typescript *To Spain in September 1936.*

43. 'the United' – VA typescript *Uncensored Letters from Barcelona 1936.*

44. 'All this is history' – ibid.

45. 'all young lads' – ibid.

46. 'like a fantastic' – VA typescript *To Spain in September 1936.*

47. 'nightmare' – VA typescript *Uncensored Letters from Barcelona 1936.*

48. 'so for that day' – VA typescript *To Spain in September 1936.*

49. 'Shut up' – ibid.

50. Field postcards, Bodleian.

51. 'Whatever wild' – VA typescript *Uncensored Letters from Barcelona 1936.*

52. 'They are not' – photographs, Bodleian; Virginia Woolf, *Three Guineas,* 1938 (London: Penguin, p125).

53. 'impetuous chivalry' – STW diary, 3 April 1970.

54. 'Telephone wires' – VA poem 'Badajoz to Chaldon, August 1936', *JfW* p117.

55. Wendy Mulford notes in *TNP* that Valentine's reportage of the actual words of working people was in the vanguard of the Mass Observation movement (p78).

56. 'Let your love' – STW letter to VA, 19 November 1936.

57. 'apparently very vital' – VA letter to STW, 24 November 1936.

58. 'If love' – STW letter to VA, 25 November 1936.

59. '*Life and Letters*' – VA diary, 4 February 1937.

60. 'One portrait' – VA poem, 'Mirror' 23 May 1937.

61. 'What am I' – VA poem, 3 February 1932.

62. 'I have had for so long' – VA letter to STW, 14 July 1936.

63. 'a depressingly puny' – STW Narrative 7, *ISBY* p155.

64. 'Lady' – Stephen Spender, *World within World*, Hamish Hamilton, London, 1951, p211.

65. 'loyal *forever*' – VA typescript *Invitation to Madrid*, July 1937.

66. 'Viva' – ibid.

67. 'a strange sentiment' – STW Narrative 7, *ISBY*, p155.

68. 'badly scared' – VA typescript *To Spain in September 1936.*

69. 'the darkness burst into flames' – ibid.
70. 'replaced her' – STW Narrative 7, *ISBY* p155.
71. 'the attitude' – VA typescript *Guests of Spain,* July 1937.

Chapter 6: Dark Entry

1. 'Everywhere' – VA poem 'By Grace of Water', 1957, *JfW* p186
2. 'It is providential' – STW letter to Elizabeth Warner, 8 Jan 1942, *Letters* p78
3. 'in the lane / scattered' – Janet Machen letter to the author, 23 January 2004.
4. 'Valentine you ask' – Ramona S Garcia letter to VA, Bodleian.
5. 'that tedious' – STW diary, nd November / December 1937.
6. 'some semblance' – VA letter to EWW, 29 November 1937, EWW Papers.
7. 'the desolation' – ibid.
8. 'In Madrid' – STW letter to VA, 29 October 1937.
9. 'Be happy' – ibid.
10. 'follow what S&V' – EWW journal, 16 May 1937, EWW Papers.
11. 'If you don't' – STW letter to EWW, 1 March 1937, EWW Papers.
12. 'personal' – Janet Machen conversation with author, 7 December 2003.
13. 'I know / built on / Elizabeth' – VA to EWW, 25 June 1936; VA to EWW, 24 September 1938, EWW Papers; STW Narrative 8, *ISBY* p162.
14. 'I cannot imagine' – STW letter to EWW, 25 September 1938, EWW Papers.
15. 'I am / impossible' – EWW journal, 21 September 1938, EWW Papers.
16. 'Seeing you this year' – STW to EWW, 24 September 1938, EWW Papers.
17. 'courage failed her' – STW Narrative 8 *ISBY* p162.
18. 'by upbringing / it would undoubtedly' – EWW letters to Mary White, 19–20 October; 15 October 1938, EWW Papers.
19. 'always / scarcely endure' – STW to EWW, 19 October 1938; VA to EWW, 19 October 1938, EWW Papers.
20. 'I WANT' – STW cable to EWW, 19 October, 1938 EWW Papers.
21. 'do not think' – STW letter to EWW, nd, EWW Papers.
22. 'plunged / at this' – STW Narrative 8 *ISBY* p165.
23. 'flight / Valentine' – STW letter to EWW, nd, EWW Papers.
24. 'It was really' – VA diary, 7 September 1951.
25. 'all the old' – EWW letter to VA, 1 January 1939, EWW Papers.
26. 'I was WRONG' – STW diary, 4 March 1970.
27. 'bitch' – STW diary, 16 April 1972.
28. 'tied / naively' – EWW letter in VA diary, 28 January 1951.
29. 'I was' – ibid.
30. 'Valentine loved' – STW Narrative 8, *ISBY* p162.
31. 'E and I' – VA diary, 21 May 1939.

32. 'two large new' – STW diary, 30 December 1949.

33. 'one can be right' – Albert Camus, quoted by Paul Preston in *The Spanish Civil War: Dreams & Nightmares* (London: Imperial War Museum, 2001), p3.

34. 'My Shirt is in Mexico' – STW *A Garland of* Straw (London: Chatto and Windus, 1943), p92–95; also see Chapter 12.

35. 'she was dressed' – William Maxwell, introduction to STW *Letters*, pxv.

36. 'her fierce commanding' – STW diary, 3 July 1975.

37. 'If only Christina' – VA diary, 1 June 1939.

38. 'small beer' – STW Narrative 8, *ISBY* p162.

39. 'the procuress' – STW Narrative 8, *ISBY* p162.

40. 'Dearest Elizabeth, I know' – STW letter to EWW, 8 June 1939, EWW Papers.

41. 'if you had cared' – EWW letter in VA diary, 28 January 1951.

42. 'Have you anything' – VA rhyme, 4 July 1939.

43. 'I am completely' – STW letter to EWW, 18 July 1939, EWW Papers.

44. 'hell-hole' – STW Narrative 8, *ISBY* p162.

45. 'wicked / it was well-aimed' – ibid.

46. 'You and I' – VA to EWW (draft letter), diary, 26 June 1941.

47. 'I should not expect' – VA diary, 1 August 1949.

48. 'lecherous' – VA memoir *For Sylvia*.

49. 'For this a tree' – VA poem 'Warren, Connecticut 31.viii.39', *JfW* p123.

50. 'Secretive' – VA poem 'Dark Entry', *JfW* p123 (where it's 'the landscape of foreboding'; this is an earlier variant ms version).

51. 'the two' – VA poem, 'There is a silence of the body', 6 July 1939.

52. 'the shadow' – STW, Narrative 8, *ISBY* p162.

53. 'A war in Europe' – STW (in VA's notebook), nd September 1939.

54. 'this epoch's' – VA poem 'Autumn's the wind', 13 September 1939.

55. 'conniving / My dear' – STW letter to EWW, 3 October 1939, EWW Papers.

56. 'My whole heart' – VA letter to EWW, nd, EWW Papers.

57. 'played the fruit-machine' – STW diary, 6 February 1970.

58. 'Down, down' – STW poem 'In a foreign country...', *STW Poems*, p267. This is one of relatively few poems written by STW during this time; in *TAH* Peter Judd suggests that the typed poem *September 1939* ('The old year's youngest fire on the hearth tonight') is a joint effort with EWW, signed with the initials 'SWW' in STW's hand. However (apart from the intrinsic unlikelihood of such a collaboration), when closely examined the initials are in fact EWW, with the lowest stroke of the E not strongly marked, and in VA's hand not STW's. The style of the poem is typical Communist-period VA, which might allow for the possibility of EWW as the imitative author, but the entire poem also exists in ms in VA's hand, and the 'EWW' on the typescript is more likely to refer to the subject-matter of the moment than the author. There is no convincing reason to accept the authorship as STW/ EWW; although it's remotely possible that the poem was by EWW in the style of VA, written out and later typed by VA, this seems highly improbable. EWW Papers.

Chapter 7: For the Duration Interned

1. 'Thank God' – STW letter to William Maxwell, 24 October 1939, *EoL* p5

2. *'in what way'* / I did' – VA letters to EWW, 19 October 1939; 29 October 1939, EWW Papers.

3. 'Whether to do well' – VA poem 'On not returning to America', nd.

4. 'except that' – STW letter to Nancy Cunard, 26 July 1941, *Letters* p86.

5. 'pretty' – STW letter to Comrade [Aitken] Ferguson, 24 June 1936, MI5 NA.

6. 'the profoundest' – STW letter to William Maxwell, 30 September 1939, *EoL* p5.

7. 'had a strong impression' – STW diary, 14 June 1940.

8. 'like a knock about' – STW letter to Paul Nordoff, 30 May 1940
   Letters p62.

9. 'America / Above ground / this mad mesh / the loved landscape / Darkness' –
   VA poems '1 March, 1940' *NM* p22; 'October, 1940' *JfW* p131; 'English Landscape,
   February 1941' *JfW* p127 ; 'On Screen and in Pictures' *JfW* p127 ; 'Black-Out' *JfW* p130,
   from *War in Progress*, described by STW as 'a running commentary' when she
   selected a group to be published in *NM* pp22–25.

10. 'But you must not / I know' – VA diary, 28 January 1951.

11. 'I shall be faithful' to 'experimental' – VA letter to EWW, 17 April 1940 [all punctuation
    and emphases in original], EWW Papers.

12. 'Valentine now' – STW letter to EWW, 12 June 1940, EWW Papers.

13. 'Her tactics' – STW letter to Paul Nordoff , 30 May 1940, *Letters* p63.

14. 'I've been seized' – ibid p64.

15. 'Now, whose teeth' – STW letter to Paul Nordoff, 13 August 1940,
    ibid p65.

16. 'my mother' – VA letter to Tom Wintringham, 20 March 1935, MI5 NA.

17. 'At middle-age' – VA poem 'Yuletide at Home', 12 December 1938.

18. 'indescribable' – STW letter to Paul Nordoff, 12 September 1940,
    Letters p65.

19. 'she emphasizes' – STW letter to Paul Nordoff, 2 October 1944, ibid p87.

20. 'on the contrary'– STW letter to Paul Nordoff, 12 September 1940, ibid p66.

21. 'integrity / the only person' – VA letter to Evelyn Holahan, 30 August 1940; EH reply
    to VA, 9 September 1940, EWW Papers.

22. 'because the record' – VA letter to STW, 14 February 1941.

23. 'Bright bar' – VA poem 'The nature of the moment', 14 January 1940, *JfW* p131.

24. 'very quietly' – STW letter to Paul Nordoff, 27 February 1941, *Letters* p70.

25. 'holiday-makers' – STW letter to Evelyn Holohan, 5 January 1941, EWW Papers.

26. 'singleness / superstitious' – VA diary, 4/5 July 1941.

27. 'others like me' – VA letter to Llewelyn Powys, November 1933, quoted in
    STW Narrative 6, *ISBY* p122.

28. 'SOLOMON / the biblical' – 26 May / 3 June 1941, MI5 NA.

29. 'was always perfectly' – STW letter to Paul Nordoff, 17 November 1940, *Letters* p69.

30. 'she is not a person' – 29 March 1944, MI5 NA.
31. 'national importance' – STW letter to Nancy Cunard, 28 April 1944, *Letters* p84.
32. 'all the disadvantages' – STW letter to Bea Howe, 4 December 1941, ibid p75.
33. 'be virtually free / provided / I do not' – MI5 internal minutes, 10 December 1942–2 February 1943, MI5 NA.
34. 'Is it wrong?' – VA diary, 29 August 1941.
35. 'Into the war' – VA poem 'Protective Custody', 13 January 1940, *JfW* p129.
36. 'chivalry' – VA diary, 19 August 1941.
37. 'county hags' – STW letter to Bea Howe, 4 December 1941, *Letters* p75.
38. 'keen passions' – VA diary, 19 August 1941.
39. 'mingy' – STW letter to Bea Howe, 4 December 1941, *Letters* p74.
40. 'stoic / how deeply' – EWW letter in VA diary, 28 January 1951.
41. 'assertions' – ibid.
42. 'in taking it' – VA letter to EWW, VA diary, 28 February 1940.
43. 'One must recognise' – VA letter to EWW, VA diary, 9 August 1941.
44. 'It is possible' – VA letter to EWW, VA diary, 10 December 1946.
45. 'beyond words' – STW diary, 5 March 1942.
46. 'a fine topcoat / a very noble' – VA letter to EWW, 20 July 1943; 13 August 1943, EWW Papers.
47. 'pleasantly various' – VA letter to EWW, 13 August 1943, EWW Papers.
48. 'fortress of books' – STW draft VA biography notes.
49. 'Teaching to Shoot' – VA poem, July 1942, *JfW* p138.
50. 'I am haunted' – STW letter to Alyse Gregory, 19 December 1942, *Letters* p82.
51. 'mental sickness' – STW Narrative 9, *ISBY* p185.
52. 'To be a poet' – ibid.
53. 'the process' – ibid.
54. 'Did I feel' – VA poem 'To Ewart Milne, 1944', 31 January 1944, *JfW* p140.
55. 'Winter Illness' – VA poem, 7 January 1944, *JfW* p140.
56. 'what went / It is probably / what you have / I do not' – VA letter to EWW 27 May 1943, EWW Papers.
57. 'it is still / because a heart' – VA letter to EWW, 20 July 1943, EWW Papers.
58. 'with scarcely' – STW letter to Nancy Cunard, 9 June 1944, *Letters* p85.
59. 'Poem in Middle Age' – VA poem, 1944, *JfW* p140.
60. 'nobody need' – STW letter to Nancy Cunard, 26 July 1944, *Letters* p86.
61. 'Sylvia says' – VA diary (draft letter to Monica Ring), 26 January 1945.
62. 'I was sure' – VA diary, 1 May 1945.
63. 'I hear them' – VA poem 'On receipt of a warning', August–September 1946, *JfW* p145.
64. 'They had destroyed' – VA diary, 7 November 1950.
65. 'I don't believe' – VA diary, 30 June 1946.
66. 'lifeless' – STW diary, 13 September 1949.

67. 'Valentine's mother' – STW to Paul Nordoff, 30 May 1947.
68. 'August 6th' – VA poem, written 6 August 1948, *JfW* p146. 6 August was also the anniversary of Robert Ackland's death.

Chapter 8: Lazarus Risen

1. 'Lord / Dearest' – VA poems 'Lord Body', 17 March 1948, *JfW* p162; 'The Dearest Child', 14 November 1947, *JfW* p155.
2. 'from where in the tossing ship' – VA poem 'Remember how, one night...', nd c 1931–33, *JfW* p44.
3. 'Whether the lost thing' – VA poem, 16 November 1947, *JfW* p155.
4. 'When one is not' – VA diary note, January 1947.
5. 'Female handkerchiefs' – VA diary, 11 April 1947.
6. '*coffee tip*' – VA, shopping list, nd.
7. 'as if Eternity / emptiness' – VA memoir *For Sylvia*.
8. 'there was nothing' – ibid.
9. 'walking in tranquillity' – ibid.
10. 'beyond a corking' – STW letter to VA, 4 October 1952.
11. 'Even after a fortnight' – STW letter to Stephen Clark, 28 December 1947, *Letters* p99.
12. 'go down quick' – STW letter to Alyse Gregory, 29 December 1947, ibid.
13. 'The New Spring' – VA poem, January 1948.
14. 'in matters / resist' – VA diary, 9 June 1948.
15. 'the desire' – ibid.
16. 'and only / I want' – VA diary, 23 June 1948.
17. 'the intensity' – ibid.
18. 'trance of desire' – STW Narrative 11, *ISBY* p239.
19. 'I remember / any rising' – VA diary, 23 June 1948.
20. 'Lord Body' – VA poem, 17 March 1948, *JfW* p162.
21. 'Forgive' – ms draft of poem, 17 March 1948.
22. 'Roll the stone' – VA poem April 1948, *JfW* p161.
23. 'On whom' – VA poem 'When from Lazarus risen', 10 April 1948.
24. 'To Now' – VA poem 'From the far past', 1 September 1948, *JfW* p159.
25. 'This I have' – VA poem 'This I have stretched out my hand to', 6 November 1948.
26. 'I wait' – VA 'Birthday Poem', 6 May 1948, *JfW* p156.
27. 'ones' to 'return' – VA poem, January 1949.
28. 'Living Near the Asylum' – VA poem, *JfW* p160.
29. 'hand-in-hand / If ever' – STW letter to Paul Nordoff, 6 June 1949, *Letters* p114.
30. 'we well might feel / I have developed / grotesque / you have this' – VA letter to EWW, 20 July 1943, EWW Papers.
31. 'I had a clear understanding' – VA diary, 15 November 1948.

32. 'at once the old love' – VA diary, 11 April 1949.

33. 'I do not believe' – VA diary, 28 January 51.

34. 'a violent desire / at a touch' – VA diary, 11 April 1949.

35. 'I never feel' – ibid.

36. 'Did Lazarus weep' – VA poem 'Did Lazarus, awakened from the dead', April 1949, *JfW* p165.

37. 'Memory returns' – VA poem, nd.

38. 'just after the war' – VA diary, 6 June 1956.

39. 'epilogue' – STW diary, 13 August 1949.

40. 'vast differences' to 'meet in love' – EWW letter in VA diary, 28 January 1951.

41. 'the one / redeemed' – ibid.

42. 'On the first night' – VA diary, 16 May 1949.

43. 'melancholy' – STW Narrative 10, *ISBY* p227.

44. 'falsehood' – ibid.

45. 'disintegration / implement' – VA diary, 4 June 1949.

46. 'because somehow she *must*' – ibid.

47. 'My serpent' – STW diary, 9 June 1949.

48. 'pale and swaying / heroic' – ibid.

49. 'Sylvia most of all' – VA diary, 11 June 1949.

50. 'The June rain' – VA poem, 11 June 1948, *JfW* p162.

51. 'A Solitary Thought' – VA poem, July 1949, *JfW* p165.

52. 'Sylvia is so deeply / the sight' – VA diary, 11 June 1949.

53. 'a sprig of rosemary' – STW diary, 10 June 1950.

54. 'Sometimes / I feel' – VA diary, 11 June 1949.

55. 'that lost' – STW diary, 31 July 1949.

56. 'it is much more' – VA diary, 31 July 1949.

57. 'When you were walking' – STW letter to VA, 31 July 1949.

58. 'Everything you say' – VA letter to STW, [1] August 1949.

59. 'dreadful' – VA diary, 1 August 1949.

60. 'half-heartedness' – STW diary, 23 August 1949.

61. 'in the unexpected' – VA diary, 1 August 1949.

62. 'mannerly / autumnal' – STW diary, 1 September 1949.

63. 'If Evelyn / Quite' – STW diary, 15 August 1949.

64. 'this baleful' – STW diary, 12 August 1949.

65. 'made the adulterous' – STW diary, 31 August 1949.

66. 'the horrified' – STW Narrative 11, *ISBY* p239.

67. 'Do GH' – STW diary list, August 1949.

68. 'I was wrong' – VA diary, 4 August 1949.

69. 'perplexed / She lives' – STW diary, 12 September 1949.

70. *'with the Sylvia'* – ibid. Sylvia recorded these strange words when she was reflecting on Alyse Gregory's comment that Valentine was unfaithful because she was so sure of Sylvia.

71. 'We have been happy' – VA letter to EWW in diary, 26 October 1949.

72. 'selfish / spectacle / how grotesque' – Evelyn Holahan letter to EWW, 14 September 1949, EWW Papers.

73. 'all I have sacrificed / getting down' – STW Narrative 12 *ISBY* p275; STW diary, 19 September 1949.

74. 'that kind of monster' – STW diary, 23 September 1949.

75. 'to do the garden' – STW diary, 26 September 1949.

76. 'almost insolently' – STW diary, 9 November 1950.

77. 'violent / If you' – STW letter to VA, 6 September 1949.

78. 'I think' – STW diary, 1 October 1949.

79. 'never felt / this creature / could not' – STW diary, 23 October 1949.

80. 'There is not' – VA poem, 'Poem in Norfolk', October 1949, *JfW* p167.

81. 'We are in such' – STW diary, 25 October 1949.

82. 'stealing from Evelyn' – STW diary, 30 November 1949.

83. 'If you can / lesser / I accept' – VA diary, 27 October 1949.

84. 'once or twice' – STW diary, 17 March 1950.

85. 'insufficient' – VA diary, 28 October 1949.

86. 'asserting' – STW diary, 22 November 1949.

87. 'risked everything' – VA diary, 9 December 1949.

88. 'Weather Forecast' – VA poem, December 1949 *JfW* p167.

Chapter 9: Lord Body

1. 'the slavery' – STW diary, 7 March 1950.

2. 'tear everything' – STW diary, 21 February 1950.

3. 'I loved' – STW diary, 23 March 1950.

4. *'such* a blight / She did not then' – VA diary, 22 June 1950.

5. 'It is at / a bitter / I took you' – STW diary, 23 March 1950.

6. 'this sudden' – STW diary, 2 May 1950.

7. 'Our years' – VA 'Poem for Sylvia', June 1950.

8. 'we shall never' – STW diary, 4 May 1950.

9. 'Sometimes I cannot' – STW diary, 2 April 1950.

10. 'a repossession' – STW diary, 10 May 1950.

11. 'one again' – STW diary, 28 April 1950.

12. 'I have had strange' – VA diary, 22 May 1950.

13. 'I felt / I do not dare' – VA diary, 25 May 1950.

14. 'I found / I *adored*' – ibid.

15. 'felt a frightful' – STW diary, 22 August 1950.
16. 'less vivid' – VA diary, 27 September 1950.
17. 'the extreme / we are deeply' – STW diary, 5 November / 20 December 1950.
18. 'never let go' – STW diary, 4 December 1950.
19. 'the black morass' – VA diary, 29 December 1950.
20. 'except when' – VA diary, 29 November 1950.
21. 'deeply / a new / more statement' – STW diary, 27 December 1950.
22. 'Salthouse, New Year's Eve' – VA poem, 27 December 1950, *JfW* p170.
23. 'like cast / their far-off / The matador / now' – VA notes, November 1950.
24. 'Do not let me' – VA poem notes, 2 December 1950.
25. 'My hand' – VA poem 'My hand and the pen', 23 June 1950, *JfW* p 168.
26. 'it most deeply' – VA diary, 18 January 1952.
27. 'I wish' – VA letter to STW, 15 February 1959.
28. 'admirably' – STW diary, 30 November 1950.
29. 'I hoped / and what small' – VA diary, 17 December / 28 December 1950.
30. 'I should not' – VA diary, 30 January 1951.
31. 'great gaunt' – STW letter to Nancy Cunard, 7 February 1951, *Letters* p126.
32. 'into miserable' – STW diary, 1 January 1951.
33. 'I resent' – STW diary, 27 January 1951.
34. 'I was a clerk' – STW diary, [–] May 1951.
35. 'I depend' – STW diary, 1 June 1951.
36. 'officially ill' – VA diary, 7 October 1951.
37. 'All joy' – VA diary, 22 December 1951.
38. 'When I was' – VA diary, 17 August 1951.
39. 'deep' – ibid.
40. 'The aftermath' – VA diary, 7 October 1951.
41. 'I *feel*' – ibid.
42. 'part of' – STW diary, 26 September 1951.
43. 'Did you say' – STW diary, 28 November 1951.
44. 'smell desolation' – STW diary, 1 September 1951.
45. 'everything' – STW diary, 10 September 1951.
46. 'a very hard / a black' – VA diary, 10 January 1952.
47. 'from time' – STW diary, 24 September 1951.
48. 'It makes my heart' – VA diary, [–] January 1952.
49. 'they can' – STW diary, 24 January 1952.
50. 'It would be most foolish' – VA poem 'It would be foolish –' 8 January 1952, *JfW* p171.
51. 'sufficient' – VA diary, 1 February 1952.
52. 'Oh, no' – Jean Larson conversation with author, 2002.
53. 'so indescribably / an unfortunate' – VA diary, 18 April 1952; [–] February 1952.

54. 'It was read' – VA diary, 27 April 1952.
55. 'justified / no such' – STW diary, 12 May 1952.
56. 'alas' – STW diary, 16 May 1952.
57. 'and knew' – VA diary, 16 May 1952.
58. 'If only' (and all quotes in para) – VA typescript '16th May in a Diary'.
59. 'mute' – ibid.
60. 'You've been / fused' – VA diary, 30 May 1952.
61. 'I love / only because' – ibid.
62. 'My mind and body' – VA diary, 31 May 1952.
63. 'modern devil / a sombre' – ibid.
64. 'noble widow' – VA diary, [–] September 1951.
65. 'Postscript to Fable' – VA poem, nd.
66. 'Poem in a Bad Year' – VA poem 21 October 1952, *JfW* p174.
67. 'I could not' – VA diary, [–] August 1952.
68. 'I wish' – VA diary, 1 August 1952.
69. 'Today it' – VA diary, 3 August 1952.
70. 'It was … her' – STW diary, 16 May 1970.
71. 'Oh! The Annunciation!' – STW diary, 13 November 1953.
72. 'an up to date / The two / Miss' – 10 November / 10 December 1952, MI5 NA.
73. '[driving] is a skill' – VA diary, 22 November 1952 [ellipses in original].
74. 'for so long' – VA diary 27 April 1953
75. 'I have worked / indolence' – VA diary, 27 December 1952 / 27 April 1953.
76. 'If only' – VA diary, September 1953.
77. 'that matchless' – VA diary, 3 February 1953.
78. 'we have no information' – MI5 internal reports 14–19 January 1953, MI5 NA.
79. 'Craig / absolutely incapable' – VA diary, 11 December 1952.
80. 'For all that takes place' – VA poem, 5 February 1952, *JfW* p172.
81. 'romantic' – VA diary, 3 June 1952.
82. 'for evidently' – VA diary, 11 May 1953.
83. 'paroxysm / the not-impossible' – VA diary, 26 May 1953.
84. 'living / we outrage' – STW diary, 23 July 1953.
85. 'I cannot write' – VA diary, 11 July 1954.
86. 'the bottom' – ibid.
87. 'Accept the cold content' – VA poem, August 1949, *JfW* p166.

Chapter 10: Saint & Rogue

1. 'to be tried' – STW diary, 28 November 1954.
2. 'asserted / would not' – VA diary, 28 November 1954.

3. 'bereft / my loss' – VA diary, 15 September; 8 September 1952.
4. 'having won / many emotions' – VA diary, 12 January 1954.
5. 'the mind / get near / It is not lack / that it should be' – VA diary, 24 December 1954.
6. 'This is the coldest' – VA poem, 8 February 1955, *JfW* p176.
7. 'If she were to rise' – VA poem, 26 March 1956, *JfW* p176.
8. 'The recurrent' – VA poem, 'The Sign on Water', nd, *JfW* p156.
9. 'O flame' – VA poem, nd, *JfW* p136.
10. 'so it is in some sense' – VA diary, 13 January 1956, 11.30am.
11. 'when she was so' – VA diary, 19 January 1954.
12. 'she has power / Artists' – VA diary, 24 September 1956; *Really Reading Gertrude Stein*, Judy Grahn (Freedom CA: The Crossing Press, 1989), p4.
13. 'the long habit / try to forget' – VA diary, 7 July 1955.
14. 'gulf / contempt' – VA diary, 17 February 1956.
15. 'to see Sylvia / never' – VA diary, 19 January 1952.
16. 'the Voltaire' – VA diary, 17 February 1956.
17. 'much more so' – VA diary, 1 March 1956.
18. 'There is hardly' – STW letter to VA, 8 September 1949.
19. 'Please never' – STW letter to VA, 17 September 1957.
20. 'disclosed as someone' – VA diary, Easter Sunday 1956.
21. 'a weakling / a tract' – VA diary, 22 April 1956.
22. 'analysis' – STW diary, 21 April 1956.
23. 'Loving' – VA diary, 6 June 1956.
24. 'I admired / and thought' – STW diary, 9 May 1957.
25. 'hates / spent her life' – VA diary, 22 September 1956.
26. 'the accumulation / poor Tib' – STW diary, 11 March 1958.
27. 'Another than EWW' – STW diary, 3 June 1957.
28. 'never happy' – STW diary, 25 January 1958.
29. 'my alarming' – STW letter to VA, 22 September 1958.
30. 'admiration' – STW diary, 20 September 1955.
31. 'I can't / At moments' – STW diary, 18 January 1957; 15 July 1956.
32. 'OF COURSE / ever / all my' – VA letter to STW 12 October 1957; ibid; VA letter to STW, 25 August 1954.
33. 'If we had no books' – VA poem, 10 January 1957.
34. 'I stand committed' – VA poem, July 1956.
35. 'an ancient permanence' – quoted by VA in *Dorset Echo*, 2 March 1956.
36. 'the general / a new' – *Dorset Echo*, 2 March 1956.
37. 'the landscape / the whole' – VA in *Dorset Echo*, 2 March 1956.
38. 'Summer' – VA poem, 24 June 1962, *JfW* p190.
39. 'melancholy doctrine' – STW diary, 27 July 1957.
40. 'It breaks' – VA letter to STW, 2 August 1958.

41. 'Meanings, moods' – Kathleen Raine, Introduction to *Selected Poems* (Ipswich MA: Golgonooza Press, 1988), p.vi.
42. 'All Souls' Night' – VA poem, 2 November 1958, *JfW* p186.
43. 'Every autumn a wind' – VA poem, 12 November 1953, *JfW* p173.
44. 'Of course' – VA diary note, 'Vigil of the Assumption', 1957.
45. 'drawn into' – VA diary, 15 October 1958.
46. 'the devil' – STW diary, 9 May 1956.
47. 'I sometimes think' – STW diary, 8 October 1958.
48. 'Don't think' – VA letter to STW, 16 September 1957.
49. 'murderous' – VA diary, 18 August 1952.
50. 'mock / Haven't you' – VA diary, 31 October 1957.
51. 'so young / scarcely' – STW diary, 9 July; 14 July 1961.
52. 'the pathos / in terms' – VA letter to STW, 12 October 1957.
53. 'gay histories' – STW diary, 19 May 1952.
54. 'observation' – VA diary note, c 4 November 1954.
55. 'incessant / who pullulate' – STW diary, 2 February 1960.
56. 'a current / Goodnight' – STW diary, 12 March / 22 January 1959.
57. 'Her wisdom' – STW diary, 3 August 1959.
58. 'standing / she has stifled' – STW diary, 17 February 1958.
59. 'Reading the book about Spain' – VA poem, 8 October 1965.
60. 'failed attempt' – VA note in poem ms book, 6 October 1965.
61. 'their faith / Only one thing' – from VA poem 'Reading the book about Spain'.
62. 'I suppose' – VA diary, 9 December 1958.
63. 'filling-in / I never' – VA diary, 15 October 1958.
64. 'While I slept' – VA poem, June 1959, *JfW* p189.

Chapter 11: The Good Englishman

1. 'call' – VA poem, 'If you and I could call ourselves together', nd, *JfW* p157.
2. 'I have tried very hard' – VA poem, 9 January 1956, revised May 1966.
3. 'closing the aperture' – VA diary, 31 October 1957.
4. 'handicapped' – STW travel diary, Presteigne, Wales, April 1960.
5. 'she lay / keen-sighted / it stands' – STW diary, 4 August / 20 March / 8 August 1960.
6. 'unassimilable / such a poet' – STW diary, 24 September 1960.
7. 'the sea' – STW diary, 17 September 1960.
8. 'Undone?' – VA poem, 3 October 1960.
9. 'After you had spoken' – VA poem, 3 October 1960, *JfW* p189.
10. '248 bloody miles' – STW diary, 13 February 1961.
11. 'gallantly / Molly / turn' – STW diary, 26 May 1961; VA diary, 6 June 1961.
12. 'like the fall' – STW letter to William Maxwell, 23 June 1961, *EoL* p107.

13. 'so elegant' – STW diary, 1 January 1962.
14. 'to condole' – STW diary, 6 June 1962.
15. 'for my present affliction' – ibid.
16. 'grieved on' – STW diary, 19 May 1962.
17. 'music' – STW diary, 6 June 1962.
18. 'Eight years' – STW diary note, 10 October 1961.
19. 'I am' – STW diary, 17 December 1956.
20. 'looking like / testudodrome' – STW diary, 13 January 1957; STW to Marchette Chute, 20 July 1962, *Letters* p201.
21. 'because I am' – VA diary, 3 August 1962.
22. 'wailing aloud / closed' – VA diary, 3 October; 3 August 1962.
23. 'Hope of Poetry' – VA poem, 13 October 1962, *JfW* p192.
24. 'lacerating' – STW diary, 23 August 1961.
25. 'After a Conversation about Pasternak' – VA poem, November 1963.
26. 'When you are ready' – U A Fanthorpe, *War, Poetry, The Child,* in *Strong Words,* ed. W N Herbert and Matthew Hollis (Tarset: Bloodaxe, 2000), p210.
27. 'stony / it is' – VA letter to STW, 4 June 1962.
28. 'I lay beside you' – VA poem, 30 November 1963, *JfW* p192.
29. 'Epithalamium' – VA poem, 'Epithalamium for Death', 30 November 1963, *JfW* p193.
30. 'love grown old' – VA diary, July 1963.
31. 'Shut your eyes' – STW diary, 4 March 1963.
32. 'I see' – STW diary, 13 March 1963.
33. 'It is what' – STW diary, 12 April 1963.
34. 'because / Valentine' – STW diary, 16 April 1963.
35. 'like a wild' – STW diary, 29 April 1963.
36. 'All perfectly' – STW diary, 22 July 1963.
37. 'never, now' – VA diary, 19 July 1963.
38. 'perfectly' – VA diary, 14 November 1963.
39. 'Severe' – VA diary, 22 November 1963.
40. 'the first one' – STW diary, 25 December 1963.
41. 'It is lovely / So far' – VA diary, 12 October 1964.
42. 'Pericles' – VA letter to Peg Manisty, nd [1965].
43. 'Skilled / He turned' – STW, *T H White* (London: Chatto & Windus, 1967), pp70, 139.
44. 'unspeakably / When I feel' – VA diary, 19 May 1965.
45. 'I remember the story' – VA poem, 6 June 1965, *JfW* p194.
46. 'I will not / very complete' – VA diary, 19 May 1965.
47. 'You could / Do you' – VA diary, 22 January 1964.
48. 'I loved' – VA diary, 18 March 1966.
49. 'the Opus / very thin / sparingly' – VA diary, 21 March 1965.

50. 'Out of the cold' – VA poem, 12 December 1954.

51. 'the thing' – VA diary, 8 September 1952.

52. 'coffee' – STW diary, 14 January 1966.

53. 'romantic' – VA diary, 12 January 1966.

54. 'dreadfully' – ibid.

55. 'the promised / An omen' – STW diary, 17 January 1966; 1 February 1970.

56. 'Middle Age' – VA diary, 19 May 1966.

57. *'holding her off'* – VA diary, 27 January 1966.

58. 'frozen out' – VA diary, 9 February 1966.

59. 'Night Poem II' – VA poem, 13 December 1966, *JfW* p196.

60. 'A not-poem about love' – VA poem, *JfW* p195.

61. 'Hold on' to 'twice in one day' – STW letter to Janet Machen, 25 June 1966, *Letters* p220.

62. 'It was all' – STW diary, 20 September 1955.

63. 'total inattention' – STW diary, 5 September 1965.

64. 'erect' – VA letter to Peg Manisty, nd [1965].

65. 'You can't win' – ibid.

66. 'No one / the long' – STW diary, 19 October 1965.

67. 'unspeakably' – VA diary, 16 April 1965.

68. 'The smell' – STW diary, 12 August 1967, (slightly mis-) quoting A E Housman's poem from *A Shropshire Lad* XL, with its sad reference to 'the land of lost content'.

69. 'one cannot' – STW diary, 10 August 1967.

70. 'shining / My heart' – VA diary, 29 January; 30 December 1967.

71. 'Vietnam (or any of the other wars)' – VA poem, 27 July 1965, *JfW* p194.

72. 'On a Calendar of Anti-War Poems' – VA poem, 5 June 1968.

73. 'June 17th 1967 China explodes the H-bomb' – VA poem, 17 June 1967.

74. 'Of course' – STW diary, 7 March 1968.

75. 'Don't grieve' – STW diary, 6 March 1968.

76. 'I totally' – STW diary, 19 March 1968.

77. 'She looked / strange' – STW diary 27; 30 March 1968.

78. 'it seems' – VA letter to Peg Manisty, March 1968.

79. 'that trousered / I'm' – VA diary, 27 May 1968.

80. 'I have written' – VA letter to Peg Manisty, 30 November 1968.

81. 'Poem in the Chinese Manner' – VA poem, 4 August 1968, *JfW* p198.

Chapter 12: How Wild and Strange A Live Man Is

1. 'We are bound / any excursions' – VA letter to STW, 10 December 1968.

2. 'I have never' – STW letter to VA, nd [18 December 1968].

3. 'greatest treasure' – VA written on STW's letter, 18 December 1968 6.45pm.

4. 'nothing amiss' – STW diary, 11 March 1969.
5. 'Reflections as I pack to go to London' – VA poem, 18 May 1969.
6. 'For an hour / we *really were*' – STW diary, 19 May 1969; VA diary 15 September 1969.
7. 'unchangeably' – VA letter to Peg Manisty, 17 June 1969.
8. 'Valentine' – Jean Larson conversation with the author, 2002.
9. 'I'm perhaps' – VA letter to EWW, 14 July 1969, EWW Papers.
10. 'June 1969' – VA poem, June 1969.
11. 'how lost' – STW diary, 1 September 1969.
12. *Poems in Pain* / 'The Crow' – VA poems, 27 November 1968, *JfW* p197; 2 June 1969, *JfW* p198.
13. 'very bad' – VA diary, 16 September 1969.
14. 'she looked so' – STW diary, 15 September 1969.
15. 'Suddenly' – VA letter to Peg Manisty, 20 September [1969].
16. 'so that / immeasurably' – VA diary, 1 April 1966.
17. 'Such a situation' – VA letter to EWW, 17 September 1969, EWW Papers.
18. 'Like the beautiful' – VA poem, 3 March 1969.
19. 'Sunt Lumina' – VA draft poem, 25 September 1969.
20. 'Absorbed' – VA draft poem, 2 October 1969.
21. 'The whole' – David Constantine, *Strong Words* (Tarset: Bloodaxe, 2000), p228.
22. 'an exemplary' – STW diary, 28 October 1969.
23. 'in the high Roman' – STW letter to Janet Machen, 2 November 1969, *Letters* p242.
24. 'its windows' – STW diary, 1 November 1969.
25. 'DON'T' – VA letter to Peg Manisty, 2 October 1969.
26. 'it is so very' – STW letter to Janet Machen, 2 November 1969, *Letters* p242.
27. 'An old marchioness' – VA diary, 24 September 1969.
28. 'please do not worry' – VA letter to EWW, 2 November 1969, EWW Papers.
29. 'revived her'– STW letter to William Maxwell, 4 November 1969, *EoL* p205.
30. 'The stormy' – STW diary, 9 November 1969.
31. 'tragic' – ibid.
32. 'strong brown' – STW diary, 10 November 1969.
33. 'in the cellular' – STW diary, 29 April 1972.
34. 'none / in our own / that happy / I do not' – VA Will, 20 June 1969.
35. 'such good / beech boughs' – STW diary, 22 November; 17 November 1969.
36. 'She can / Maureen' – VA Will, 20 June 1969.
37. 'I am a part' – STW diary, 7 August 1970.
38. 'when Valentine' – STW letter to William Maxwell, 3 October 1973, *EoL* p260.
39. 'The bell / The Practice' – STW diary, 22 May 1970.
40. 'I woke' – STW diary, 23, 24, 25 September 1972.
41. 'the long room' – STW diary, 4 September 1971.

42. 'her corduroy' – STW diary, 17 March 1970.

43. 'her *shirts*' – STW diary, 30 September 1970.

44. 'We remember' – STW diary, 27 June 1970.

45. 'agonies' – ibid.

46. 'she was so brave' – STW diary, 24 June 1970.

47. 'O WHY' – STW diary, 6 May 1970.

48. 'the misery / the agony' – STW diary, 21 September 1970.

49. 'She couldn't have' – STW diary, 6 January 1970. The friend was Angela Debenham, widow of Piers.

50. 'How *can* I' – STW diary, 27 April 1975.

51. 'I am / A false' – STW diary, 14 February 1976.

52. 'All her trees / A day' – STW diary 7 September 1971; 19 May 1973.

53. 'remembered' – STW diary, 25 February 1970.

54. 'was an admirer' – STW letter to Mr Ferguson, 10 April 1975, Collection Ray Russell.

55. 'lyrical / Extremely observant' – STW draft VA biography for *NM*.

56. 'sardonic' – ibid.

57. 'I think' – VA diary, Easter Sunday 1956.

58. 'Began' – STW diary, 17 June 1942.

59. 'So much / Every line' – STW letter to William Maxwell, 18 January 1971, *EoL* p217; STW diary, 12 January 1971.

60. 'My love' – STW diary, 1 October 1970.

61. 'I had never seen' – STW Introduction, *The Cat's Cradle Book* (London: Chatto & Windus, 1960), p12.

62. 'incantation / love-poem' – STW diary, 31 July 1972.

63. 'My mind' – STW diary, 20 January 1971.

64. 'more rational' – STW Introduction, *The Cat's Cradle Book,* ibid p36.

65. 'And by her death' – VA poem 'Sleep'. STW wondered whether 'In a dream-sense this could mean that by my death she recaptured the wild black-haired Sylvia of when she first loved me', or was the swan 'her poetry – which tending me had impeded'? STW diary, 24 May; August 1971.

66. 'there, lolling / Thomas' – STW story, 'The Five Black Swans', *Kingdoms of Elfin* (London: Chatto & Windus, 1977), pp19, 22.

67. This is discussed in more detail in 'The Practice of the Presence of Valentine', my contribution to *Critical Essays on Sylvia Townsend Warner*, ed. Gill Davies, David Malcolm and John Simons (Lampeter & New York: Edwin Mellen Press, 2006), pp29–43.

68. 'as the great English' – Julius Lipton letter to unnamed recipient, 3 February 1981, Warner-Ackland Archive.

69. 'You know' – William Maxwell letter to STW, April 1978, *EoL* p339.

70. 'I do not / Poems' – VA Will, 20 June 1969.

71. 'I can imagine' – VA letter to STW, 12 April 1934.

72. 'a bloody' – VA diary, 16 October 1932.

73. 'clearly identifiable' – Emily Hamer, *Britannia's Glory: A History of Twentieth-Century Lesbians* (London: Cassell, 1996), p129.

74. 'a thousand' – VA letter to Julius Lipton, 13 May 1935, quoted in *TNP* p245.

75. 'prejudice' – Sarah Shulman, *Hooters*, documentary film dir. Anna Margarita Albelo, 2010.

76. 'first public' – STW letter to William Maxwell 2 May 1967, *Letters* p225.

77. 'lesbian companion' – Frances Partridge, 27 December 1965, *Other People: Diaries 1963–1966* (London: HarperCollins, 1993), p189. This namelessness or invisibility continues, for instance in Virginia Nicholson's delightful *Among the Bohemians* (London: Penguin, 2003), in an entirely sympathetic portrait of STW's 'fulfilment beyond her wildest dreams' with 'her lover Valentine' – no surname, p48.

78. 'Bill Empson' – VA diary, 6 June 1952.

79. For instance, in Julia Blackburn's *Threads: The Delicate Life of John Craske* (London: Jonathan Cape, 2015) the author describes VA as the 'woman who looks like a man' (p207), and 'a bit like [ex-prime minister] David Cameron' (p6). In a *Guardian* article about Craske, 'Life on the Ocean Wave' (13 March 2015), she again comments on being struck by VA's 'resemblance to David Cameron'. This may seem superficially amusing, but is analogous to saying that 'all tall, dark-haired, white Englishmen (or other racial stereotype) look the same'; the observation actually being made is that VA comically resembles a *man*. (Gender diverse people may well find this offensive.) The point being missed is that twenty-first century Old Etonian Tories also represent an archetype, perpetuating the style, suits and haircuts of the 1930s to indicate their allegiance to an outmoded patriarchal caste system which VA was committed to undermining when she wore contemporary male attire.

80. 'I have served' – VA diary, 24 March 1957.

81. The poem Sylvia misattributed to VA was 'where the hills make a home hollow' by Mary Casey (see note 54); VA's poems 'Never love unless you can' (first line 'Lesbian love is equally'), and 'Towards the place to which we would or would not come' have in the past been mistakenly attributed to STW, and 'A Hard Winter' to Katie Powys.

82. 'read on' – VA diary, 8 February 1933.

83. 'Darling London' – STW diary, 7 December 1952.

84. 'thinking' – Virginia Woolf, *Orlando* (London: The Hogarth Press, 1928), p240.

85. 'because I had a habit' – VA Will, 20 June 1969.

86. 'Strange to think' – STW diary, 12 July 1970. Susanna Pinney was the typist-reader.

87. 'When you' – VA poem, 5 September 1954, *JfW* p175.

A Personal Note: The Quest for Valentine

1. 'every one' – A J A Symons, *The Quest for Corvo: An Experiment in Biography,* Cassell, 1934 (London: Penguin, 2018), p251.

2. 'there is a great deal' – Janet Machen letter to the author, 17 September 2001.

3. 'a biographer' – Sybille Bedford (quoting a saying of Desmond MacCarthy), 'Afterword', in *Jigsaw* (London: Eland Publishing, 2005), p353.

4. 'Nothing' – Symons, ibid, p251.

5. 'when I am' – VA memoir *For Sylvia*.

Select Bibliography

Valentine Ackland and Sylvia Townsend Warner, *Whether a Dove or Seagull* (New York: Viking Press, 1933; London: Chatto & Windus, 1934).

Valentine Ackland, *Country Conditions* (London: Lawrence & Wishart, 1936).

Valentine Ackland, *Twenty-Eight Poems* (Wells: Clare, Son & Co, 1957).

Valentine Ackland, *Later Poems* (Wells: Clare, Son & Co, nd [1970]).

Valentine Ackland, *The Nature of the Moment* (London: Chatto & Windus, 1973).

Valentine Ackland, *Further Poems* (Beckenham: Welmont Publishing, 1978).

Valentine Ackland, *For Sylvia: An Honest Account* (London: Chatto & Windus, 1985).

Frances Bingham (ed.), *Journey from Winter: Selected Poems of Valentine Ackland* (Manchester: Carcanet, 2008).

Gill Davies et al (eds.), *Critical Essays on Sylvia Townsend Warner, English Novelist 1893–1978* (Lampeter & New York: Edwin Mellen Press, 2006).

Claire Harman, *Sylvia Townsend Warner: A Biography* (London: Chatto & Windus, 1989).

Claire Harman (ed.), *Sylvia Townsend Warner: New Collected Poems* (Manchester: Carcanet, 2008).

Claire Harman (ed.), *The Diaries of Sylvia Townsend Warner* (London: Chatto & Windus, 1994).

Peter Haring Judd, *The Akeing Heart: Letters between Sylvia Townsend Warner, Valentine Ackland & Elizabeth Wade White* (Reading: Handheld Press, 2018).

William Maxwell (ed.), *Sylvia Townsend Warner Letters* (London: Chatto & Windus, 1982).

Wendy Mulford, *This Narrow Place. Sylvia Townsend Warner and Valentine Ackland: Life, Letters and Politics, 1930–1951* (London: Pandora Press, 1988).

Susanna Pinney (ed.), *I'll Stand by You: The Letters of Sylvia Townsend Warner & Valentine Ackland* (London: Pimlico, 1998).

Michael Steinman (ed.), *The Element of Lavishness: Letters of Sylvia Townsend Warner & William Maxwell* (Washington DC: Counterpoint, 2001).

Judith Stinton, *Chaldon Herring: The Powys Circle in a Dorset Village* (Woodbridge: The Boydell Press, 1988).

Index

Page numbers in italics refer to illustrations.

E

F

G

H

I

J

K

L

M

N

O

P

Q

R

S

Y

The Akeing Heart

Letters between Sylvia Townsend Warner, Valentine Ackland and Elizabeth Wade White

by Peter Haring Judd

The Akeing Heart is the story of the tormented relationships between the British novelist and poet Sylvia Townsend Warner; her life partner Valentine Ackland; the American who invaded their happiness, Elizabeth Wade White; and Elizabeth's neglected lover Evelyn Holahan. Valentine was the serial seducer, and Elizabeth the demanding lover claiming her sexuality for the first time. Sylvia kept faith in anger and despair, while Evelyn offered Elizabeth realistic fidelity to balance Valentine's romanticism.

Originally self-published, this revised edition of correspondence over twenty years between the four women makes this book one of the finest collections of twentieth-century literary letters about love and its betrayals.

'*The Akeing Heart* is the most important and startling addition in decades to what we know about these perennially fascinating writers.'
— Claire Harman, author of *Sylvia Townsend Warner. A Biography* and *The Diaries of Sylvia Townsend Warner*

'Judd's story is an engrossing one, and the best of the Warner letters evince her characteristic joy in language and observation.'
— Michael Caines, *The Times Literary Supplement*